Reading/Language Arts Framework for California Public Schools

Kindergarten Through Grade Twelve

Developed by the
Curriculum Development and Supplemental
Materials Commission

Adopted by the
California State Board of Education

Published by the
California Department of Education

Publishing Information

When the *Reading/Language Arts Framework for California Public Schools, Kindergarten Through Grade Twelve* was adopted by the California State Board of Education on December 10, 1998, the members of the State Board were the following: Yvonne W. Larsen, President; Robert L. Trigg, Vice-President; Timothy Draper; Kathryn Dronenburg; Marion Joseph; Marion McDowell; Janet G. Nicholas; Gerti B. Thomas; Marina Tse; and Richard Weston.

The framework was developed by the Curriculum Development and Supplemental Materials Commission. (See pages x–xii for the names of the members of the commission and the names of the principal writers and others who made significant contributions to the framework.)

This publication was edited by Edward O'Malley, working in cooperation with Nancy Brynelson, Consultant, Elementary Education Division, Curriculum and Instructional Leadership Branch, California Department of Education. It was prepared for printing by the staff of CDE Press. The cover and interior design were created and prepared by Cheryl McDonald. Typesetting was done by Jamie Contreras. The framework was published by the California Department of Education, 721 Capitol Mall, Sacramento, California (mailing address: P.O. Box 944272, Sacramento, CA 94244-2720). It was distributed under the provisions of the Library Distribution Act and *Government Code* Section 11096.

ISBN 0-8011-1462-4

Photo Credits

Photographs were provided by Glen Korengold, working in cooperation with Mark Hopkins Elementary School, Sacramento City Unified School District, and the following schools in the Washington Unified School District: Bryte Elementary, Elkhorn Village Elementary, Golden State Middle, River City High, and Southport Elementary.

Ordering Information

Copies of this publication are available for $17.50 each, plus shipping and handling charges. California residents are charged sales tax. Orders may be sent to CDE Press, Sales Office, California Department of Education, P.O. Box 271, Sacramento, CA 95812-0271; FAX (916) 323-0823. See page 292 for complete information on payment, including credit-card purchases, and a partial list of other educational resources available from the Department.

In addition, an illustrated *Educational Resources Catalog* describing publications, videos, and other instructional media available from the Department can be obtained without charge by writing to the address given above or by calling the Sales Office at (916) 445-1260. Prices for all publications are subject to change.

To
Wilson C. Riles

Teacher, statesman, tireless champion of children
State Superintendent of Public Instruction, 1971–1983

We saw the vision through his eyes.
We felt the passion through his spirit.
His legacy was to kindle the flame,
and ours is to keep it burning,
for the children.

Contents

Note: The corresponding text from the *English–Language Arts Content Standards* can be found at the end of each grade-level section.

Foreword

When parents bring their children to the classroom door, they are entrusting our schools with this nation's most precious resource. No more important public service exists than to ensure that when children leave our schools as young adults, they are empowered with the language skills they need to be successful, contributing members of an information society that relies increasingly on the power and richness of language for effective communication. We take this responsibility seriously and invite you to participate with us as we implement a system that will ensure that every student will be reading at least by the third grade and will graduate with a full range of abilities in the language arts.

Reading has been described as emancipation because it allows the mind access to all previously recorded human thought. Its corollary, writing, allows us to communicate with the future. And listening and speaking, tools of the present, allow us to connect with people throughout the world. Without the ability to read, write, listen, and speak well, our students will find themselves lost in a world where even basic transactions assume facility with language. The importance of our responsibility to teach students to read with comprehension and enthusiasm, to listen with understanding and compassion, to speak with conviction and effect, and to write with clarity and persuasion cannot be overstated.

To accomplish that ambitious task, we are providing a framework that offers a blueprint for implementation of the language arts content standards adopted by the California State Board of Education in 1997. Those world-class standards, comprehensive and balanced, may require changes in instructional programs, instructional materials, staff development, and assessment strategies. A standards-based system of curricular and instructional programs that accelerates and sustains the early and continued achievement in reading and the language arts by all students in California's public education system, kindergarten through grade twelve, is described in this framework. That system cannot and will not be implemented, however, without the participation and contributions of teachers, administrators, parents, students, and all other stakeholders in a literate society. Teaching our children to use and enjoy the power of language is a shared responsibility. We look forward to working with you to ensure that all students attain the highest possible levels of language and literacy.

DELAINE EASTIN
State Superintendent of Public Instruction

YVONNE LARSEN
President, California State Board of Education

Preface

Responsibility for ensuring that all students develop proficiency in the language arts is not new. The increasing social, economic, and technological demands for students to be proficient in reading, writing, listening, and speaking are urgent and unforgiving. For high school graduates in California to proceed to institutions of higher education or to be employable and meet the unprecedented civic, economic, and technological challenges of the twenty-first century, they must be more than merely literate. They must be able to read all forms of text fluently and independently, communicate effectively and creatively in oral and written form, and comprehend and deliver complex forms of discourse. In addition to those pragmatic and economic purposes of language arts proficiency, the role of California educators is to instill in students (1) a lifelong love of reading; (2) a facility and joy of communicating through language; and (3) a deep appreciation of literary and informational text and the ways in which print expands our universe and our understanding of history and humanity.

Our students will require higher levels of literacy skills than ever before. California has put in place a system of support to respond to that reality and to achieve the goal that all students who graduate are proficient in the language arts. An integral component of that system is the *Reading/ Language Arts Framework for California Public Schools, Kindergarten Through Grade Twelve*. Content standards, well-designed materials, skilled teachers, and a comprehensive program of assessment complete the system.

This framework is based on the rigorous English–language arts content standards adopted by the State Board in November of 1997. Those standards form the basis of curriculum development at every grade level and a statewide assessment and accountability system. *Education Code* Section 60605(f) requires that this framework be aligned with the standards.

The *Reading/Language Arts Framework* replaces the 1987 *English–Language Arts Framework* and relies heavily on the converging research base in beginning reading. It responds to the charge of the State Superintendent of Public Instruction and the State Board of Education to ensure that all students can read at grade level at least by the end of the third grade. The framework observes the commitment to a balanced and comprehensive language arts program, defining balance as the differential instructional emphasis on specific skills and strategies at strategic points in a learner's instruction to ensure proficiency according to all language arts standards.

This framework addresses reading, writing, speaking, listening, and written and oral English-language conventions for the full range of learners and across the full kindergarten through grade twelve educational span. The standards and the framework give special emphasis to continuity and progression in the language arts curriculum and to the reality that standards in the earlier grades are building blocks for proficiency in the later grades. Educators must make a commitment to provide the necessary support to ensure that all students reach proficiency. The framework further recognizes and addresses the critical linkages among curriculum, instruction, and assessment to enhance student learning. Effective, well-trained teachers and quality instructional materials that select and sequence information to optimize learning and the retention of information are at the core of effective programs. The framework emphasizes the important content and instructional connections that can and should be made across domains and standards to provide a coherent, effective, and efficient program of language arts instruction.

The standards describe the content students should master by the end of each grade level. The framework elaborates on those standards and describes the curriculum and instruction necessary to help students achieve the levels of mastery. It also focuses on specific grade-level, standards-based instruction and, as such, has a purpose much different from frameworks of the past. Most important, this framework focuses on developing the highest levels of language arts proficiency to enable students to participate fully in society and the world of work and to unlock the power and pleasure of communicating effectively in the English language.

LESLIE FAUSSET
Chief Deputy Superintendent
Educational Policy, Curriculum, and
*   Department Management*

SONIA HERNANDEZ
Deputy Superintendent
Curriculum and Instructional Leadership Branch

WENDY HARRIS
Assistant Superintendent and Director
Elementary Division

CATHERINE BARKETT
Administrator
Curriculum Frameworks and Instructional
*   Resources Office*

Acknowledgments

Fifteen California educators selected from 200 applicants were appointed in 1996 by the Curriculum Development and Supplemental Materials Commission (Curriculum Commission) and confirmed by the California State Board of Education to serve on the Curriculum Framework and Criteria Committee for English–Language Arts and English as a Second Language. More than half of the diverse group taught students in kindergarten through grade twelve. Other members were school principals, a coordinating field librarian, a reading specialist, county office curriculum coordinators, and university educators.

After more than a year of intensive meetings and writing focused on creating a comprehensive and balanced document, the committee produced a preliminary draft. During the summer of 1997, that draft underwent an in-depth review and evaluation by a prominent California reading researcher to ensure that it was grounded in relevant research and practice. Simultaneously, the newly developed English–language arts content standards were being finalized by the Commission for the Establishment of Academic Content and Performance Standards. In addition, new legislation was enacted that called for all frameworks to be fully aligned with the corresponding content standards. Adoption of the standards by the State Board and the new legislation required that the preliminary draft of the framework be revised to reflect a new focus on the implementation of the standards and the instruction students must receive to meet those standards successfully.

An invitation to bid was issued to obtain assistance in reshaping the preliminary draft to meet the new criteria. The draft was submitted to new writers, who then created a draft for field review that was aligned with the English–language arts content standards and contained an instructional context for those standards. More than 2,000 copies of the draft framework were distributed to educators and other experts across the state and nation during the field review process in June and July 1998. The Curriculum Commission held two public hearings to receive feedback on the draft in July and August 1998 and directed the writers and Department of Education staff to make necessary revisions. The State Board conducted two public hearings on the framework in fall 1998 and adopted the *Reading/Language Arts Framework for California Public Schools, Kindergarten Through Grade Twelve* in December 1998.

The principal writers of the framework were:

Edward J. Kame'enui, University of Oregon, Eugene

Deborah C. Simmons, University of Oregon, Eugene

The following members of the Subject-Matter Committee for English–Language Arts and English as a Second Language were responsible for overseeing the development of the framework:

Chair
Lillian Vega Castaneda, California State University, San Marcos

Vice-Chair
Marilyn Astore, Sacramento County Office of Education

Members
Patrice Abarca, Los Angeles Unified School District
Eleanor Brown, San Juan Unified School District
Ken Dotson, Turlock Joint Elementary School District
Lisa Jeffery, Los Angeles Unified School District
Susan Stickel, Elk Grove Unified School District
Jean Williams (Retired), Fresno Unified School District

The work of the Subject-Matter Committee was greatly supported by the State Board of Education liaisons:

Kathryn Dronenburg
Marion Joseph

The other members of the Curriculum Commission were:

Kirk Ankeney (Chair, 1998), San Diego City Unified School District
Roy Anthony, Grossmont Union High School District
Michele Garside, Laguna Salada Union Elementary School District
Viken Hovsepian, Glendale Unified School District
Joseph Nation, San Rafael
Richard Schwartz, Torrance Unified School District
Barbara Smith, San Rafael City Elementary and High School Districts
Sheri Willebrand, Ventura Unified School District

The Curriculum Commission benefited from the work of the Curriculum Framework and Criteria Committee for English–Language Arts and English as a Second Language. The committee members were:

Kathy Allen, Palos Verdes Peninsula Unified School District
Gladys Frantz, San Francisco Unified School District
Magdalena Ruz Gonzalez, Pacific Oaks College
Dewey Hall, Rowland Unified School District
Carol Jago, Santa Monica-Malibu Unified School District
Nancy Kotowski, Monterey County Office of Education
Kathy Marin, Whittier City School District
Jo Anne Polite, Los Angeles Unified School District
Marilyn Robertson, Los Angeles Unified School District
John Shefelbine, California State University, Sacramento
George Sheridan, Black Oak Mine Unified School District
Takako Suzuki, Los Angeles Unified School District
Jerry Treadway, San Diego State University, Framework Committee Chair
Sharon Ulanoff, California State University, San Marcos
Kami Winding, New Haven Unified School District

The writer for the committee was
Lisa Ray Kelly, Ukiah.

California Department of Education staff members who contributed to developing the framework were:

Sonia Hernandez, Deputy Superintendent, Curriculum and Instructional Leadership Branch

Catherine Barkett, Administrator, Curriculum Frameworks and Instructional Resources Office

Christine Bridges, Analyst, Curriculum Frameworks and Instructional Resources Office

Nancy Brynelson, Consultant, Reading and Mathematics Policy and Leadership Office

Wendy Harris, Assistant Superintendent and Director, Elementary Division

Diane Levin, Language Arts Consultant, Curriculum Frameworks and Instructional Resources Office

Christine Rodrigues, Consultant, Curriculum Frameworks and Instructional Resources Office

Nancy Sullivan, Administrator, Education Technology Office

Special appreciation is extended to:

Karen Buxton, Curriculum Specialist for Language Arts, Grades 7–12, San Juan Unified School District, for her assistance in revising the final version of the framework for grades seven through twelve

Marjorie DeBuse, University of Oregon, for her assistance in writing sections of the framework related to advanced learners

Claude Goldenberg, California State University, Long Beach, for his assistance in revising sections of the framework related to beginning reading

Robin Scarcella, University of California, Irvine, for her assistance in writing sections of the framework related to English learners

Introduction to the Framework

The framework uses the English–language arts content standards as its curricular platform and aligns curriculum, assessment, instruction, and organization to provide a comprehensive, coherent structure for language arts teaching and learning.

The purpose of the California *Reading/Language Arts Framework* is to provide a blueprint for organizing instruction so that every child meets or exceeds the language arts content standards. It will guide the implementation of the standards by specifying the design of instructional materials, curriculum, instruction, and professional development. The standards designate what to teach at specific grade levels, and this framework provides guidelines and selected research-based approaches for implementing instruction to ensure optimal benefits for all students, including those with special learning needs (e.g., English learners, students with learning disabilities and reading difficulties, and advanced learners).

Teachers should
not be expected
to be the
composers
of the music as
well as the
conductors of
the orchestra.

*Kathi Cooper,
Sacramento City
Unified School District*

Audiences for the Framework

The framework has two primary audiences: (1) teachers and other educators involved in English–language arts instruction; and (2) developers and publishers of language arts programs and materials. Parents, members of the community, and policymakers can be guided by the framework as they review language arts programs at the local and state levels. Educators will use this framework and the content standards as a road map for curriculum and instruction. Publishers must attend to the content and pedagogical requirements specified in the content standards and the framework to ensure that all California students have access to research-based instructional and practice materials. Carefully articulated curricular sequences and quality instructional materials enable teachers to invest more energy in delivering instruction and assessing the effectiveness of instruction for the full range of learners in their classrooms.

The Context of the Language Arts

In a suburban elementary school, seven-year-old Joshua enters the second grade reading two correct words in a minute and scoring at the ninth percentile on a standardized measure of receptive vocabulary. He cannot read the words *mom* or *can* or identify pictures that represent the meanings of *group* or *pair*. In the same second-grade classroom, seven-year-old Ricardo reads third-grade material fluently and provides a detailed and vivid recall of the story depicting the race between a tortoise and a hare. Judith, an eleven-year-old student with a reading disability, is repeating the fourth grade in an urban school in another part of the state. She labors over each of the words in a history passage on the California Gold Rush and has extreme difficulty in writing basic sentences to summarize the major points in the text.

Michael, an eighth-grade student in a rural school, reads and comprehends Guy de Maupassant's short story "The Necklace" with ease, carefully comparing and contrasting the theme with that of other short stories and communicating his ideas fluently and eloquently in writing. In a suburban high school on the coast, the instructional diversity of an eleventh-grade classroom poses particular challenges as students with reading abilities that span more than six grade levels read *Of Mice and Men* by John Steinbeck and orally support their viewpoints and positions with details from the text.

The individual differences of the students just mentioned are as varied as their educational performances. Many plausible factors can explain why Michael excels and Judith struggles. Previous instructional experiences, prior knowledge of concepts and content, the socioeconomic level of the family, and motivation are all part of the complex equation of factors that can determine children's literacy success. The common denominator of the students is the need to develop competence in the language arts to ensure that they will be able to access information with ease, apply language skills at levels demanded in the twenty-first century, appreciate literature, and obtain the liberty society offers to those who can use the English language with facility. The mission of all public schools must be to ensure that students acquire that proficiency to enhance their civic participation and their academic, social, personal, and economic success in today's society and tomorrow's world.

The Challenge in the Language Arts

Facility in the language arts is the enabling skill that traverses academic disciplines and translates into meaningful personal, social, and economic outcomes for individuals. Literacy is the key to becoming an independent learner in all the other disciplines. Society has long recognized the importance of successful reading. But only recently have we begun to understand the profound, enduring consequences of not learning to read well and the newly found evidence of the critical abbreviated period in which to alter patterns of reading failure (California Department of Education 1995; Juel 1988; Lyon and Chhabra 1996). Most important, we recognize the convergence of evidence to guide instruction in the language arts (National Research Council 1998).

One need not look beyond school dropout data, prison rosters, or public assistance rolls to find that the problem of illiteracy is pervasive and is especially common to many who are not succeeding in a society whose literacy demands continue to exacerbate the divisions between the haves and the have-nots. Studies of individuals who are resilient in facing personal and social adversity indicate that the ability to read and write well renders powerful, far-reaching positive effects. Literacy levels are positively associated with both higher annual income and lower unemployment. On the other hand, the absence of proficient reading and writing skills is associated not only with academic failure and dropping out of school but also with unemployment and involvement with the judicial system (Cornwall and Bawden 1992; Werner 1993).

Stanovich (1986) observes that students who read early and successfully not only reap the advantages of early literacy but also accumulate experiences with print that continue to differentiate good readers from poor readers throughout their academic careers. Unfortunately, the rich-get-richer phenomenon known as the Matthew Effect (see glossary) has been verified in both the academic and the economic domains. Individuals who test at the least-proficient levels of literacy are often unemployable because even low-skill jobs today demand adequate ability in reading (Whitman and Gest 1995).

In 1993 Peter Drucker described the advent of the knowledge society in which knowledge workers will replace blue-collar workers as the dominant class in the twenty-first century. According to Drucker society will demand more sophisticated print-oriented skills than are currently required of the American workforce. America will be greatly challenged in general to develop competitive knowledge workers. In 1996 Simmons and Kame'enui remarked that those referred to as vulnerable learners would be especially challenged; that is, students who, because of their instructional, socioeconomic, experiential, physiological, and neurological characteristics, bring different and often additional requirements to instruction and curriculum.

The Charge to Educators

Reading/language arts and related disciplines are the beneficiaries of an abundance of converging research that produces a professional knowledge base related to fostering and sustaining competence in the language arts, particularly beginning reading. Noteworthy advances have identified the features of curricular and instructional interventions to offset negative factors that can accompany

Students who read early and successfully not only reap the advantages of early literacy but also accumulate experiences with print that continue to differentiate good readers from poor readers throughout their academic careers.

children when they enter school (Hanson and Farrell 1995; Lipson and Wixson 1986). As educational leaders it is our charge to use that knowledge base responsibly and strategically to ensure that all children educated in California public schools will graduate with the knowledge and skills that allow them to access and employ the power of the printed word. Toward that end this framework is designed to provide a blueprint for curriculum and instruction to enhance all students' potential as producers and users of language.

Guiding Principles

In an effort to accelerate and sustain all learners' proficiency in the language arts, ten principles are used to guide this framework and address the complexity of the content and context of language arts instruction. The principles direct the purpose, design, delivery, and evaluation of instruction. Accordingly, the framework:

- *Uses the English–language arts content standards as its curricular platform and aligns curriculum, assessment, instruction, and organization* to provide a comprehensive, coherent structure for language arts teaching and learning. The standards serve as curricular guideposts for teachers and provide clear-cut curricular goals for all learners. Genuine alignment of curriculum, assessment, instruction, and organization rests at the school level. There the components must be identified, implemented, and adjusted to fit the conditions and contexts of the school and the needs of the learners.
- *Stresses the importance of a balanced, comprehensive program. Balanced* is defined as the strategic selection and scheduling of instruction to ensure

that students meet or exceed those standards, and *comprehensive* is defined as the inclusion of all content standards. Although more or less emphasis is placed on particular strands, depending on students' needs at a given time, all strands are to be developed simultaneously.

—*Balanced* does not mean that all skills and standards receive equal emphasis at a given point in time. Rather, it implies that the overall emphasis accorded to a skill or standard is determined by its priority or importance relative to students' language and literacy levels and needs. For example, in kindergarten and the first grade, students first learn to apply and practice decoding and word-attack skills in carefully controlled, decodable texts. Later in the first grade and in subsequent grades the emphasis on decodable texts shifts to less-controlled passages and literature as students develop proficiency in the skills needed for reading in an alphabetic writing system.

—A *comprehensive* program ensures that students learn to read and write, comprehend and compose, appreciate and analyze, and perform and enjoy the language arts. They should spend time immersed in high-quality literature and work with expository text, learn foundational skills in the alphabetic writing system, and study real books. A comprehensive program ensures that students master foundational skills as a gateway to using all forms of language as tools for thinking, learning, and communicating (Bay Area Reading Task Force 1997).

- *Emphasizes that students must be fluent readers at least by the end of the third grade* and that third-grade competence depends on the specific and cumulative mastery of skills in kindergarten through grade three together with the development of positive attitudes toward reading and writing. Consistent with the content standards, the framework recognizes that the advanced skills of comprehending narrative and informational text and literary response and analysis and the creation of eloquent prose all depend on solid vocabulary, decoding, and word-recognition skills fostered in the early grades and sustained throughout the school years.

- *Describes the important skills, concepts, and strategies that students must be able to use after the third grade* and attends specifically to those advanced higher-order skills from grades four through twelve that require explicit and systematic instruction.

- *Provides guidance to ensure that all educators and learners understand* that (1) specific skills in reading, writing, speaking, and listening must be taught and learned; (2) the language arts are related, reciprocal processes that build on and strengthen one another; and (3) the language arts can be learned across all academic disciplines.

- *Promotes a preventive rather than remedial approach.* The most effective instructional approach is to prevent reading/language arts problems before they begin. The key to success is to make the first instruction students receive their best instruction.

- *Assumes that all learners will work toward the same standards* yet recognizes that not all learners will acquire skills and knowledge at the same rate. Intervention strategies must be in place to identify students who are not progressing adequately and to intervene at all levels as early and as long as necessary to support their acquisition of learning in the language arts.

- *Addresses the full range of learners in classrooms*, with specific attention being given to language arts instruction and the learning needs of English learners, special education students, students with learning difficulties, and advanced learners. The framework addresses students with special needs at both ends of the academic continuum; that is, those who enter with less-than-adequate skills and struggle to develop fundamental competence and those who enter with advanced skills that require curriculum modifications to foster optimal achievement.

- *Assumes that virtually all students can learn to read* and that older struggling readers will benefit from refocusing instruction on building the skills, strategies, and knowledge that are the foundation for subsequent success in reading/language arts.

- *Is designed to be useful to a wide range of consumers*, including professional developers, reading specialists, library media teachers, principals, district and county leaders of curriculum and instruction, college and university teacher educators, teachers, parents, community members, and publishers. However, the framework is first and foremost a tool for teachers and a guide for publishers and developers of educational materials.

Organization of the Framework

The organization of this framework is based on the content of the *English–Language Arts Content Standards* (California Department of Education 1998a). Accordingly, the framework:

- Presents the goals and key components of an effective language arts program (Chapter 2)
- Describes the curriculum content and instructional practices needed for students to master the *English–Language Arts Content Standards* (Chapter 3 for K–3, Chapter 4 for grades 4–8, and Chapter 5 for grades 9–12)
- Guides the development of appropriate assessment tools and methods to ensure that each student's progress toward achieving specific knowledge, skills, and understanding in language arts is measured (Chapter 6)
- Suggests specific strategies to promote access to appropriately challenging curriculum for students with special needs (Chapter 7)
- Describes the systems of support, including professional development, that should be in place for effective implementation of a rigorous and coherent language arts curriculum (Chapter 8)
- Specifies requirements for instructional resources, including print and electronic learning resources (Chapter 9)

Chapters 3, 4, and 5, which detail standards-based curriculum content and instructional practices for the major grade-level clusters (K–3, 4–8, and 9–12), are further organized according to (1) curriculum content overview for each grade-level cluster; (2) overview of standards and

instruction for each grade; (3) classroom connections indicating sample integration points (K–8); and (4) curricular and instructional profiles illustrating a selected standard for each grade. *Note:* The corresponding text from the *English–Language Arts Content Standards* can be found at the end of each grade-level section.

Essential to the organization of this framework is the structure of the standards themselves. They are categorized by domain: reading, writing, written and oral English-language conventions, and listening and speaking. Within each domain, strands and substrands are also used to categorize the standards. The structure of the content standards is illustrated on the following page in the sample table for the first grade. Appendix A provides an overview of the domain strands and substrands by grade.

The standards (e.g., 1.1–1.3) within substrands and strands serve as benchmarks by which to gauge what students should learn at designated points in time and over time. The strands are not intended to suggest that each standard is to be given equal weight in a given year. Instead, the weight and emphasis of a particular strand must be determined by (1) the role of the standards within the strand to developing competence within a specific domain, such as reading or writing; and (2) the performance of the learners. The English–language arts content standards illustrate the complexity of teaching the language arts, the multiple components that must be examined and integrated to create a comprehensive program, and the critical and integral relation of earlier and later skills.

The standards are mastery standards, meaning that students should master or be proficient in the knowledge, skills, and strategies specified in a particular standard, at least by the end of the designated grade. Instruction to develop such proficiency is not, however, restricted to a specific grade.

The standards are mastery standards, meaning that students should master or be proficient in the knowledge, skills, and strategies specified in a particular standard, at least by the end of the designated grade.

Structure of the Content Standards

DOMAIN	STRAND		SUBSTRAND	STANDARD	
Reading	1.0	Word analysis, fluency, and systematic vocabulary development	Concepts about print	1.1	Match oral words to printed words.
				1.2	Identify the title and author of a reading selection.
				1.3	Identify letters, words, and sentences.

Essential to the organization of this framework is the structure of the standards themselves.

Publishers and teachers should consider the prerequisite skills and sequence of instruction students will need to master a standard by the end of the grade and introduce and sequence instruction within and between grades to ensure mastery at least by the grade in which the standard is identified. For example, Reading Standard 1.9 specifies that students will be able to divide single-syllable words into their components (e.g., /c/ /a/ /t/ = cat). This standard does not propose that students wait until the first grade to begin sequential segmentation but that they master the skill at least by the end of the first grade.

In recognition that a substantial portion of the instructional day must be devoted to language arts instruction, educators and publishers of instructional materials should address the history–social science and science content standards simultaneously with the language arts standards, particularly for kindergarten through grade three.

Two considerations regarding the treatment of standards are that (1) the complexity of the language arts and the number of content standards preclude a comprehensive, detailed analysis of each standard in the framework; and (2) the discussion of the standards in the framework parallels their organization by domains, strands, and substrands, whereas in practice those features are interwoven. *No attempt is made to address every standard within the grade-level discussions; rather, standards important to understanding the domains or standards new to a particular grade are highlighted and discussed.* Standards may be paraphrased or restated to illustrate the descriptions. The full text of the *English–Language Arts Content Standards* is included in the corresponding grade-level sections. Similarly, the connections between standards are not thoroughly explored in the descriptions of grade-level standards. Instead, they are addressed in (1) the samples of integration points in the grade-level sections; and (2) the representative content standards and instructional connections in Appendix B.

Curricular and instructional profiles serve as a starting point for curriculum planning and instruction for a selected standard at each grade level. Profiles include critical dimensions that should be components of effective language arts lessons. Ideally, the components would be incorporated into published commercial materials. But if the components are not fully developed in existing materials, the profiles offer a model for teachers to use in modifying and strengthening instruction for the full range of learners. It is not suggested, however, that profiles be developed for all standards. Instead, designers will want to consider the interrelationship of standards across domains and strands in curriculum planning and instruction and in the development of instructional resources. (See the following "Key to Curricular and Instructional Profiles" for details on the elements of the curricular and instructional profiles.)

Key to Curricular and Instructional Profiles

Domain, Strand, Substrand, and Standard

Prerequisite or corequisite standards (or both) are listed at the beginning of the profile for each grade.

Curricular and Instructional Decisions

Instructional Objectives	Definitions of what is to be taught and learned.
Instructional Design	Strategic selection and sequencing of information to be taught. Features of instructional design include what to teach, when to introduce skills and concepts, how to select examples, how to integrate standards, and how to teach for transference and generalization.
Instructional Delivery	Procedures and strategies teachers use to develop students' skills and knowledge. Materials should provide clear steps of how to introduce the skill or strategy. This dimension includes what teachers and students do. Modeling, pacing, reinforcement, questioning, corrections, and feedback are also included. It further involves the structure of delivery, including teacher demonstration or modeling, guided practice, peer-mediated instruction, and independent practice and application.
Assessment	Three critical purposes are addressed:

1. *Entry-level assessment for instructional planning:* how to determine the skill level of students through the use of meaningful indicators of reading and language arts proficiency prior to instruction
2. *Monitoring student progress toward the instructional objective:* how to determine whether students are making adequate progress on skills and concepts taught directly
3. *Post-test assessment toward the standard:* how to determine the effectiveness of instruction and students' proficiency after instruction

**Universal
Access**

Although all learners work toward mastery of the same standards, curriculum and instruction are differentiated to meet students' needs. Some students may meet more than one of the following descriptions:

1. *Students with reading difficulties or disabilities.* Are the standard and objective appropriate for the learner in content and number of objectives? Can students use the same materials? Or will materials need to be modified to accommodate the speaking, listening, reading, or writing competence of the learners?

2. *Students who are advanced learners.* Determine whether the content has been mastered by the student. Do the content and activities need to be accelerated or enriched? Are the content and objectives appropriate for the learners? If not, how can the materials and requirements of the task be modified?

3. *Students who are English learners.* Is more extensive instruction of vocabulary or other English-language features necessary to achieve the standard? Is the rate of introduction of new information manageable for learners? Is there sufficient oral and written modeling of new skills and concepts and reinforcement of previously taught information? Have linguistic elements in the lesson or materials been modified as appropriate for the proficiency level of the students?

**Instructional
Materials**

Criteria to consider include the following:

1. Introduction of content, skills, and strategies is carefully sequenced.
2. Number and range of examples are adequate.
3. Prerequisite skills are addressed, and materials provide sufficient review of previously taught skills and strategies.
4. Assessment tasks parallel the requirements of the standard.

Goal and Key Components of Effective Language Arts Instruction

The child's first instruction must employ the most valid and effective methods available to ensure mastery of the skills that lay the foundation for further reading achievement.

The *Reading/Language Arts Framework* specifies the strategic and systematic reading and language skills and knowledge that students should learn and teachers should teach to achieve competence in the language arts. A primary assumption is that students master particular skills and knowledge at designated points in time and that earlier skills are foundational and requisite for later, more complex higher-order skills and knowledge. Those skills and knowledge are carefully mapped out in the *English–Language Arts Content Standards.* A critical feature of the standards and this framework is that gaps, delays, and deficits in skills and knowledge experienced in previous grades must still be addressed responsively and responsibly.

11

Chapter 2
Goal and Key
Components
of Effective
Language Arts
Instruction

Goal of Effective Language Arts Instruction

The knowledge and skills that enable eleventh- and twelfth-grade students to verify facts from public documents and critique their truthfulness, write carefully constructed persuasive essays, and develop and present a research question and supporting evidence with multimedia do not begin in the eleventh grade but originate in the early grades through careful development of language arts competence in specific and integrated skills and knowledge. The task of California schools, then, is to develop and deliver a language arts curriculum that is systematic and carefully articulated and establishes specific, continuing standards leading to competence and alignment with the *English–Language Arts Content Standards.*

The goal of developing lifelong readers and writers begins early in students' lives and represents a unique balance of competence, motivation, accessibility, and experiences with print. When students develop competence in the fundamentals of reading and writing, they increase their motivation to achieve. Educators should be keenly aware of the inherent difficulty of learning to read and write in English and of the integral linkage between proficiency and motivation. Difficulties in mastering the elements of reading, writing, listening, and speaking can easily and directly "stifle motivation . . . [and] in turn hamper instructional efforts" (National Research Council 1998, 316). The child's first instruction must employ the most valid and effective methods available to ensure mastery of the skills that lay the foundation for further reading achievement.

Key Components of Effective Language Arts Instruction

Assumption: The effectiveness of instruction is measured by student performance according to valid, reliable assessment aligned with the language arts content standards.

Knowledge gained over the past three decades reveals the multiple contexts that shape the quantity and quality of learning (Carroll 1963, 1989; Mosenthal 1984, 1985). Effective language arts programs are dynamic and involve professionals, policies, instructional materials, and practices that interact in complex ways. The best practices of any profession are not gained in a vacuum but are implemented and sustained in environments that support, enhance, and reinforce those practices and include several dimensions (Smith, Simmons, and Kame'enui 1998).

In 1995 the California Reading Task Force identified four components that a balanced, comprehensive approach to reading must contain: (1) a strong literature, language, and comprehension program that includes a balance of oral and written language; (2) an organized, explicit skills program that includes phonemic awareness (sounds in words), phonics, and decoding skills to address the needs of the emergent reader; (3) ongoing diagnosis that informs teaching and assessment that ensures accountability; and (4) a powerful early intervention program that provides individual tutoring for students at risk of failure in reading.

The key components of an effective language arts program (an expansion of

The goal of developing lifelong readers and writers begins early in students' lives and represents a unique balance of competence, motivation, accessibility, and experiences with print.

the four elements contained in *Every Child a Reader* [California Department of Education 1995]) are assessment, instruction, instructional time, instructional programs and materials, instructional grouping and scheduling, differentiated instruction, classroom instructional and management practices, professional development, administrative practices, parent and community involvement, motivation, effort, and academic language. Each of the components is described in the following sections. *Note:* Both the strength of the components and their strategic integration are required for effective instruction in the language arts.

Assessment in the Language Arts

Assessment anchored to important learning objectives should provide the basis for instruction. Different types of assessment used at strategic points (before, during, and after instruction) provide information critical to determining what to teach, how much the students are learning, and whether the students have achieved mastery. Characteristics of the assessment component in an effective language arts program are as follows:

Assessment of student performance is used to determine what students need to learn and what teachers need to teach.

- Assessment of student performance is used to determine what students need to learn and what teachers need to teach. It is also used to determine what students have already learned well and what teachers do not have to teach.
- Indicators of critical skills and strategies are used to identify students at risk of difficulty and in need of specialized instruction.
- Ongoing assessment of student performance is linked closely to instruction and curriculum activities as well as school-site goals, district and state standards, and state assessments.

- Teachers receive training and support to manage assessment. Teachers or trained paraprofessionals can make quick, focused checks of an individual student's progress while the remaining students are engaged in meaningful work.
- Formal and informal as well as formative and summative measures are used to document student performance.
- Summative assessment assists sites, districts, and the state in monitoring the effectiveness of established programs.

Instruction in the Language Arts

High-quality instruction is at the heart of all good language arts programs. A comprehensive, balanced language arts program in which curriculum and instruction are differentiated according to assessed needs should be provided to all students. Characteristics of the instruction component in an effective language arts program are as follows:

- The curriculum for reading and the language arts in kindergarten through grade three provides explicit and systematic instruction and diagnostic support in:

  —Phonemic awareness
  —Phonics
  —Decoding
  —Word-attack skills
  —Spelling
  —Vocabulary
  —Comprehension skills
  —Writing skills and strategies and their application
  —Listening and speaking skills and strategies

- The curriculum for reading and the language arts in grades four through

13

Chapter 2
Goal and Key
Components
of Effective
Language Arts
Instruction

twelve provides explicit and systematic instruction and diagnostic support in:

—Word-attack skills (e.g., decoding and structural as applied to multisyllabic words)
—Spelling
—Vocabulary
—Comprehension skills, including contextual skills
—Text-handling and strategic reading skills
—Writing skills and strategies and their application
—Listening and speaking skills and their application

- For students in grades four through twelve who do not demonstrate competence in the skills and knowledge required in kindergarten through grade three, assessments are conducted and systematic instruction is provided in the necessary prerequisite skills, such as:

—Phonemic awareness
—Specific instruction in decoding and phonics
—Fluency
—Vocabulary and language development
—Comprehension strategies

- Teachers adapt learning contexts to challenge and extend the skills of advanced learners. Opportunities for acceleration and enrichment are provided.
- Even with the highest-quality classroom instruction, some students have difficulty progressing according to grade-level expectations. For those students assessment tools to diagnose specific instructional needs, together with instructional support and age-appropriate materials, are essential to address foundational skill deficits.

Instructional Time

Opportunities for students to learn are determined in part by the amount and use of time allocated for instruction. For proficiency in the language arts to be achieved, an adequate amount of time must be allocated to instruction, and that time must be protected from interruptions. Characteristics of the instructional time component in an effective language arts program are as follows:

- At the primary level a minimum of two and one-half hours of instructional time is allocated to language arts instruction daily. This time is given priority and is protected from interruption.
- In grades four through eight, two hours of instructional time are allocated to language arts instruction daily through core instructional periods or within a self-contained classroom.
- In grades nine through twelve, all students participate in a minimum of one course per semester of language arts instruction.
- Engaged academic time (the time students actively participate in appropriately challenging tasks) is maximized.
- Classroom and school time are allocated to activities and content highly correlated with essential reading and literacy skills.
- Students with special learning needs are provided additional instructional time and support. Additional time is allocated within the school day, before school, after school, and during vacation periods as necessary. At the secondary level additional courses and opportunities outside the school day and year are provided for students having difficulties with reading.

Chapter 2
Goal and Key
Components
of Effective
Language Arts
Instruction

Effective
instructional
programs and
materials can
greatly influence
the amount and
rate of learning
in classrooms.

- The school extends learning time for all students by promoting independent reading outside school in daily at-home reading assignments and expectations, use of summer reading lists, and family and community literacy activities.

Instructional Programs and Materials

Effective instructional programs and materials based on the English–language arts content standards and current and confirmed research can greatly influence the amount and rate of learning in classrooms. Characteristics of the instructional programs and materials component in an effective language arts program are as follows:

- Instructional materials incorporate specific strategies, teaching/instructional activities, procedures, examples, and opportunities for review and application consistent with current and confirmed research.
- Instructional materials prioritize and sequence essential skills and strategies in a logical, coherent manner and demonstrate the relationship between fundamental skills (e.g., decoding, vocabulary, and comprehension).
- Instructional materials address or reinforce content-area standards in mathematics, science, and history–social science whenever feasible.
- Instructional materials include activities that relate directly to the learning objectives. Extraneous material is kept to a minimum.
- In support of practice and motivation, students at every grade level have access to and are encouraged to use a collection of interesting and suitable library books in addition to their required texts.

- Curricular programs and instructional materials provide specific suggestions for special-needs students.
- Instructional materials for students in grades four through twelve who have reading difficulties align with age-appropriate interests and offer systematic practice of needed skills. Materials are available on topics that motivate learners to read.
- Instructional materials for English learners address the same curricular content described in this framework for English speakers and give additional emphasis to the structures and systems of English, including phonology, morphology, syntax, and semantics.
- A validated process is used to select both print and electronic instructional materials to promote high levels of achievement for the full array of learners.

Instructional Grouping and Scheduling

The purpose of instructional grouping and scheduling is to maximize opportunities to learn. First of all, content must govern instruction. Then instructional grouping and scheduling are used to enhance learning opportunities. Characteristics of the instructional grouping and scheduling component in an effective language arts program are as follows:

- Instruction is provided in flexible groupings to maximize student performance. Whole-group instruction or heterogeneous grouping may be used when the objectives are appropriate for the range of learners in the classroom. Homogeneous grouping may be used to customize specific instruction for assessed student needs.

15

Chapter 2
Goal and Key
Components
of Effective
Language Arts
Instruction

- Group size and composition are adjusted to accommodate and reflect student progress and instructional objectives (flexible and dynamic grouping).
- Tutoring (peer or adult or both) is used judiciously to supplement (not supplant) explicit teacher-delivered instruction. It aligns with classroom objectives and instruction.
- Cross-class or cross-grade grouping is used when appropriate to maximize opportunities to tailor instruction to students' performance levels. Such grouping is appropriate when it facilitates teaching students within a similar age span and achievement range. As a general rule, differences should be within one year in kindergarten through grade three, two years in grades four through eight, and three years in grades nine through twelve.
- Centers and independent activities are used judiciously and are aligned with instructional goals and objectives focused on achieving grade-level standards.

Differentiated Instruction

All students are expected to meet or exceed the grade-level expectations set forth in the *English–Language Arts Content Standards.* Differentiated instruction aims to optimize learning opportunities and outcomes for all students by tailoring instruction to meet their current level of knowledge and prerequisite skills. Students with a wide range of learning needs can be expected in almost any classroom, and their needs are addressed more fully in Chapter 7. Characteristics of the differentiated instruction component in an effective language arts program are as follows:

- Students with reading difficulties or disabilities are provided with oppor-

tunities for more intensive, systematic teaching and practice to learn the skills and strategies needed for meeting the standards. Those students with more intensive needs requiring special education services may need outside assistance and further instructional differentiation based on their individualized education programs.
- Teachers adapt learning contexts to stimulate and extend the proficiency of students who are advanced learners. Opportunities for acceleration and enrichment are provided.
- English learners develop proficiency in English and in the concepts and skills contained in the *English–Language Arts Content Standards.* Emphasis is placed on (1) instruction in reading and writing; and (2) simultaneous instruction in the acquisition of academic vocabulary and the phonological, morphological, and syntactical structures of English already understood by English speakers.
- Teachers adapt instruction for students with multiple needs (e.g., gifted English learners or students identified as gifted and eligible for special education services).

Classroom Instructional and Management Practices

Classroom and instructional management practices promote student engagement and maximize instructional time and effectiveness. Characteristics of the classroom instructional and management practices component in an effective language arts program are as follows:

- Classrooms are highly interactive and provide instruction, constructive feedback, and high levels of engage-

Chapter 2
Goal and Key
Components
of Effective
Language Arts
Instruction

ment together with appropriate activities and resources.

- Academic and social expectations are well established and are explicitly taught at the school and classroom levels. Classroom and schoolwide discipline plans and procedures are implemented consistently by all staff.

- The links between instruction, behavior, and the curriculum are so clear and strong that tasks and instruction are assigned at appropriate levels, students have a high probability of being successful, lessons are well paced, and the classroom/school environment is supportive.

- Teachers plan and manage whole-class and small-group lessons, independent student work, assessment tasks, and instructional materials efficiently and effectively so that the students are actively engaged, instructional time is maximized, and lesson objectives are achieved.

Professional Development

The preparation of teachers and ongoing support for their continuing professional development are critical to the quality of schools and increases in student achievement. Characteristics of the professional development component in an effective language arts program are as follows:

- Professional development for teachers focuses on student learning, with attention given to tailoring curriculum and instruction to students' needs, all of which is compatible with current research and the English–language arts content standards.

- Educators participate in the planning of their own professional learning.

- Activities are designed to be ongoing and in-depth and include a variety of strategies to help educators apply what they have learned and sustain improved instruction.

- Time is allocated for educators to reflect, discuss, analyze, and refine their own professional practices and to plan and refine instruction accordingly.

- The administration makes a commitment to ensure support, ongoing follow-up, and evaluation of professional development.

Administrative Practices

Administrative support of language arts instruction reminds all those involved in education that reform efforts are not considered effective unless they contribute to increased student achievement. Strong instructional leadership characterizes effective schools and can help maintain a focus on high-quality instruction. Characteristics of the administrative practices component in an effective language arts program are that administrators:

- Are knowledgeable about the English–language arts content standards and effective language arts programs. They work with teachers to create a coherent plan in the school for language arts instruction that is based on assessment and provides access to such programs for all students.

- Maximize and protect instructional time for language arts and organize the resources and personnel needed to support classroom assessment and instruction.

The preparation
of teachers and
ongoing support
for their
continuing
professional
development are
critical to the
quality of schools
and increases
in student
achievement.

17

Chapter 2
Goal and Key
Components
of Effective
Language Arts
Instruction

- Support the development of explicit schoolwide, grade-level, and individual performance goals, are aware of school and classroom language arts performance, institute practices to provide school-level performance information in a timely manner, and act to ensure that learning is adequate and is sustained over time.
- Ensure that all teachers are well trained in reading and the language arts and support teachers in their implementation of effective programs.
- Allocate resources, time, and staff in all grades for students who have not demonstrated competence on reading and writing standards. A commitment and plan of action are established to ensure that all students read and write at or above grade level.

Parent and Community Involvement

Ensuring that California's students are proficient in the language arts is everyone's concern. As stakeholders in that goal, parents, community members, college and university partners, and business and industry can all make significant contributions toward expanding student learning opportunities and designing and implementing exemplary language arts programs. Characteristics of the parent and community involvement component in an effective language arts program are as follows:

- Parents are well informed about the English–language arts content standards, the district's curriculum and assessment program, and the progress of their children in learning to read, write, speak, and listen.
- Parents are encouraged to involve themselves in education and are supported in their efforts to improve

their children's learning in reading and the language arts.
- Materials and programs are organized so that parents, siblings, and community members can provide extended learning experiences.
- College and university partners collaborate with schools and districts in designing and providing professional development, tutoring, and other programs to support increased student proficiency in language arts.
- The community is used as a classroom abundant in examples of how and why the language arts are important in our lives, our work, and our thinking.

Other Considerations

All stakeholders in the promotion of literacy should understand that the inclusion of the key instructional components described previously is the goal for all schools. Additional factors that are important in a successful language arts program are students' personal attributes, such as motivation and effort, and development of academic language.

Motivation

Successful teachers help students develop fundamental skills in reading that provide the foundation for all later work in the language arts. As students begin to develop those skills, effective teachers nurture the students' desire or motivation to learn for a number of reasons, including recognition of the critical link between the amount of reading students do and their vocabulary development. In language arts instruction motivation not only enhances the learning process but is also a necessary precursor for students choosing to read on their own. Motivation to read is especially important in light of the English–language

Chapter 2
Goal and Key
Components
of Effective
Language Arts
Instruction

In language arts instruction motivation not only enhances the learning process but is also a necessary precursor for students choosing to read on their own.

arts content standards, which call for students to do a significant amount of reading in addition to their regular school reading: by the fourth grade, one-half million words annually; by the eighth grade, one million words annually; and by the twelfth grade, two million words annually.

The important dimensions of motivation to read are an individual's self-concept as a reader and the value placed on reading (Gambrell et al. 1996). Self-concept derives in large part from the individual's skill in reading; that is, by mastering standards in reading, the student becomes motivated. The value of reading can be promoted by teachers in many ways, such as by:

- Displaying their own enthusiasm for reading and appreciation of its value
- Providing appropriate reading materials (readable and interesting)
- Creating a stimulating learning environment
- Modeling positive reading behaviors (Ediger 1988)
- Encouraging students to take home books that are appropriate to their reading levels
- Encouraging parents to read to their children and to model the value of reading at home for pleasure and information

Motivation and reading for pleasure are mutually reinforcing. Reading for pleasure should be promoted in every classroom, and the school should supply a wide variety of interesting reading materials at the students' independent reading levels, allow time to read (Shefelbine 1991), and assign reading as homework. Motivation is also linked to four key features of literacy learning: providing access to books, offering a choice of texts, establishing familiarity with a topic, and promoting

social interactions about books (Gambrell et al. 1996).

Reading programs should reflect a desire for students to "compose lives in which reading matters" (Calkins 1996, 32–33). Encouraging the habit of independent reading is crucial in helping students understand and appreciate the value of reading. Independent classroom reading, particularly in kindergarten through grade six, can serve as a practical way of linking vocabulary and comprehension and complementing other instructional approaches while expanding word knowledge in a realistic setting. The teacher should schedule time for independent reading daily and should serve as a model of how to read well as students engage in silent reading with books selected by themselves or by the teacher. A balance of encouraging wide and varied reading as much as possible and of using modeling at appropriate times in clear, demonstrative, and motivational ways is very beneficial (Sanacore 1988).

Effort

Together with motivation, student effort is an essential element for successful learning. Research on high achievers—whether in mathematics, athletics, the arts, science, or business—reveals that successful people exert enormous effort (Gardner 1983; Bloom 1985). Of all the variables affecting success, effort is the one most within the control of the students. They must learn that in the language arts a direct relationship exists between effort and achievement, just as in sports, music, and every other discipline. Effective teachers teach that principle explicitly and create opportunities for students to demonstrate it (Hunter and Barker 1987).

Holding students to high standards conveys respect for them as learners.

19

Chapter 2
Goal and Key
Components
of Effective
Language Arts
Instruction

Feedback to students about failure on a task that could have been accomplished with more effort communicates to students that they have the abilities necessary to succeed and need to exert them. Conversely, a teacher's acceptance of less than standard work from students while knowing that they are capable of more serves only to convince students that they do not have to try or that the teacher does not believe that the students can succeed (Hunter and Barker 1987).

Successful classrooms are places of expectation and responsibility. Young people are expected to work hard, think things through, and produce their best work. Teachers support students with a range of guides and structures, organizing the curriculum to stimulate learning and thinking, inviting and answering questions, providing positive and corrective feedback, encouraging peer support and assistance, and creating a trusting classroom atmosphere. In successful classrooms students contribute to the flow of events and help shape the direction of discussion.

Proficiency in Academic Language

Proficiency in decoding and encoding skills is necessary but not sufficient for comprehending and writing about academic subject matter. Students also have to understand, use, and ultimately live the academic language of books and schooling.
(Shefelbine 1998)

Academic language refers to the language of literacy and books, tests, and formal writing. Shefelbine proposes a framework of reading that includes academic language as a key component of reading comprehension (see the chart on the following page).

A number of studies and researchers have shown that academic language

proficiency and its subcomponents are related to achievement in reading and writing as early as the third grade. Vocabulary is a critical element of academic language. In a study in which achievement trends of low-income students beginning in the second grade through the seventh grade were observed, a decline in word-meaning scores was identified after the third grade and in oral and silent reading comprehension in the sixth and seventh grades. Difficulties with comprehension were attributed to the challenging texts that "use more difficult, abstract, specialized, and technical words; the concepts used in textbooks also become more abstract, and understanding them requires more sophisticated levels of background knowledge and cognition" (Chall, Jacobs, and Baldwin 1990, 46).

Some researchers view academic language as different enough from conversational speech to be considered a second language (Maylath 1994, cited in Corson 1995). Shefelbine (1998) identifies several interrelated characteristics of academic language that differ from conversational speech. Some of those aspects include language function, vocabulary, background knowledge, text structure, syntactic complexity, and abstract thinking.

Academic language is learned by being repeated and extended while learning subject matter, including literature, science, and history–social science. It is difficult to learn quickly because of its peculiar characteristics, especially its requirement for extensive knowledge of vocabulary and background. Key components of developing academic language are reading, writing, and talking about books and school subject matter. Hearing language is not enough for students to

Academic language refers to the language of literacy and books, tests, and formal writing.

Note: The content of this section on proficiency in academic language has been provided by John Shefelbine, California State University, Sacramento.

20

Chapter 2
Goal and Key
Components
of Effective
Language Arts
Instruction

Decoding					Comprehension				
Word recognition strategies				Fluency	Academic language			Comprehension strategies	
Concepts about print	Phonemic awareness	Phonics	Sight words	Automaticity	Background Knowledge	Vocabulary	Syntax - - - - Text structure	Comprehension monitoring	(Re)organizing text

The central
importance of
students reading
widely at
increasingly more
challenging levels
cannot be
overemphasized.

learn academic language. They must produce it by speaking and writing it. Talking about text is necessary for them to develop their active vocabulary (Corson 1995). They must *use* words rather than just receive them passively in order to retain new vocabulary. Four strategies suggested for developing academic language are the following:

1. *Reading aloud to students.* Reading aloud to students is a powerful way to build language and vocabulary (Chall, Jacobs, and Baldwin 1990; Dickinson and Smith 1994; Wells 1986). In doing so it is important to select narrative and informational books with content linguistically and conceptually challenging but still engaging and understandable (Chall, Jacobs, and Baldwin 1990). Focus should be placed on building language, vocabulary, and knowledge of content rather than on developing knowledge of print or decoding strategies. Larger proportions of analysis, prediction, and vocabulary-related talk by teachers and children are associated with higher gains in vocabulary and comprehension (Dickinson and Smith 1994). Teachers should focus briefly on the meanings of certain words during reading and ask questions that require increased amounts of language and thinking from students.

2. *Instructional discussions.* Opportunities for students to initiate and participate in discussions on instructional topics build academic language. Suggested strategies for structuring those discussions include instructional conversations (Goldenberg 1992-93) and questioning the author (Beck et al. 1997). Both strategies employ open-ended questions that require students to interpret a text or topic. Students respond to one another and to the teacher. In questioning the author, the teacher and students pose queries that facilitate group discussion about an author's ideas and prompt student-to-student interactions.

3. *Reading by students.* One of the strongest predictors of reading comprehension in general and of vocabulary development in particular is the amount of time students spend reading (Anderson, Wilson, and Fielding 1988; Corson 1995; Cunningham and Stanovich 1998). Although reading aloud to students is helpful in developing academic language, the central importance of students reading widely at increasingly more challenging levels cannot be overemphasized. High-interest, low-vocabulary texts, although often appropriate for building fluency, are not as likely to produce growth in

academic language. To obtain such growth, students must read a great deal at school and at home. Classroom and schoolwide strategies to encourage and inspire student independent reading are essential. Students should master skills in reading early and well so that they will be able to read independently. Those who are not fluent readers and do not have the foundation skills to understand a variety of types of print do not engage willingly and joyfully in reading.

4. *Writing by students.* Students also practice and develop academic language in their writing as they respond to and analyze literature and compose essays and reports on a variety of topics. Incorporating advanced vocabulary and complex language structures appropriately into their own writing is the eventual goal of development in academic language, and frequent opportunities to write for a variety of purposes are essential to consolidating gains. Teachers should analyze and use student writing to guide further instruction and application of academic language features and conventions.

Chapter 2
Goal and Key
Components
of Effective
Language Arts
Instruction

Content Standards and Instructional Practices

Kindergarten Through Grade Three

Although all the skills within strands are important, no greater responsibility exists for educators of students in kindergarten through grade three than to ensure that each student in their care leaves the third grade able to read fluently, effortlessly, independently, and enthusiastically.

The period spanning kindergarten through grade three is the most critical for instruction in the language arts. During that time students acquire the foundational skills needed for later academic, social, and economic success. By the end of the third grade, students should be able to (1) read complex word forms accurately and fluently in connected texts and decode multisyllabic words independently; (2) read grade-level narrative and expository texts and recall sequence, main ideas, and supporting details; and (3) write compositions that describe familiar events

23

Chapter 3
Content Standards
and Instructional
Practices—
Kindergarten
Through Grade
Three

and experiences and construct complete, correct sentences to communicate their ideas. In addition, they should be able not only to respond to questions but also to make well-organized oral presentations centered on major points of information. As a result of their new skills, they are beginning to enjoy the richness of ideas expressed in books. Achievement of those skills by the end of the third grade is the goal for all students. Students achieve those skills by building on a progression of carefully specified and strategically sequenced content standards and instruction that begins in kindergarten.

Proficiency is based on critical building blocks in each grade. Some of the building blocks (e.g., vocabulary development, analysis of narrative text) span kindergarten through grade three, and others (e.g., phonemic awareness, concepts about print) are mastered in specific grades. The building blocks and their importance to overall language arts success in kindergarten through grade three are profiled in this chapter. An overview is followed by grade-specific summaries and instructional analyses for kindergarten through grade three.

Reading Word Analysis, Fluency, and Systematic Vocabulary Development

The standards for word analysis, fluency, and systematic vocabulary development are a key part of development in kindergarten through grade three. Although readers access words in many ways (whole words, decoding, word parts, and context), research has found that decoding, or the ability to apply knowledge of letter-sound correspondences to identify words, is fundamental to independent word recognition. Good readers rely

primarily on the letters in a word rather than context or pictures to identify familiar and unfamiliar words (Ehri 1994). The fluency good readers have with word recognition makes us think they read whole words at a time. In fact, fluent readers process virtually every letter in a word (Adams 1990). The speed and facility with which they recognize words differentiate good readers from less successful readers.

Automaticity is the ability to recognize a word (or series of words in text) effortlessly and rapidly. The foundations of automatic word recognition begin in kindergarten through developing phonemic awareness and learning the sounds associated with letters as well as concepts about print. Phonemic awareness, the ability to hear and manipulate the sounds of language, is a key indicator for students who learn to read easily versus children who continue to have difficulty. Instruction in phonemic awareness begins in kindergarten and concludes with more complex activities by the middle of the first grade. By the middle of kindergarten, students should be tested on phonemic awareness. Beginning in kindergarten and continuing into the first grade, children should be explicitly taught the process of blending individual sounds into words. For example, the printed word *man* is converted into its component letters (*m a n*), then into its corresponding sounds, each sound being held as readers progress to the next sound (*mmmmmaaaaannnn*). This explicit blending process is temporary yet critical as children advance in the word-recognition process.

In the late first grade and continuing through the second and third grades, students focus on two dimensions of word recognition—advanced word recognition skills and automaticity. In the first grade they progress from vowel-consonant and

Research has found that decoding, or the ability to apply knowledge of letter-sound correspondences to identify words, is fundamental to independent word recognition.

Chapter 3
Content Standards
and Instructional
Practices—
Kindergarten
Through Grade
Three

consonant-vowel-consonant word types to consonant blends, vowel digraphs, and *r*-controlled letter-sound associations. Inflected endings and word roots are added to extend word-recognition abilities. In the second grade decoding and word-recognition skills take on greater sophistication with the addition of multisyllabic words and more complex spelling patterns. In both the second grade and the third grade, more advanced decoding strategies focus on how to break up multisyllabic words and employ morphemic analysis (analyzing affixes and word roots). The second-grade and third-grade curriculum also focuses on orthographic knowledge; that is, recognizing larger, more complex chunks of letters (e.g., *ight, ierce*) to enhance fluency.

Proficient readers, writers, and speakers develop fluency with the fundamental skills and strategies. *Fluency is defined as the accuracy and rate with which students perform reading tasks.* In oral reading it includes additional dimensions that involve the quality of such reading (e.g., expression and intonation). To be considered fluent readers, students must perform a task or demonstrate a skill or strategy accurately, quickly, and effortlessly.

Fluency in kindergarten through grade three involves a wide range of skills and strategies (e.g., identifying letter names, producing sounds associated with letters, blending letter-sounds into words, reading connected text, spelling words, and writing sentences). Instruction in developing fluency must focus first on explicit opportunities for the student to learn the skill or strategy. Once a skill is learned, fluency develops as a result of multiple opportunities to practice the skill or strategy with a high rate of success. For early decoding in the first grade, students read stories in which there is a high percentage of words composed of taught

letter-sound correspondences and a few previously taught sight words.

An important feature of language arts instruction in kindergarten through grade three is vocabulary development, beginning in kindergarten with direct instruction in specific categories of words and progressing to understanding the relations of such words as synonyms and antonyms and the importance of structural features of words (affixes) to word meaning. Wide reading is essential to learning vocabulary and must be an integral component of instruction. At first the teacher should read literary and expository texts to students, exposing them to vocabulary they are not yet able to read. As students develop proficiency in word recognition, they are taught independent word-learning strategies, such as learning meanings from context and using dictionaries and glossaries as instructional resources.

The primary means by which students learn new words is through independent reading. The volume of that reading is crucial (Cunningham and Stanovich 1998). The authors acknowledge the strong relationship between decoding and vocabulary, noting that decoding skill mediates reading volume and thus vocabulary size. Therefore, one of the most effective strategic strikes educators can make in helping students develop vocabulary growth is to teach them to become fluent readers and encourage them to read extensively. In a study of independent reading, Anderson, Wilson, and Fielding (1988) found that the difference between children scoring at the ninetieth percentile in the amount of out-of-school independent reading and those scoring at the second percentile was approximately 21 minutes of independent reading per day. By the fourth grade students should read one-half million words of running text

The primary means by which students learn new words is through independent reading.

25

Chapter 3
Content Standards
and Instructional
Practices—
Kindergarten
Through Grade
Three

independently (see Chapter 4, page 114). Therefore, the process and benefits of independent reading must begin in the earlier grades.

Reading   **Reading
Comprehension**

An important building block in kindergarten through grade three is instruction in strategies related to reading comprehension, including how to predict what will happen in a text, how to compare information between sources, and how to answer essential questions. The foundation for this proficiency begins in kindergarten, when students receive explicit instruction and opportunities to answer simple questions about *who* and *what*. More abstract *why* and *what if* questions are mastered in the first and second grades. Although kindergarten nonreaders use the strategies orally in response to the teacher reading the text, more proficient readers also apply the strategies to the text they themselves read. Direct teaching and modeling of the strategies and readers' application of the strategies to the text they hear and read increase the ability of students to develop literal and inferential understanding, increase vocabulary, and make connections between parts of a text, between separate texts, and between text and personal experience.

Most students require explicit instruction in strategies related to reading comprehension, just as they do for decoding. Before the students listen to or read a story or informational passage, the teacher must bring to bear relevant student experiences and prior knowledge, develop knowledge of the topic, and teach critical, unfamiliar vocabulary. And the students should engage in predictions about upcoming text that are based on titles and pictures. While the students are reading, the teacher should introduce questions strategically to focus attention on critical information and encourage the students to monitor comprehension by self-questioning and returning to the text to fill in gaps in comprehension. When the students have finished reading, they should engage in analysis and synthesis, retelling, summarizing, and acting on information, such as placing events in sequential order. *Recommended Readings in Literature, Kindergarten Through Grade Eight* (California Department of Education 1996a) lists high-quality, complex materials to be read by students.

Reading   **Literary Response
and Analysis**

In kindergarten through grade three, students develop their ability to analyze literature and distinguish between the structural features of narrative text (e.g., characters, theme, plot, setting) and the various forms of narrative (e.g., myths, legends, fables). They learn the commonalities in narrative text and develop a schema or map for stories. Again, the standards progress from kindergarten, where analysis focuses on the characters, settings, and important events, to more sophisticated story elements (e.g., plot in the first grade, comparison of elements in the second grade, and theme in the third grade). Although kindergartners and early first graders also develop the strategies orally in response to text that has been read aloud, older students increasingly develop comprehension strategies through text they read and in conjunction with direct teaching and modeling of strategies.

Most students require explicit instruction in strategies related to reading comprehension, just as they do for decoding.

Chapter 3
Content Standards
and Instructional
Practices—
Kindergarten
Through Grade
Three

Writing

Writing Strategies and Applications

Students in kindergarten through grade three develop foundational writing strategies, applications, and conventions. They begin by forming uppercase and lowercase letters and using their knowledge of letters and sounds to write words. That knowledge of the alphabetic principle continues in the first grade as students write sentences. By the second grade writing extends to paragraphs, and by the third grade students write paragraphs with topic sentences. In penmanship students progress from legible printing in the first grade to the use of cursive or jointed italic in the third grade.

The systematic progression of instruction and application from kindergarten through grade three prepares students to write clear and coherent sentences and paragraphs that develop a central idea. Their writing shows clear purpose and awareness of audience as they refine their ability to use writing to describe and explain objects, events, and experiences (see page 93 in this chapter).

In the first grade another essential building block is introduced; that is, writing as a process. The act of writing is made up of a set of thinking and composing processes used selectively by a writer. Students learn that writing consists of several iterative phases (i.e., prewriting, drafting, revising, editing, and postwriting) that vary depending on the purpose and audience for writing. Students are also taught, however, that they are not limited to using the various phases all the time or in any fixed order. Instruction continues in the second and third grades and beyond. Throughout those grades the dimensions of organization, grammar, sentence structure, spelling, basic punctuation and capitalization, and handwriting are introduced and extended progressively.

With its emphasis on planning and revising for clarity, the writing process helps students understand that writing is not the same as speech written down. Direct instruction in more specific writing strategies also helps students understand how to go beyond writing down conversation. Of particular interest here are ideas, organization, voice, word choice, sentence fluency, and conventions. The first five involve content (rather than spelling and mechanics) and directly address aspects of decontexualized communication that many students find challenging. They are discussed fully in Spandel (1998).

Written and Oral English-Language Conventions

In kindergarten through grade three, written and oral English-language conventions are integrated with the respective strands (writing applications, speaking applications) where they are most directly applied. Over the course of the four-year span, students learn to write and punctuate declarative, interrogative, imperative, and exclamatory sentences.

Spelling instruction and proficiency progress in the first grade from phonetic stages, during which children learn to represent all of the prominent phonemes in simple words, to more advanced phonetic, rule-governed, and predictable patterns of spelling in the second and third grades (Moats 1995). Kindergarten and first-grade students will progress from prephonetic to phonetic stages of spelling as they begin to write. The National Research Council (1998, 8) states that temporary spellings, specifically those used in the phonetic stage, can be "helpful for developing understanding of the identity and segmentation of speech sounds and

27

Chapter 3
Content Standards
and Instructional
Practices—
Kindergarten
Through Grade
Three

sound-spelling relationships. Conventionally correct spelling should be developed through focused instruction and practice. Primary children should be expected to spell previously studied words and spelling patterns correctly in their final writing products." Fundamental skills in sentence structure, grammar, punctuation, capitalization, and spelling become building blocks for more advanced applications.

Listening and Speaking

Listening and Speaking Strategies and Speaking Applications

In kindergarten through grade three, students develop listening and speaking strategies and speaking applications that parallel and reinforce instruction in the other language arts. For example, as students learn to identify the major elements in stories, they practice retelling stories and include characters, settings, and major events. When speaking, they need systematic opportunities to use the vocabulary introduced in reading and writing. Students are taught to listen and follow instructions that begin as one-step directions in kindergarten and progress to three and four steps in the second and third grades.

Making Connections for Students

Instructional materials must help students make connections between standards and between skills and strategies. For example, students must learn not only to hear and manipulate the sounds in words but also to practice skills and integrate them into beginning reading and spelling activities. However, if they

practice writing sentences with correct punctuation and capitalization but never apply those skills in larger contexts or for authentic purposes, instruction is fragmented and the skills without purpose. The goal in language arts instruction must, therefore, be to ensure that component parts (skills, strategies, structures) are identified; are carefully sequenced according to their complexity and use in more advanced writing applications; are developed to mastery; and are progressively and purposefully connected and then incorporated with authentic learning exercises, including those presented in the study of history–social science, mathematics, and science.

A transformation takes place in learners between kindergarten and the third grade. A typical kindergartner enters school with little formal knowledge of academic requirements and uses of language. Exiting third graders who have mastered the code are able to access, comprehend, compose, discuss, and enjoy a wide range of literature and informational text. Their transformation comes from the systematic and strategic design and delivery of instruction anchored to the English–language arts content standards. Students who acquire necessary skills and knowledge early have a high probability of continued academic success. But students who fail to learn the fundamental skills and knowledge of the alphabetic writing system by the third grade will find themselves in relentless pursuit of the standards and will need extra support to arrive at grade level. Critical to the task are well-trained classroom teachers and teaching specialists who plan and implement lessons and assessments based on standards and current research and who are tireless in their efforts to teach all children to read, write, speak, and listen well.

Exiting third graders who have mastered the code are able to access, comprehend, compose, discuss, and enjoy a wide range of literature and informational text.

Chapter 3
Content Standards
and Instructional
Practices—
Kindergarten
Through Grade
Three

No greater
responsibility
exists for
educators of
students in
kindergarten
through grade
three than to
ensure that each
student in their
care leaves the
third grade able
to read fluently,
effortlessly,
independently, and
enthusiastically.

Teaching Students to Read: A Special Priority

Although all the skills within strands are important, no greater responsibility exists for educators of students in kindergarten through grade three than to ensure that each student in their care leaves the third grade able to read fluently, effortlessly, independently, and enthusiastically. Each student must understand the relation of print to speech, the sound structure of language, and the alphabetic principle and be able to apply those abilities to grade-level text. Effective instruction in reading nurtures both comprehension and fluency in word recognition. Concentration on the skills that build word recognition are critically important in the early primary grades.

Learning to read is the most important skill that students develop during their early academic years. Moreover, converging evidence reveals that the kindergarten through grade three span is the optimal period of time for such learning. Students who fail to read fluently by the end of the third grade have only a minimal chance of achieving literacy competence without specific interventions (Juel 1988; Felton and Pepper 1995).

What is particularly intriguing and elusive about reading is that despite its complexity, skillful reading looks like an easy and natural thing to do. On the contrary, reading requires deliberate and systematic human intervention and context (Kame'enui 1996). The process of reading is learned. Although some students become skillful readers without systematic instruction, many others need intense, systematic instruction in reading to succeed—a need that has not been fully recognized or addressed. Scientific re-

search has made considerable progress in gaining an understanding of what the components of reading instruction should be and how many more students can be helped to learn to read successfully. Our knowledge is not yet absolute in some areas, and many important questions remain to be answered. Nevertheless, we know that learning to read in an alphabetic writing system requires that we attend tenaciously to the features of that writing system and make explicit and conspicuous the key features of the system. Otherwise, large numbers of students will be at risk of not learning to read well.

Becoming a fluent and skillful reader requires extensive engagement with the English language, including:

- Listening to words and to the sounds inside of words
- Hearing and talking about stories
- Gaining facility with the concepts of print
- Understanding the sounds that make up our language
- Manipulating the sounds and relating the specific sounds to printed letters and words
- Connecting words with events, actions, things, and ideas and expressing those ideas in writing
- Learning about the connection between sounds, letters, syllables, words, and concepts
- Gaining an understanding of the structure of stories and informational text and relating events to personal experiences

Reading as a process is more than it appears to be. Because it does not come naturally to many students, the parts, especially the important parts, must be taught strategically and intentionally as an absolute priority. To improve reading achievement, we must fully understand

Chapter 3
Content Standards
and Instructional
Practices—
Kindergarten
Through Grade
Three

and appreciate the complexity and primacy of early reading instruction. The dimensions of beginning reading are like the strands of a strong rope. Like such a rope, the strength of the reading process depends on the strength of the individual strands, the strategic integration of all the strands, and the effective binding or connecting of the strands (Chard, Simmons, and Kame'enui 1998). First, it is critical that the strands, including vocabulary acquisition, concepts about print, phonemic awareness, decoding and word recognition, knowledge of the structure of stories, and listening comprehension are robust, stable, and reliable. Next, the strength of the reading process depends on strategic integration of the strands to produce readers who can apply their skills in a variety of contexts and tasks.

An important principle in early reading instruction is that skills from all strands must be part of the students' reading programs from kindergarten on. Emphasis on particular skills will differ over time and from student to student. For example, word-recognition skills should be trans-ferred and applied, first with decodable text where students can apply and practice the skills reliably and then with quality literature and informational texts as students demonstrate an ability to apply skills and strategies successfully.

A second essential principle is that new skills must be integrated across strands to reinforce and extend learning. For example, words learned in word-reading exercises can be used in writing, and vocabulary from a story can be incorporated with speaking. Systematically establishing connections between new skills and authentic applications and between skills in one strand and applications in another is essential to retention and generalization.

The following sections profile and summarize the content of the language arts program for each grade level in kindergarten through grade three. Each grade-level description includes a summary of the content, relevant instructional analyses, content connections across domains, and curricular and instructional profiles.

Chapter 3
Content Standards
and Instructional
Practices—
Kindergarten
Through Grade
Three

Kindergarten

Standards and Instruction

Students enter kindergarten with a wide range of individual differences in prior opportunities to hear, see, and learn the English language and alphabetic writing system. Thus, the challenge for educators is to determine the essential skills kindergartners must master and the way to organize and deliver instruction of maximum effectiveness and efficiency that addresses the range of (1) the skills and knowledge to be taught; and (2) the capacity of the learners. Instruction in kindergarten is focused on developing foundational skills that prepare students for later learning in the language arts. The strands to be emphasized at the kindergarten level are listed in the adjacent column under the appropriate domains.

Each of the strands is addressed separately in the following section with the exception of the written and oral English-language conventions strand, which is integrated into appropriate sections.

Reading

1.0 Word Analysis, Fluency, and Systematic Vocabulary Development
2.0 Reading Comprehension
3.0 Literary Response and Analysis

Writing

1.0 Writing Strategies

Written and Oral English-Language Conventions

1.0 Written and Oral English-Language Conventions

Listening and Speaking

1.0 Listening and Speaking Strategies
2.0 Speaking Applications (Genres and Their Characteristics)

Chapter 3
Content Standards
and Instructional
Practices—
Kindergarten
Through Grade
Three

Kindergarten

Standards and
Instruction

Reading Word Analysis, Fluency, and Systematic Vocabulary Development

Concepts About Print

A primary focus of language arts instruction in kindergarten is making sense of the alphabet and its role in reading. Familiarity with the letters of the alphabet is a powerful predictor of early reading success (Ehri and McCormick 1998). Moreover, letter-sound knowledge is not optional in an alphabetic writing system. By the end of kindergarten, students should be able to name all uppercase and lowercase letters and match all letters with their associated sounds.

Whether to teach letter names or letter-sound relationships first remains unsettled. Some reading programs recommend introducing letter names first because they are typically easier and more familiar to children. Others teach letter-sound relationships before letter names. Likewise, the treatment of uppercase and lowercase letters has varied. In some programs both uppercase and lowercase letters are introduced concurrently; in others the introduction of capital letters dissimilar to their lowercase letters is delayed.

The kindergarten experience should also expose students to a range of print forms and functions. Students learn to use conventions of print not only to negotiate print but also to aid comprehension (e.g., Reading Comprehension Standard 2.1). A recommended sequence is to present (1) the particular concept of print (e.g., books are read front to back, print moves from left to right), as would be done with any other basic concept; and (2) a learning activity in which books are used.

Phonemic Awareness

The most essential element of language arts instruction in kindergarten is the development of phonemic awareness; that is, teaching students the sound structure of language. Seven content standards (Reading Standards 1.7–1.13) progressively address phonemic awareness and its multiple dimensions. Phonemic awareness is:

1. The ability to hear and manipulate the sounds in spoken words and the understanding that spoken words and syllables are made up of sequences of speech sounds (Yopp 1988). Early phonemic awareness is all auditory; it does not involve print.
2. Fundamental to later mapping speech to print. If a child cannot hear that *man* and *moon* begin with the same sound or cannot blend the sounds /rrrrruuuuunnnn/ to *run*, that child typically has difficulty connecting sounds with their written symbols.
3. Essential to learning to read in an alphabetic writing system because letters represent sounds or phonemes. Without phonemic awareness, phonics makes little sense.
4. A strong predictor of early reading success.

Instruction in phonemic awareness can span two years, kindergarten and first grade. But in this aspect of teaching as in others, the teacher must be guided by the students' developing competencies. Some students require little training in phonemic awareness; others might require quite a bit. Although early phonemic awareness is oral, the teacher must be careful not to delay in providing learning opportunities with print. Learning phonics and learning to decode and write words all help

Chapter 3
Content Standards
and Instructional
Practices—
Kindergarten
Through Grade
Three

Kindergarten

Standards and
Instruction

students continue to develop phonemic awareness. In addition, students who have developed or are successfully developing phonemic awareness should not have to spend an unnecessary amount of time being instructed in such awareness. Adequate, ongoing assessment of student progress is essential. Oral activities in kindergarten should focus on such simple tasks as rhyming, matching words with beginning sounds, and blending sounds into words. Midyear screening of all students to determine their phonemic awareness and need for further instruction is also important.

In a review of phonemic awareness interventions to enhance the early reading achievement of students with and without disabilities, the following instructional strategies were found effective (Smith, Simmons, and Kame'enui 1998):

1. Modeling phonemic awareness tasks and responses orally and following with students' production of the task

2. Making students' cognitive manipulations of sounds overt by using concrete representations (e.g., markers, pictures, and Elkonin boxes) or auditory cues that signal the movement of one sound to the next (e.g., claps)

3. Teaching skills explicitly and systematically

4. Adding letter-sound correspondence instruction to phonological awareness interventions after students demonstrate early phonemic awareness

5. Progressing from the easier phonemic awareness activities to the more difficult—from rhyming and sound matching to blending, segmentation, and manipulation

6. Focusing on segmentation or the combination of blending and segmenting

7. Starting with larger linguistic units (words and syllables) and proceeding to smaller linguistic units (phonemes)

8. Focusing beginning instruction on the phonemic level of phonological units with short words (two to three phonemes; e.g., *at, mud, run*)

9. Focusing first on the initial sound (*sat*), then on the final sound (*sat*), and lastly on the medial sound (*sat*) in words

10. Introducing several continuous sounds first (e.g., /m/, /r/, /s/) before introducing stop sounds (e.g., /t/, /b/, /k/) because stop sounds are more difficult to isolate

11. Providing brief instructional sessions (Significant gains in phonemic awareness are often made in 15 to 20 minutes of daily instruction and practice over a period of 9 to 12 weeks.)

Decoding and Word Recognition

In kindergarten students begin to work with words in three important ways: decoding, spelling, and writing. Decoding is of primary importance. The students learn the prerequisites (phonemic awareness, letter-sound correspondences) and requisites (blending individual letter-sound correspondences to read whole words) of decoding. The ability to associate consonant and vowel sounds with appropriate letters is fundamental to reliable decoding and will be the focus of the curricular and instructional profile presented later in this section.

The selection, sequencing, review, and practice of letter-sound correspondences require careful analysis to optimize

Chapter 3
Content Standards
and Instructional
Practices—
Kindergarten
Through Grade
Three

Kindergarten

Standards and
Instruction

successful early reading. Selected guidelines include:

- Scheduling high-utility letter sounds early in the sequence (e.g., /m/, /s/, /a/, /r/, /t/)
- Including a few short vowels early in the sequence so that students can use letter-sound knowledge to form and read words
- Sequencing instruction, separating the introduction of letter sounds that are easily confused (e.g., /p/, /b/, /v/; /e/, /i/)
- Using student knowledge of letter-sounds to help them read and spell words (The difficulty of the words students spell should parallel the difficulty of the word patterns they read. Further specifications for the procedures for teaching word reading are found in the first-grade presentation.)

Vocabulary and Concept Development

Curriculum and instruction in kindergarten must also develop understanding of concepts and vocabulary as building blocks of language: categories of color, shape, and words used in kindergarten instruction (e.g., *group, pair, same*). Vocabulary is developed through direct instruction in specific concepts and vocabulary and exposure to a broad and diverse vocabulary while listening to stories. For students who enter kindergarten with limited knowledge of vocabulary, special instruction in concept and language development should be provided to help close the widening vocabulary gap between them and their peers.

Teachers should identify vocabulary words critical to listening comprehension and teach those words directly. Factors that influence the learning of vocabulary are (1) providing multiple exposures to words; (2) selecting and teaching words that are important to understanding a story or are high-utility words; (3) having students process words deeply and in multiple contexts; and (4) providing definitional and contextual support.

Reading   Reading Comprehension

Most students are not able to read sophisticated stories in kindergarten on their own but learn to identify and use strategies to comprehend the stories that are read to them daily. In the kindergarten curriculum important strategies for teaching comprehension as students listen to stories are (1) using pictures and context to make predictions; (2) retelling familiar stories; and (3) answering and asking questions about essential elements.

Factors to be considered when introducing comprehension strategies are:

1. Easing into instruction, beginning with stories containing obvious information and considering the complexity of the text
2. Controlling the difficulty of the task initially by introducing the strategy first in sentences and paragraphs and then in stories
3. Modeling multiple examples and providing extensive guided practice in listening-comprehension strategies
4. Inserting questions at strategic intervals to reduce the memory load for learners when introducing strategies in stories. (For example, have students retell the important events after each page rather than wait for the end of the story.)
5. Using both narrative and expository text

Chapter 3
Content Standards
and Instructional
Practices—
Kindergarten
Through Grade
Three

Kindergarten

Standards and
Instruction

Reading Literary Response and Analysis

One of the most powerful structures students learn in kindergarten is the schema or map of stories. The elements of *story grammar* (see glossary) can be applied to most stories and provide students with an important anchor when listening to stories, recalling them, and eventually writing their own. Story grammar can be used as a framework for beginning to teach higher-level comprehension skills. Students who have learned story grammar can begin to summarize by using the elements to retell the story. In kindergarten three elements are introduced: setting, characters, and important events. The remaining elements are gradually introduced in successive grades. Suggested strategies for teaching story elements are to:

- Introduce stories where elements are explicit (e.g., setting is described specifically).
- Focus on only a few important elements and introduce additional elements when the students can reliably identify those previously taught.
- Model and guide the students through stories, thinking out loud as the elements are being identified.
- Have students discuss the elements orally and compare with other stories.
- Use elements of story grammar as a structure for recalling and retelling the story. Model retelling, using the setting, characters, and important events as recall anchors. Provide picture cues to help students learn the essential elements.
- Provide plentiful opportunities to listen to and explore a variety of text forms and to engage in interactive discussion of the messages and meanings of the text. As students retell stories or answer questions about stories, they are provided with models of oral English-language conventions together with opportunities to produce complete, coherent sentences.

Writing Writing Strategies

Kindergarten students learn not only to recognize, identify, and comprehend but also to write letters, words, and beginning narratives. The connections in content between reading and writing are important in reinforcing essential skills. As students study the sound structure of language and learn how to read phonetically regular words and to write letters, they begin to use that knowledge to document their ideas in words. The National Research Council (1998, 187) states that "at the earliest stages, writing may consist of scribbling or strings of letter-like forms. If opportunities to write are ample and well complemented by other literacy activities and alphabetic instruction, kindergartners should be using real letters to spell out words phonetically before the school year is out. The practice of encouraging children to write and spell words as they sound (sometimes called temporary spelling) has been shown to hasten refinement of children's phonemic awareness and to accelerate their acquisition of conventional spelling when it is taught in first grade and up."

Listening and Speaking Listening and Speaking Strategies; Speaking Applications

Kindergarten instruction focuses on the development of receptive and expressive

Chapter 3
Content Standards
and Instructional
Practices—
Kindergarten
Through Grade
Three

language. Initially, preschool students learn to process and retain sentence-level instructions. Eventually, they begin to use their knowledge of sentence structure to produce their own clear, coherent sentences. To do so, the students must have models of such sentences and opportunities to produce them. For some, instruction begins first with statement repetition and progresses to statement production. Instruction in this focus area must be carefully organized to include:

1. Explicit modeling of standard English
2. Carefully constructed linguistic units that progress from short sentences to longer sentences
3. Frequent opportunities to repeat sentences
4. Additional, gentle modeling emphasizing specific elements of sentences omitted or pronounced incorrectly
5. Strategically designed instruction that shifts from statement repetition to statement production
6. Structured statement production whereby students first generate responses to questions from pictures or prompts and then generate questions or responses without prompts

Kindergarten students expand their speaking skills by reciting poems, rhymes, and songs. They make brief oral presentations about familiar experiences or interests and learn to describe people, places, things, location, size, color, shape, and action.

Content and Instructional Connections

The following activities integrate standards across domains, strands, and academic disciplines. Teachers may wish to:

1. Read aloud and discuss quality literature to extend students' oral vocabulary, concepts about print, and understanding of characters, settings, and important events.
2. Begin letter-sound instruction when students demonstrate some phonemic awareness. Then incorporate instruction in letter sounds and simple decoding to help phonemic awareness develop further.
3. Use only previously taught letters and letter-sound associations to spell words.
4. Use words students can read in writing activities.
5. Incorporate words from vocabulary instruction throughout the day and across subject disciplines.
6. Provide multiple opportunities for students to hear and practice new vocabulary.
7. Provide opportunities for students to retell stories and model retelling familiar stories, emphasizing English-language conventions.
8. Read aloud and discuss expository text consistent with the kindergarten science, mathematics, and history–social science standards.

Please see Appendix B for examples of standards that span domains and strands.

Chapter 3
Content Standards
and Instructional
Practices—
Kindergarten
Through Grade
Three

Kindergarten

Curricular and Instructional Profile

Reading Standard   1.14

DOMAIN	STRAND	SUBSTRAND	STANDARD
Reading	1.0 Word analysis, fluency, and systematic vocabulary development	Decoding and word recognition	1.14 Match all consonant and short-vowel sounds to appropriate letters.

Prerequisite or corequisite standards. **Kindergarten Word Analysis, Fluency, and Systematic Vocabulary Development Standards 1.6, 1.7, 1.8, 1.9.**

Standard 1.6: Recognize and name all uppercase and lowercase letters.

Standard 1.7: Track and represent the number, sameness or difference, and order of two and three isolated phonemes.

Standard 1.8: Track and represent changes in simple syllables and words with two and three sounds.

Standard 1.9: Blend vowel-consonant sounds orally to make words or syllables.

Curricular and Instructional Decisions

Instructional Objectives

1. Determine whether letters and letter sounds will be introduced simultaneously or separately. This consideration is extremely critical for students who have difficulty acquiring and retaining information.

2. Define the task for learners. *Match* implies that students produce the sound in response to a letter.

3. Determine when each letter-sound correspondence will be learned. To enable students to accomplish Reading Standard 1.15 (Read simple one-syllable and high-frequency words; i.e., sight words), the teacher must introduce more than just one letter-sound per week.

37

Chapter 3
Content Standards
and Instructional
Practices—
Kindergarten
Through Grade
Three

Kindergarten

Curricular and
Instructional
Profile

Instructional Design

1. Schedule the introduction of letter sounds to optimize learning.

2. Separate easily confused letters and sounds.

3. Introduce early in the sequence those letter sounds that occur in a large number of words.

4. Introduce early those letter sounds that relate to letter names (e.g., /s/, /r/, /m/) to facilitate learning.

5. Include a few short vowels early to allow students to build words easily.

6. Use several continuous sounds early that can be stretched (e.g., /m/, /n/, /s/) rather than stop or abrupt sounds (e.g., /t/, /b/, /d/) because continuous sounds facilitate blending.

7. Review letter sounds cumulatively to promote retention.

8. Determine whether students can handle uppercase and lowercase letters simultaneously. If so, introduce those letters in which uppercase and lowercase are similar (e.g., *S s, P p, C c*) before ones that are different (e.g., *D d*). For dissimilar letters withhold introducing the uppercase letter until later in the sequence.

9. Teach students to use letter sounds in simple word reading as soon as they have a group of letter sounds (four to six) from which to build words.

10. Include a phonemic awareness objective and parallel instruction focused on the phoneme level (e.g., Reading Standards 1.7, 1.8, 1.9).

11. Introduce simple word reading (e.g., vowel-consonant, as in *an*, or consonant-vowel-consonant, as in *sat*) once students have mastered a small number of letter-sound correspondences contained in those words.

Instructional Delivery

1. Model the process of producing the sound and matching it with the letter. *Ensure that sounds are correctly pronounced* and not turned into nonexistent syllables (not *muh* but *mmm*).

2. Use and allow students to use a variety of media (chalkboard, magnetic letters, magic slates, and sounds written on chart paper) to reinforce letter-sound practice.

3. Divide instruction into (a) new letter-sound instruction; and (b) discrimination practice in which previously introduced letter-sounds are reviewed and distinguished from the newly introduced sound. If students do not know the sound, model the sound, provide an opportunity for them to identify or match the sound, and return to the letter sound later in the lesson to reinforce and review.

Chapter 3
Content Standards
and Instructional
Practices—
Kindergarten
Through Grade
Three

Kindergarten

Curricular and
Instructional
Profile

**Instructional
Delivery**
(Continued)

4. Teach letter sounds explicitly, using a *teacher model, guided practice, and independent practice sequence.*

5. Provide frequent, short periods of instruction and practice during the day.

6. Relate letter-sound instruction to the standard of hearing sounds in words (phonemic awareness). Discuss the connection of hearing sounds (aural) and mapping those sounds to print (alphabetic).

Assessment

Entry-Level
Assessment

1. *Entry-Level Assessment for Instructional Planning*

   a. Before instruction assess student knowledge by showing an array of all the letters ordered randomly on a page. An alternative is to order the letter sounds in the sequence to be introduced in the instruction.

      The font should be large enough that the letters can be easily distinguished. Model the task on a couple of letter sounds. Show a row or column of letters and ask the child to tell you the sound of the letter. If the child tells you the name, say, "That's the name of the letter. Can you tell me the sound it makes?" Continue until the student has completed the task or you have sufficient information about the student's knowledge of letter sounds. If the student misses five consecutive sounds, stop testing.

   b. This stage of assessment is important because it provides direct information for instruction. Examine the letter-sound profiles of students in the class to determine whether consistent errors on specific letter-sound correspondences are evident.

   c. Determine whether you are assessing for accuracy or for fluency. Accuracy measures simply document whether letter sounds are identified correctly or incorrectly.

      An alternative measurement procedure is to assess for fluency of letter-sound knowledge. Provide the student a page of letter-sound correspondences arranged in rows in random order on the page. Ask the student to say the sound for each letter on the page. Allow one minute for the exercise. Record the letter-sound correspondences correctly identified and those in error. Subtract the errors from the total. The resulting score will be the number of letter sounds per minute. This method allows you to monitor student growth over time by periodically administering one-minute assessments of letter-sound fluency.

Chapter 3
Content Standards
and Instructional
Practices—
Kindergarten
Through Grade
Three

Kindergarten

Curricular and
Instructional
Profile

Assessment
(Continued)

d. Knowledge of letter-sound correspondence is an important indicator for establishing flexible skill-based instructional groups. Review the class profile to determine which students have considerable knowledge, moderate knowledge, or limited knowledge. Design flexible groupings to accommodate instruction to the learners' entry performance level.

Monitoring
Student
Progress

2. *Monitoring Student Progress Toward the Instructional Objective.* This assessment phase is designed to determine students' progress and mastery of letter-sound knowledge. The options available are:

   a. Maintaining a set of letter sounds that have been taught and assessing student performance at least biweekly to evaluate progress on those sounds. Document letter sounds students can and cannot identify.

   b. Monitoring progress toward the long-term goal of knowledge of all letter-sound correspondences. Use a format similar to the entry-level assessment and monitor progress at least once every two weeks. Document performance (numbers of correct letter sounds and those in need of further instruction). Again, if a student makes five consecutive errors, discontinue the assessment.

Post-test
Assessment

3. *Post-test Assessment Toward the Standard.* On completion of letter-sound instruction, assess student performance according to the procedures used to assess entry-level performance. The focus at this point should be on letter-sound fluency, and the goal of instruction is that students identify letter sounds accurately and automatically, enabling the students to apply letter sounds to read simple *vowel-consonant* (VC) or *consonant-vowel-consonant* (CVC) words. A target for achievement is for students to read letter-sound correspondences at a rate of one per second. Post-test assessment should include a fluency rate if it was not part of entry-level assessment. *Note:* Instruction in word reading can begin once students have learned a small number of consonants and vowels that enable them to read words.

**Universal
Access**

Reading
Difficulties
or Disabilities

1. *Students with Reading Difficulties or Disabilities*

   a. Determine whether the rate of introduction is acceptable for students with special needs. If the pace is too rapid, provide additional instruction, such as an extra preteaching period (before the lesson). If students are grouped heterogeneously, the entire group is given extra scaffolded instruction. Homogeneous groups will allow

Chapter 3
Content Standards
and Instructional
Practices—
Kindergarten
Through Grade
Three

Kindergarten
Curricular and
Instructional
Profile

Universal Access
(Continued)

Advanced Learners

English Learners

the teacher to preteach only those students who need the extra help.

b. For students having difficulty in retaining letter-sound knowledge, schedule a booster session sometime during the day. Review troublesome letter sounds or newly introduced information for one to two minutes.

2. *Students Who Are Advanced Learners.* Assess students for both accuracy and fluency. Keep in mind that when many advanced learners enter kindergarten, they may be reading at three to four or more grade levels above their age peers and may not need instruction in this skill area. Suggested procedures to follow are to:

a. Provide explicit instruction if many letter sounds are unfamiliar to students. Keep in mind that some students may acquire letter-sound knowledge very quickly. Accelerate movement through instructional materials if appropriate.

b. Design an instructional schedule to address any unknown skills if students have mastered the majority of letter-sound correspondences.

c. Assess higher-level reading skills if students are proficient in all letter sounds (i.e., can produce the sounds accurately and fluently). On the basis of a thorough assessment, they should be placed at an appropriate instructional level that provides academic challenge. For advanced students who have already mastered the language arts standards for kindergarten, grouping those students with first graders for language arts instruction is a simple and inexpensive way to provide the appropriate level of instruction. Their rate of learning should be subject to ongoing monitoring to ensure that they are learning at a rate commensurate with their ability.

3. *Students Who Are English Learners.* The following suggestions assume that students will begin language arts instruction in English and that literacy instruction will be augmented by concurrent formal linguistic instruction in English (English-language development). If language arts instruction is provided in part in a primary language, instruction in the primary language should be designed according to the same standards and principles indicated for language arts instruction in this framework. Suggested procedures to follow are to:

a. Ensure that students have had sufficient opportunities through prior activities in phonemic awareness to hear, distinguish, and produce sounds being introduced.

41

Chapter 3
Content Standards
and Instructional
Practices—
Kindergarten
Through Grade
Three

Kindergarten

Curricular and
Instructional
Profile

Universal Access (Continued)

Teachers should be aware of phonological differences between English and the students' primary language and provide additional exposure to and practice with the difficult sounds.

b. Provide students with additional systematic guidance and practice if they are unable to match all consonant and short-vowel sounds to appropriate letters.

c. Schedule additional brief practice sessions for English learners who have difficulty in learning letter-sound correspondences. They should benefit from additional review and practice of particularly difficult letter sounds.

d. Ensure that (1) students receive instruction or have had experiences (or both) with the words to be used in simple word reading; and (2) they understand the meaning of the words.

e. Encourage English learners to take home age-appropriate materials (e.g., flash cards, decodable text, handouts) related to the teaching objective.

Instructional Materials

1. Sequence the introduction of letter-sound correspondences, strategically separating easily confused sounds (e.g., /p/, /b/, /v/ and vowel sounds, especially /e/ and /i/) and introducing high-utility sounds first.

2. Scan the introduction of letter sounds for potential problems. The goal of letter-sound instruction is to provide the tools needed for word reading. Instructional texts should first introduce letter sounds in isolation. Then sounds that have been taught should be incorporated into words.

3. Include entry-level and progress-monitoring measures as well as assessments that allow teachers to identify advanced learners.

4. Ensure that similar skills (e.g., phonemic awareness and word reading) are correlated and that connections are made in instructional materials and instruction.

5. Proceed to simple instruction in word reading once students develop a set of letter sounds that allow them to read vowel-consonant or consonant-vowel-consonant words (not necessarily all sounds).

Chapter 3
Content Standards
and Instructional
Practices—
Kindergarten
Through Grade
Three

Kindergarten

English–Language Arts Content Standards

Reading

1.0 Word Analysis, Fluency, and Systematic Vocabulary Development

Students know about letters, words, and sounds. They apply this knowledge to read simple sentences.

Concepts About Print

1.1 Identify the front cover, back cover, and title page of a book.

1.2 Follow words from left to right and from top to bottom on the printed page.

1.3 Understand that printed materials provide information.

1.4 Recognize that sentences in print are made up of separate words.

1.5 Distinguish letters from words.

1.6 Recognize and name all uppercase and lowercase letters of the alphabet.

Phonemic Awareness

1.7 Track (move sequentially from sound to sound) and represent the number, sameness/difference, and order of two and three isolated phonemes (e.g., /f, s, th/, /j, d, j/).

1.8 Track (move sequentially from sound to sound) and represent changes in simple syllables and words with two and three sounds as one sound is added, substituted, omitted, shifted, or repeated (e.g., vowel-consonant, consonant-vowel, or consonant-vowel-consonant).

1.9 Blend vowel-consonant sounds orally to make words or syllables.

1.10 Identify and produce rhyming words in response to an oral prompt.

1.11 Distinguish orally stated one-syllable words and separate into beginning or ending sounds.

1.12 Track auditorily each word in a sentence and each syllable in a word.

1.13 Count the number of sounds in syllables and syllables in words.

Decoding and Word Recognition

1.14 Match all consonant and short-vowel sounds to appropriate letters.

1.15 Read simple one-syllable and high-frequency words (i.e., sight words).

1.16 Understand that as letters of words change, so do the sounds (i.e., the alphabetic principle).

Vocabulary and Concept Development

1.17 Identify and sort common words in basic categories (e.g., colors, shapes, foods).

1.18 Describe common objects and events in both general and specific language.

2.0 Reading Comprehension

Students identify the basic facts and ideas in what they have read, heard, or viewed. They use comprehension strategies (e.g., generating and responding to questions, comparing new information to what is already known). The selections in *Recommended Readings in Literature, Kindergarten Through Grade Eight* (California Department of Education, 1996) illustrate the quality and complexity of the materials to be read by students.

Chapter 3
Content Standards
and Instructional
Practices—
Kindergarten
Through Grade
Three

Kindergarten

English–Language
Arts Content
Standards

Structural Features of Informational Materials

2.1 Locate the title, table of contents, name of author, and name of illustrator.

Comprehension and Analysis of Grade-Level-Appropriate Text

2.2 Use pictures and context to make predictions about story content.

2.3 Connect to life experiences the information and events in texts.

2.4 Retell familiar stories.

2.5 Ask and answer questions about essential elements of a text.

3.0 Literary Response and Analysis

Students listen and respond to stories based on well-known characters, themes, plots, and settings. The selections in *Recommended Readings in Literature, Kindergarten Through Grade Eight* illustrate the quality and complexity of the materials to be read by students.

Narrative Analysis of Grade-Level-Appropriate Text

3.1 Distinguish fantasy from realistic text.

3.2 Identify types of everyday print materials (e.g., storybooks, poems, newspapers, signs, labels).

3.3 Identify characters, settings, and important events.

Writing

1.0 Writing Strategies

Students write words and brief sentences that are legible.

Organization and Focus

1.1 Use letters and phonetically spelled words to write about experiences, stories, people, objects, or events.

1.2 Write consonant-vowel-consonant words (i.e., demonstrate the alphabetic principle).

1.3 Write by moving from left to right and from top to bottom.

Penmanship

1.4 Write uppercase and lowercase letters of the alphabet independently, attending to the form and proper spacing of the letters.

Written and Oral English Language Conventions

The standards for written and oral English language conventions have been placed between those for writing and for listening and speaking because these conventions are essential to both sets of skills.

1.0 Written and Oral English Language Conventions

Students write and speak with a command of standard English conventions.

Sentence Structure

1.1 Recognize and use complete, coherent sentences when speaking.

Spelling

1.2 Spell independently by using pre-phonetic knowledge, sounds of the alphabet, and knowledge of letter names.

Listening and Speaking

1.0. Listening and Speaking Strategies

Students listen and respond to oral communication. They speak in clear and coherent sentences.

Comprehension

1.1 Understand and follow one- and two-step oral directions.

1.2 Share information and ideas, speaking audibly in complete, coherent sentences.

2.0. Speaking Applications (Genres and Their Characteristics)

Students deliver brief recitations and oral presentations about familiar experiences or interests, demonstrating command of the organization and delivery strategies outlined in Listening and Speaking Standard 1.0.

Using the listening and speaking strategies of kindergarten outlined in Listening and Speaking Standard 1.0, students:

2.1 Describe people, places, things (e.g., size, color, shape), locations, and actions.

2.2 Recite short poems, rhymes, and songs.

2.3 Relate an experience or creative story in a logical sequence.

44

Chapter 3
Content Standards
and Instructional
Practices—
Kindergarten
Through Grade
Three

First Grade

Standards and Instruction

First-grade students extend their knowledge of language arts in significant and exciting ways as they learn skills that enable them to read and write more independently. Instruction should be focused on helping students improve the skills they had begun to develop in kindergarten. An instructional priority must be that the students learn to read and exit the grade with the ability to decode and recognize increasingly complex words accurately and automatically. Moreover, they should be able to write and spell those words and use them to communicate ideas and experiences. Concurrently, students must have broad and rich experiences to expand their knowledge of vocabulary and concepts and extend their exposure and understanding of literary forms. As they write and speak, they should be able to apply the conventions and structures of sentences.

Of foremost importance is the availability of quality instructional materials that will allow students to achieve and apply different standards in the first grade. Specifically, students will need decodable texts with which to practice the decoding skills they are learning. In addition, they will need a broad array of high-quality literature and informational texts for the teacher to read to them as they develop listening comprehension skills prerequisite for reading comprehension. The separate forms of text are necessary because neither by itself is suitable or adequate to develop the full range of skills expected of first graders. Each type of text has a distinct and significant role in beginning reading instruction.

The strands to be emphasized at the first-grade level are listed on the following page under the appropriate domains.

Each of the strands is addressed separately in the following section, with the exception of the written and oral English-language conventions strand, which is integrated into appropriate sections.

Chapter 3
Content Standards
and Instructional
Practices—
Kindergarten
Through Grade
Three

First Grade

Standards and
Instruction

Reading

1.0   Word Analysis, Fluency,
       and Systematic Vocabulary
       Development
2.0   Reading Comprehension
3.0   Literary Response and Analysis

Writing

1.0   Writing Strategies
2.0   Writing Applications (Genres and
       Their Characteristics)

Written and Oral English-Language Conventions

1.0   Written and Oral English-Language
       Conventions

Listening and Speaking

1.0   Listening and Speaking Strategies
2.0   Speaking Applications (Genres and
       Their Characteristics)

Reading   **Word Analysis,
              Fluency, and
              Systematic Vocabulary
              Development**

Concepts About Print

First-grade students refine their understanding of the relationship between print and language and extend that understanding to more specific applications. Specifically, they should be able not only to discriminate letters from words and words from sentences but also to match a spoken word (e.g., *cat*) with a printed word. This awareness of words and their relation to speech is reinforced by instruction and practice in phonemic awareness.

First graders further their understanding of books and stories by learning the standard conventions of print, including titles and authors. Instruction in concepts about print is focused on teaching students to (1) match oral words with printed words; (2) learn the conventions of stories, books, and other forms of literature (titles, authors); and (3) discriminate letters, words, and sentences. A recommended instructional method is to teach a particular convention of print (e.g., title) as any other basic concept, using a wide range of examples. Once students learn the basic concept, it should be incorporated into a wide array of text forms and be reviewed systematically.

Phonemic Awareness

The first-grade curriculum and instruction in phonemic awareness prepare learners by making explicit the relationship between the words they hear and the phonemic structure of the language. Students must possess phonemic awareness if they are to understand the relationship between speech and print and therefore develop proficiency in reading and writing increasingly complex words and word types. Instruction in language at the phoneme level and student proficiency in that area are the hallmarks of the curriculum standards for the first grade. Through systematic instructional sequences, students should become not only phonemically aware but also phonemically proficient in identifying and producing a range of phonemic awareness skills. (*Note:* For a more complete discussion of phonemic awareness and its relation to early reading and spelling success, see the kindergarten section in this chapter.)

First-grade students should be provided with systematic and extensive instruction and practice in:

- Learning to analyze words at the phoneme level (i.e., working with individual sounds within words)
- Working with phonemes in all positions in words (initial, final, medial)

Chapter 3
Content Standards
and Instructional
Practices—
Kindergarten
Through Grade
Three

First Grade

Standards and
Instruction

- Progressing from identifying or distinguishing the positions of sounds in words to producing the sound and adding, deleting, and changing selected sounds
- Allocating a significant amount of time to blending, segmenting, and manipulating tasks
- Working with increasingly longer words (three to four phonemes)
- Expanding beyond consonant-vowel-consonant words (e.g., *sun*) to more complex phonemic structures (consonant blends)
- Incorporating letters into phonemic awareness activities
- Aligning the words used in phonemic awareness activities with those used in reading

Instruction in phonemic awareness can span two years, kindergarten and first grade. But in this aspect of teaching as in others, the teacher must be guided by the students' developing competencies. Some students require little training in phonemic awareness; others might require quite a bit. Although early phonemic awareness is oral, the teacher must be careful not to delay in providing learning opportunities with print. Learning phonics and learning to decode and write words all help students continue to develop phonemic awareness. In addition, students who have developed or are successfully developing phonemic awareness should not have to spend an unnecessary amount of time being instructed in such awareness. Adequate, ongoing assessment of student progress is essential.

Decoding and Word Recognition

Students who enter the first grade should possess two critical skills: (1) fundamental understanding of the phonemic structure of words; and (2) association of letters and sounds. Some

students combine the two skills intuitively through alphabetic insight; that is, the process of hearing sounds in words and using the sequence of letters in words and their associated sounds to read words. A priority of the first-grade curriculum must be to ensure that all students develop alphabetic insight and extend their ability to decode words independently and read words automatically. Automaticity comes from reading many decodable texts in which most words are composed of taught letter-sound correspondences and some words are taught directly as sight words. Decodable text should be used as an intervening step between explicit skill acquisition and the student's ability to read quality trade books. It should contain the phonic elements with which students are familiar. However, the text should be unfamiliar to the student so that they are required to apply word-analysis skills and not reconstruct text they have memorized.

A review of the content standards indicates that in the first grade students progress from being able to generate the sounds for all consonants and vowels to reading compound words, words with inflectional endings, and common word families. Decoding plays an essential role in this evolution from a time when students enter with limited knowledge of how to recognize words to a time when they leave fully able to recognize unfamiliar words. Beginning decoding (or more technically, phonological recoding) is the ability to (1) read from left to right simple, new regular words; (2) generate sounds from all the letters; and (3) blend those sounds into a recognizable word. Explicit instruction and attention to specific letters in words and repeated opportunities to practice words successfully result in automaticity—the ability to recognize a word effortlessly and rapidly. Decoding is essential to reading unfamiliar

Decoding is
the key students
use to unlock
unfamiliar words.
Marion Joseph

Chapter 3
Content Standards
and Instructional
Practices—
Kindergarten
Through Grade
Three

First Grade

Standards and
Instruction

words and reading words independently and is a critical benchmark in a student's reading development.

Because the English language is alphabetic, decoding is an essential and primary means of recognizing words. English has too many words for the user to rely on memorization as a primary strategy for identifying words (Bay Area Reading Task Force 1997). In the first grade the skills and strategies learned in decoding and word recognition are extended in the standards for writing conventions. For example, as students learn to read compound words and contractions, economy in instruction can be gained by having the students write the words and use them in speaking. Similarly, as students learn to read three- and four-letter short-vowel words and sight words, they should be given instruction and opportunities to practice spelling those words.

Decoding instruction in the first grade should:

- Progress systematically from simple word types (e.g., consonant-vowel-consonant) and word lengths (e.g., number of phonemes) and word complexity (e.g., phonemes in the word, position of blends, stop sounds) to more complex words.
- Model instruction at each of the fundamental stages (e.g., letter-sound correspondences, blending, reading whole words).
- Sequence words strategically to incorporate known letters or letter-sound combinations.
- Provide initial practice in controlled connected text in which students can apply their newly learned skills successfully.
- Include repeated opportunities to read words in contexts in which students can apply their knowledge of letter-sound correspondences.

- Use decodable text based on specific phonics lessons in the early part of the first grade as an intervening step between explicit skill acquisition and the students' ability to read quality trade books. Decodable text should contain the phonics elements and sight words that students have been taught. However, the text should be unfamiliar to students so that they are required to apply word-analysis skills and not simply reconstruct text they have memorized.
- Teach necessary sight words to make more interesting stories accessible.

First-grade instruction in word analysis should teach students high-frequency irregular words systematically. Words with high utility should be selected and used judiciously in early reading. Teachers should point out irregularities while focusing student attention on all letters in the word and should provide repeated practice. The number of irregular words introduced should be controlled so that the students will not be overwhelmed. High-frequency words (e.g., *was, saw; them, they, there*), often confused by students, should be strategically separated for initial instruction as well.

Instruction in word families and word patterns (i.e., reading orthographic units of text, such as *at, sat, fat, rat*) should begin after students have learned the letter-sound correspondences in the unit (Ehri and McCormick 1998). Teaching students to process larger, highly represented patterns will increase fluency in word recognition. However, the instruction should be carefully coordinated and should build on knowledge gained from instruction in letter-sound correspondence.

The benchmark for facile word readers in the first grade is their ability to read aloud fluently in a manner that resembles natural speech. Although important in its

Chapter 3
Content Standards
and Instructional
Practices—
Kindergarten
Through Grade
Three

First Grade

Standards and
Instruction

own right, fluency has significant implications for comprehension. A primary reason for its importance is that *if students are not fluent, automatic decoders, they will spend so much mental energy decoding words that they will have too little energy left for comprehension* (Stanovich 1994). Comprehension clearly involves more than fluent word recognition but is dependent on fluent word recognition. On average, first graders increase their reading fluency approximately 2.10 correct words per minute per week (Fuchs et al. 1993). After an estimated 30 weeks of instruction, students should leave the first grade reading approximately 60 words per minute correctly. Practice in fluency is most appropriate when students are accurate word readers. One technique that has been used to increase fluency is repeated readings of the same text to develop familiarity and automaticity (Samuels 1979).

Vocabulary and Concept Development

The curriculum and instruction offered in the first grade extend the understanding of concepts and vocabulary in English. Instruction should focus on two types of vocabulary development, basic categorization of grade-appropriate concepts (e.g., animals, foods) and the words students hear and read in stories and informational text that are instrumental to comprehension. Vocabulary development occurs through both direct instruction in specific concepts and words and through exposure to a broad and diverse range of words in stories and informational text that have been read.

In addition to learning specific vocabulary, first-grade students also learn to use context and surrounding text to understand the meaning of unknown words. They are provided instruction and opportunities that prepare them to use new and descriptive vocabulary in their speaking and writing.

Reading   Reading Comprehension

Reading comprehension can be developed through listening and reading. For kindergarten students and all other students whose decoding and word-recognition skills do not yet allow them access to story-level passages, systematic opportunities must be provided to listen to stories and answer comprehension questions orally. The oral readings should have more complex vocabulary, syntactic structures, and story lines than are found in the text used for decoding and word recognition.

Key comprehension strategies for first graders include:

- Identifying text that uses sequence or other logical order
- Following one-step written instructions
- Responding to or posing *who, what, when, where,* and *how* questions
- Recognizing the commonalities that occur across stories and narrative text
- Using context to resolve ambiguities about the meaning of words and sentences
- Confirming predictions by identifying supporting text
- Relating prior knowledge to textual information
- Retelling the central ideas of simple expository or narrative passages

Instruction in comprehension is designed with the same precision as instruction in word recognition. For comprehension to occur, the words in the text, along with their meanings, must first be accessible to the learner. Initial reading comprehension is practiced with texts students can read at their level. When

Chapter 3
Content Standards
and Instructional
Practices—
Kindergarten
Through Grade
Three

First Grade

Standards and
Instruction

appropriate, the complexity of comprehension instruction may be simplified by allowing students to learn and practice the strategy from information presented in speech or in pictures. If the forms of presentation are not appropriate, initial instruction in comprehension can begin with manageable textual units (e.g., sentences, short paragraphs before longer passages, and complete stories).

Additional instruction in comprehension may include:

- Modeling multiple examples and providing extensive guided practice in comprehension strategies
- Helping students recognize the features of text that facilitate comprehension
- Brainstorming central ideas from the text (e.g., What do we know about what frogs eat? What do we know about where they live? What do we know about their appearance? What else would we like to know about frogs?)

The text for initial instruction in comprehension should (1) begin with linguistic units appropriate for the learner; (2) use familiar vocabulary; (3) be based on a topic with which the learner is familiar; and (4) use simple syntactical structures. Instruction in comprehension should also require students to determine which strategy to use and why and provide extensive opportunities for students to read and apply the strategies throughout the year. For example, instruction designed to teach children to answer *who, what, when, where,* and *how* questions (Reading Comprehension Standard 2.2) would consist of determining which type of question to ask first. *Who* and *what* questions are typically easier to answer than *when* and *where* questions. For *when* and *where* questions, instruction in how to identify the when and where in text may

be necessary. These examples would be presented orally because the wording may be too difficult for first graders to decode:

After the baseball game tells when.

On Saturday tells when.

On the table tells where.

In San Francisco tells where.

When students can correctly identify and discriminate between when and where, they learn to answer questions from sentences. *Example:*

Text: "Nick went home after the baseball game."

Question: "When did Nick go home?" (After the baseball game)

A simple instructional design would teach each type of question separately. After one type is clearly understood and applied (e.g., *who*), a second type (e.g., *what*) would be introduced. After both types are understood, *who* and *what* questions can be combined in an instructional session.

At the very beginning of instruction, first-grade students should be given a linguistic structure they can comprehend. Sentences are, therefore, a plausible starting point because they provide a manageable unit of language that conveys information. Once students can answer questions at the sentence level, the teacher can proceed to multiple sentences and eventually to paragraphs. Students who are more advanced can be prompted to ask and answer the questions.

Reading Literary Response and Analysis

First-grade students should extend their schema or structure of stories to the organizational structure that narrative text has a beginning, a middle, and an end. In

Chapter 3
Content Standards
and Instructional
Practices—
Kindergarten
Through Grade
Three

First Grade

Standards and
Instruction

addition, they should learn the sequence or logical order of informational text. They use those structures to comprehend text as well as retell stories. The elements of plot are added to the previously taught setting, characters, and important events. For a description of instructional design for elements of story grammar, see the kindergarten section in this chapter.

The importance of understanding the structures of text is reflected in the number of related standards. For Literary Response and Analysis Standard 3.1, for example, students read about and learn the elements of stories. They also learn that stories have a beginning, middle, and end. These structures are directly connected to Writing Application Standard 2.1, for which students write brief narratives describing an experience. Further related is Speaking Application Standard 2.2, the objective of which is for students to retell stories, using basic story grammar elements.

Content standards in mathematics, history–social science, and science can be addressed simultaneously as students read (or have read to them) stories or expository text that develop concepts and vocabulary in those academic areas. Economic, effective curricular programs and instruction will draw upon those relationships to expedite and reinforce language arts learning across the curriculum.

Strategies recommended in teaching organizational sequences of text (informational or narrative) are:

- Ensuring that students have a conceptual understanding of beginning, middle, and end
- Introducing text where the components of text are explicit (beginning, middle, and end being obvious)

- Beginning with short passages to reduce the memory load for learners
- Focusing on only one component at a time (e.g., beginning)
- Introducing an additional component when students can reliably identify those previously taught
- Guiding students through sample text in which teachers think out loud as they identify the components
- Having students discuss the elements orally and make comparisons with other stories
- Using the beginning, middle, and end as a structure for recalling and retelling the story or information

Writing   Writing Strategies and Writing Applications

First-grade writing combines the important skills of idea formation and documentation, penmanship, and spelling. Spelling assumes increased importance as students are responsible for communicating their ideas through recognized conventions. At this stage spelling instruction takes three forms. Students should be taught explicitly how to use their knowledge of the phonemic structure of words and letter-sound correspondences to spell *the words they do not know*. As students begin to read words, they should be taught to spell *the words they can read*. In addition, students need to learn to spell *high-frequency words* correctly. The ability to use phonetic spelling, although temporary, indicates that children "have achieved an essential milestone toward mastery of decoding in reading" (Moats 1995).

Moats reports that although some students easily learn to spell correctly, many others do not. Guidelines for

Chapter 3
Content Standards
and Instructional
Practices—
Kindergarten
Through Grade
Three

First Grade

Standards and
Instruction

instruction in spelling for students who do not easily learn to spell correctly include:

1. Systematic, teacher-directed instruction and practice with controlled amounts of new information

2. Regulation of the amount of information presented at one time (Introduce smaller sets of words as opposed to entire lists at one time.)

3. Plentiful opportunities to practice newly introduced spellings

4. Presentation of only one spelling rule or generalization at a time

5. Provision of immediate corrective feedback

6. Organized, sequential instruction that builds on phonological awareness and letter-sound correspondences and regular one-syllable patterns.

Students in the first grade are introduced to writing as a means of communicating. They begin to understand that writing is a process and learn to apply the process appropriately to write brief narratives and brief descriptions of objects, persons, places, or events. As students learn to apply process writing to narrative and descriptive structures, they also learn the different types of sentences along with the conventions for recording their ideas (e.g., capitalization, punctuation). They learn to apply writing conventions, with particular emphasis being placed on the fundamentals of grammar, punctuation, and capitalization.

General guidelines for writing instruction include:

1. Selecting and emphasizing those sentence types most useful for communicating ideas

2. Focusing on one form of punctuation until learners achieve mastery

and then introducing a second form

3. Sequencing student writing activities so that they first see good models, edit other writing, and then generate their own sentences or text

As students learn the various stages of writing as a process (prewriting, drafting, revising, editing, and publishing), they should have a structure for incorporating varying combinations of the stages into their writing that is based on the purpose of a specific piece of writing. Using a story grammar structure or a simple structure for descriptive text helps students apply the stages of writing.

Listening and Speaking

Listening and Speaking Strategies and Speaking Applications

First-grade students are increasingly responsible for comprehending information presented orally, communicating their ideas through speaking and writing, recalling important information from narratives and informational text, and answering questions. Their responses should incorporate greater diversity into the words they use and greater mastery of grammatical structures. To respond to or produce complete, coherent sentences that use descriptive words or correct singular and plural nouns, students need models of those structures along with many opportunities to produce their own sentences.

Instructional considerations to improve sentence production include:

1. Providing explicit models

2. Eliciting student responses that progress from identification to production

Chapter 3
Content Standards
and Instructional
Practices—
Kindergarten
Through Grade
Three

First Grade

Standards and
Instruction

3. Carefully selecting, sequencing, and scheduling instructional targets that allow learners to master one form (e.g., *my*) before progressing to the next (e.g., *his/her* or *your/yours*)

4. Providing frequent opportunities to repeat sentences

5. Strategically integrating instruction requiring students to discern the correct usage (e.g., *his/her, your/ yours*)

In addition to learning sentence-level standards for listening and speaking, students should learn to comprehend and reconstruct sequences of information, including multiple-step directions, poems, songs, and stories. Incremental instruction in which students are taught to recall increasingly longer units should build on the sentence-level guidelines previously outlined.

Content and Instructional Connections

The following activities integrate standards across domains, strands, and academic disciplines. Teachers may wish to:

1. Use known letters, phonemic awareness, letter-sound associations, and encoding skills to read, write, and spell words.

2. Reinforce the connections between phonemic awareness, translating a printed word into its letter-sound correspondences, reading the whole word, and spelling. Use words that students can read in spelling and writing activities.

3. Introduce words from stories in various instructional activities. Provide frequent opportunities for students to hear and practice new vocabulary.

4. Provide ample opportunities for students to hear stories read aloud and then discuss those stories.

5. Provide opportunities for students to retell stories based on their knowledge of story elements. Model how to retell familiar stories, emphasizing coherent English-language conventions.

6. Use the story grammar structure to comprehend, retell, and compose stories.

7. Have students read (and read to them) stories and informational text that address the first-grade content standards in mathematics, science, and history–social science.

Please see Appendix B for examples of standards that span domains and strands.

53

Chapter 3
Content Standards
and Instructional
Practices—
Kindergarten
Through Grade
Three

First Grade

Curricular and Instructional Profile

Reading Standard   1.10

DOMAIN	STRAND	SUBSTRAND	STANDARD
Reading	1.0 Word analysis, fluency, and systematic vocabulary development	Decoding and word recognition	1.10 Generate the sounds from all the letters and letter patterns, including consonant blends and long- and short-vowel patterns (i.e., phonograms), and blend those sounds into recognizable words.

Prerequisite standard. **Kindergarten Word Analysis, Fluency, and Systematic Vocabulary Development Standard 1.14:** Match all consonant and short-vowel sounds to appropriate letters.

Prerequisite or corequisite standards. **First-Grade Word Analysis, Fluency, and Systematic Vocabulary Development Standards 1.8, 1.9.**

Standard 1.8: Blend two to four phonemes into recognizable words.

Standard 1.9: Segment single-syllable words into their components.

Corequisite standard. **First-Grade Written and Oral English-Language Conventions Standard 1.8:** Spell three- and four-letter short-vowel words and grade-level-appropriate sight words correctly.

Curricular and Instructional Decisions

Instructional Objectives

1. The standard addressing the year-end goal of being able to blend all letters and letter patterns into words involves a minimum of three skills:
   a. Knowledge of some letter-sound correspondences
   b. Ability orally to blend and segment words of three to four phonemes

Chapter 3
Content Standards
and Instructional
Practices—
Kindergarten
Through Grade
Three

First Grade

Curricular and
Instructional
Profile

**Instructional
Objectives**
(Continued)

c. Ability to blend letter-sound correspondences taken from written words

Assessment, instruction, and practice should address each of the components.

2. Before teaching students to recognize the sounds associated with each letter and blend those sounds into a word, determine whether students have the prerequisite skills (see 1a and 1b). Students do not have to know all the letter sounds before initiating blending and word reading. However, to satisfy the prerequisite for this standard, they must know some letter sounds and be able to blend and segment words auditorily.

3. Blending is a focused and distributed instructional priority. That is, during initial instruction there is an intense focus on this strategy. Teachers provide extensive instruction (delivered in short increments) and practice in learning to blend easy word types. Instruction and practice in blending must be reintroduced when new word types are introduced. Although this instructional period may be brief, students must understand that blending is used not only with short words (e.g., *sun*) but with longer words as well (e.g., *splash*).

**Instructional
Design**

Successful word reading depends largely on:

1. Systematic selection and sequencing of letters in the words to maximize students' ability to blend
2. Progression of word difficulty based on length and configuration of consonants and vowels within the word
3. Explicit instruction and modeling in how to blend letter sounds into words
4. Sufficient practice in transitioning from reading each letter sound at a time to reading the whole word
5. Explicit instruction in how to "sound out words in your head"

Systematic Selection and Sequencing of Letters in Words

Letter sounds in words have properties that can enhance or impede blending and word reading. For initial instruction in blending, the letters in words should be:

- Continuous sounds because they can be prolonged or stretched (e.g., /m/, /s/)
- Letters students know
- Used in a large number of words for high utility
- Lowercase unless the uppercase and lowercase letters have highly similar shapes (e.g., *S s; V v*)

Note: Visually and auditorily similar (e.g., /b/ and /d/) letter sounds should not be in the same initial blending activities.

Chapter 3
Content Standards
and Instructional
Practices—
Kindergarten
Through Grade
Three

**Instructional
Design**
(Continued)

**Progression of Word Difficulty Based on Length
and Configuration of Consonants and Vowels
Within the Word**

Words used in blending instruction and practice should:

- Progress from the short vowel-consonant and consonant-vowel-consonant (two- or three-letter words in which letters represent their most common sounds) to longer words (four- or five-phoneme words in which letters represent their most common sounds).
- Reserve consonant blends (e.g., /st/, /tr/, /pl/) until the students are proficient in working with consonant-vowel-consonant configurations.
- Begin with continuous sounds in early exercises to facilitate blending. Stop sounds (sounds that cannot be prolonged in the breath stream, such as /t/, /p/, and /ck/) may be used in the final positions of words.
- Represent vocabulary and concepts with which students are familiar.

**Progression from Oral Blending to Oral Whole-Word Reading
to "Sounding It Out in Your Head"**

- Orally blending the letter-sound associations of a word is a first step in word reading. In this process students produce each sound orally and sustain that sound as they progress to the next. This process focuses student attention on the individual letters in the word and on their importance.
- Once proficient in blending the individual sounds orally, students are taught to put those sounds together into a whole word. This important step must be modeled and practiced.
- The final step in this sequence involves students sounding out the letter-sound correspondences "in their head" or silently producing the whole word.

This systematic progression is important because it makes public the necessary steps involved in reading a whole word.

**Instructional
Delivery**

Orally Blending Individual Letter Sounds

1. Model the process of blending the sounds in the word ("I'll read this word, blending the sounds *mmmmmmmmaaaaaaaannnnnn*"). Do not stop between the sounds. Make certain that the sounds are not distorted as you stretch them out. You may want to use language that helps make the process more vivid (stretching out the sounds, keeping the sounds going).
2. Use your finger or hand to track under each letter as you say each individual sound.

Chapter 3
Content Standards
and Instructional
Practices—
Kindergarten
Through Grade
Three

First Grade

Curricular and
Instructional
Profile

**Instructional
Delivery**
(Continued)

3. Hold each sound long enough for the students to hear it individually. Stop sounds cannot be prolonged without distortion. When introducing words that begin with stop sounds (such as *t, k,* and *p*), teach the students that those sounds should be pronounced quickly and should not be stretched out.
4. Use an explicit teaching sequence in which you model examples first and then have the students blend the words with you. Finally, the students should blend the words on their own.
5. Include a sufficient number of examples to assess students' proficiency. This instructional segment should be relatively brief (five to ten minutes) in the daily language arts lesson.

Producing the Whole Word

1. Introduce the whole-word step in which students say the word at a regular pace once they can blend the sounds in the word.
2. Provide sufficient time for students to put the sounds together. The sequence involves orally blending the individual letter sounds in the word and then saying the whole word.

Internalizing the Blending Process

1. In the final step of the blending process, students sound out the word to themselves and then produce the whole word.
2. Two important dimensions of this phase are:
   a. Showing students how to internalize
   b. Providing sufficient time for all students to blend the word in their head and say the word
3. On average, students should be able to blend sounds and retrieve a word at a rate of a maximum of one second per letter sound in the word. If they require more time, they may not have mastered the prerequisite skills.
   Because blending is now an overt process, teachers must use strategies to show students the transition steps. Teachers might wish to model how to trace a finger under each sound, subvocalizing the sounds of the word.

General Design

1. Provide frequent, short periods of instruction and practice on blending. Examples should include newly introduced letter sounds and newly introduced word types—consonant-vowel-consonant-consonant (e.g., *rest*).
2. Relate blending instruction to spelling when students master blending and reading words at a regular rate. Teaching students the relationship between reading and spelling strengthens alphabetic understanding and the connections between reading and writing.

Chapter 3

Content Standards
and Instructional
Practices—
Kindergarten
Through Grade
Three

First Grade

Curricular and
Instructional
Profile

Assessment

Entry-Level
Assessment

1. *Entry-Level Assessment for Instructional Planning*

   a. Assess student knowledge of letter sounds to identify letter sounds to use in initial blending and word-reading instruction. Students should be fluent in some letter-sound correspondences prior to beginning word-reading instruction.

   b. Assess students' phonemic blending ability (e.g., the ability to blend three to four phonemes into a word).

   c. Determine whether students can read words in lists of word types or in passages containing high percentages of words that are phonetically regular. Identify word types (length and consonant-vowel configuration) that students can read and begin instruction at that point.

   d. Use nonsense words or pseudo words as measures to assess blending ability. Nonsense words are phonetically regular but have no commonly recognized meaning (e.g., *rin, sep, tist*). With nonsense words you can determine students' knowledge of individual letter-sound correspondences and blending ability.

   e. Most first graders will have a limited repertoire of words they can read depending on the kindergarten instruction they have received. Many students may have a core of sight words they can identify and may look like readers. However, they may not have adequate decoding skills.

Monitoring
Student
Progress

2. *Monitoring Student Progress Toward the Instructional Objective*

   a. This assessment phase is designed to determine students' progress and mastery of letter-sound knowledge. The options available are:

      • Maintaining a set of taught letter sounds and word types. To evaluate progress, assess student performance at least once every two weeks on words containing familiar letter sounds. Record performance and document particular letter sounds or blending patterns with which they have difficulty (e.g., stopping between sounds; not being able to read whole words).

      • Monitoring progress toward the long-term goal with a list of words selected randomly from the first-grade curriculum. Although all word types will have been introduced during the early months of the academic year, this measure provides a common measure by which to evaluate students' change in word-reading ability over time.

   b. Once students are reading individual words at a rate of one word per three seconds or less, introduce connected text as an assessment tool.

Chapter 3
Content Standards
and Instructional
Practices—
Kindergarten
Through Grade
Three

First Grade

Curricular and
Instructional
Profile

Assessment
(Continued)

Post-test
Assessment

3. *Post-test Assessment Toward the Standard*

a. Blending is a temporary and distributed instructional priority. Students may be able to blend some word types but not others. Therefore, there may be ongoing post-tests depending on the word type being studied.

b. Post-tests should be distributed throughout the year. To assess overall growth, administer a test that measures fluency through the use of a nonsense-word measure to determine entry-level skills. Or have the students read a passage that represents the range of word types and blending requirements for the year.

**Universal
Access**

Reading
Difficulties
or Disabilities

1. *Students with Reading Difficulties or Disabilities*

a. These students need a firm understanding of prerequisite skills before beginning blending. If they cannot blend sounds auditorily or know only a few letter-sound correspondences, provide appropriate instruction before introducing blending.

b. Some first graders will continue to stop between the sounds in a word. Provide extra models of not stopping between the sounds and provide sufficient waiting time for students to process the sounds into the whole word.

c. Assess whether the rate of introduction of new letter sounds into blending or new word types is manageable for students with special needs. If the pace is too rapid, provide additional instruction.

d. If students have difficulty in retaining the blending strategy, schedule a booster session sometime during the day for one to two minutes.

Advanced
Learners

2. *Students Who Are Advanced Learners*

a. Use entry-level assessment to determine the need for instruction in blending. Keep in mind that some students may have memorized a large repertoire of words but still lack blending strategies. Use the nonsense words measure to assess their ability.

b. Determine the word type(s) for which students need instruction. They may learn the blending strategy and immediately generalize to more complex word types, making further or extensive instruction in blending unnecessary.

c. If isolated word types are unfamiliar to students, design an instructional schedule to address the missing skills. If the students are proficient in decoding phonetically regular words, proceed to introductory passage-reading standards.

59

Chapter 3
Content Standards
and Instructional
Practices—
Kindergarten
Through Grade
Three

**Universal
Access**
(Continued)

d. Provide explicit instruction in targeted skill areas, keeping in mind that the students may acquire the blending strategy very quickly. Accelerate movement through instructional objectives.

e. If the students can demonstrate mastery of the grade-level standards, consider grouping the students within or across grade levels to work on the second-grade standards.

Because many advanced learners enter the first grade reading well above grade level, the teacher should determine their overall reading ability in addition to their performance in specific skill areas. On the basis of a comprehensive assessment, give students challenging instructional materials and monitor their progress carefully to ensure they are learning at a rate commensurate with their abilities.

Note: Unnecessary drill and practice in areas of high performance can be very discouraging for advanced learners because they are being asked to learn something they already know.

English Learners

3. *Students Who Are English Learners*

The following suggestions assume that students will begin language arts instruction in English and that literacy instruction is augmented by concurrent formal linguistic instruction in English (English-language development). If instruction is provided in part in the primary language and that language is alphabetic, the instruction in the primary language should be designed according to the same standards and principles established for language arts instruction in this framework. It is suggested, therefore, that the teacher:

a. Reassess the students' knowledge of letter-sound correspondences and phonological awareness of the sounds included in the lesson before teaching English learners to blend sounds. Additional phonological and letter-sound instruction should be provided as needed. Teachers should be aware of phonological differences between English and the students' primary languages and provide additional exposure to and practice with the difficult sounds.

b. Provide additional modeling and practice for those English learners who need further assistance. Appropriate modeling can be provided by the teacher or by native English-speaking peers. Be sure to provide sufficient waiting time to process and produce sounds.

c. Assess whether the rate of introduction of new letter sounds into blending or of new word types is manageable. If not manageable for some students, determine a way to provide additional systematic, guided instruction so that they will be able to catch up with their classmates and accomplish the lesson objective.

Chapter 3
Content Standards
and Instructional
Practices—
Kindergarten
Through Grade
Three

First Grade

Curricular and
Instructional
Profile

**Universal
Access**
(Continued)

d. Ensure that students have had previous instruction or experiences (or both) with the words included in the instruction and that they understand their meaning.
e. Assess what knowledge is assumed before each unit of instruction. That is, determine what knowledge the typical English speaker already brings to the classroom and provide preteaching of key concepts.
f. Have English learners who have acquired literacy skills in their first language draw on those skills in English. Teachers can build on the knowledge of reading skills that students have acquired in their first languages when teaching English letter-sound correspondences.
g. Provide English learners with explicit models of the letter-sound correspondences that students are expected to know and correct errors as would be done for other learners. Correction of errors should always be conducted in a way that encourages students to keep trying and helps them see the progress they are making.

**Instructional
Materials**

1. Texts should contain explicit instruction in the blending process as well as in the transition from blending to the reading of whole words.

2. The letter-sound correspondences included in the words and the word types should be carefully selected.

3. Measures for assessing entry level and progress throughout instruction should be included in curricular materials.

4. Related skills (e.g., phonemic awareness, spelling) should be correlated, and connections should be made in instructional materials and instruction.

5. Decodable texts should be provided as an intervening step between explicit skill acquisition and the student's ability to read quality trade books. Decodable texts should contain the phonics elements with which students are familiar. However, the text should be unfamiliar to the student because the student should apply word-analysis skills, not reconstruct text already memorized.

61

Chapter 3
Content Standards
and Instructional
Practices—
Kindergarten
Through Grade
Three

First Grade

English–Language Arts Content Standards

Reading

1.0 Word Analysis, Fluency, and Systematic Vocabulary Development

Students understand the basic features of reading. They select letter patterns and know how to translate them into spoken language by using phonics, syllabication, and word parts. They apply this knowledge to achieve fluent oral and silent reading.

Concepts About Print

1.1 Match oral words to printed words.

1.2 Identify the title and author of a reading selection.

1.3 Identify letters, words, and sentences.

Phonemic Awareness

1.4 Distinguish initial, medial, and final sounds in single-syllable words.

1.5 Distinguish long- and short-vowel sounds in orally stated single-syllable words (e.g., *bit/bite*).

1.6 Create and state a series of rhyming words, including consonant blends.

1.7 Add, delete, or change target sounds to change words (e.g., change *cow* to *how; pan* to *an*).

1.8 Blend two to four phonemes into recognizable words (e.g., /c/a/t/ = cat; /f/ l/a/t/ = flat).

1.9 Segment single syllable words into their components (e.g., /c/a/t/ = cat; /s/p/l/a/t/ =splat; /r/i/ch/ = rich).

Decoding and Word Recognition

1.10 Generate the sounds from all the letters and letter patterns, including consonant blends and long- and short-vowel patterns (i.e., phonograms), and blend those sounds into recognizable words.

1.11 Read common, irregular sight words (e.g., *the, have, said, come, give, of*).

1.12 Use knowledge of vowel digraphs and *r*-controlled letter-sound associations to read words.

1.13 Read compound words and contractions.

1.14 Read inflectional forms (e.g., *-s, -ed, -ing*) and root words (e.g., *look, looked, looking*).

1.15 Read common word families (e.g., *-ite, -ate*).

1.16 Read aloud with fluency in a manner that sounds like natural speech.

Vocabulary and Concept Development

1.17 Classify grade-appropriate categories of words (e.g., concrete collections of animals, foods, toys).

2.0 Reading Comprehension

Students read and understand grade-level-appropriate material. They draw upon a variety of comprehension strategies as needed (e.g., generating and responding to essential questions, making predictions, comparing information from several sources). The selections in *Recommended Readings in Literature, Kindergarten Through Grade Eight*

Chapter 3
Content Standards
and Instructional
Practices—
Kindergarten
Through Grade
Three

First Grade

English–Language
Arts Content
Standards

illustrate the quality and complexity of the materials to be read by students. In addition to their regular school reading, by grade four, students read one-half million words annually, including a good representation of grade-level-appropriate narrative and expository text (e.g., classic and contemporary literature, magazines, newspapers, online information). In grade one, students begin to make progress toward this goal.

Structural Features of Informational Materials

2.1   Identify text that uses sequence or other logical order.

Comprehension and Analysis of Grade-Level-Appropriate Text

2.2   Respond to *who, what, when, where,* and *how* questions.

2.3   Follow one-step written instructions.

2.4   Use context to resolve ambiguities about word and sentence meanings.

2.5   Confirm predictions about what will happen next in a text by identifying key words (i.e., signpost words).

2.6   Relate prior knowledge to textual information.

2.7   Retell the central ideas of simple expository or narrative passages.

3.0   Literary Response and Analysis

Students read and respond to a wide variety of significant works of children's literature. They distinguish between the structural features of the text and the literary terms or elements (e.g., theme, plot, setting, characters). The selections in *Recommended Readings in Literature, Kindergarten Through Grade Eight* illustrate the quality and complexity of the materials to be read by students.

Narrative Analysis of Grade-Level-Appropriate Text

3.1   Identify and describe the elements of plot, setting, and character(s) in a story, as well as the story's beginning, middle, and ending.

3.2   Describe the roles of authors and illustrators and their contributions to print materials.

3.3   Recollect, talk, and write about books read during the school year.

Writing
1.0   Writing Strategies

Students write clear and coherent sentences and paragraphs that develop a central idea. Their writing shows they consider the audience and purpose. Students progress through the stages of the writing process (e.g., prewriting, drafting, revising, editing successive versions).

Organization and Focus

1.1   Select a focus when writing.

1.2   Use descriptive words when writing.

Penmanship

1.3   Print legibly and space letters, words, and sentences appropriately.

2.0   Writing Applications (Genres and Their Characteristics)

Students write compositions that describe and explain familiar objects, events, and experiences. Student writing demonstrates a command of standard American English and the drafting, research, and organizational strategies outlined in Writing Standard 1.0.

Using the writing strategies of grade one outlined in Writing Standard 1.0, students:

2.1   Write brief narratives (e.g., fictional, autobiographical) describing an experience.

2.2   Write brief expository descriptions of a real object, person, place, or event, using sensory details.

Chapter 3
Content Standards
and Instructional
Practices—
Kindergarten
Through Grade
Three

First Grade

English–Language
Arts Content
Standards

Written and Oral English Language Conventions

The standards for written and oral English language conventions have been placed between those for writing and for listening and speaking because these conventions are essential to both sets of skills.

1.0 Written and Oral English Language Conventions

Students write and speak with a command of standard English conventions appropriate to this grade level.

Sentence Structure

1.1 Write and speak in complete, coherent sentences.

Grammar

1.2 Identify and correctly use singular and plural nouns.

1.3 Identify and correctly use contractions (e.g., *isn't, aren't, can't, won't*) and singular possessive pronouns (e.g., *my/mine, his/her, hers, your/s*) in writing and speaking.

Punctuation

1.4 Distinguish between declarative, exclamatory, and interrogative sentences.

1.5 Use a period, exclamation point, or question mark at the end of sentences.

1.6 Use knowledge of the basic rules of punctuation and capitalization when writing.

Capitalization

1.7 Capitalize the first word of a sentence, names of people, and the pronoun *I*.

Spelling

1.8 Spell three- and four-letter short-vowel words and grade-level-appropriate sight words correctly.

Listening and Speaking

1.0 Listening and Speaking Strategies

Students listen critically and respond appropriately to oral communication. They speak in a manner that guides the listener to understand important ideas by using proper phrasing, pitch, and modulation.

Comprehension

1.1 Listen attentively.

1.2 Ask questions for clarification and understanding.

1.3 Give, restate, and follow simple two-step directions.

Organization and Delivery of Oral Communication

1.4 Stay on the topic when speaking.

1.5 Use descriptive words when speaking about people, places, things, and events.

2.0 Speaking Applications (Genres and Their Characteristics)

Students deliver brief recitations and oral presentations about familiar experiences or interests that are organized around a coherent thesis statement. Student speaking demonstrates a command of standard American English and the organizational and delivery strategies outlined in Listening and Speaking Standard 1.0.

Using the speaking strategies of grade one outlined in Listening and Speaking Standard 1.0, students:

2.1 Recite poems, rhymes, songs, and stories.

2.2 Retell stories using basic story grammar and relating the sequence of story events by answering *who, what, when, where, why,* and *how* questions.

2.3 Relate an important life event or personal experience in a simple sequence.

2.4 Provide descriptions with careful attention to sensory detail.

64

Chapter 3
Content Standards
and Instructional
Practices—
Kindergarten
Through Grade
Three

Second Grade

Standards and Instruction

Before they enter the second grade, most students have already learned the foundational skills of word analysis and have a rudimentary understanding of the elements of narrative text. They are able to spell three- and four-letter short vowel words and some common sight words (e.g., *the, have, said, come, give, of*). In addition, they possess basic skills in penmanship and in the use of writing to communicate knowledge and ideas. In the second grade the language arts curriculum and instruction are focused on enhancing word-recognition fluency, extending understanding of dimensions of narrative and informational text, and increasing proficiency in written and oral communication.

The second-grade curriculum and instruction should emphasize increasing students' facility with the alphabetic writing system and with larger and more complex units of text and on applying knowledge of letter-sound correspondences to decode unfamiliar words. Further efforts should be made to help students link phonemic awareness of words and knowledge of letter-sounds to build lexicons of familiar words; use knowledge of spelling patterns, prefixes, and suffixes; and increase sight vocabulary through extensive practice. Adequate

initial reading instruction requires that students use reading to obtain meaning from print and have frequent opportunities to read.

They should extend their repertoire of reading-comprehension strategies for both narrative and informational text with instructional adjuncts (e.g., graphs, diagrams) and more sophisticated techniques for analyzing text (e.g., comparison and contrast). Initial skill in editing and revising text must be developed at this grade level, and increased emphasis should be placed on legible and coherent writing. Students should continue to work on written and oral English-language conventions as they develop their awareness of the parts of speech and the correct spelling of more complex word types. Listening comprehension and speaking expectations increase as second graders learn to paraphrase, clarify, explain, and report on information they hear, experience, and read.

The strands to be emphasized in the second grade are listed on the following page under the appropriate domains.

Each of the strands is addressed separately with the exception of the written and oral English-language conventions strand, which is integrated within appropriate sections.

65

Chapter 3
Content Standards
and Instructional
Practices—
Kindergarten
Through Grade
Three

Second Grade

Standards and
Instruction

Reading

1.0	Word Analysis, Fluency, and Systematic Vocabulary Development
2.0	Reading Comprehension
3.0	Literary Response and Analysis

Writing

| 1.0 | Writing Strategies |
| 2.0 | Writing Applications (Genres and Their Characteristics) |

Written and Oral English-Language Conventions

| 1.0 | Written and Oral English-Language Conventions |

Listening and Speaking

| 1.0 | Listening and Speaking Strategies |
| 2.0 | Speaking Applications (Genres and Their Characteristics) |

Reading   **Word Analysis, Fluency, and Systematic Vocabulary Development**

Decoding and Word Recognition

At the *beginning* of the second grade, students should be able to (1) generate the sounds for all consonants, consonant blends, and long and short vowels; (2) recognize common sight words; and (3) process word families and inflectional endings of words.

Development of word-analysis and word-recognition skills in the second grade proceeds systematically, building on first-grade skills and extending those fundamental understandings purposefully and interdependently. Instruction should carefully sequence the introduction of new skills and strategies. If students lack proficiency in prerequisite skills, those

skills must be taught before more advanced word structures are presented.

Early in the second grade, decoding operations are mechanical and not automatic for many learners. During this year students typically make great strides in decoding fluency (Ehri and McCormick 1998). Over the course of the year, they develop fluency through instruction in advanced phonics units (e.g., vowel diphthongs) and in the use of larger orthographic units of text, such as onset and rime. (Onset is the consonant or consonants that come before the first vowel; rime is the remainder of the word beginning with the first vowel [e.g., *h-ill, p-ill*] to read words.) Redundancy in letter sounds and orthographic units in words allows students to process words more efficiently. They learn to read phonetically regular words more fluently as they become familiar and facile with chunks of text. *Note*: Students have not merely memorized the larger units but, when necessary, can apply their knowledge of letter-sound correspondences to work their way through the words.

Students in the second grade should also continue instruction and practice in learning reliable rules to assist in decoding. For example, learning that an *e* at the end of a word usually causes the medial vowel to be long (or say its name) is a rule that advances word-analysis skills. A primary goal of second-grade word-analysis instruction is to increase systematically students' ability to read words because of their knowledge of more complex spelling patterns.

Another essential component of fluency development is the opportunity for students to practice unfamiliar words many times in text, allowing them to use their decoding skills with a high degree of success. Text that students practice should be at their instructional level, with no more than one in ten words read inaccurately.

Chapter 3
Content Standards
and Instructional
Practices—
Kindergarten
Through Grade
Three

Second Grade

Standards and
Instruction

Advanced instruction in decoding is more effective if it relies on the following principles of design and delivery. Suggested procedures to follow are to:

- Teach the advanced phonic-analysis skills as explicitly as was done for the earlier letter-sound correspondences: first in isolation, then in words and connected text, and, when the students become proficient, in trade books.
- Avoid assuming that learners will automatically transfer skills from one word type to another. When introducing a new letter combination, prefix, or word ending, model each of the fundamental stages (e.g., letter-combination, prefixes), blending the word and then reading the whole word.
- Separate auditorily and visually similar letter combinations in the instructional sequence (e.g., do not introduce both sounds for *oo* simultaneously; separate *ai, au*).
- Sequence words and sentences strategically to incorporate known phonics units (e.g., letter combinations, inflectional endings).
- Ensure that students know the sounds of the individual letters prior to introducing larger orthographic units (e.g., *ill, ap, ing*).
- Provide initial practice in controlled contexts in which students can apply newly learned skills successfully.
- Offer repeated opportunities for students to read words in contexts where they can apply their advanced phonics skills with a high level of success.
- Use decodable text, if needed, as an intervening step between explicit skill acquisition and the student's ability to read quality trade books.

- Incorporate spelling to reinforce word analysis. After students can read words, provide explicit instruction in spelling, showing students how to map the sounds of letters onto print.
- Make clear the connections between decoding (symbol to sound) and spelling (sound to symbol). At this point students have three powerful tools to facilitate word learning: ability to hear sounds in words, knowledge of the individual letter sounds or letter-sound combinations, and knowledge of the letters. Teach and remind students to rely on those skills and strategies when they encounter unfamiliar words or need to spell a word. However, ensure that students understand that some words are not spelled as they sound. The spelling of those words must be memorized at this stage.
- Teach decoding strategies initially, using words with meanings familiar to students.

Multisyllabic word reading. As students progress in word-analysis skills, they encounter more complex words, particularly words with more than one syllable. In the second grade students learn the rules of syllabication. Two strategies aid multisyllabic word recognition—breaking the word into syllables and learning prefixes and suffixes.

Sight-word reading. Second-grade word-analysis instruction must systematically teach children sight-word recognition of high-frequency words. When sight words (high-frequency irregular words) are being taught, it is important for the teacher to:

1. Select words that have high utility; that is, words that are used frequently in grade-appropriate literature and informational text.

67

Chapter 3
Content Standards
and Instructional
Practices---
Kindergarten
Through Grade
Three

Second Grade

Standards and
Instruction

2. Sequence high-frequency irregular words to avoid potential confusion. For example, high-frequency words that are often confused by students should be strategically separated for initial instruction.

3. Limit the number of sight words introduced at one time (five to seven new words).

4. Preteach the sight words prior to reading connected text.

5. Provide a cumulative review of important high-frequency sight words as part of daily reading instruction (two to three minutes).

Fluency. The benchmark of fluent readers in the second grade is the ability to read grade-level material aloud and accurately in a manner that sounds like natural speech. The essential questions to be asked: What should second-grade speech sound like? How do we define fluency for second graders? Research studies indicate that students reading at the fiftieth percentile in spring in the second grade read 90 to 100 words per minute correct orally (Hasbrouck and Tindal 1992) and that, on average, they increase their reading fluency approximately 1.46 correct words per minute per week (Fuchs et al. 1993).

Vocabulary and Concept Development

In the second grade curriculum and instruction extend the understanding of concepts and vocabulary in four primary ways:

- Knowledge and use of antonyms and synonyms
- Use of individual words in compounds to predict the meaning
- Use of prefixes and suffixes to assist in word meaning
- Learning multiple-meaning words

Two emphases in vocabulary development initiated in kindergarten should carry through into the second grade: (1) direct instruction of specific concepts and vocabulary essential to understanding text; and (2) exposure to a broad and diverse vocabulary through listening to and reading stories and informational texts.

Of the new vocabulary skills introduced in the second grade, the use of prefixes and suffixes to aid in word meaning is a skill that students may use frequently as they read more complex and challenging texts. When teaching prefixes and suffixes to assist in word meaning, teachers should emphasize those that occur with the greatest frequency in second-grade material. Prefixes and suffixes that are most useful in understanding word meaning should be introduced before less useful ones.

In presenting instruction in prefixes and suffixes, the teacher should:

1. Introduce the prefix or suffix in isolation, indicating its meaning and then connecting it in words.

2. Illustrate the prefix or suffix with multiple examples.

3. Use examples when the roots are familiar to students (e.g., *remake* and *replay* as opposed to *record* and *recode*) (Cunningham 1998).

4. Integrate words into sentences and ask students to tell the meaning of the word in the sentence.

5. Review previously introduced words cumulatively.

6. Separate prefixes that appear similar in initial instructional sequences (e.g., *pre, pro*).

Reading Comprehension

In the second grade informational text gains greater prominence than before as students learn to (1) use conventions of informational text (e.g., titles, chapter

Chapter 3
Content Standards
and Instructional
Practices—
Kindergarten
Through Grade
Three

Second Grade

Standards and
Instruction

headings) to locate important information; (2) ask clarifying questions; and (3) interpret information from graphs, diagrams, and charts. Concurrently, students learn the importance of reading in locating facts and details in narrative and informational text and recognizing cause-and-effect relationships.

Given the great number of comprehension skills and strategies to be learned, instruction should be organized in a coherent structure. A question that might be asked here is, Which skills and strategies should be used during prereading, reading, and postreading?

Instruction in reading comprehension is the intentional teaching of information or strategies to increase a student's understanding of what is read. When the second-grade standards are considered in conjunction with the big picture of instruction in reading comprehension, it is important to recognize that such instruction consists of three phases. In the *acquisition phase* the skill or strategy is taught explicitly with the aid of carefully designed examples and practice. This phase may consist of one or more days depending on the skill or strategy being taught. The *focused application phase* should continue across several instructional sessions to illustrate the applicability and utility of the skill or strategy. The *strategic integration phase*, occurring over the course of the year, is designed to connect previously taught skills and strategies with new content and text. Curriculum and instruction should cumulatively build a repertoire of skills and strategies that are introduced, applied, and integrated with appropriate texts and for authentic purposes over the course of the year. As students begin to develop reading-comprehension skills, effective

teachers foster interest and motivation to read and assist students in developing an appreciation of the rewards and joys of reading.

Reading   Literary Response and Analysis

In the second grade students work extensively in analyzing the elements of narrative text and comparing and contrasting elements within and among texts. Building on their prior schemata of stories, students read versions of stories written by different authors to gain an understanding of the influence of the writer and the culture. They use the narrative text structure to write brief narratives (Writing Applications Standard 2.1) and retell stories (Listening and Speaking Standard 2.1). Emphasis on comprehension is centered on teaching students to analyze narratives, compare and contrast, and generate alternative endings. The connections with the listening, speaking, and writing domains are clear in this strand. Instructional effectiveness and efficiency can be gained by employing inherent connections in content.

As students learn to compare and contrast, many will benefit from a structure specifying the dimensions that will be compared and contrasted. The story grammar structure works elegantly in this instance as a tool for prompting information to compare and contrast, organizing information, and grouping related ideas to maintain a consistent focus (Writing Strategies Standard 1.1). This feature will be the focus of the instructional and curricular profile that appears at the end of the second-grade section.

69

Chapter 3
Content Standards
and Instructional
Practices---
Kindergarten
Through Grade
Three

Writing   Writing Strategies and Writing Applications

Students become more comfortable and familiar with writing when it is a regular and frequent activity. In the second grade writing progresses to narratives in which students move through a logical sequence of events. They learn to write about an experience in the first grade and to write for different audiences and purposes in the second grade. The narrative structure and requirements expand in the second grade to multiple paragraphs that integrate knowledge of setting, characters, objectives, and events to develop more complex and complete narratives. In addition, second graders learn an additional text structure, the friendly letter, as a form of written communication.

Applications of narrative and letter writing depend on well-developed writing strategies, including grouping of related ideas, facility with various stages of writing, and legible handwriting. In the second grade students focus on learning to revise text to improve sequence and increase descriptive detail. Concurrently, they require instruction in distinguishing between complete and incomplete sentences, extending grammatical proficiency with parts of speech, applying correct capitalization and punctuation, and expanding their repertoire of correctly spelled words. Spelling instruction progresses to include inflected endings and irregular or exception words (e.g., *said, who, what, why*). The instructional guidelines for systematic instruction introduced in the first grade are equally important in the second grade. They consist of small sets of words that are introduced explicitly, reviewed frequently, and integrated into writing exercises.

The standards on which writing strategies and applications are based may be conceived as discrete skills that learners apply. Alternatively, and more effectively, the individual skills can be conceptualized in strands. Within a single writing lesson, instruction might occur along each of the major strands in writing strategies (e.g., organization, penmanship, revision) and written and oral English conventions (e.g., sentence structure, grammar, punctuation, capitalization, spelling). Instruction in each strand can address the specific dimensions of grammar and punctuation appropriate to the individual student.

In instruction according to strands, incremental and progressive skills and strategies within and across a range of strands related to a larger domain are introduced and learned to provide a precise, coherent course of study. Such instruction, both specific and related, which focuses on specific skills and strategies and incorporates them into exercises once learners are proficient with individual skills, is especially appropriate for writing. Features of this instruction are as follows:

1. Dimensions of a complex task are analyzed, and the strands are identified (e.g., organization, grammar, sentence structure, and stages of writing).

2. Specific objectives within a strand are identified and sequenced individually.

3. Cross-strand skills are integrated once learners are proficient in individual strand skills and strategies.

4. Previously taught skills and strategies are reviewed cumulatively.

5. The instructional analysis of the content and proficiency of the learner will prescribe the length of the instructional sequence.

Chapter 3
Content Standards
and Instructional
Practices—
Kindergarten
Through Grade
Three

Second Grade

Standards and
Instruction

Listening and Speaking
Listening and Speaking Strategies; Speaking Applications

In the second grade the students' proficiency in speaking and listening expands quantitatively and qualitatively. The students are responsible for comprehending larger amounts of information presented orally (e.g., three- to four-step instructions) and for communicating their ideas with increased attention to detail and substance (e.g., reporting on a topic with supportive facts and details). Speaking strategies are applied in two primary formats—recounting experiences or stories and reporting on a topic with facts and details.

Narrative experiences or stories and reports, which are the focus of second-grade instruction, have identifiable and generalizable structures taught in reading and writing and can be used to communicate ideas orally. Although students may be quite facile in identifying the common elements of stories by the second grade, identifying or recognizing is a simpler task in most cases than generating and producing the elements of text in oral reports. Instruction to prepare students to recall stories or experiences or to report on a topic should proceed from (1) the reading of text for which students know the elements (e.g., characters, setting, problem, important events, resolution to the problem, conclusion); to (2) the identification of those elements in stories and topics; and (3) the production or generation of the elements.

Students should be introduced to the simple strategy of organizing both narrative and expository texts chronologically. That type of organization is particularly applicable to language arts activities that reinforce the history–social science standards for this grade level. In addition to understanding chronological organization, students can build on the *who, what, when, where,* and *how* strategy learned in the first grade as another way of organizing oral and written communication.

Content and Instructional Connections

The following activities integrate standards across domains, strands, and academic disciplines. Teachers may wish to:

1. Reinforce the connections between phonemic awareness (hearing the sounds in words), phonological recoding (translating a printed word into its letter-sound correspondences), and translating sounds into print (spelling).
2. Extend the words that students can read (e.g., special vowel spellings, plurals) into their spelling and writing.
3. Incorporate words taken from vocabulary instruction (e.g., synonyms, words with prefixes) into exercises providing systematic opportunities to use words in sentences throughout the day.
4. Incorporate comprehension strategies into other content areas (e.g., reading a science textbook when appropriate) and practice those strategies.
5. Use story grammar elements as a common structure for comprehending, retelling, and composing stories.
6. Select appropriate content standards in science, mathematics, and history–social science to address within the instructional time allotted for instruction in the language arts.

Please see Appendix B for examples of standards that span domains and strands.

71

Chapter 3
Content Standards
and Instructional
Practices—
Kindergarten
Through Grade
Three

Second Grade

Curricular and Instructional Profile

Reading Standard 3.1

DOMAIN	STRAND	SUBSTRAND	STANDARD
Reading	3.0 Literacy response and analysis	Narrative analysis of grade-level-appropriate text	3.1 Compare and contrast plots, settings, and characters presented by different authors.

Prerequisite standards. **Kindergarten Literary Response and Analysis Standard 3.3:** Identify characters, settings, and important events.

First-Grade Literary Response and Analysis Standard 3.1: Identify and describe the elements of plot, setting, and characters in a story as well as the story's beginning, middle, and ending.

Curricular and Instructional Decisions

Instructional Objectives	1. Identify the major events (plot), settings, and characters of stories. 2. Compare and contrast those elements. Successful comparison and contrast of story elements depend on the ability to identify the major elements of individual stories. In this standard second graders use the literary elements of stories to identify similarities and differences between and among a wide, varied sampling of children's literature.
Instructional Design	Comparing and contrasting textual elements involve a host of factors that make this task either manageable or extraordinarily difficult. Initial instruction is likely to be most effective and efficient if it adheres to the following guidelines. Teachers may wish to: 1. Begin with a review and practice of identifying story grammar elements (e.g., setting, characters, problems, attempts to solve

Chapter 3
Content Standards
and Instructional
Practices—
Kindergarten
Through Grade
Three

Second Grade

Curricular and
Instructional
Profile

**Instructional
Design**
(Continued)

the problem or sequence of events, and resolution of the problem or conclusion).

2. Support readers' identification of story grammar elements with a think sheet or story note sheet that outlines the elements students should identify.

3. Select stories with parallel structures that adhere to conventional story lines.

4. Use stories in which elements are explicit and clearly identifiable.

5. Do not proceed to a comparison and contrast analysis until students can identify elements of individual stories reliably. (Provide additional practice if necessary.)

6. Model how to compare and contrast explicitly, focusing on specific elements.

7. Begin with an oral comparison and contrast analysis. Have the students read the same story as a group and use a comparison and contrast version of the story grammar elements to indicate whether elements are the same or different.

8. Include stories in which some elements are comparable and some are different.

9. Begin with shorter stories and proceed to longer ones.

10. Use stories with largely familiar vocabulary. Stories that are not presented orally should be within the readability level of students.

11. Support learners in initial analyses by providing a concrete, overt strategy for comparing and contrasting elements that designates similarities and differences.

12. Provide sufficient practice in both components of instruction: (a) identifying elements; and (b) comparing and contrasting elements between and among stories.

Progression of Examples for Comparison and Contrast Analysis

- *First teaching sequence:* two stories, relatively brief, with explicit story grammar elements. Some elements in both stories should be comparable and some should differ (e.g., Peter Rabbit and Curious George are both "curious, mischievous").
- *Second teaching sequence:* two stories of moderate length, with explicit story grammar elements. Some elements in both stories should be comparable, and some should differ.
- *Third teaching sequence:* two or three stories that parallel the reading requirements of second graders. Elements are explicit.

Note: Each teaching sequence may require several days of instruction and practice for students to become proficient. This sequence is not intended to connote that this range of proficiency can be mastered in three days.

Chapter 3
Content Standards
and Instructional
Practices—
Kindergarten
Through Grade
Three

Second Grade

Curricular and
Instructional
Profile

**Instructional
Delivery**

1. Begin the instructional sequence with a review of the elements of an individual story in which the students identify setting, characters, problems, attempts to solve the problem or sequence of events, and resolution of the problem or conclusion. One of the stories should be included in the subsequent comparison and contrast analysis.

2. Identify explicitly for the students the critical elements; that is, read a section of the story and talk students through the process of identifying individual elements (see the previous description). If the students have difficulty with specific elements, provide further practice with additional stories.

3. Follow up teacher-directed identification of the elements with guided practice during which the students (as a whole class or in respective reading groups) identify the elements with the teacher's assistance.

4. Conclude this segment of instruction with independent practice. Students should use story note sheets or summary sheets to identify the elements of a story.

5. Model the process of comparing and contrasting story elements by using a structured tool. Walk students through the comparison and contrast process, thinking out loud as you model. (For example, "In *Peter Rabbit* the story takes place in a small garden in the country. In *Curious George* the story takes place in a busy city. The settings of these stories are different.") Continue modeling through all the elements in the story.

6. Explain the steps in the strategy: "When you read stories, they often have the same parts or elements. We are going to look at those parts to see how the stories are the same and how they are different."

7. Model multiple examples.

8. Guide students through the process of using the story elements to compare and contrast stories, using questions: "Where do these stories take place? Who are the characters? How are they the same? How are they different?" Provide corrective feedback. In this phase decrease prompts and assign greater responsibility to students.

9. Test students, using the same text format as in the teaching sequences. Do so immediately after the last teaching example to determine whether the students have acquired the strategy.

10. If students cannot use the strategy to compare and contrast story elements, analyze their responses to determine (1) whether the difficulties are specific to certain elements or are more generic; or (2) whether the difficulties are specific to certain students. Provide appropriate instruction and practice.

11. Present additional examples to assess student understanding.

Chapter 3
Content Standards
and Instructional
Practices—
Kindergarten
Through Grade
Three

Second Grade

Curricular and
Instructional
Profile

Assessment

Entry-Level Assessment

1. *Entry-Level Assessment for Instructional Planning*

   a. The most important entry-level assessment information for this standard is the extent to which students are already familiar with the elements of stories. The most direct assessment is for students to read a story and identify the elements either in response to a list of elements or on their own.

   b. Determine whether further instruction is needed in the identification of the basic elements of story grammar.

Monitoring Student Progress

2. *Monitoring Student Progress Toward the Instructional Objective.* This assessment phase is designed to determine the effectiveness of instruction and students' mastery of what has been taught. By designing tasks that align with the sequence of instruction, student performance can be used to determine whether to proceed to the next phase of instruction or to conduct further instruction and practice at the current phase.

Post-test Assessment

3. *Post-test Assessment Toward the Standard.* Analyzing stories by comparing and contrasting critical elements is a strategy that begins in the second grade and continues for many grades. This strategy should not be seen as a discrete skill that is taught and assessed at one time of the year. Narrative analysis should be distributed throughout the second grade to assess students' retention of the skill and to demonstrate the broad utility of the strategy. Published materials should emphasize this strategy and distribute its use across literature read in the second grade.

For a summative analysis a grid may be used that compares and contrasts story elements. Or students can be assigned to write a composition comparing and contrasting stories.

Universal Access

Reading Difficulties or Disabilities

1. *Students with Reading Difficulties or Disabilities*

   a. Students reading below grade level will require reading selections taken from below-grade-level literature. At this stage the goal is for students to learn the elements of story grammar and the comparison and contrast analysis strategy. This strategy can be introduced, discussed, and applied to stories that are read aloud to students. They can then use the analysis strategies with texts they read on their own.

   b. Students with disabilities or learning difficulties may need more extensive instruction in comparison and contrast. Materials should include examples of elements easily identifiable for basic comparison and contrast exercises.

Chapter 3
Content Standards
and Instructional
Practices—
Kindergarten
Through Grade
Three

Second Grade

Curricular and
Instructional
Profile

**Universal
Access**
(Continued)

Advanced
Learners

English Learners

c. Students may need scaffolded story sheets that not only identify the story grammar elements, such as setting or resolution, but also define setting—where and when the story takes place; and resolution—how the problem was solved.

d. Instructional materials should provide a range of examples to allow more extensive practice.

2. *Students Who Are Advanced Learners*

a. Advanced learners who have demonstrated above-grade-level comprehension skills and who have extensive reading experience may be grouped and given higher-level materials and a more sophisticated analysis of story elements. Regardless of how they are grouped, the teacher should substitute an advanced assignment for the regular lesson.

b. Advanced students might develop their own stories, orally or in writing, that compare and contrast a given story provided in class. They might compare and contrast two versions of the same story by different authors. Or they might rewrite a portion of a story to illustrate differences. These students may make connections that vary from the expected, given their ability to think creatively and abstractly and to generalize at an age earlier than that of their chronological peers.

3. *Students Who Are English Learners*

a. Through carefully designed instruction students should learn the process of identifying elements of stories and comparing and contrasting those elements. For students whose primary language is not English (English learners), a foremost problem can be the vocabulary used in the stories. The concepts and vocabulary may require more extensive development than is necessary for other students.

English learners can be helped to develop vocabulary through preteaching; providing vocabulary instruction; modeling the pronunciation of words; scaffolding (e.g., through summary sheets, visuals, realia, and compare and contrast sheets); and encouraging the students to use the vocabulary from the stories in class discussions and writing assignments. These students should learn more than the meaning of words. To accomplish grade-level objectives, they need to know how to use in their writing the words they have learned. To do so, they must learn the grammatical rules governing the use of words. When teaching words, the teacher should make sure to provide students with numerous examples of sentences containing

Chapter 3
Content Standards
and Instructional
Practices—
Kindergarten
Through Grade
Three

Second Grade

Curricular and
Instructional
Profile

Universal Access (Continued)

the words, encourage them to use words in their speech and writing, and provide corrective feedback when appropriate.

b. English learners may require more extensive instruction in comparison and contrast. Resources should include explicit instruction in words and expressions used to compare and contrast ("In comparison with . . . , X is different from Y because . . . ; both X and Y have a similar setting").

c. English learners benefit from extensive exposure to narrative models, comparison and contrast analyses, and multiple opportunities to use story elements to compare and contrast stories.

d. The teacher should select some texts that children of diverse cultures can relate to easily. Whenever possible, the texts should be authentic. Simplified texts should be used only with students with weak proficiency in English. Students who use the simplified texts need intensive English-language instruction to enable them to catch up with their peers.

Instructional Materials

1. Instructional materials should contain explicit instruction in strategies for comparing and contrasting stories. Enough selections should be made available at each level of instruction to ensure student mastery of the strategy.

2. Texts should be carefully selected and should contain critical features, including explicitness of the elements, length, familiarity of vocabulary, and readability.

3. Materials should include a range of selections and a corresponding set of assessment tasks to evaluate student performance at each stage of learning.

4. Materials should further include reproducible scaffolds or supports for students, including summary sheets that outline the story grammar elements and grids that use story grammar elements for comparison and contrast.

77

Chapter 3
Content Standards
and Instructional
Practices—
Kindergarten
Through Grade
Three

Second Grade

English–Language Arts Content Standards

Reading

1.0 Word Analysis, Fluency, and Systematic Vocabulary Development

Students understand the basic features of reading. They select letter patterns and know how to translate them into spoken language by using phonics, syllabication, and word parts. They apply this knowledge to achieve fluent oral and silent reading.

Decoding and Word Recognition

1.1 Recognize and use knowledge of spelling patterns (e.g., diphthongs, special vowel spellings) when reading.

1.2 Apply knowledge of basic syllabication rules when reading (e.g., vowel-consonant-vowel = *su/per;* vowel-consonant/consonant-vowel = *sup/per*).

1.3 Decode two-syllable nonsense words and regular multisyllable words.

1.4 Recognize common abbreviations (e.g., *Jan., Sun., Mr., St.*).

1.5 Identify and correctly use regular plurals (e.g., *-s, -es, -ies*) and irregular plurals (e.g., *fly/flies, wife/wives*).

1.6 Read aloud fluently and accurately and with appropriate intonation and expression.

Vocabulary and Concept Development

1.7 Understand and explain common antonyms and synonyms.

1.8 Use knowledge of individual words in unknown compound words to predict their meaning.

1.9 Know the meaning of simple prefixes and suffixes (e.g., *over-, un-, - ing, -ly*).

1.10 Identify simple multiple-meaning words.

2.0 Reading Comprehension

Students read and understand grade-level-appropriate material. They draw upon a variety of comprehension strategies as needed (e.g., generating and responding to essential questions, making predictions, comparing information from several sources). The selections in *Recommended Readings in Literature, Kindergarten Through Grade Eight* illustrate the quality and complexity of the materials to be read by students. In addition to their regular school reading, by grade four, students read one-half million words annually, including a good representation of grade-level-appropriate narrative and expository text (e.g., classic and contemporary literature, magazines, newspapers, online information). In grade two, students continue to make progress toward this goal.

Structural Features of Informational Materials

2.1 Use titles, tables of contents, and chapter headings to locate information in expository text.

Comprehension and Analysis of Grade-Level-Appropriate Text

2.2 State the purpose in reading (i.e., tell what information is sought).

Chapter 3
Content Standards
and Instructional
Practices—
Kindergarten
Through Grade
Three

Second Grade

English–Language
Arts Content
Standards

2.3 Use knowledge of the author's purpose(s) to comprehend informational text.

2.4 Ask clarifying questions about essential textual elements of exposition (e.g., *why, what if, how*).

2.5 Restate facts and details in the text to clarify and organize ideas.

2.6 Recognize cause-and-effect relationships in a text.

2.7 Interpret information from diagrams, charts, and graphs.

2.8 Follow two-step written instructions.

3.0. Literary Response and Analysis

Students read and respond to a wide variety of significant works of children's literature. They distinguish between the structural features of the text and the literary terms or elements (e.g., theme, plot, setting, characters). The selections in *Recommended Readings in Literature, Kindergarten Through Grade Eight* illustrate the quality and complexity of the materials to be read by students.

Narrative Analysis of Grade-Level-Appropriate Text

3.1 Compare and contrast plots, settings, and characters presented by different authors.

3.2 Generate alternative endings to plots and identify the reason or reasons for, and the impact of, the alternatives.

3.3 Compare and contrast different versions of the same stories that reflect different cultures.

3.4 Identify the use of rhythm, rhyme, and alliteration in poetry.

Writing

1.0 Writing Strategies

Students write clear and coherent sentences and paragraphs that develop a central idea. Their writing shows they consider the audience and purpose. Students progress through the stages of the writing process (e.g., prewriting, drafting, revising, editing successive versions).

Organization and Focus

1.1 Group related ideas and maintain a consistent focus.

Penmanship

1.2 Create readable documents with legible handwriting.

Research

1.3 Understand the purposes of various reference materials (e.g., dictionary, thesaurus, atlas).

Evaluation and Revision

1.4 Revise original drafts to improve sequence and provide more descriptive detail.

2.0 Writing Applications (Genres and Their Characteristics)

Students write compositions that describe and explain familiar objects, events, and experiences. Student writing demonstrates a command of standard American English and the drafting, research, and organizational strategies outlined in Writing Standard 1.0.

Using the writing strategies of grade two outlined in Writing Standard 1.0, students:

2.1 Write brief narratives based on their experiences:
   a. Move through a logical sequence of events.
   b. Describe the setting, characters, objects, and events in detail.

2.2 Write a friendly letter complete with the date, salutation, body, closing, and signature.

Written and Oral English Language Conventions

The standards for written and oral English language conventions have been placed between those for writing and for listening and speaking because these conventions are essential to both sets of skills.

Chapter 3
Content Standards
and Instructional
Practices—
Kindergarten
Through Grade
Three

Second Grade

English–Language
Arts Content
Standards

1.0 Written and Oral English Language Conventions

Students write and speak with a command of standard English conventions appropriate to this grade level.

Sentence Structure

1.1 Distinguish between complete and incomplete sentences.

1.2 Recognize and use the correct word order in written sentences.

Grammar

1.3 Identify and correctly use various parts of speech, including nouns and verbs, in writing and speaking.

Punctuation

1.4 Use commas in the greeting and closure of a letter and with dates and items in a series.

1.5 Use quotation marks correctly.

Capitalization

1.6 Capitalize all proper nouns, words at the beginning of sentences and greetings, months and days of the week, and titles and initials of people.

Spelling

1.7 Spell frequently used, irregular words correctly (e.g., *was, were, says, said, who, what, why*).

1.8 Spell basic short-vowel, long-vowel, *r*-controlled, and consonant-blend patterns correctly.

Listening and Speaking

1.0 Listening and Speaking Strategies

Students listen critically and respond appropriately to oral communication. They speak in a manner that guides the listener to understand important ideas by using proper phrasing, pitch, and modulation.

Comprehension

1.1 Determine the purpose or purposes of listening (e.g., to obtain information, to solve problems, for enjoyment).

1.2 Ask for clarification and explanation of stories and ideas.

1.3 Paraphrase information that has been shared orally by others.

1.4 Give and follow three- and four-step oral directions.

Organization and Delivery of Oral Communication

1.5 Organize presentations to maintain a clear focus.

1.6 Speak clearly and at an appropriate pace for the type of communication (e.g., informal discussion, report to class).

1.7 Recount experiences in a logical sequence.

1.8 Retell stories, including characters, setting, and plot.

1.9 Report on a topic with supportive facts and details.

2.0 Speaking Applications (Genres and Their Characteristics)

Students deliver brief recitations and oral presentations about familiar experiences or interests that are organized around a coherent thesis statement. Student speaking demonstrates a command of standard American English and the organizational and delivery strategies outlined in Listening and Speaking Standard 1.0.

Using the speaking strategies of grade two outlined in Listening and Speaking Standard 1.0, students:

2.1 Recount experiences or present stories:
   a. Move through a logical sequence of events.
   b. Describe story elements (e.g., characters, plot, setting).

2.2 Report on a topic with facts and details, drawing from several sources of information.

Chapter 3
Content Standards
and Instructional
Practices—
Kindergarten
Through Grade
Three

Third Grade

Standards and Instruction

The curriculum and instruction offered in the third grade should enable students to (1) read grade-level fiction and nonfiction materials independently with literal and inferential comprehension; (2) develop a knowledge of common spelling patterns, roots, and affixes; (3) use conventions of spelling and conventions of print (e.g., paragraphs, end-sentence punctuation); (4) clarify new words, make predictions, and summarize reading passages; (5) answer questions that require analysis, synthesis, and evaluation of grade-level narrative and informational text; and (6) support answers to questions about what they have read by drawing on background knowledge and specific details from the text.

The third grade is often considered the last period of formal instruction in decoding for students who still need it, although they continue to recognize new words beyond this grade level. At the end of this pivotal year, instruction in phonics is phased out from the formal curriculum as a focal point for students who have learned to decode. Increased and extended emphasis is placed on vocabulary acquisition, comprehension strategies, text analysis, and writing. Students are also taught to use context as an independent vocabulary strategy.

Instruction in identifying the main idea, prior-knowledge connections, and literal and inferential comprehension assumes greater prominence, as does increased variety in the narratives selected for reading (e.g., fairy tales, fables, textbooks). Building strategies for writing sentences and paragraphs is also emphasized. Students learn formal sentence structure, the four basic types of sentences, and the use of the sentences in written paragraphs. Finally, students take a big step forward, learning how to use speaking strategies and applications and how to deliver prose, poetry, and personal narratives and experiences with fluency, intonation, and expression. The strands to be emphasized at the third-grade level are listed on the following page under the appropriate domains.

Each of the strands is addressed separately with the exception of the written and oral English-language conventions strand, which is integrated within appropriate sections.

Chapter 3
Content Standards
and Instructional
Practices—
Kindergarten
Through Grade
Three

Third Grade

Standards and
Instruction

Reading

1.0 Word Analysis, Fluency, and Systematic Vocabulary Development
2.0 Reading Comprehension
3.0 Literary Response and Analysis

Writing

1.0 Writing Strategies
2.0 Writing Applications (Genres and Their Characteristics)

Written and Oral English-Language Conventions

1.0 Written and Oral English-Language Conventions

Listening and Speaking

1.0 Listening and Speaking Strategies
2.0 Speaking Applications (Genres and Their Characteristics)

Reading **Word Analysis, Fluency, and Vocabulary Development**

Decoding and Word Recognition

Specific decoding instruction in the earlier grades and redundancy of exposure through repeated practice have developed a stable and reliable strategy for analyzing words. As with earlier instruction in decoding and word recognition, students will need explicit instruction for word families (phonograms). Many of the same principles for selecting and sequencing instruction in the early grades apply here: (1) separating word parts that are highly similar (e.g., *ight* and *aight*); (2) introducing word parts that occur with high frequency over those that occur in only a few words; and (3) teaching the word parts first and then incorporating the words into sentences and connected text.

The word-recognition substrand in the third grade emphasizes reading harder and bigger words (i.e., multisyllabic words) and reading all words more fluently. Students further their word-analysis and fluency skills through instruction centered on orthographically larger and more complex units (e.g., *ight, aught, own).* They may learn to apply the orthographic unit *ight* first in such simple words as (pl)*ight*, (m)*ight*, and (sl)*ight*. When students are successful in reading simpler words with *ight,* word analysis should be extended to more complex words in which *ight* occurs in different positions (e.g., l*ight*ning, overn*ight*, br*ight*ness, forthr*ight*, del*ight*, and kn*ight*).

In the third grade students will also need to learn strategies to decode multisyllabic words. They can be taught to use the structural features of such word parts as affixes (e.g., *pre-, mis-, -tion*) to aid in word recognition. Economy can be achieved by teaching both the word part (e.g., *un*) and its meaning (*not*), then applying the strategy to words that follow the rules. In this structural analysis of the word, students are taught to look for the affix(es) and then find the root or base word.

Guidelines for reading big or multisyllabic words (Nagy et al. 1992, cited in Cunningham 1998) call for:

1. Providing explicit explanations, including modeling, "think-alouds," guided practice, and the gradual transfer of responsibility to students
2. Relying on examples more than abstract rules (Begin with familiar words. Show "nonexamples." Use word parts rather than have students search for little words within a word. *Examples:* depart, report.)

Chapter 3
Content Standards
and Instructional
Practices—
Kindergarten
Through Grade
Three

Third Grade

Standards and
Instruction

3. Teaching what is most useful
4. Making clear the limitations of structural analysis
5. Using extended text in opportunities for application

Cunningham provides a model for reading big words that combines reading, meaning, and spelling and extends the steps by teaching (1) prefixes that are useful from a meaning standpoint (e.g., *re-*); (2) suffixes that are most useful (e.g., *-ly, -er, -ful*); and (3) a few useful roots (e.g., *play, work, agree*). Students are also taught to spell words that have high utility for meaning, spelling, and decoding.

In addition to being taught structural analysis, students should be taught strategies to confirm the fit of the word in context. Although contextual analysis has limited usefulness as a single word-recognition strategy, it expands students' capacity for word analysis and recognition when used to confirm the accuracy of words identified by decoding and structural analysis. Words identified through the decoding of letter sounds or letter combinations are followed by recognition of larger units of words, including onsets and rimes and common word parts, such as prefixes and suffixes. After decoding and structural analysis have occurred, contextual analysis can be used to verify the accuracy and fit of the word in the sentence.

Extended word-analysis skills and ample opportunities to practice skills in connected text should enable third-grade students to read grade-appropriate text accurately and fluently. A study addressing target rates found that in third-grade classrooms students typically read 79 correct words per minute in the fall and 114 in the spring (Hasbrouck and Tindal 1992). Markell and Deno (1997) found

that a minimum threshold for acceptable comprehension was an ability to read correctly 90 words per minute. That is, students who read 90 or more words per minute correctly scored 80 percent or above on a measure of comprehension. On average a third grader's weekly reading fluency increases approximately 1.08 words per minute (Fuchs et al. 1993). As students learn to recognize words automatically, they should have opportunities to hear and practice reading text aloud, emphasizing pacing, intonation, and expression. Fluency or facility with print frees up cognitive resources for comprehension.

Vocabulary and Concept Development

In the early grades students learn approximately 3,000 new words per year *if* they read one-half million to one million words of running text per year. Obviously, it is educationally impossible for students to learn even a sizable portion of the 3,000 words through direct instructional approaches alone. Students in the third grade further their knowledge of vocabulary in significant ways, primarily through independent reading but also through independent vocabulary-learning strategies. In addition to direct instruction in synonyms, antonyms, and so on and explicit strategies for teaching the hierarchical relationship among words (e.g., living things/animal/mammal/dog), students are introduced to two strategies for independent learning of vocabulary. The first strategy is to learn to use the dictionary to understand the meaning of unknown words—a complex task with special constraints for third graders. The words in the dictionary definition are often more difficult than the target word itself. Dictionary usage should be taught explicitly with grade-appropriate dictio-

Chapter 3
Content Standards
and Instructional
Practices—
Kindergarten
Through Grade
Three

Third Grade

Standards and
Instruction

naries that allow students to access and understand the meaning of an unknown word. Moreover, understanding the definition of words alone has limited staying power unless the words are used in context and are encountered frequently.

A second independent vocabulary strategy introduced in the third grade is using context to gain the meaning of an unfamiliar word. Context includes the words surrounding the unfamiliar word that provide information to its meaning. Because not all contexts are created equal, however, initial instruction must be designed carefully to enable learners to acquire this important vocabulary strategy. Students should learn to use context effectively because most word meanings are learned from context. The third-grade curricular and instructional profile focuses on that strategy. In addition to the independent word-learning strategies, the third-grade curricula and instruction extend the understanding of concepts and vocabulary of the English language through (1) learning and using antonyms and synonyms; (2) using individual words in compound words to predict the meaning; (3) using prefixes and suffixes to assist in word meaning; and (4) learning simple multiple-meaning words.

Two vocabulary emphases initiated in kindergarten should carry through in the third grade; that is, direct instruction in specific concepts and vocabulary essential to understanding text and exposure to a broad and diverse vocabulary through listening to and reading stories. Of the new vocabulary skills introduced in the third grade, using prefixes and suffixes to aid in word meaning is one that students will use frequently as they read more complex and challenging text. (See the earlier discussion for guidance in teaching prefixes and suffixes.)

Reading   Reading Comprehension

In the third grade emphasis is placed on narrative and expository texts and literal and inferential comprehension. Third-grade students expand comprehension skills and strategies by:

- Using conventions of informational text (e.g., titles, chapter headings, glossaries) to locate important information
- Using prior knowledge to ask questions, make connections, and support answers
- Recalling major points in text and modifying predictions
- Recalling main ideas from expository text
- Demonstrating comprehension by identifying answers in the text
- Extracting information from text
- Following simple, multiple-step instructions

A major advancement in comprehension for the third grade focuses on identifying and recalling the main idea and supporting details of expository texts. In writing there is a related standard (Writing Standard 1.1) according to which students write paragraphs that include topic sentences (i.e., main ideas) and supporting facts and details. Expository text is typically more difficult to comprehend than narrative text. The ability to comprehend expository text is essential for achievement in school, especially in the later elementary grades and in the middle school years.

Successful instruction in complex comprehension strategies, such as finding the main idea, depends largely on the design of the information taught. Well-designed text enables readers to identify relevant information, including main ideas

Chapter 3
Content Standards
and Instructional
Practices—
Kindergarten
Through Grade
Three

Third Grade

Standards and
Instruction

and the relations between ideas
(Seidenberg 1989). In a review of text-processing research, Seidenberg (1989)
found that general education students
from elementary school through college
demonstrated difficulty in analyzing the
main ideas in textbooks, especially if the
main ideas were implied rather than stated
clearly.

For initial instruction in the acquisition
of main ideas, the teacher should consider:

- Beginning with linguistic units
  appropriate to the learner; for
  example, using pictures and a set of
  individual sentences before present-ing paragraph or passage-level text to
  help students learn the concept of
  main idea
- Using text in which the main idea is
  explicitly stated and is clear and in
  which the ideas follow a logical order
- Using familiar vocabulary and
  passages at appropriate readability
  levels for learners
- Using familiar topics
- Using familiar, simple syntactical
  structures and sentence types
- Progressing to more complex
  structures in which main ideas are
  not explicit and passages are longer

Reading   Literary Response and Analysis

The third-grade curriculum and
instruction are focused on (1) broadening
the type of narrative texts students read
and study (e.g., fairy tales, fables);
(2) distinguishing literary forms (poetry,
prose, fiction, and nonfiction); and
(3) deepening students' understanding
of elements in narrative text.

In the third grade students read a wide
variety of literature (poems, fiction,
nonfiction) and narrative text structures

(fairy tales, legends). They should also
begin to examine the commonalities
(e.g., plots, characters, settings) in story
structure, particularly the plots in different
types of stories and the uniqueness of each
story. The structural element of theme is
added to the story elements to extend the
schema for the comprehension of stories.
Students should begin to identify the
speaker and articulate the purpose.

Particular emphasis should be placed
on extending the understanding of
character development by studying what
characters say and do. The actions,
motives, attributes, and feelings of charac-ters may be abstract concepts for many
third graders. Just as students need a
framework such as basic story grammar to
aid in the comprehension of the basic
elements of stories, they may also need
prompts or structures to assist in the
identification and analysis of character.
This framework or map may be a simple
structure that makes visible and obvious
the features of characters to which stu-dents should attend. For example, in the
chart on the following page, the main
characters from *Charlotte's Web* (White
1952) are identified, and critical character
features are specified. The sections in the
chart serve to allow students to trace
changes in characters over the course of
the text.

As in all well-designed instruction in
comprehension, a carefully designed
sequence of examples should be provided
when students are in the acquisition phase
of learning to extend their understanding
and facility with character development.
The sequence should first be modeled and
then guided by the teacher and, finally,
practiced by the students. Opportunities
for corrective feedback should also be
provided.

Chapter 3
Content Standards
and Instructional
Practices—
Kindergarten
Through Grade
Three

Third Grade

Standards and
Instruction

Character	Section	Section	Section
Charlotte	How she feels:	Changes:	Changes:
	How she acts:	Changes:	Changes:
	How she looks:	Changes:	Changes:
Wilbur	How he feels:	Changes:	Changes:
	How he acts:	Changes:	Changes:
	How he looks:	Changes:	Changes:

Writing   Writing Strategies and Writing Applications

In the third grade students extend their writing strategies by (1) creating a single paragraph with a topic sentence and supporting details; (2) refining the legibility of their writing; (3) learning to access information from a range of reference materials (e.g., thesaurus, encyclopedia); (4) revising drafts to improve coherence and progression of ideas; and (5) progressing through the stages of the writing process.

Using these strategies, students continue to advance skills in written conventions as they learn to use declarative, interrogative, imperative, and exclamatory sentences. Advanced grammatical conventions, particularly subject-verb agreement and use of the tense, are the focus of third-grade instruction, along with continued development in capitalization, punctuation, and spelling.

As students learn to read words with double consonants, inflected endings, *y*-derivatives (e.g., *baby/ies*), and so forth, they are ready to learn to spell the words. Guidelines outlined in the first grade for spelling instruction are applicable in this grade. *Homophones* (i.e., words that sound alike but have different spellings and meanings: *their, there,* and *they're*) pose particular spelling problems. Homo-phones should be introduced a few at a time. It is recommended that a single homophone be introduced first. After mastery of that homophone, another may be presented. Once both homophones are mastered, they may be used in discrimination exercises in which meaning and context are emphasized.

In practice students apply those strategies and conventions as they learn and extend proficiency in writing narratives, descriptions, and personal and formal correspondence. This strategic integration of skills, strategies, and structures requires (1) explicit instruction in each of the individual components (e.g., sentence types, writing of paragraphs, use of tense); and (2) systematic connections of components to demonstrate the utility of the individual parts and communicate to students the big picture of writing. A common flaw in instructional materials is that they often fail to make the important connections for students. For example, students may learn to write declarative sentences but do not practice them or integrate them into other writing activities. Similarly, if students practice writing sentences with correct punctuation and capitalization but never apply the skills in larger contexts or for authentic purposes, instruction is fragmented. The skills are seemingly without purpose.

Chapter 3
Content Standards
and Instructional
Practices—
Kindergarten
Through Grade
Three

Third Grade

Standards and
Instruction

The goal in writing instruction must, therefore, be to ensure that component parts (skills, strategies, structures) are (1) identified; (2) carefully sequenced according to their complexity and use in more advanced writing applications; (3) developed to mastery; and (4) progressively and purposefully connected within and across content standards in the four academic areas and then incorporated into authentic writing exercises.

Listening and Speaking

Listening and Speaking Strategies; Speaking Applications

In the third grade emphasis is placed on listening and speaking strategies and on speaking applications. Fourteen standards signify the importance of students' speaking and listening development, the amount and type of information they should comprehend, and the formats and methods they should use to communicate their knowledge and ideas.

The connections across the language arts domains (reading, writing, listening, and speaking) have been stressed in other sections of this framework but bear repeating because they have particular significance for developing students' speaking and listening skills. Just as students need structures, maps, or anchors to facilitate their understanding of narrative or expository text, they will require the same types of supporting structures when learning what to listen for and what to speak about. Simplistic as it may seem, students may not know what to include when summarizing (e.g., organizing descriptions or sequencing events). The parallels of the structures students learn in reading and writing apply directly to the goals of listening and speaking, and those connections require explicit, carefully

designed instruction. The benefits of earlier teaching should be readily apparent because students already know the elements of stories, descriptions, and sequences of events from previous instruction in reading and writing.

It is typically easier to retell than to create and easier to comprehend than to compose. Therefore, instructional materials and instruction should honor those inherent complexities and ensure that students first have opportunities to listen to and read narratives, descriptives, and sequences of events before being asked to write and orally present narratives, descriptives, and sequences of events. Instructional design must address further (1) the length of the information to be listened to or spoken; (2) familiarity with the topic; (3) familiarity with the vocabulary; and (4) syntactical complexity of the information.

Initial listening and speaking applications should be shorter in length, should be centered on more familiar topics, and should be less complex syntactically.

Content and Instructional Connections

The following activities integrate standards across domains, strands, and academic disciplines. Teachers may wish to:

1. Reinforce the connections between decoding, word recognition, spelling, and writing. Word families, multisyllabic words, and structural units (e.g., prefixes) that students learn to read should be incorporated into spelling and writing instruction and practice.

2. Incorporate words or word parts from vocabulary instruction (e.g., prefixes, synonyms) in

systematic opportunities that use those words in sentences. Practice throughout the day and over a period of time.

3. Make connections between structures used for comprehension and composition. Demonstrate how text structures can be used across domains to enhance recall and composition.

4. Teach rules that generalize across reading materials and make explicit the connections of their use in a variety of subject areas (e.g., use context to help learn the meanings of words you do not know).

5. Make connections by incorporating and reinforcing specific skills and conventions (e.g., grammar, main idea, sentence types) across all writing assignments and exercises.

6. Select appropriate content standards for science, mathematics, and history–social science to address within language arts instructional time.

Please see Appendix B for examples of standards that span domains and strands.

Chapter 3
Content Standards
and Instructional
Practices—
Kindergarten
Through Grade
Three

Third Grade

Standards and
Instruction

Chapter 3
Content Standards
and Instructional
Practices—
Kindergarten
Through Grade
Three

Third Grade

Curricular and Instructional Profile

Reading Standard   1.6

DOMAIN	STRAND		SUBSTRAND	STANDARD	
Reading	1.0	Word analysis, fluency, and systematic vocabulary development	Vocabulary and concept development	1.6	Use sentence and word context to find the meaning of unknown words.

Prerequisite standards. **First-Grade Reading Comprehension Standards 2.4, 2.5.**

Standard 2.4: Use context to resolve ambiguities about word and sentence meanings.

Standard 2.5: Confirm predictions about what will happen next in a text by identifying key words.

Curricular and Instructional Decisions

Instructional Objective	When given a text (sentence or sentences) with unfamiliar vocabulary used in close proximity, students should first decode the word and then use the context to determine the word meaning. Learning words from context involves a range of variables that enhance or impede the success of the strategy, including the student's previous knowledge about the subject matter, the proximity of other words in the passage that may serve as clues, and the difficulty of the reading selection.
Instructional Design	Successful learning from context depends largely on practice. Teachers can teach this strategy through: 1. Systematic selection and sequencing of examples (contexts) 2. Progression of context difficulty from shorter passages (e.g., 40 to 60 words with two or three unfamiliar words) to longer ones (e.g., 80 to 100 words with five or six unfamiliar words)

Chapter 3
Content Standards
and Instructional
Practices—
Kindergarten
Through Grade
Three

Third Grade

Curricular and
Instructional
Profile

Instructional Design (Continued)

3. Explicit instruction and modeling in how to use context to learn word meaning

Contexts for Initial Instruction:

1. Unfamiliar words are limited to a manageable number (one every two to three sentences).
2. Unfamiliar words are kept within the students' readability level.
3. Contexts focus on a familiar topic.
4. Contexts include a range of examples in which new vocabulary is accessible through surrounding context and a few examples in which a dictionary must be used.
5. Contexts focus on vocabulary of high utility.

Instructional Delivery

1. Model the process of using context to learn new word meanings. Think out loud as you model: "I don't know the meaning of this word. I'll read the words around it to see if they help me." Show the conventions used to define new words (e.g., appositives).
2. Model multiple positive and negative examples (i.e., vocabulary for which the context does or does not provide meaning). Show students how to use a dictionary in the latter case.
3. Invite students to suggest which other words or passages provide clues to the meaning of the unfamiliar word.
4. Ask students to suggest synonyms for the unknown word and substitute the synonyms to see whether the meaning of the sentence changes or remains the same.
5. Guide students through the process of using the context to learn new word meanings. Provide corrective feedback.

Assessment

Entry-Level Assessment

Monitoring Student Progress

Post-test Assessment

1. *Entry-Level Assessment for Instructional Planning.* At the entry level assess student knowledge of the strategy to determine whether students need instruction in the strategy.

2. *Monitoring Student Progress Toward the Instructional Objective.* Determine whether students can use context to understand unfamiliar word meanings. Use a range of examples, including shorter and longer passages as well as simple and complex contexts in which defining information is in close or far proximity to the unfamiliar word.

3. *Post-test Assessment Toward the Standard.* Use post-tests throughout the year to measure whether students are able to use context to understand unfamiliar word meanings and whether they are retaining the meaning of the unfamiliar words over time.

Chapter 3
Content Standards
and Instructional
Practices—
Kindergarten
Through Grade
Three

Third Grade

Curricular and
Instructional
Profile

Universal Access

Reading Difficulties or Disabilities

1. *Students with Reading Difficulties or Disabilities*

   a. Students with reading difficulties or disabilities must be very firm in prerequisite skills to benefit from context. The prerequisite skills include:

   • Decoding and word-recognition skills that enable students to read the text with 90 to 95 percent accuracy (If students cannot read the grade-level text, identify materials that are appropriate and teach the same strategy.)

   • Knowledge of words in context that define or explain the unfamiliar word

   b. Students with reading difficulties or disabilities may need more controlled examples with shorter length, fewer unknown words, and so forth.

Advanced Learners

2. *Students Who Are Advanced Learners*

   a. Entry-level assessment should be used to determine the necessity of teaching students to determine the meaning of unfamiliar words from context. Advanced learners are often characterized by their extensive vocabulary, making necessary the use of materials beyond their grade level to assess their skills.

   b. The level and type of instruction needed should be established. Students may progress rapidly to learning word meanings if context is separated from the target vocabulary once the basic strategy is known.

   c. Students with a high level of proficiency in this skill may benefit from exposure to more sophisticated alternate activities for vocabulary development instead of this instruction.

English Learners

3. *Students Who Are English Learners*

   a. For English learners to benefit from context, they must know the grammatical features, idioms, and vocabulary words used to define or explain the unfamiliar word. They should also understand the concepts presented in the text. English learners may need additional prereading activities that explain cultural references and develop their grammatical competence and knowledge of English vocabulary. Entry-level assessment should also be used to determine the appropriateness of texts for English learners. Whenever possible, authentic texts not simplified for English learners should be used. However, simplified texts may be needed if students have difficulty in learning and if initial entry-level

Chapter 3
Content Standards
and Instructional
Practices—
Kindergarten
Through Grade
Three

Third Grade

Curricular and
Instructional
Profile

**Universal
Access**
(Continued)

assessment shows that students are unable to use context to
determine word meanings

b. Entry-level assessment should also be used to determine the
appropriateness of this objective. English learners do not
rely on the strategy of learning the meanings of words from
context without also learning the necessity of attending to
the specific ways in which words are used in writing.
Teachers should not assume that English learners will
acquire the grammatical rules governing the use of words at
the same time they are acquiring the meaning of the words.
To teach students the rules, teachers need to provide
students with explicit instruction, model the words in
speech and writing, encourage students to use words in
sentences and in longer text, and provide students with
corrective feedback on their use of words.

c. Curricular materials should provide English learners with
additional opportunities to read texts that contain similar
vocabulary words and grammatical structures so that
students are repeatedly exposed to new words and structures. Some texts should be relevant to the interests and
needs of English learners from diverse cultures.

**Instructional
Materials**

1. Texts should contain explicit instruction strategies for identifying words from near-proximity contexts and far-proximity
contexts. Sufficient examples of each type should be provided
to ensure student mastery of the strategy.

2. Texts should be carefully selected and designed according to
critical features, including proximity of the defining context,
number of unfamiliar word meanings, richness of the context,
readability of the text, text length, and syntactical complexity.

3. Measures for conducting assessment at the entry level and
throughout the period of instruction must be included in the
curricular materials.

Chapter 3
Content Standards
and Instructional
Practices—
Kindergarten
Through Grade
Three

Third Grade

English–Language Arts Content Standards

Reading

1.0 Word Analysis, Fluency, and Systematic Vocabulary Development

Students understand the basic features of reading. They select letter patterns and know how to translate them into spoken language by using phonics, syllabication, and word parts. They apply this knowledge to achieve fluent oral and silent reading.

Decoding and Word Recognition

1.1 Know and use complex word families when reading (e.g., *-ight*) to decode unfamiliar words.

1.2 Decode regular multisyllabic words.

1.3 Read aloud narrative and expository text fluently and accurately and with appropriate pacing, intonation, and expression.

Vocabulary and Concept Development

1.4 Use knowledge of antonyms, synonyms, homophones, and homographs to determine the meanings of words.

1.5 Demonstrate knowledge of levels of specificity among grade-appropriate words and explain the importance of these relations (e.g., *dog/mammal/animal/living things*).

1.6 Use sentence and word context to find the meaning of unknown words.

1.7 Use a dictionary to learn the meaning and other features of unknown words.

1.8 Use knowledge of prefixes (e.g., *un-, re-, pre-, bi-, mis-, dis-*) and suffixes (e.g., *-er, -est, -ful*) to determine the meaning of words.

2.0 Reading Comprehension

Students read and understand grade-level-appropriate material. They draw upon a variety of comprehension strategies as needed (e.g., generating and responding to essential questions, making predictions, comparing information from several sources). The selections in *Recommended Readings in Literature, Kindergarten Through Grade Eight* illustrate the quality and complexity of the materials to be read by students. In addition to their regular school reading, by grade four, students read one-half million words annually, including a good representation of grade-level-appropriate narrative and expository text (e.g., classic and contemporary literature, magazines, newspapers, online information). In grade three, students make substantial progress toward this goal.

Structural Features of Informational Materials

2.1 Use titles, tables of contents, chapter headings, glossaries, and indexes to locate information in text.

Comprehension and Analysis of Grade-Level-Appropriate Text

2.2 Ask questions and support answers by connecting prior knowledge with literal

Chapter 3
Content Standards
and Instructional
Practices—
Kindergarten
Through Grade
Three

Third Grade

English–Language
Arts Content
Standards

information found in, and inferred from, the text.

2.3 Demonstrate comprehension by identifying answers in the text.

2.4 Recall major points in the text and make and modify predictions about forthcoming information.

2.5 Distinguish the main idea and supporting details in expository text.

2.6 Extract appropriate and significant information from the text, including problems and solutions.

2.7 Follow simple multiple-step written instructions (e.g., how to assemble a product or play a board game).

3.0 Literary Response and Analysis

Students read and respond to a wide variety of significant works of children's literature. They distinguish between the structural features of the text and literary terms or elements (e.g., theme, plot, setting, characters). The selections in *Recommended Readings in Literature, Kindergarten Through Grade Eight* illustrate the quality and complexity of the materials to be read by students.

Structural Features of Literature

3.1 Distinguish common forms of literature (e.g., poetry, drama, fiction, nonfiction).

Narrative Analysis of Grade-Level-Appropriate Text

3.2 Comprehend basic plots of classic fairy tales, myths, folktales, legends, and fables from around the world.

3.3 Determine what characters are like by what they say or do and by how the author or illustrator portrays them.

3.4 Determine the underlying theme or author's message in fiction and nonfiction text.

3.5 Recognize the similarities of sounds in words and rhythmic patterns (e.g., alliteration, onomatopoeia) in a selection.

3.6 Identify the speaker or narrator in a selection.

Writing

1.0 Writing Strategies

Students write clear and coherent sentences and paragraphs that develop a central idea. Their writing shows they consider the audience and purpose. Students progress through the stages of the writing process (e.g., prewriting, drafting, revising, editing successive versions).

Organization and Focus

1.1 Create a single paragraph:
 a. Develop a topic sentence.
 b. Include simple supporting facts and details.

Penmanship

1.2 Write legibly in cursive or joined italic, allowing margins and correct spacing between letters in a word and words in a sentence.

Research

1.3 Understand the structure and organization of various reference materials (e.g., dictionary, thesaurus, atlas, encyclopedia).

Evaluation and Revision

1.4 Revise drafts to improve the coherence and logical progression of ideas by using an established rubric.

2.0 Writing Applications (Genres and Their Characteristics)

Students write compositions that describe and explain familiar objects, events, and experiences. Student writing demonstrates a command of standard American English and the drafting, research, and organizational strategies outlined in Writing Standard 1.0.

Using the writing strategies of grade three outlined in Writing Standard 1.0, students:

2.1 Write narratives:
 a. Provide a context within which an action takes place.

Chapter 3
Content Standards
and Instructional
Practices—
Kindergarten
Through Grade
Three

Third Grade

English–Language
Arts Content
Standards

b. Include well-chosen details to develop the plot.

c. Provide insight into why the selected incident is memorable.

2.2 Write descriptions that use concrete sensory details to present and support unified impressions of people, places, things, or experiences.

2.3 Write personal and formal letters, thank-you notes, and invitations:

a. Show awareness of the knowledge and interests of the audience and establish a purpose and context.

b. Include the date, proper salutation, body, closing, and signature.

Written and Oral English Language Conventions

The standards for written and oral English language conventions have been placed between those for writing and for listening and speaking because these conventions are essential to both sets of skills.

1.0 Written and Oral English Language Conventions

Students write and speak with a command of standard English conventions appropriate to this grade level.

Sentence Structure

1.1 Understand and be able to use complete and correct declarative, interrogative, imperative, and exclamatory sentences in writing and speaking.

Grammar

1.2 Identify subjects and verbs that are in agreement and identify and use pronouns, adjectives, compound words, and articles correctly in writing and speaking.

1.3 Identify and use past, present, and future verb tenses properly in writing and speaking.

1.4 Identify and use subjects and verbs correctly in speaking and writing simple sentences.

Punctuation

1.5 Punctuate dates, city and state, and titles of books correctly.

1.6 Use commas in dates, locations, and addresses and for items in a series.

Capitalization

1.7 Capitalize geographical names, holidays, historical periods, and special events correctly.

Spelling

1.8 Spell correctly one-syllable words that have blends, contractions, compounds, orthographic patterns (e.g., *qu*, consonant doubling, changing the ending of a word from *-y* to *-ies* when forming the plural), and common homophones (e.g., *hair-hare*).

1.9 Arrange words in alphabetic order.

Listening and Speaking

1.0 Listening and Speaking Strategies

Students listen critically and respond appropriately to oral communication. They speak in a manner that guides the listener to understand important ideas by using proper phrasing, pitch, and modulation.

Comprehension

1.1 Retell, paraphrase, and explain what has been said by a speaker.

1.2 Connect and relate prior experiences, insights, and ideas to those of a speaker.

1.3 Respond to questions with appropriate elaboration.

1.4 Identify the musical elements of literary language (e.g., rhymes, repeated sounds, instances of onomatopoeia).

Organization and Delivery of Oral Communication

1.5 Organize ideas chronologically or around major points of information.

1.6 Provide a beginning, a middle, and an end, including concrete details that develop a central idea.

Chapter 3
Content Standards
and Instructional
Practices—
Kindergarten
Through Grade
Three

1.7 Use clear and specific vocabulary to communicate ideas and establish the tone.

1.8 Clarify and enhance oral presentations through the use of appropriate props (e.g., objects, pictures, charts).

1.9 Read prose and poetry aloud with fluency, rhythm, and pace, using appropriate intonation and vocal patterns to emphasize important passages of the text being read.

Analysis and Evaluation of Oral and Media Communications

1.10 Compare ideas and points of view expressed in broadcast and print media.

1.11 Distinguish between the speaker's opinions and verifiable facts.

2.0 Speaking Applications (Genres and Their Characteristics)

Students deliver brief recitations and oral presentations about familiar experiences or interests that are organized around a coherent thesis statement. Student speaking demon-strates a command of standard American English and the organizational and delivery strategies outlined in Listening and Speaking Standard 1.0.

Using the speaking strategies of grade three outlined in Listening and Speaking Standard 1.0, students:

2.1 Make brief narrative presentations:

   a. Provide a context for an incident that is the subject of the presentation.

   b. Provide insight into why the selected incident is memorable.

   c. Include well-chosen details to develop character, setting, and plot.

2.2 Plan and present dramatic interpretations of experiences, stories, poems, or plays with clear diction, pitch, tempo, and tone.

2.3 Make descriptive presentations that use concrete sensory details to set forth and support unified impressions of people, places, things, or experiences.

4

Content Standards and Instructional Practices

Grades Four Through Eight

The stages of learning to read and reading to learn help establish a further stage that extends through grade eight. That stage is perhaps best characterized as reading and learning for life, during which students begin to grapple with the full and complex range of lifelong language and literacy skills.

The standards for grades four through eight are expansive, revealing the important and weighty transitions in knowledge and skills expected of all students after the primary grades. The first significant transition for students occurs when they move from the stage popularly referred to as learning to read in kindergarten through grade three to that of reading to learn in grade four (National Center to Improve the Tools of Educators 1997). Emphasis on subject-matter reading begins to exert its full force on all students at this stage as they begin to study history–social science and science. The stages of learning to read and reading to learn help establish a further stage that extends through grade eight. That stage is perhaps best characterized as reading and learning

97

Chapter 4
Content Standards
and Instructional
Practices—
Grades Four
Through Eight

for life, during which students begin to grapple with the full and complex range of lifelong language and literacy skills.

For example, students are expected by the end of the eighth grade to demonstrate command of the following standards: (1) evaluating the unity, coherence, logic, internal consistency, and structural patterns of text; (2) achieving an effective balance between researched information and original ideas; (3) evaluating the credibility of a speaker; (4) presenting detailed evidence, examples, and reasoning to support arguments, differentiating between facts and opinion; and (5) identifying the sequence of activities needed to design a system, operate a tool, or explain the bylaws of an organization. Clearly, the expectations reach far beyond the stages of learning to read and reading to learn to knowing what is important and why. Students will not be able to grasp those important advanced skills and experiences if they are still struggling to decipher the alphabetic writing system. Therefore, the important transitions to engagement with more complex informational text in print and electronic form should not detract from the continuing importance of ensuring that all students are competent and fluent readers in grades four through eight.

A priority in the reading domain for each of the grades in the four through eight cluster is ensuring that students are able to read aloud narrative and expository text fluently and accurately. To do so, students must continue to recognize increasingly complex words accurately and automatically in grade-level-appropriate narrative and expository text ranging from classical literature to on-line information. In addition, they must continue to develop their vocabulary knowledge and skills in more sophisticated ways, such as analyzing idioms, analogies, metaphors, and similes to infer literal and figurative meanings of phrases and understanding historical influences on the meanings of English words. Students must also learn to write clear, coherent, and focused essays and conduct multiple-step information searches as part of the research process, using the learning resources and technology in the library media center and the classroom. In grades five through eight, students extend their writing applications as they compose narrative, expository, persuasive, and descriptive texts of at least 500 to 700 words each. They are expected to use correct conventions in writing as they express their newly found knowledge and understanding and to exhibit increasing sophistication in sentence structure, grammar, punctuation, capitalization, and spelling.

The strands for grades four through eight are the same as those for kindergarten through grade three except for a change of emphasis. The introduction of new emphases, however, does not diminish the importance of some well-established strands, such as word analysis, fluency, and systematic vocabulary development, which continues to be a central strand in grades four through six. This focus recognizes the fundamental importance to reading comprehension of skillful and fluent decoding. *If students in grades four through eight are unable to comprehend the complexities of narrative and expository text, a highly probable source of the problem is inability to decode words accurately and fluently.* Therefore, word-recognition activities and fluency practice for students who continue to struggle with the alphabetic writing system continue to be critical in this grade span.

A primary focus in grades four through eight is having students learn words and concepts. Students study the origins, derivations, and use of words over time and in different types of text. Although

Chapter 4
Content Standards
and Instructional
Practices—
Grades Four
Through Eight

extensive independent reading is the primary means of increasing vocabulary knowledge, many children need direct instruction in word-learning strategies to develop their vocabularies and enhance their ability to learn new words while reading. Because vocabulary knowledge is not acquired genetically or without extensive and sustained engagement with print, the classroom environment, instruction, and extensive opportunities to read are essential.

Vocabulary knowledge, which typically doubles during grades four through eight, is a direct result of how much a student reads. The more a student reads, the more the vocabulary knowledge increases. For example, students who read one-half million to one million words of running text generally learn approximately 3,000 new words per year. Voracious readers—those who read five million or more words of running text per year—in the middle school years will obviously learn more than 3,000 new words. The goal by the eighth grade is that students independently read one million words of running text annually (see page 176 in this chapter). Therefore, the process and benefits of independent reading must be instilled and reinforced from the fourth grade forward if students are to attain that goal. Ours is an age in which teachers can encourage independent reading through a variety of strategies. Access to outstanding age-appropriate multicultural literature as well as a variety of print and electronic informational materials in school and in public libraries is important for all students, particularly for those who do not have reading material at home.

Other standards extended and emphasized in grades four through eight include:

- Use of the research process and a variety of learning resources and technologies in the school library,

classrooms, the community, and the home as tools and strategies for preparing various types of documents, reports, and presentations

- Writing applications in a full range of text structures, including narratives, biographies, autobiographies, short stories, responses to literature, research reports, persuasive compositions, technical documents, and documents related to career development

- Speaking applications that require students to deliver well-organized formal presentations employing traditional rhetorical strategies

- Literary forms and devices that help to define and clarify an author's ideas, purpose, tone, point of view, and intentions

Students who have not become fluent readers by the end of the third grade can and must still be taught to become successful readers. However, the evidence and message are clear: without systematic and explicit instruction in the alphabetic code, little chance exists of their ever catching up (Felton and Pepper 1995). Reasons for students failing to learn to read in the upper elementary school, middle school, and high school grades include the following (Greene 1998):

- Instructional materials in grades four and above contain too many unfamiliar words, making the text unmanageable for struggling readers.

- Text in grades four and above contains complex word types and phonic elements that exceed learners' current skills.

- Word-recognition efforts drain cognitive resources, leaving little for comprehension.

- The sentence and text structures are complex (e.g., parenthetical

99

Chapter 4
Content Standards
and Instructional
Practices—
Grades Four
Through Eight

elements, passive voice), making comprehension more difficult.

- Teachers of middle school and high school students have often not been taught how to teach students to read.

The problems experienced by students in grades four and above who continue to struggle with the alphabetic code are difficult if not impossible to overcome with the traditional curriculum. What is known about students who do not learn to read easily is that they need explicit, carefully designed instruction in the alphabetic code. What differs from the traditional curriculum is that these students no longer have three or four years to learn to read, making the curricular requirements all the more important. Some strategic interventions that must be made to alter the learning patterns of students who have not yet learned to read are to:

1. Adopt a program of documented effectiveness that teaches students the fundamentals of systematic decoding and sequentially extends their abilities to read and write more complicated word types and text structures. The early curriculum should include research-based components: phonemic awareness, alphabetic understanding (e.g., letter-sound correspondences); phonological recoding (decoding and encoding); reading accuracy and fluency; vocabulary; and comprehension (Greene 1998). The curriculum should progress to more complex word-recognition skills that parallel those described in the *English–Language Arts Content Standards.*

2. Administer measures of assessment and assign to students the materials and programs that will enable them to read successfully (with 90 to 95 percent accuracy).

3. Design and schedule special instruction to maximize resources. One-on-one instruction by a qualified teacher, although desirable, is often not affordable. Identify small groups of students who are at similar levels of ability and schedule instruction for those groups.

4. Schedule a sufficient amount of time for reading instruction and protect that time. Struggling readers in grades four through eight should receive at least two hours of language arts instruction each day.

5. Monitor student progress and adjust the instruction and time allocations accordingly.

The proficiency of all students in the fundamental areas of reading, including word recognition, fluency, academic language, and comprehension strategies, must be determined. Once students have mastered the code, they may need additional assistance in a number of areas. Some who have reading difficulties at these grade levels may have rudimentary skills in word recognition but need practice in developing fluency. Others may be reasonably proficient in word recognition and fluency but need support to develop the vocabulary and background information they need to understand more advanced expository and narrative text. Still others may need explicit instruction in comprehension strategies to help them in their understanding and analysis of text. Many students need encouragement and structures to read independently outside class so that they can strengthen all aspects of their reading development.

Students with diagnosed needs in word recognition and fluency will require the most intensive interventions in grades four through eight. However, teachers in self-contained classrooms and content areas

Chapter 4
Content Standards
and Instructional
Practices—
Grades Four
Through Eight

can assist in a number of ways those readers who may not require the most intensive interventions but still need to improve their reading ability substantially. They can assist those readers by (1) scheduling opportunities for practice in developing fluency, providing age-appropriate materials that match the students' instructional levels; (2) providing vocabulary and information needed to understand literary readings and textbook chapters; (3) teaching strategies directly for comprehending different forms of text; and (4) organizing opportunities for independent reading both in class and at home.

101

Chapter 4
Content Standards
and Instructional
Practices—
Grades Four
Through Eight

Fourth Grade

Standards and Instruction

The fourth-grade content standards collectively represent an important transformation for students. When students advance from the third grade to the fourth grade, they make a critical transition from learning to read to reading to learn in subject-matter content. This changeover requires students to be fluent and automatic readers by the end of the third grade so that they are prepared to read and comprehend complex narrative and expository texts in such content areas as history–social science and science. An instructional priority for grades four through six is a continuing focus on ensuring that all students are able to read fluently and accurately. In addition, students are beginning a technological adventure of acquiring a new set of skills, such as basic keyboarding and familiarity with computer terminology.

The strands to be emphasized at the fourth-grade level are listed in the adjacent column under the appropriate domain.

The following sections profile focus areas within each of the strands and identify content and instructional connections that span domains, strands, and standards.

Reading

1.0 Word Analysis, Fluency, and Systematic Vocabulary Development
2.0 Reading Comprehension
3.0 Literary Response and Analysis

Writing

1.0 Writing Strategies
2.0 Writing Applications (Genres and Their Characteristics)

Written and Oral English-Language Conventions

1.0 Written and Oral English-Language Conventions

Listening and Speaking

1.0 Listening and Speaking Strategies
2.0 Speaking Applications (Genres and Their Characteristics)

Chapter 4
Content Standards
and Instructional
Practices—
Grades Four
Through Eight

Reading   Word Analysis, Fluency, and Systematic Vocabulary Development

Word Recognition

The continuing focus on decoding words fluently and accurately is both appropriate and necessary for the fourth grade. Students unable to decode words automatically will not be able to comprehend grade-appropriate narrative or expository text. Those who are not reading at grade level should receive continued systematic and explicit instruction in decoding, with particular attention being paid to the study of multisyllabic words and unfamiliar technical terminology as well as to systematic practice in reading fluency. Every effort should be made to ensure that students who are *not* reading at grade level will:

- Receive intensive decoding instruction.
- Be placed in small homogeneous groups for language arts instruction.
- Be given ample opportunities to practice reading in text designed to reinforce instruction and written at each student's level.
- Receive an additional period of reading instruction.
- Be offered a research-based reading curriculum.
- Be systematically monitored in reading progress throughout the school year.
- Be held to a high level of reading performance.

Vocabulary and Concept Development

Vocabulary and concept development has broad applications across the domains of reading, writing, and listening and speaking. Although the standards empha-size the use of external context cues at earlier grade levels, emphasis shifts strategically in the fourth grade (and continues through the tenth grade) to the use of internal, morphological, etymological, and historical word cues. Knowledge of affixes and roots—their meanings and origins—should be limited to the most common (and useful) morphological components; that is, those immediately applicable to the students' current level of vocabulary acquisition.

In addition, the standards at this level target synonyms, antonyms, idioms, and words with multiple meanings (the vast majority of nontechnical words in English). Students should be required to use a dictionary and a thesaurus to determine related words and concepts. Instruction in new conceptual knowledge should include clear examples in addition to verbal definitions of words.

Extensive independent reading is the primary means for increasing vocabulary knowledge (Nagy 1998). Students who read more learn more about words and their meanings. Although direct, explicit teaching of word meanings is effective and important, it cannot produce the needed growth in students' vocabulary knowledge that should occur in the fourth grade. Students should be given ample opportunities to read in school and outside school. The teacher should (Baker, Simmons, and Kame'enui 1998):

- Specify for students a clear purpose for reading.
- Establish objectives for each reading activity.
- Assess students' independent reading to determine what material they can read.
- Target specific vocabulary words to be learned and clarify why they are important.

103

Chapter 4
Content Standards
and Instructional
Practices—
Grades Four
Through Eight

Fourth Grade

Standards and
Instruction

- Hold students accountable for the content of what they read and the unfamiliar but important vocabulary words they read.
- Ensure multiple exposure to unfamiliar vocabulary words.
- Teach students vocabulary-learning strategies for use during independent reading.

Reading   Reading Comprehension

Structural Features of Informational Materials

The standards focus primarily on the structural features of informational (expository) text. The features of informational discourse emphasized at this level are fundamental: patterns such as compare and contrast; central focus or theme; and use of facts, details, and examples. Many of the fundamentals are incorporated across other text structures and genres at later grade levels. Similarly, narratives that form the focus of literary reading at this level are the object of writing standards as well. The fundamentals of narratives are also emphasized: elements of plot, character traits and motivations, setting, and the interactions between the fundamentals.

Because some of the text forms will be new to students in the fourth grade, the structural features of text should be introduced systematically (i.e., from easy text structures to more complex) and judiciously (i.e., a text structure is taught for a substantial amount of time initially to foster understanding rather than for a day here or there). Once taught, text structures should be reviewed cumulatively.

We finally seem to be getting the message that kids learn what they are taught and get to practice. . . . The point is simple: When we

identify a variable, including a text structure variable, that looks like it might make a difference in comprehension, we ought to adopt a frontal assault strategy when considering its instructional power—teach about it systematically and make certain students have a chance to practice it.
(Pearson and Camperell 1985, 339)

Text Appropriate to Grade Level

The features of reading comprehension in grade-level-appropriate text introduced in the fourth grade are extensions of comprehension instruction at earlier grade levels and include, for example: (1) identifying main idea and significant important details; (2) reading for different purposes; (3) making predictions; (4) distinguishing between fact and opinion and cause and effect; (5) comparing and contrasting information on the same topic; and (6) reading multiple-step directions in technical manuals. In the later grades students are required to apply those skills in more complex tasks and contexts (e.g., using information from a variety of consumer, workplace, or public documents).

Reading   Literary Response and Analysis

Students in the fourth grade will continue to learn about fundamental elements of literature that will allow them to appreciate the rich quality and complexity of materials they read. The elements include describing the structural differences between fables, myths, fantasies, legends, and fairy tales as well as defining and identifying simile, metaphor, hyperbole, and personification in literary works. To ensure that students are not overwhelmed or confused by the introduction of the complex range of literary

Chapter 4
Content Standards
and Instructional
Practices—
Grades Four
Through Eight

Fourth Grade

Standards and
Instruction

elements specified in the standards, teachers should concentrate on:

- Identifying and introducing the least complex element of literature before the more complex elements
- Providing ample opportunities for students to understand, study, and apply the individual elements before testing them on a combination of elements
- Ensuring that the literature is not overly complex for the fourth-grade level (e.g., unfamiliar text structure, high density of unfamiliar vocabulary, complex syntactical structure)
- Using literature (e.g., fable, myth, legend) that is of manageable length to allow students to comprehend and understand the target element
- Providing explicit and guided instruction during the initial phases of learning and ensure that students are provided with the appropriate instructional supports (e.g., a think sheet or note sheet for the particular type of text) during initial opportunities for independent reading.

The elements of story grammar (e.g., plot, setting, characters, motivation) continue to be a priority.

Writing   Writing Strategies

Although students continue to use all stages of writing (i.e., prewriting, drafting, revising, editing, postwriting) at this level, the standards specifically address revising and editing. (See the discussion on writing as a process at the beginning of Chapter 3.) They particularly emphasize the importance of revising and editing for coherence and progression by adding, deleting, consolidating, and rearranging text (see the fourth-grade curricular and instructional profile in a later section).

Such a standard assumes that students are able to create multiple-paragraph compositions and use traditional structures (e.g., chronological order, cause and effect, similarity and difference) for conveying information. It also assumes that students can select a focus, organizational structure, and point of view based on purpose, audience, and format. Fundamental to students progressing through the stages of writing as a process is their being able to write clear, coherent sentences and construct paragraphs that develop a central idea, focus on a particular audience, and reveal a clear purpose. Students plan their writing by creating outlines and using other organizational techniques. The conventions of written discourse, such as penmanship (i.e., writing fluidly and legibly in cursive or joined italic), continue to be emphasized.

A new substrand is research and technology. Research introduces students to a variety of print and electronic reference materials and other sources of information, such as almanacs, newspapers, and periodicals. Students are also expected to demonstrate basic keyboarding skills and familiarity with the basics of computer usage (e.g., cursor, software, memory, disk drive, hard drive).

Writing   Writing Applications

Students are expected to demonstrate a command of standard English by writing narratives, responses to literature, information reports, and summaries. In doing so, they are required to illustrate a range of skills, such as using concrete sensory details, supporting judgments, drawing from multiple sources of information, and framing a central question about an issue or situation.

Teachers should clarify the linkages between the students' reading and com-

105

Chapter 4
Content Standards
and Instructional
Practices—
Grades Four
Through Eight

Fourth Grade
Standards and
Instruction

prehending different types of text structures and composing the same types of texts. During the *initial* stages of instruction for the fourth grade in which students are learning to write narratives, information reports, summaries, or responses to literature, teachers should concentrate on:

- Presenting to students clear, simple, uncluttered models of narratives, information reports, summaries, and responses to literature
- Introducing one form of writing at a time
- Using prompts, such as a note sheet (i.e., an outline that students use to take notes) when appropriate that identifies the essential elements of the text structure and allows students to record the essential elements of a particular writing form (e.g., narrative) *before* they generate a written example on their own
- Introducing simpler forms of writing (e.g., narratives) before introducing more complex forms (e.g., responses to literature)
- Presenting a range of examples of a particular form of writing before introducing a new form
- Devoting extensive time and presenting multiple opportunities for students to develop proficiency with each form of writing

Written and Oral English-Language Conventions

The correct use of mechanics and the conventions of oral and written discourse continues to be emphasized at this level and include:

- Sentence structure—using simple and compound sentences and combining short sentences with appositives, participial phrases, and prepositional phrases

- Grammar—identifying and using regular and irregular verbs, adverbs, prepositions, and coordinating conjunctions in writing and speaking
- Punctuation and capitalization—using parentheses, commas in direct quotations, apostrophes in the possessive case, underlining, quotation marks, and italics; capitalizing titles of magazines, newspapers, works of art, musical compositions, and the first word in quotations
- Spelling—spelling roots, inflections, prefixes, suffixes, and syllable constructions

Note: The fifth-grade instructional guidelines for written and oral conventions should also apply to the fourth grade. And the guidelines for spelling instruction presented in Chapter 3 for the first grade will be useful in the fourth grade and above for students who still have considerable difficulty in spelling correctly.

Listening and Speaking
Listening and Speaking Strategies

In the fourth grade students should continue to listen critically and respond appropriately to oral communications. The content standards require students to ask thoughtful questions, summarize major ideas, use supporting evidence to substantiate conclusions, identify how language usages reflect regional and cultural differences, and give precise directions and instructions.

During their delivery of oral communications, students are expected to present effective introductions and conclusions; use traditional structures for conveying information; emphasize points that make clear to listeners or viewers the important ideas and concepts; and employ details, anecdotes, examples, volume, pitch, phrasing,

Chapter 4
Content Standards
and Instructional
Practices—
Grades Four
Through Eight

Fourth Grade

Standards and
Instruction

pace, modulation, and gestures to explain, clarify, or enhance meaning. Finally, students are expected to evaluate the role of the news media in focusing attention on events and in forming opinions on issues.

Listening and Speaking
Speaking Applications

Fourth graders are expected to use speaking strategies to make narrative and informational presentations. In doing so, students should demonstrate their ability to relate ideas, frame a key question, provide a context for listeners to imagine an event or experience, provide insight into why a selection is memorable, and incorporate more than one source of information. They are also expected to deliver oral summaries of articles and books and to recite brief poems, soliloquies, or dramatic dialogues, using clear diction, tempo, volume, and phrasing.

Teachers should emphasize the linkages between the students' experiences in reading and composing different types of text structures and making oral presentations from those texts. For example, compositions that students have written can be used to create outlines they will work from in their oral presentations. Also needed will be an ample number of model presentations in which specific elements (e.g., volume, pace, gestures) are demonstrated. The models should focus on a few elements at a time rather than introduce all elements at once.

Content and Instructional Connections

The teacher can help students integrate mastery of standards across domains, strands, and academic disciplines by having students:

1. Read narrative and expository text aloud with grade-appropriate fluency and accuracy and with appropriate pacing, intonation, and expression.

2. Use knowledge of root words to determine the meaning of unknown words within a passage and provide opportunities for students to use the words in written compositions.

3. Use appropriate strategies when reading for different purposes (e.g., full comprehension, location of information, personal enjoyment) and in a range of contexts.

4. Make connections between the main events of the plot, their causes, and the influence of each event on future actions.

5. Answer questions about their knowledge of the situation and setting and of a character's traits and motivations to determine the causes of the character's actions.

6. Make connections between the focus of a composition, its organizational structure, and its point of view according to purpose, audience, length, and format.

7. Create multiple-paragraph compositions.

8. Complete writing and oral assignments in the language arts that provide opportunities to attain content standards simultaneously in history–social science, science, and mathematics.

Please see Appendix B for examples of standards that span domains and strands.

107

Chapter 4
Content Standards
and Instructional
Practices—
Grades Four
Through Eight

Fourth Grade
Curricular and Instructional Profile

Writing Standard 1.10

DOMAIN	STRAND	SUBSTRAND	STANDARD
Writing	1.0 Writing strategies	Evaluation and revision	1.10 Edit and revise selected drafts to improve coherence and progression by adding, deleting, consolidating, and rearranging text

Note: Keep in mind the two related objectives in this standard—revising and editing. Students will need explicit instruction in both.

Prerequisite standards. **Third-Grade Writing Strategies Standard 1.4:** Revise drafts to improve the coherence and logical progression of ideas by using an established rubric.

Corequisite standards. **Fourth-Grade Writing Strategies Standards 1.1, 1.2, 1.3.**

Standard 1.1: Select a focus, an organizational structure, and a point of view.

Standard 1.2: Create multiple-paragraph compositions.

Standard 1.3: Use traditional structures for conveying information.

Curricular and Instructional Decisions

Instructional Objectives	1. Introduce a dimension for revision (e.g., adding). No prescribed sequence exists for introducing the dimensions. However, the earlier dimensions should be easier to introduce and are commonly represented in students' writing.
	2. Introduce a second dimension for revision (e.g., deleting) once students are successful with the first. Add other revision components as students develop competence.
	3. Integrate new and previously taught revision components through instruction and examples that require students to discriminate and apply all taught components.

Chapter 4
Content Standards
and Instructional
Practices—
Grades Four
Through Eight

Fourth Grade

Curricular and
Instructional
Profile

Instructional Design

Objective:
Identifying Text
That Needs
Revising

Decisions must be made about three critical design features in the deletion objective:

1. What sequence of instruction will allow students to revise? For example, when in the sequence will students identify information that is missing in the composition?
2. What amount of information should students revise?
3. What strategy will students use to rewrite or edit text on the basis of the revision phase?

Textual Unit Size and Sequence

The sequence of writing models is critical. Carefully selected models allow students first to learn the strategies for revising and then to apply those strategies to their own writing. Initial text models should control the difficulty of the task by beginning with focused revising tasks. Later texts should progress to increasingly complex compositions. Each phase of revising requires multiple models. A possible design sequence for adding follows.

Adding Information to a Text

The first models should contain obvious places for addition to and expansion of the text, including statements that require supporting details and development. Adding information may range from providing a specific illustration to support a claim or adding a word or a short phrase to clarify a concept.

Example:

Josh's dog Rex was overweight and lazy. He weighed too much and sat around all day. He didn't get much exercise. He only got excited when it was time to eat. Josh was at school during the day. Dinner was Rex's favorite time. Dinner was the time he liked the best. At dinner time Rex moved quickly, jumping and hopping and dashing and running around until Josh put the food in his dish. Josh did his homework in the evening.

Providing Strategies for Students

This strategy involves reading the model with the students while adding information to the text. The teacher reads the text first. Subsequent readings are done by student volunteers. Then the teacher provides the students with questioning strategies aimed at identifying segments of the text that need development, addition, and expansion. After the students have had enough experience with the text to make appropriate comments, the teacher asks the students to identify the first segment of the text that requires additional information (supporting details).

Example: The writer's topic sentence or claim is the following: "Josh's dog was overweight and lazy." The teacher asks, "How can

109

Chapter 4
Content Standards
and Instructional
Practices—
Grades Four
Through Eight

Fourth Grade

Curricular and
Instructional
Profile

**Instructional
Design**
(Continued)

we provide the reader with proof that Josh's dog was overweight and lazy?" Students add appropriate details that develop the writer's claim. The teacher records the students' suggestions for additions. They should include appropriate words, phrases, and supporting details.

When the first paragraph is complete, the teacher asks the students to identify the next idea that requires additional information. The teacher asks, "Does Josh ever get excited? If so, how can the writer prove it?" The teacher records appropriate additions to this section of the text. Then the teacher says, "We have two pictures of Rex. What proof do we have that he is overweight and lazy?" The students identify the supporting details. "What proof do we have that he is sometimes active and excited?" The students identify the supporting details, and the teacher records the additions.

The teacher asks, "On the basis of the information that we have gathered, what can we conclude about Josh's dog, Rex?" The teacher records the conclusion.

Deletion (Extending the Lesson)

Once the students have identified the areas that require additions and have composed and placed the additions, they eliminate information no longer germane to the text. The teacher asks the students, "What information remains in this story that does not fit with the writer's topic?"

The students are then asked to:

1. Eliminate complete sentences or phrases that do not tell more about the topic.
2. Delete individual words that do not tell more about the topic.
3. Rewrite sentences by combining sentences or sentence parts that tell the same thing about the topic and deleting unnecessary words.
4. Proceed from paragraph to paragraph.
5. Edit the revised text to ensure that the written-language conventions (e.g., grammar, capitalization, punctuation, spelling) are correct.

The teacher records the deletions.

Internalizing and Applying Writing Strategies

The teacher asks the students to rewrite the completed composition. When the rewriting is complete, the teacher asks the students to identify the strategies used to revise the original model. They should include the following:

- Identifying topic sentences
- Providing additional information for each topic identified

Chapter 4
Content Standards
and Instructional
Practices—
Grades Four
Through Eight

Fourth Grade

Curricular and
Instructional
Profile

**Instructional
Design**
(Continued)

- Drafting an appropriate conclusion
- Deleting information not pertinent to the topic

Next Steps

The teacher types up the strategies identified by the students, and the students keep the list of strategies in a writing folder. The strategies should also be posted in the classroom in poster form. Students should have multiple opportunities for teacher-directed revision. Progress should proceed from explicit teacher-directed instruction to guided practice to independent practice.

Objective:
Revising
the Student-
Generated
Text

When students can edit models provided by the teacher, they are ready to practice revising their own work by systematically applying the strategies for revision to their own prose. They are asked to:

1. Identify topic sentences that need further development.
2. Add clearer words, phrases, and supporting details.
3. Create appropriate paragraphs determined by the topics identified for addition.
4. Delete information that does not fit the composition, using steps for deletion.
5. Edit while using appropriate language conventions.

**Instructional
Delivery**

1. Define revising and tell why it is important to know when to add and delete information in a text.
2. Establish rules for adding and deleting.
3. Present the steps in adding and deleting information to revise text effectively.
4. Model multiple paragraphs containing information that needs to be revised. The text should include vocabulary familiar to the students, and the information to be revised should represent various parts of speech.
5. Encourage students to think out loud as they read the paragraph and (a) locate the sentences that need expansion; (b) locate the sentences or phrases that do not tell more about the topic; and (c) use the proofreader's deletion mark to eliminate segments that need to be deleted.
6. Repeat the lesson, using appropriate materials.
7. Begin the editing phase once revising and rewriting are complete. Students should edit text to ensure that the written language conventions are correct.
8. Do not underestimate the amount of time and practice needed to develop proficiency in revising and editing.

Chapter 4
Content Standards
and Instructional
Practices—
Grades Four
Through Eight

Assessment

Entry-Level Assessment

1. *Entry-Level Assessment for Instructional Planning.* Conduct an entry-level assessment of the students' overall proficiency on the standard. *Revise and edit selected drafts to improve coherence and progression by adding, deleting, consolidating, rearranging text, and correcting.* On the basis of that assessment, identify the dimensions of revision and editing that need to be taught and the level of instruction necessary. Use the entry-level assessment as your guide for instructional planning. With the assessment you can identify students who are proficient in revising and editing and those who need systematic instruction.

Monitoring Student Progress

2. *Monitoring Student Progress Toward the Instructional Objective*
   a. The assessment phase is designed to determine students' progress and mastery of skills that have been taught as well as the retention of those skills. The assessment measures progress toward components (i.e., specific objectives) of the standard rather than the entire standard.
   b. A series of tasks should be constructed to assess students' mastery in revising at several levels (paragraph, multiple paragraph, self-composition). Assessment tasks should parallel the objectives and requirements of instruction. The sequence of tasks should progress toward the goal of the instructional unit, beginning with simpler units and requirements and progressing to more complex applications. These measures are administered on the completion of a particular unit of instruction. For example, the paragraph assessment should be made on the completion of revising and editing at the paragraph level.
   c. On completion of instruction *in revising through adding or deleting,* a measure is administered to assess progress toward the objective. The integration of addition and deletion is assessed on completion of the specific instruction unit.
   d. This assessment sequence continues through the remaining components of instruction necessary to achieve the standard.

Post-test Assessment

3. *Post-test Assessment Toward the Standard.* On completion of all instructional units, assess student performance according to the procedures used to assess entry-level performance. Give students a multiple-paragraph composition to revise and edit. You may also want to have students write their compositions on a standard topic to assess their ability to revise and edit their own writing. During the year systematically assess the students' retention of editing and revising skills and proficiency in meeting other writing standards.

Fourth Grade

Curricular and
Instructional
Profile

Chapter 4
Content Standards
and Instructional
Practices—
Grades Four
Through Eight

Fourth Grade

Curricular and
Instructional
Profile

**Universal
Access**

Reading
Difficulties
or Disabilities

1. *Students with Reading Difficulties or Disabilities*

    a. Passages should be appropriate to the instructional reading levels of students. If not, students may work with peers or an aide for assistance with word recognition. In addition, teachers may need to use supplementary examples from the instructional resources designed for universal access. The examples control more carefully the amount and type of information to be added or deleted. At first, exercises might focus only on missing or redundant information; later, more subtle forms would be introduced, such as colorless descriptions or irrelevant information.

    b. Expository text may be used that provides information related to grade-level content standards in the other disciplines (history–social science, science, and mathematics).

Advanced
Learners

2. *Students Who Are Advanced Learners.* Use the entry-level assessment to determine whether students are proficient according to the standard or need instruction. If found proficient in the grade-level assessment, consider assessing performance according to the parallel standards for successively higher grades until the appropriate instructional level is determined. Instruction at that level should be provided to ensure that students are challenged. The students' rates of learning should be subject to ongoing monitoring to ensure that they are progressing at rates commensurate with their abilities. If students are not proficient according to the standard, the teacher may wish to:

    a. Adjust the pace of instruction because the students may not require the same number of examples or amount of practice as their peers do.

    b. Introduce more than one revising or editing dimension at a time.

    c. Use supplementary examples from the instructional materials designed for universal access that increase the complexity of the passages students edit for independent work.

English Learners

3. *Students Who Are English Learners*

    a. English learners can learn to add and delete text well without developing knowledge of the rhetorical devices that enable them to write cohesive, coherent text. To help English learners achieve Writing Standard 1.10, provide them with specific, explicit instruction concerning transition phrases (e.g., *first, second, third, next, in conclusion*) and pronoun reference (e.g., *he, she, it, they*). Cohesive devices (such as transition phrases and pronouns), which are often used differently in the students' first languages, are useful in

113

Chapter 4
Content Standards
and Instructional
Practices—
Grades Four
Through Eight

**Universal
Access**
(Continued)

establishing cohesive, coherent texts. *Note:* Many Asian students use full noun phrases to establish cohesion instead of the pronouns used by native English speakers.

b. English learners benefit greatly from sentence-combining exercises. They need extensive guidance and practice in using such grammatical structures as relative clauses (e.g., I like the man *who lives on the corner*); conditional statements (e.g., *If I were you,* I would not do that); and subordinate clauses (e.g., She received good grades *because she worked hard*).

c. Because English learners are still developing proficiency in English, care should be taken in organizing peer revision and peer editing. Individual students should receive feedback from the teacher on their writing and any grammatical or other errors they have made. Errors in grammar or other mistakes common to many students in the class should be the subject of additional classroom instruction and practice.

d. In an English-language mainstream classroom, it is important to group English learners with students proficient in English. When to do so is impossible, the teacher will need to provide additional models of input for students as well as opportunities to use the models.

e. Consider using expository text that provides information related to grade-level content standards in the other disciplines (history–social science, science, and mathematics).

**Instructional
Materials**

Instructional materials should carefully sequence the introduction of the dimensions of revising and editing. Focus first on the number of objectives introduced, then on the number and range of examples. Are the examples adequate? Or will you need to invest time creating your own examples? Are assessment passages and examples included? Assessment tasks should be available for each phase of assessment: entry-level assessment for instructional planning, monitoring of progress toward the instructional objective, and post-test assessment toward the standard.

Chapter 4
Content Standards
and Instructional
Practices—
Grades Four
Through Eight

Fourth Grade

English–Language Arts Content Standards

Reading

1.0 Word Analysis, Fluency, and Systematic Vocabulary Development

Students understand the basic features of reading. They select letter patterns and know how to translate them into spoken language by using phonics, syllabication, and word parts. They apply this knowledge to achieve fluent oral and silent reading.

Word Recognition

1.1 Read narrative and expository text aloud with grade-appropriate fluency and accuracy and with appropriate pacing, intonation, and expression.

Vocabulary and Concept Development

1.2 Apply knowledge of word origins, derivations, synonyms, antonyms, and idioms to determine the meaning of words and phrases.

1.3 Use knowledge of root words to determine the meaning of unknown words within a passage.

1.4 Know common roots and affixes derived from Greek and Latin and use this knowledge to analyze the meaning of complex words (e.g., *international*).

1.5 Use a thesaurus to determine related words and concepts.

1.6 Distinguish and interpret words with multiple meanings.

2.0 Reading Comprehension

Students read and understand grade-level-appropriate material. They draw upon a variety of comprehension strategies as needed (e.g., generating and responding to essential questions, making predictions, comparing information from several sources). The selections in *Recommended Readings in Literature, Kindergarten Through Grade Eight* illustrate the quality and complexity of the materials to be read by students. In addition to their regular school reading, students read one-half million words annually, including a good representation of grade-level-appropriate narrative and expository text (e.g., classic and contemporary literature, magazines, newspapers, online information).

Structural Features of Informational Materials

2.1 Identify structural patterns found in informational text (e.g., compare and contrast, cause and effect, sequential or chronological order, proposition and support) to strengthen comprehension.

Comprehension and Analysis of Grade-Level-Appropriate Text

2.2 Use appropriate strategies when reading for different purposes (e.g., full comprehension, location of information, personal enjoyment).

2.3 Make and confirm predictions about text by using prior knowledge and ideas presented in the text itself, including

115

Chapter 4
Content Standards
and Instructional
Practices—
Grades Four
Through Eight

Fourth Grade
English–Language
Arts Content
Standards

illustrations, titles, topic sentences, important words, and foreshadowing clues.

2.4 Evaluate new information and hypotheses by testing them against known information and ideas.

2.5 Compare and contrast information on the same topic after reading several passages or articles.

2.6 Distinguish between cause and effect and between fact and opinion in expository text.

2.7 Follow multiple-step instructions in a basic technical manual (e.g., how to use computer commands or video games).

3.0 Literary Response and Analysis

Students read and respond to a wide variety of significant works of children's literature. They distinguish between the structural features of the text and the literary terms or elements (e.g., theme, plot, setting, characters). The selections in *Recommended Readings in Literature, Kindergarten Through Grade Eight* illustrate the quality and complexity of the materials to be read by students.

Structural Features of Literature

3.1 Describe the structural differences of various imaginative forms of literature, including fantasies, fables, myths, legends, and fairy tales.

Narrative Analysis of Grade-Level-Appropriate Text

3.2 Identify the main events of the plot, their causes, and the influence of each event on future actions.

3.3 Use knowledge of the situation and setting and of a character's traits and motivations to determine the causes for that character's actions.

3.4 Compare and contrast tales from different cultures by tracing the exploits of one character type and develop theories to account for similar tales in diverse cultures (e.g., trickster tales).

3.5 Define figurative language (e.g., simile, metaphor, hyperbole, personification) and identify its use in literary works.

Writing

1.0 Writing Strategies

Students write clear, coherent sentences and paragraphs that develop a central idea. Their writing shows they consider the audience and purpose. Students progress through the stages of the writing process (e.g., prewriting, drafting, revising, editing successive versions).

Organization and Focus

1.1 Select a focus, an organizational structure, and a point of view based upon purpose, audience, length, and format requirements.

1.2 Create multiple-paragraph compositions:

a. Provide an introductory paragraph.
b. Establish and support a central idea with a topic sentence at or near the beginning of the first paragraph.
c. Include supporting paragraphs with simple facts, details, and explanations.
d. Conclude with a paragraph that summarizes the points.
e. Use correct indention.

1.3 Use traditional structures for conveying information (e.g., chronological order, cause and effect, similarity and difference, and posing and answering a question).

Penmanship

1.4 Write fluidly and legibly in cursive or joined italic.

Research and Technology

1.5 Quote or paraphrase information sources, citing them appropriately.

1.6 Locate information in reference texts by using organizational features (e.g., prefaces, appendixes).

1.7 Use various reference materials (e.g., dictionary, thesaurus, card catalog, encyclopedia, online information) as an aid to writing.

1.8 Understand the organization of almanacs, newspapers, and periodicals and how to use those print materials.

Chapter 4
Content Standards
and Instructional
Practices—
Grades Four
Through Eight

Fourth Grade

English–Language
Arts Content
Standards

1.9 Demonstrate basic keyboarding skills and familiarity with computer terminology (e.g., cursor, software, memory, disk drive, hard drive).

Evaluation and Revision

1.10 Edit and revise selected drafts to improve coherence and progression by adding, deleting, consolidating, and rearranging text.

2.0 Writing Applications (Genres and Their Characteristics)

Students write compositions that describe and explain familiar objects, events, and experiences. Student writing demonstrates a command of standard American English and the drafting, research, and organizational strategies outlined in Writing Standard 1.0.

Using the writing strategies of grade four outlined in Writing Standard 1.0, students:

2.1 Write narratives:

   a. Relate ideas, observations, or recollections of an event or experience.

   b. Provide a context to enable the reader to imagine the world of the event or experience.

   c. Use concrete sensory details.

   d. Provide insight into why the selected event or experience is memorable.

2.2 Write responses to literature:

   a. Demonstrate an understanding of the literary work.

   b. Support judgments through references to both the text and prior knowledge.

2.3 Write information reports:

   a. Frame a central question about an issue or situation.

   b. Include facts and details for focus.

   c. Draw from more than one source of information (e.g., speakers, books, newspapers, other media sources).

2.4 Write summaries that contain the main ideas of the reading selection and the most significant details.

Written and Oral English Language Conventions

The standards for written and oral English language conventions have been placed between those for writing and for listening and speaking because these conventions are essential to both sets of skills.

1.0 Written and Oral English Language Conventions

Students write and speak with a command of standard English conventions appropriate to this grade level.

Sentence Structure

1.1 Use simple and compound sentences in writing and speaking.

1.2 Combine short, related sentences with appositives, participial phrases, adjectives, adverbs, and prepositional phrases.

Grammar

1.3 Identify and use regular and irregular verbs, adverbs, prepositions, and coordinating conjunctions in writing and speaking.

Punctuation

1.4 Use parentheses, commas in direct quotations, and apostrophes in the possessive case of nouns and in contractions.

1.5 Use underlining, quotation marks, or italics to identify titles of documents.

Capitalization

1.6 Capitalize names of magazines, newspapers, works of art, musical compositions, organizations, and the first word in quotations when appropriate.

Spelling

1.7 Spell correctly roots, inflections, suffixes and prefixes, and syllable constructions.

Chapter 4
Content Standards
and Instructional
Practices—
Grades Four
Through Eight

Fourth Grade

English–Language
Arts Content
Standards

Listening and Speaking

1.0 Listening and Speaking Strategies

Students listen critically and respond appropriately to oral communication. They speak in a manner that guides the listener to understand important ideas by using proper phrasing, pitch, and modulation.

Comprehension

1.1 Ask thoughtful questions and respond to relevant questions with appropriate elaboration in oral settings.

1.2 Summarize major ideas and supporting evidence presented in spoken messages and formal presentations.

1.3 Identify how language usages (e.g., sayings, expressions) reflect regions and cultures.

1.4 Give precise directions and instructions.

Organization and Delivery of Oral Communication

1.5 Present effective introductions and conclusions that guide and inform the listener's understanding of important ideas and evidence.

1.6 Use traditional structures for conveying information (e.g., cause and effect, similarity and difference, and posing and answering a question).

1.7 Emphasize points in ways that help the listener or viewer to follow important ideas and concepts.

1.8 Use details, examples, anecdotes, or experiences to explain or clarify information.

1.9 Use volume, pitch, phrasing, pace, modulation, and gestures appropriately to enhance meaning.

Analysis and Evaluation of Oral Media Communication

1.10 Evaluate the role of the media in focusing attention on events and in forming opinions on issues.

2.0 Speaking Applications (Genres and Their Characteristics)

Students deliver brief recitations and oral presentations about familiar experiences or interests that are organized around a coherent thesis statement. Student speaking demonstrates a command of standard American English and the organizational and delivery strategies outlined in Listening and Speaking Standard 1.0.

Using the speaking strategies of grade four outlined in Listening and Speaking Standard 1.0, students:

2.1 Make narrative presentations:

a. Relate ideas, observations, or recollections about an event or experience.

b. Provide a context that enables the listener to imagine the circumstances of the event or experience.

c. Provide insight into why the selected event or experience is memorable.

2.2 Make informational presentations:

a. Frame a key question.

b. Include facts and details that help listeners to focus.

c. Incorporate more than one source of information (e.g., speakers, books, newspapers, television or radio reports).

2.3 Deliver oral summaries of articles and books that contain the main ideas of the event or article and the most significant details.

2.4 Recite brief poems (i.e., two or three stanzas), soliloquies, or dramatic dialogues, using clear diction, tempo, volume, and phrasing.

Chapter 4
Content Standards
and Instructional
Practices—
Grades Four
Through Eight

Fifth Grade

Standards and Instruction

The fifth-grade standards and instruction build on and extend the foundational and transitional skills begun in the fourth grade. The instructional priority for both the fourth grade and the fifth grade is a continued focus on ensuring that all students are able to read fluently and accurately and are therefore prepared to read and comprehend complex narrative and expository texts in the content areas. In addition, students in the fifth grade are introduced to new, advanced forms of evaluation, such as expository critique and literary criticism in the reading domain.

The strands to be emphasized at the fifth-grade level are listed in the adjacent column under the appropriate domains.

The following sections profile focus areas within each of the strands and identify content and instructional connections that span domains, strands, and standards.

Reading

1.0 Word Analysis, Fluency, and Systematic Vocabulary Development
2.0 Reading Comprehension (Focus on Informational Materials)
3.0 Literary Response and Analysis

Writing

1.0 Writing Strategies
2.0 Writing Applications (Genres and Their Characteristics)

Written and Oral English-Language Conventions

1.0 Written and Oral English-Language Conventions

Listening and Speaking

1.0 Listening and Speaking Strategies
2.0 Speaking Applications (Genres and Their Characteristics)

Chapter 4
Content Standards
and Instructional
Practices—
Grades Four
Through Eight

Fifth Grade

Standards and
Instruction

Reading   Word Analysis, Fluency, and Systematic Vocabulary Development

Word Recognition

The fifth-grade standards continue to focus on decoding words fluently and accurately. Students are required to read aloud narrative and expository text fluently and accurately and use appropriate pacing, intonation, and expression. As in the fourth grade, students who are not reading at grade level should receive continued systematic, explicit instruction in decoding or comprehension strategies or both. (See the fourth-grade section earlier in this chapter for a discussion of systematic, explicit instruction in reading.)

Vocabulary and Concept Development

The vocabulary and concept development standards at this level require students to understand and explain words, including using figurative and metaphorical words in context and abstract roots and affixes derived from Greek and Latin to analyze the meaning of complex words. The standards continue to emphasize the use of internal, morphological, etymological, and historical word cues. In addition, students are expected to understand and explain frequently used synonyms, antonyms, and homographs.

Students should continue to engage in extensive independent reading as the primary means of increasing vocabulary knowledge (Nagy 1998). Students should be given ample opportunities to read. In addition, vocabulary instruction must continue to be systematic (see the vocabulary guidelines for the fourth grade).

Reading   Reading Comprehension (Focus on Informational Materials)

The fifth-grade standards focus primarily on the structural features of informational materials, comprehension and analysis of grade-level-appropriate text, and expository critique. Students are expected to understand how text structures (e.g., formats, graphics, sequences, diagrams, illustrations, charts, maps) make information accessible and usable and analyze text organized in sequential or chronological order. In addition, students should use basic comprehension strategies, such as (1) discerning main ideas and concepts in texts; (2) identifying and assessing evidence that supports ideas; (3) drawing inferences, conclusions, or generalizations about text; and (4) identifying textual evidence and prior knowledge to support those inferences, conclusions, and generalizations. The expository critique, introduced at this level, requires students to distinguish facts, supported inferences, and opinions in text.

Instruction in reading comprehension in the fifth grade should:

- Use texts in which complex linguistic and syntactical features are appropriate for the fifth-grade level. Similarly, the number of unfamiliar vocabulary words should be carefully controlled to be manageable for students.
- Ensure that students have the prerequisite knowledge and skills to comprehend the text.
- Begin with teacher-directed instruction, including modeling and guidance, and gradually shift responsibility to the student.
- Include repeated opportunities for students to answer comprehension questions during the reading of the text.

Chapter 4
Content Standards
and Instructional
Practices—
Grades Four
Through Eight

Fifth Grade

Standards and
Instruction

- Require students to read some of the text aloud, at least initially.
- Provide sufficient practice for students to reach a high level of performance for one level of text complexity before introducing the next level.

Reading   Literary Response and Analysis

As they did in the fourth grade, students in the fifth grade will continue to learn about the fundamental elements of literature, including identifying and analyzing the characteristics of poetry, drama, fiction, and nonfiction and explaining the appropriateness of the literary forms chosen. In addition, the elements of narrative texts are emphasized. Students are required to (1) identify the main problem or conflict of the plot and explain how it is resolved; (2) contrast the actions, motives, and appearances of characters; (3) understand and recognize themes in sample works; and (4) describe the function and effect of common literary devices (e.g., imagery, metaphor, symbolism).

An effective instructional strategy for teaching the elements of narrative text is to employ the structure of story grammar, which has been described in previous grade-level overviews. The strategy involves (1) introducing and sequencing the elements of narrative text from easy to complex; (2) using a note sheet that allows students to record information about each story element (e.g., character information, conflict or problem, theme) as they read a story or text; and (3) using a think-aloud strategy in conjunction with the note sheet whereby the teacher summarizes and points out how to anticipate elements of story grammar in the text. This strategy can also be extended and used with contrasting information on character according to which students locate, record, and contrast the motives of two characters. However,

this extension requires students to be proficient in identifying character elements before they are contrasted.

Students are also required to evaluate the meaning of archetypal patterns and symbols and the author's use of various techniques (e.g., appeal of characters in a picture or book, logic and credibility of plots and settings) to influence the readers' perspectives.

Writing   Writing Strategies

Organization and Focus

As students in the fifth grade continue to progress through the stages of writing as a process, they are required to create multiple-paragraph narrative and expository compositions. To do so, they must establish and develop a topic or plot, describe the setting or details that link one paragraph to another, and present an ending or concluding paragraph that summarizes important ideas and details.

Important instructional considerations for the writing process include:

- Ensuring that students understand the text structure before they begin to employ that structure in their writing
- Using that text structure as a tool for organizing a written composition
- Demonstrating that writing is composed of several different stages: prewriting, drafting, revising, editing, and postwriting
- Providing examples or models of writing that make clear the important features (e.g., main problem, conflict, character motives, theme, imagery) of narrative and expository compositions
- Using strategies that make conspicuous for students exactly how to identify, comprehend, and record the critical features of compositions on a note sheet (For example, the

121

Chapter 4
Content Standards
and Instructional
Practices—
Grades Four
Through Eight

Fifth Grade

Standards and
Instruction

teacher reads aloud a piece of writing and explicitly identifies it.)

- Demonstrating a range of examples of *one* particular feature at a time (e.g., conflict) in one type of text (e.g., narrative), then introducing new features (e.g., main problem or conflict, plot)

Research and Technology

Students must learn to (1) use organizational features of printed or electronic text to locate relevant information; (2) create simple documents, using electronic media and employing organizational features (e.g., passwords, entry and pull-down menus, word searchers, spell checks); and (3) use a thesaurus to identify alternative word choices and meanings.

Instruction in the research and technology standard of locating relevant information should:

- Involve a topic that is familiar and interesting to students.
- Begin with a clear and unambiguous set of examples of information relevant to the topic.
- Include examples of information obviously irrelevant to the topic.
- Consist of teacher-directed or guided instruction that reveals to students the requirements for locating relevant information.
- Progress from examples involving clearly relevant information to those that require more critical discrimination of relevant and irrelevant information.

Evaluation and Revision

Students are expected to continue to revise and edit manuscripts to improve the meaning and focus of writing by adding, deleting, consolidating, clarifying, rearranging words and sentences, and making final corrections. (See the instructional profile of this standard for the fourth grade.)

Writing   Writing Applications (Genres and Their Characteristics)

Students are expected to write narrative, expository, persuasive, and descriptive texts of at least 500 to 700 words for each text and continue to demonstrate a command of standard English. They are also required to write narratives; responses to literature; research reports about important ideas, issues, or events; and persuasive letters or compositions.

General instructional guidelines for teaching the different types of text structures include:

1. Providing students with ample opportunities to compose each text structure and receive written, systematic, and instructive feedback on their writing
2. Using procedural facilitators such as think sheets or note sheets to help structure and organize information
3. Modeling each stage of the writing process (prewriting, drafting, revising, editing, postwriting) and providing ample opportunities for students to become proficient at each stage.
4. Providing explicit, clear criteria (e.g., use of an editor's checklist) for students to follow in editing written compositions

Written and Oral English-Language Conventions

Students are expected to have a command of the English-language conventions, including sentence structure, grammar, punctuation, capitalization, and spelling. The conventions can be conceptualized as discrete skills and taught in strands. Instruction by strand employs an

Chapter 4
Content Standards
and Instructional
Practices—
Grades Four
Through Eight

incremental and progressive approach to teaching specific skills and strategies within and across a larger domain. For example, a writing lesson might include separate and individual strands of instruction in punctuation, grammar, and sentence structure. Each strand is specific to the particular written convention (e.g., conventions for grammar and punctuation) and is related to the larger domain of writing applications (e.g., persuasive letter or composition).

The parts of speech can be confusing to students if instruction is not clear. Teaching demonstrations should include an adequate number of examples, both positive and negative, of a part of speech that the student is able to identify. For example, students must learn that the words *eat, ate, has eaten,* and *will eat* are all verbs. Verbs in the present and past tenses can be presented first and followed at a later time by two-word verbs, such as *has eaten, will eat,* and *is eating.*

When teaching students to identify the parts of speech, the teacher should sequence the instruction so that the students can learn that many words can serve as different parts of speech according to how the word is used in a sentence. For example, the word *running* may function as a noun (e.g., *Running* is fun); as an adjective (e.g., The *running* water in the stream moved us along quickly); or as part of a verb (e.g., We were *running*).

Cumulative review is particularly important in teaching the parts of speech. Once students learn a new part of speech, they should be given exercises in which sentences include examples of the new part of speech along with previously introduced and taught parts of speech. Review and practice should be frequent enough to provide for understanding and retention.

When showing students how to use a particular word or phrase or other struc-

ture, the teacher should include a range of positive examples and carefully selected and sequenced negative examples. The negative examples serve to rule out likely misinterpretations.

When introducing a new type of sentence structure, the teacher should provide adequate practice in writing sentences before requiring students to use the new sentence type in writing passages. Those assignments should be structured to prompt usage of the new sentence type. In addition, the teacher should provide adequate cumulative review to facilitate understanding and retention as well as exercises requiring the students to revise existing passages by combining sentences and thereby create a new type of sentence structure. Students should be taught not only *how* to create new sentence types but *when* to use them. For example, some students will need careful instruction to determine when words, phrases, or clauses should be joined by *and, or,* or *but.*

When a new mark of punctuation is introduced, exercises should be included that provide adequate practice first in *how* to use the new mark and then in *when* to use it. For example, when students learn how to write sentences that begin with a clause that tells *when* (e.g., *After the sun went down,* the mosquitoes became unbearable), some students are likely to begin using commas even when the clause comes at the end of the sentence. Students need adequate practice to determine when *not* to use the new punctuation.

Listening and Speaking
Listening and Speaking Strategies

Like fourth-grade students, fifth-grade students are expected to continue to listen critically and respond appropriately to oral communications. However, they are also

123

Chapter 4
Content Standards
and Instructional
Practices—
Grades Four
Through Eight

Fifth Grade

Standards and
Instruction

expected to be more engaged as listeners and speakers by asking questions that seek information already discussed; interpreting a speaker's verbal and nonverbal messages, purposes, and perspectives; and making inferences or drawing conclusions based on an oral report. The standards for the organization and delivery of oral communication are the same as those for the fourth grade (i.e., select a focus, organizational structure, and point of view for an oral presentation).

Students are also expected to identify, analyze, and critique persuasive techniques (e.g., promises, dares, flattery, glittering generalizations) and identify logical fallacies used in oral presentations and media messages. Finally, they are to take an active role in analyzing the media as sources of information, entertainment, persuasion, interpretation of events, and transmission of culture.

Listening and Speaking
Speaking Applications (Genres and Their Characteristics)

Fifth graders are expected to use speaking strategies to deliver narrative and informative presentations and oral responses to literature. Specific skills to be integrated include establishing a situation or plot, showing the listener what happens; framing questions to direct an investigation; establishing a controlling idea or topic; developing a topic with simple facts, details, examples, and explanations; summarizing significant events and details; articulating an understanding of several ideas or images; and using examples or textual evidence from the work to support conclusions.

A systematic schedule for introducing, teaching, and linking speaking strategies

with similar standards in reading and writing should be developed. Students will require clear examples of each type of presentation and adequate practice and feedback for each of the requirements of the presentations (e.g., establishing a situation or plot; showing the listener what happens, framing questions to direct an investigation, and establishing a controlling idea or topic).

Content and Instructional Connections

The teacher can help students integrate mastery of standards across domains, strands, and academic disciplines by having students:

1. Read aloud narrative and expository text fluently and accurately and with appropriate pacing, intonation, and expression.
2. Use knowledge of word origins to determine the meaning of unknown words.
3. Demonstrate how print and electronic text features (e.g., format, graphics, sequence, diagrams, illustrations, charts, maps) make information accessible and usable.
4. Create multiple-paragraph narrative compositions, using electronic media and employing organizational features.
5. Add, delete, consolidate, clarify, and rearrange words and sentences.
6. Use topics and examples for speaking, writing, and editing assignments that relate to grade five history–social science and science content standards.

Please see Appendix B for examples of standards that span domains and strands.

Chapter 4
Content Standards
and Instructional
Practices—
Grades Four
Through Eight

Fifth Grade

Curricular and Instructional Profile

Reading Standard   3.2

DOMAIN	STRAND	SUBSTRAND	STANDARD
Reading	3.0 Literacy response and analysis	Narrative analysis of grade-level-appropriate text	3.2 Identify the main problem or conflict in the plot and explain how it is resolved.

Corequisite standards. **Fifth-Grade Literary Response and Analysis Standard 3.3:** Contrast the actions, motives, and appearances of characters in a work of fiction and discuss the importance of the contrasts to the plot or theme.

Fifth-Grade Writing Strategies Standard 1.1: Create multiple-paragraph narrative compositions.

Curricular and Instructional Decisions

Instructional Objective	Identify the main problem or conflict of the plot, explain how it is resolved, and employ that analysis in written and oral presentations.
Instructional Design	The identification of conflict and resolution in the plots of novels and short stories is fundamental for more sophisticated aspects of literary analysis. In addition, those elements of plot are central to quality narrative compositions and oral presentations.

Following the suggested sequence for systematic instruction, the teacher might:

1. Begin the sequence with Literary Response and Analysis Standard 3.2, analyzing and evaluating conflict and resolution in narratives.
2. Teach students explicitly, through direct instruction or guided discussion, the basic critical attributes of a good plot: a protagonist with a problem (conflict), an antagonist who

125

Chapter 4
Content Standards
and Instructional
Practices—
Grades Four
Through Eight

Fifth Grade

Curricular and
Instructional
Profile

**Instructional
Design**
(Continued)

interferes with the protagonist's attempts to solve the problem, some unsuccessful efforts (because of the antagonist's interference) to solve the problem, and a final successful solution (conflict resolution).

3. Note that at this level the antagonist should be concrete (e.g., a "bad person"). Students will learn the elements better *initially* if they do not have to analyze abstract conflicts, such as mental conflict within the protagonist.

4. Focus as much on unsuccessful attempts to resolve the conflict as on the final resolution. Students should note the ways in which the protagonist learns from the lack of success.

5. Emphasize the importance of a *satisfying* resolution for readers. One way to do so is through examples of *unsatisfying* resolutions.

6. Have the students apply the basic elements in their own writing once they have mastered them (Writing Strategies Standards 1.1a–c, 2.1a–b).

7. Provide students with an overt strategy for planning their narrative compositions (prewriting). For instance, you might have the students first identify the protagonist and antagonist and the conflict between them, then skip to planning a satisfying resolution, and finally go back to outline unsuccessful attempts to resolve the conflict. This strategy should be implemented flexibly to capture the reiterative process of planning narratives.

8. Require students to develop plots that are promising as they draft a piece of writing. Because drafting is a difficult task at this level, a good plan will help ensure a successful draft.

9. Incorporate other standards into the instruction (e.g., Writing Strategies Standard 1.6).

10. Once students have successfully written and revised a narrative with strong plot elements, have them modify their stories for oral presentation (Speaking Applications Standard 2.1).

11. Compare and contrast the written and oral presentations of the same story. Emphasize, for example, how plot elements are the same for both but that oral presentations allow for rhetorical devices that cannot be used in written documents. Students can *show* their audience some elements of a story that have to be *told* in written documents.

**Instructional
Delivery**

Some standards presented in the earlier grades address the basic elements of story grammar. Therefore, students should be assessed initially to determine the extent to which they might have already mastered the key elements of plot (see "Assessment" following).

Chapter 4
Content Standards
and Instructional
Practices—
Grades Four
Through Eight

Fifth Grade

Curricular and
Instructional
Profile

Instructional Delivery (Continued)

Assuming that most students will need more instruction or more in-depth instruction in the elements of plot, teachers should:

1. Have students examine several short stories to learn the commonality of plot elements across stories. One or more stories should be weak, especially as to conflict resolution.
2. Walk through a few stories with students, beginning with very strong hints about the plot elements in each but gradually reducing the hints to ensure that students can recognize the elements on their own.
3. Consider establishing cooperative work groups, especially during the planning phase of writing a narrative. Serving as an audience for one another, the students should tell their story to their peers in their group, working off their plot outline. In that way they are likely to learn whether the plot resolution they have in mind is satisfying before they commit themselves too much to their stories. Cooperative work is most appropriate either before students begin to write or between the drafting and revising stages of the writing process.
4. Present students with a strategy for developing a good plot outline and assist students liberally during the plot-planning phase of writing.

Assessment

Entry-Level Assessment

1. *Entry-Level Assessment for Instructional Planning.* The most important pretest information for this standard is the extent to which students are already familiar with the fundamentals of narrative plots. Students might be asked to work from a good short story to identify the fundamentals present in that story.

Monitoring Student Progress

2. *Monitoring Student Progress Toward the Instructional Objective.* Assessing students' achieving the objectives of narrative plots will be facilitated greatly if instruction follows well-differentiated steps as outlined previously. Teachers can use the work produced at each step to evaluate whether to spend a little more time on that step or to move forward confidently.

Post-test Assessment

3. *Post-test Assessment Toward the Standard.* Usual state- or district-required formal assessments contribute to part of the picture of student achievement toward standards. In addition, the types of assignments teachers routinely use in determining a major part of student grades serve an important role toward giving a complete picture of achievement. For example, a final written composition in published form should be part of the summative evaluation for students. However, a summative evaluation should assess individual accountability. Writing assignments that students complete on their own meet that requirement better than assignments in which students work cooperatively.

127

Chapter 4
Content Standards
and Instructional
Practices—
Grades Four
Through Eight

**Universal
Access**

Reading
Difficulties
or Disabilities

1. *Students with Reading Difficulties or Disabilities*

   a. Some reading selections used to illustrate plot elements can be taken from below-grade-level discourse. At this stage the most important goal is for students to learn the fundamental elements of plot (rather than demonstrate grade-level reading ability).

   b. Some lower-performing students might lack the ability to create a good conflict and resolution on their own. To facilitate the inclusion of such students in the regular curriculum, teachers can provide those students with more prompting.

   c. Students who do have difficulty in making oral presentations should (1) be allowed to read their presentations; and (2) be given ample opportunities to practice the delivery of their presentations (with constructive feedback) before being required to make a final presentation to the entire group.

Advanced
Learners

2. *Students Who Are Advanced Learners.* Because these students are more likely to have a good command of plot elements, they may be encouraged, after the teacher has determined the extent of their competence, to work with examples in which conflict and resolution are more subtle. Note that high-achieving students may be given opportunities to interact with each other in homogeneous cooperative groups. Advanced learners may also occasionally serve from time to time as mentors in mixed-ability groups. These students may read stories above their grade level that have more sophisticated plots (e.g., stories based upon a psychological conflict within a single character.) Note that creating a good plot can be challenging for any student at any level. (One form of professional writer's block is the inability to come up with a satisfying plot resolution.)

   Although advanced learners should be challenged, the teacher should base expectations for achievement on observed performance and information gained from periodic teacher-student conferences regarding the difficulty of the material, the pacing, and the level of student motivation.

English Learners

3. *Students Who Are English Learners.* In classes with English learners, teachers should consider reading aloud from one or two of the models used to teach fundamental plot elements. The students may experience no difficulty in learning plot elements conceptually but may be limited in their ability to comprehend the written material and express their conceptual

Chapter 4
Content Standards
and Instructional
Practices—
Grades Four
Through Eight

Fifth Grade

Curricular and
Instructional
Profile

Universal Access (Continued)

knowledge in writing. To assist English learners in their work, teachers should:

a. Simplify the task for English learners by focusing more attention initially on the plot elements in a narrative composition and less on other aspects of writing.

b. Note that although all students have difficulty in focusing on all aspects of written discourse at once, English learners especially may need additional time to complete tasks and additional practice.

c. Teach students how to switch between past and present tenses to develop narrative plots. ("This is a story about a girl who fell in love with a toad.")

d. Provide corrective feedback to students on their compositions to help them with standard English conventions. The feedback needs to be shaped to the specific needs of English learners and should always be presented gently and positively.

e. Encourage English learners to practice their English-speaking skills. They should be allowed to practice their oral presentations before presenting them in class and should be allowed to use visual aids as prompts if necessary.

Instructional Materials

Instructional materials should supply teachers with instructional strategies, procedural facilitators, and the types of model text described above. Relatively *poor* models—which are effective instructional tools—are not the types of discourse teachers can locate easily on their own. (However, teachers should consider using some anonymous examples of student writing from previous years.) Publishers should give special care to providing effective tools for teachers to help students with special needs.

129

Chapter 4
Content Standards
and Instructional
Practices—
Grades Four
Through Eight

Fifth Grade

English–Language Arts Content Standards

Reading

1.0 Word Analysis, Fluency, and Systematic Vocabulary Development

Students use their knowledge of word origins and word relationships, as well as historical and literary context clues, to determine the meaning of specialized vocabulary and to understand the precise meaning of grade-level-appropriate words.

Word Recognition

1.1 Read aloud narrative and expository text fluently and accurately and with appropriate pacing, intonation, and expression.

Vocabulary and Concept Development

1.2 Use word origins to determine the meaning of unknown words.
1.3 Understand and explain frequently used synonyms, antonyms, and homographs.
1.4 Know abstract, derived roots and affixes from Greek and Latin and use this knowledge to analyze the meaning of complex words (e.g., *controversial*).
1.5 Understand and explain the figurative and metaphorical use of words in context.

2.0 Reading Comprehension (Focus on Informational Materials)

Students read and understand grade-level-appropriate material. They describe and connect the essential ideas, arguments, and perspectives of the text by using their knowledge of text structure, organization, and purpose. The selections in *Recommended Readings in Literature, Kindergarten Through Grade Eight* illustrate the quality and complexity of the materials to be read by students. In addition, by grade eight, students read one million words annually on their own, including a good representation of grade-level-appropriate narrative and expository text (e.g., classic and contemporary literature, magazines, newspapers, online information). In grade five, students make progress toward this goal.

Structural Features of Informational Materials

2.1 Understand how text features (e.g., format, graphics, sequence, diagrams, illustrations, charts, maps) make information accessible and usable.
2.2 Analyze text that is organized in sequential or chronological order.

Comprehension and Analysis of Grade-Level-Appropriate Text

2.3 Discern main ideas and concepts presented in texts, identifying and assessing evidence that supports those ideas.

Chapter 4
Content Standards
and Instructional
Practices—
Grades Four
Through Eight

Fifth Grade

English–Language
Arts Content
Standards

2.4　Draw inferences, conclusions, or generalizations about text and support them with textual evidence and prior knowledge.

Expository Critique

2.5　Distinguish facts, supported inferences, and opinions in text.

3.0　Literary Response and Analysis

Students read and respond to historically or culturally significant works of literature. They begin to find ways to clarify the ideas and make connections between literary works. The selections in *Recommended Readings in Literature, Kindergarten Through Grade Eight* illustrate the quality and complexity of the materials to be read by students.

Structural Features of Literature

3.1　Identify and analyze the characteristics of poetry, drama, fiction, and nonfiction and explain the appropriateness of the literary forms chosen by an author for a specific purpose.

Narrative Analysis of Grade-Level-Appropriate Text

3.2　Identify the main problem or conflict of the plot and explain how it is resolved.

3.3　Contrast the actions, motives (e.g., loyalty, selfishness, conscientiousness), and appearances of characters in a work of fiction and discuss the importance of the contrasts to the plot or theme.

3.4　Understand that *theme* refers to the meaning or moral of a selection and recognize themes (whether implied or stated directly) in sample works.

3.5　Describe the function and effect of common literary devices (e.g., imagery, metaphor, symbolism).

Literary Criticism

3.6　Evaluate the meaning of archetypal patterns and symbols that are found in myth and tradition by using literature from different eras and cultures.

3.7　Evaluate the author's use of various techniques (e.g., appeal of characters in a picture book, logic and credibility of plots and settings, use of figurative language) to influence readers' perspectives.

Writing

1.0　Writing Strategies

Students write clear, coherent, and focused essays. The writing exhibits the students' awareness of the audience and purpose. Essays contain formal introductions, supporting evidence, and conclusions. Students progress through the stages of the writing process as needed.

Organization and Focus

1.1　Create multiple-paragraph narrative compositions:

　　a. Establish and develop a situation or plot.

　　b. Describe the setting.

　　c. Present an ending.

1.2　Create multiple-paragraph expository compositions:

　　a. Establish a topic, important ideas, or events in sequence or chronological order.

　　b. Provide details and transitional expressions that link one paragraph to another in a clear line of thought.

　　c. Offer a concluding paragraph that summarizes important ideas and details.

Research and Technology

1.3　Use organizational features of printed text (e.g., citations, end notes, bibliographic references) to locate relevant information.

1.4　Create simple documents by using electronic media and employing organizational features (e.g., passwords, entry and pull-down menus, word searches, the thesaurus, spell checks).

1.5　Use a thesaurus to identify alternative word choices and meanings.

Chapter 4
Content Standards
and Instructional
Practices—
Grades Four
Through Eight

Evaluation and Revision

1.6   Edit and revise manuscripts to improve the meaning and focus of writing by adding, deleting, consolidating, clarifying, and rearranging words and sentences.

2.0   Writing Applications (Genres and Their Characteristics)

Students write narrative, expository, persuasive, and descriptive texts of at least 500 to 700 words in each genre. Student writing demonstrates a command of standard American English and the research, organizational, and drafting strategies outlined in Writing Standard 1.0.

Using the writing strategies of grade five outlined in Writing Standard 1.0, students:

2.1   Write narratives:

a. Establish a plot, point of view, setting, and conflict.

b. Show, rather than tell, the events of the story.

2.2   Write responses to literature:

a. Demonstrate an understanding of a literary work.

a. Support judgments through references to the text and to prior knowledge.

c. Develop interpretations that exhibit careful reading and understanding.

2.3   Write research reports about important ideas, issues, or events by using the following guidelines:

a. Frame questions that direct the investigation.

b. Establish a controlling idea or topic.

c. Develop the topic with simple facts, details, examples, and explanations.

2.4   Write persuasive letters or compositions:

a. State a clear position in support of a proposal.

b. Support a position with relevant evidence.

c. Follow a simple organizational pattern.

d. Address reader concerns.

Written and Oral English Language Conventions

The standards for written and oral English language conventions have been placed between those for writing and for listening and speaking because these conventions are essential to both sets of skills.

1.0   Written and Oral English Language Conventions

Students write and speak with a command of standard English conventions appropriate to this grade level.

Sentence Structure

1.1   Identify and correctly use prepositional phrases, appositives, and independent and dependent clauses; use transitions and conjunctions to connect ideas.

Grammar

1.2   Identify and correctly use verbs that are often misused (e.g., *lie/lay, sit/set, rise/ raise*), modifiers, and pronouns.

Punctuation

1.3   Use a colon to separate hours and minutes and to introduce a list; use quotation marks around the exact words of a speaker and titles of poems, songs, short stories, and so forth.

Capitalization

1.4.   Use correct capitalization.

Spelling

1.5   Spell roots, suffixes, prefixes, contractions, and syllable constructions correctly.

Chapter 4
Content Standards
and Instructional
Practices—
Grades Four
Through Eight

Listening and Speaking

1.0 Listening and Speaking Strategies

Students deliver focused, coherent presentations that convey ideas clearly and relate to the background and interests of the audience. They evaluate the content of oral communication.

Comprehension

1.1 Ask questions that seek information not already discussed.

1.2 Interpret a speaker's verbal and nonverbal messages, purposes, and perspectives.

1.3 Make inferences or draw conclusions based on an oral report.

Organization and Delivery of Oral Communication

1.4 Select a focus, organizational structure, and point of view for an oral presentation.

1.5 Clarify and support spoken ideas with evidence and examples.

1.6 Engage the audience with appropriate verbal cues, facial expressions, and gestures.

Analysis and Evaluation of Oral and Media Communications

1.7 Identify, analyze, and critique persuasive techniques (e.g., promises, dares, flattery, glittering generalities); identify logical fallacies used in oral presentations and media messages.

1.8 Analyze media as sources for information, entertainment, persuasion, interpretation of events, and transmission of culture.

2.0 Speaking Applications (Genres and Their Characteristics)

Students deliver well-organized formal presentations employing traditional rhetorical strategies (e.g., narration, exposition, persuasion, description). Student speaking demonstrates a command of standard American English and the organizational and delivery strategies outlined in Listening and Speaking Standard 1.0.

Using the speaking strategies of grade five outlined in Listening and Speaking Standard 1.0, students:

2.1 Deliver narrative presentations:
   a. Establish a situation, plot, point of view, and setting with descriptive words and phrases.
   b. Show, rather than tell, the listener what happens.

2.2 Deliver informative presentations about an important idea, issue, or event by the following means:
   a. Frame questions to direct the investigation.
   b. Establish a controlling idea or topic.
   c. Develop the topic with simple facts, details, examples, and explanations.

2.3 Deliver oral responses to literature:
   a. Summarize significant events and details.
   b. Articulate an understanding of several ideas or images communicated by the literary work.
   c. Use examples or textual evidence from the work to support conclusions.

133

Chapter 4
Content Standards
and Instructional
Practices—
Grades Four
Through Eight

Sixth Grade

Standards and Instruction

In the sixth grade students focus on active engagement with the text. They are required to analyze, identify, define, explain, and critique rather than merely understand, describe, use, know, and distinguish as they were required to do in the fifth grade. However, the standards still require students to read aloud narrative and expository text fluently and accurately and with appropriate pacing, intonation, and expression.

As in the fifth grade, an instructional priority in the sixth grade is an increased focus on advanced forms of evaluation in expository critique and literary criticism and advanced presentations on problems and solutions.

The strands to be emphasized at the sixth-grade level are listed in the adjacent column under the appropriate domains.

The following sections profile focus areas within each of the strands and identify content and instructional connections across domains, strands, and standards.

Reading

1.0 Word Analysis, Fluency, and Systematic Vocabulary Development
2.0 Reading Comprehension (Focus on Informational Materials)
3.0 Literary Response and Analysis

Writing

1.0 Writing Strategies
2.0 Writing Applications (Genres and Their Characteristics)

Written and Oral English-Language Conventions

1.0 Written and Oral English-Language Conventions

Listening and Speaking

1.0 Listening and Speaking Strategies
2.0 Speaking Applications (Genres and Their Characteristics)

Chapter 4
Content Standards
and Instructional
Practices—
Grades Four
Through Eight

Sixth Grade

Standards and
Instruction

Reading **Word Analysis, Fluency, and Systematic Vocabulary Development**

Word Recognition

The sixth-grade standards continue to focus on decoding words fluently and accurately. Students are required to read aloud narrative and expository text fluently and accurately, with appropriate pacing, intonation, and expression. As in the fourth and fifth grades, students not reading at grade level should receive continued systematic and explicit instruction in decoding or comprehension strategies or both. (See the fourth-grade section on reading for a discussion of systematic, explicit instruction in reading.)

Vocabulary and Concept Development

The vocabulary and concept development standards for the sixth grade shift from a focus on word origins and roots and affixes derived from Greek and Latin to a focus on interpreting figurative language and recognizing meanings of frequently used foreign words with multiple meanings. In addition, students are required to understand and explain shades of meaning in related words (e.g., *softly* and *quietly*).

As in the fourth and fifth grades, students should continue to engage in extensive independent reading as the primary means for increasing vocabulary knowledge. They must continue to be given ample opportunities and encouragement to read. Vocabulary instruction must still be systematic (see the vocabulary guidelines for the fourth grade). Instruction in word derivation should be a common component of instruction across the academic year, emphasizing and coordinating vocabulary analysis with words students will encounter in the instructional materials they read. In an effort to increase the likelihood that students will retain vocabulary, words that have been studied previously should be interspersed in instructional materials and lessons.

Reading **Reading Comprehension (Focus on Informational Materials)**

The sixth-grade standards require students to (1) identify the structural features of the popular media (e.g., newspapers, magazines, on-line information) and use those features to obtain information; and (2) analyze instructional materials that use a compare-and-contrast organizational pattern. In addition, comprehension strategies include (1) connecting and clarifying main ideas and identifying their relationships to other sources and related topics; (2) clarifying the understanding of instructional materials by creating outlines, logical notes, summaries, or reports; and (3) following multiple-step instructions for preparing applications (e.g., for a public library card, bank savings account, sports club or league membership). Expository critique continues at this level and requires students, for example, to determine the adequacy and appropriateness of evidence for an author's conclusions and to note instances of unsupported inferences, fallacious reasoning, unreasonable persuasion, and propaganda in instructional materials.

The advanced form of expository critique at this level relies heavily on students' prerequisite skills in identifying adequate and appropriate evidence and distinguishing conclusions substantiated with ample and appropriate evidence from those not substantiated. The teacher should initially model multiple examples

135

Chapter 4
Content Standards
and Instructional
Practices—
Grades Four
Through Eight

Sixth Grade

Standards and
Instruction

for which the students evaluate the evidence to support conclusions. The examples should contain evidence clearly appropriate or inappropriate and progress to evidence more subtle and complex. After the teacher's modeling has been completed, the students can work in pairs or cooperative groups to evaluate the validity of conclusions. Independent practice should be the culminating assignment.

The reading-comprehension strategy described previously (see the fifth-grade Reading Comprehension Strand 2.0) may be extended effectively to the sixth grade with more complex narrative and informational texts.

Reading Literary Response and Analysis

Literary response and analysis in the sixth grade should extend the strategies described in the fifth grade (see story grammar strategies) to more complex narrative and informational text that allows students to:

- Analyze the effect of qualities of character (e.g., courage or cowardice, ambition or laziness) on plot and resolution of conflict.
- Analyze the influence of setting on the problem and its resolution.
- Determine how tone or meaning is conveyed in poetry through word choice, figurative language, sentence structure, line length, punctuation, rhythm, repetition, and rhyme.
- Identify the speaker and recognize the difference between first-person and third-person narration (e.g., autobiography compared with biography).
- Identify and analyze features of themes conveyed through characters, actions, and images.

- Explain the effects of common literary devices (e.g., symbolism, imagery, metaphor) in a variety of fictional and nonfictional texts.

Students are also required to evaluate the meaning of archetypal patterns and symbols and the author's use of various techniques (e.g., appeal of characters in a picture or book, logic and credibility of plots and settings) to influence the readers' perspectives.

Although the element of *theme* has been an instructional focus for several grades, it remains a difficult concept that requires systematic instruction. Using characters' actions as evidence of a theme, for example, will require explicit instruction and prompting initially (directing students to read for how the character's actions influence the story). Students will need to learn to document character actions by reading and analyzing several examples under teacher-guided conditions. Once students become familiar with the requirements of this analysis, they can conduct analyses independently. They should also work with poetry, determining how tone or meaning is conveyed through word choice, figurative language, sentence structure, line length, punctuation, rhythm, repetition, and rhyme.

The general instructional guidelines specified for the literary response and analysis strand in the fourth grade are also appropriate here (see the overview for the fourth grade).

Writing Writing Strategies

Organization and Focus

When students advance to the sixth grade, they also advance their writing to (1) selecting forms of writing that best suits the intended purpose; (2) creating multiple-paragraph expository composi-

Chapter 4
Content Standards
and Instructional
Practices—
Grades Four
Through Eight

Sixth Grade

Standards and
Instruction

tions; and (3) using a variety of effective and coherent organizational patterns, including comparison and contrast; organization by categories; and arrangement by spatial order, order of importance, or climactic order.

Because the requirements of this strand are complex, sixth-grade students should be eased into this complexity of writing forms, purposes, and organizational patterns. To ensure that all students are successful as they advance in more complex writing, teachers should:

- Select clear examples or models of the different forms of writing (e.g., autobiographical and persuasive writing) so that students are able to distinguish the features of each form. The examples selected to represent each form must not be overly complex or subtle or cluttered in purpose or structure.
- Make explicit the specific purpose and intended audience for each of the different forms of writing. Provide ample opportunities for students to discern the specific purpose and intended audience for each form before requiring them to generate examples of each form of writing on their own.
- Use an adequate number of examples of each different form of writing. The examples should reveal a modest range of the distinguishing features of each form (It is not essential initially to show students the full range of distinguishing features of each.)
- Employ a teaching strategy (e.g., explicit modeling, think-aloud strategy, facilitative questioning strategy) that makes conspicuous for students the distinguishing features of each writing form.

- Construct a review schedule that provides students with ample opportunities to revisit and reinforce the distinguishing features of each form.

Research and Technology

Research or information problem solving is an application of all of the language arts skills learned to date, especially reading comprehension (Eisenberg and Berkowitz 1990). Research is a recursive process in which the learner uses steps to access, evaluate, discard, select, and use information from multiple sources. Many models for the research process exist. Users must eventually construct their own mental model of the process as they use it (Loertscher 1998). Students prepare formal documents (e.g., term papers or research reports) in response to assignments and may also use research in formal debates or multimedia presentations. The skills students learn as they master standards in this strand relate directly to career preparation in a variety of fields.

Students must learn to use organizational features of electronic text (e.g., Internet searches, databases, keyword searches, E-mail addresses) to locate relevant information. They must learn to compose documents with appropriate formatting (e.g., margins, tabs, spacing, columns, page orientation), using their word-processing skills.

Teaching students the organizational features of electronic text for locating information and creating documents is potentially a troublesome task for at least two reasons. First, the software features and requirements of electronic text vary greatly—from a library database to Web sites on the Internet to a word-processing document. Second, many features of an electronic text involve functions

137

Chapter 4
Content Standards
and Instructional
Practices—
Grades Four
Through Eight

Sixth Grade

Standards and
Instruction

(e.g., keyword searches using a find command) or other features (e.g., e-mail addresses) not technically part of an electronic text. The electronic text environment must be simplified significantly if students are to learn about the organizational features of electronic text.

Teachers should work with library media teachers to ease students into this complex computer-based, electronic text environment by:

- Teaching students about different electronic sources available to them in their classroom, school library, and community libraries or computer centers and labs (e.g., CD-ROM encyclopedias and dictionaries, library databases, other online databases, newsgroups, web pages)
- Teaching students the names, purposes, methods, and limitations of different electronic sources (e.g., automated library catalog, web sites, e-mail)
- Teaching students the methods necessary for using electronic sources, such as navigating within one source and searching one source or a database for a specific topic before searching in multiple sources and for multiple topics
- Providing students ample opportunities to explore and learn in one type of electronic text, such as the automated library catalog or electronic magazine indexing before introducing another type of electronic text
- Selecting and establishing access for all students to one type of electronic text (e.g., automated library catalog)
- Creating a clearly defined task with specific objectives and outcomes to ensure that students will gain appropriate experience from working

in the electronic text (e.g., automated library catalog).

- Ensuring that students have the prerequisite knowledge, skills, and experience with the computer environment to benefit from working tasks specific to the research and technology standards

Learning to use a word-processing program to compose documents requires that students understand the basics of operating the computer system they will be using at school and, it is hoped, at home as well. The instructional guidelines for teaching sixth-grade students to compose documents with appropriate formatting by using word-processing skills and principles of design (e.g., margins, tabs, spacing, columns, page orientation) include, for example, teaching students to:

- Open existing files, save files, and create new files in the word-processing program they will use most frequently.
- Understand the basics of navigation, text manipulation, and editing within the word processor, including use of (1) the control to change the location of the cursor, highlight text, or access menus, commands, and icons; (2) navigation keys, such as the page up, page down, and arrow keys; (3) common commands on the keyboard (e.g., typing control and the letter *S* to save a document); and (4) copy, cut, and paste command functions for text manipulation and editing. Show students how to manipulate, create, and edit documents before teaching them to format documents. Easier formatting techniques include line and paragraph spacing; bold, italics, and underlining; and different fonts and font sizes. Formatting techniques of

Chapter 4
Content Standards
and Instructional
Practices—
Grades Four
Through Eight

Sixth Grade

Standards and
Instruction

midlevel difficulty include margins, page numbers, tabs, and page breaks. Advanced formatting techniques include insertion of tables, embedded objects, borders and shading, and automatic bulleted lists.

- Use the spelling and grammar checks judiciously and wisely. For example, students should learn not to depend solely on the word-processing functions. Examples of errors that would pass a spelling and grammar check but would be caught by a proofreader should be used to demonstrate the limits of those functions.

Evaluation and Revision

Students are expected to continue to revise their writing to improve the organization and consistency of ideas within and between paragraphs. This instruction should take place throughout the year as students progress from easy text to more complex forms of composition. In addition, a specific part of a period each day should be devoted to revising and editing written compositions.

Writing Writing Applications (Genres and Their Characteristics)

As in the fifth grade, students in the sixth grade are expected to write narrative, expository, persuasive, and descriptive texts (e.g., responses to literature and research reports about important ideas, issues, or events) of at least 500 to 700 words in each genre and continue to demonstrate a command of standard English.

A new requirement in the sixth-grade standards is writing expository compositions (e.g., description, explanation, comparison and contrast, problem and

solution). Students must (1) state their thesis or purpose; (2) explain the situation; (3) follow an organizational pattern appropriate to the type of composition; and (4) offer persuasive evidence to validate arguments and conclusions as needed.

Instructional guidelines for writing expository compositions include:

1. Introducing and teaching one type of expository composition at a time
2. Selecting clear and appropriate examples of each type of expository composition, including examples of students' writing to use as models
3. Using a think sheet or note sheet to provide an outline for learning the essential structure of each type of expository composition
4. Reading and summarizing the important information in one type of expository text (e.g., a social studies text involving a problem and solution) by using a think sheet or note sheet before writing the specific type of expository composition
5. Establishing a process to provide students with sufficient comments and feedback for their expository compositions, such as a partner system for editing that uses an editing checklist on selected assignments and teacher comments on others

Written and Oral English-Language Conventions

Students are expected to have a command of English-language conventions, including sentence structure (e.g., simple, compound, complex, and compound-complex sentences); grammar (e.g., identifying and using indefinite pronouns and

139

Chapter 4
Content Standards
and Instructional
Practices—
Grades Four
Through Eight

Sixth Grade

Standards and
Instruction

present perfect, past perfect, and future perfect tenses); punctuation (e.g., using colons, semicolons, and commas correctly in contexts); capitalization; and spelling.

Listening and Speaking
Listening and Speaking Strategies

As in the fourth and fifth grades, students in the sixth grade listen critically and respond appropriately to oral communications. However, sixth graders are also expected to deliver focused, coherent presentations. They continue to be engaged as listeners and speakers and (1) relate the speaker's verbal communication to the nonverbal message; (2) identify the tone, mood, and emotion conveyed in the oral communication; and (3) restate and execute multiple-step oral instructions and directions.

The standards for the organization and delivery of oral communication are both similar to those for the fourth and fifth grades (e.g., select a focus, an organizational structure, and a point of view for an oral presentation) and different (e.g., emphasize salient points to assist the listener; support opinions with detailed evidence; use effective rate, volume, pitch, and tone; and align nonverbal elements to sustain audience interest and attention). Students are also expected to analyze the use of rhetorical devices (e.g., cadence, repetitive patterns, onomatopoeia) for intent and effect. Finally, they are to identify persuasive and propaganda techniques used in television programs and identify false and misleading information.

To identify techniques of persuasion and propaganda, students must learn their basic structure through observation of models and instruction by the teacher. The basic elements of persuasive argument (thesis, support for argument or thesis,

counter arguments to rebut alternative positions on a topic) are used in written and oral discourse. By addressing the structural elements in writing and listening to persuasive arguments, the teacher can make instruction effective.

Listening and Speaking
Speaking Applications (Genres and Their Characteristics)

Sixth-grade students are expected to deliver well-organized formal presentations employing traditional rhetorical strategies. Specifically, they are required to deliver narrative, informative, and persuasive presentations as well as oral responses to literature and presentations on problems and solutions.

Students are expected to demonstrate a range of speaking skills and strategies that include establishing a context, plot, and point of view; posing relevant questions sufficiently limited in scope to be competently and thoroughly answered; developing an interpretation exhibiting careful reading, understanding, and insight; engaging the listener and fostering acceptance of the proposition or proposal; and theorizing on the causes and effects of a problem and establishing connections between the defined problem and at least one solution.

Content and Instructional Connections

The teacher can help students integrate mastery of standards across domains, strands, and academic disciplines by having students:

1. Read aloud narrative and expository text fluently and accurately, with appropriate pacing, intonation, and expression.

Chapter 4
Content Standards
and Instructional
Practices—
Grades Four
Through Eight

Sixth Grade

Standards and
Instruction

2. Use opportunities for narrative reading to identify and interpret figurative language and words with multiple meanings.

3. Make connections between main ideas and their relationships to other sources and related topics. They should be able to demonstrate that the connections and relationships are found in different forms of fiction or expository text, such as students' sixth-grade history–social science or science instructional materials.

4. Select a form of writing (e.g., personal letter, letter to the editor, review, poem, narrative, report on a historical figure or scientific phenomenon) and demonstrate how it best suits the intended purpose.

5. Use organizational features of electronic text (e.g., bulletin boards, databases, keyword searches, e-mail addresses) to locate information related to history or science standards.

Please see Appendix B for examples of standards that span domains and strands.

141

Chapter 4
Content Standards
and Instructional
Practices---
Grades Four
Through Eight

Sixth Grade

Curricular and Instructional Profile

Writing Standard 2.3

DOMAIN	STRAND	SUBSTRAND	STANDARD
Writing	2.0 Writing applications (genres and their characteristics)		2.3 Write research reports.

Corequisite standards. **Sixth-Grade Writing Strategies Standards 1.2, 1.3, 1.4 1.5, 1.6.**

Standard 1.2: Create multiple-paragraph expository compositions.

Standard 1.3: Use a variety of effective and coherent organizational patterns.

Standard 1.4: Use organizational features of electronic text.

Standard 1.5: Compare documents with appropriate formatting by using word-processing skills and principles of design.

Standard 1.6: Revise writing to improve the organization and consistency of ideas within and between paragraphs.

Curricular and Instructional Decisions

Instructional Objectives	Write research reports that: 1. Pose relevant questions and are sufficiently narrow in scope. 2. Offer support from several authoritative sources. 3. Include a bibliography.
Instructional Design	The sixth grade is the first level at which the standards require students to read and create informational discourse supported by references. Students are required to do so—at increasing levels of sophistication—in grades seven through twelve, making the instruction they receive in the sixth grade the foundation for much of their language arts work throughout the rest of their school years. The transition to expository writing based on outside sources is often difficult for students. Although sixth-grade students may

Chapter 4
Content Standards
and Instructional
Practices—
Grades Four
Through Eight

Sixth Grade

Curricular and
Instructional
Profile

**Instructional
Design**
(Continued)

know how to use reference materials (e.g., encyclopedias, online resources), they may not know how to read and take notes from those materials in a way that facilitates writing research reports. (If students do not know how to use reference materials, they should be given direct instruction so that they can satisfy this important prerequisite. The library media teacher should be a willing partner in this process.) The following guidelines can help reduce that difficulty and make research writing successful for more students:

1. When reading reference materials, students should:

   a. Write all bibliographic information for a source on index cards. Make sure that all necessary information is noted. Then number the cards. The information does not have to be put in a particular style at this point.

   b. Make a separate index card for each important point in the source. Place direct quotations in quotation marks. Write on each card the bibliographic number of the source for the notes.

   c. Repeat this process for a number of sources.

2. Begin outlining as usual during this prewriting phase. Locate source cards that support each entry in the outline. Create piles of source cards according to the entries.

3. Elaborate on the outline by ordering source cards for each entry and indicating their order on the outline. Cards can now be coded by using a system, such as point I, card 1; point II, card 3; and so on.

4. During this prewriting phase, the students should make decisions about whether their topic is too broad or too narrow. They are likely to find that they do not need some of the sources for some points and need a few more sources for other points.

5. The key to writing a good research report lies in doing extensive preparation as shown. Once the teacher is convinced that the students are well prepared, the students should begin drafting and working reiteratively through the phases of the writing process.

6. Instruction on how to incorporate source material into text should be overt. The students need to know that they may state someone else's point of view in their own words but must credit the source.

7. Once the students know which sources are to be used in their report, they should go back to their bibliographic cards and order the entries according to a formal style. (See, for example, the guidelines published by the Modern Language Association or the American Psychological Association. Or perhaps the

Chapter 4
Content Standards
and Instructional
Practices—
Grades Four
Through Eight

Sixth Grade

Curricular and
Instructional
Profile

Instructional Design
(Continued)

school has adopted a style to be used.) Bibliographic formats may often appear to be senseless to students. The teacher should instruct the students to use a style book and should demonstrate some of the major bibliographic formats and the rationale behind bibliographies. Discuss, for example, the difficulties the students would have in trying to find sources if bibliographic entries were incomplete.

8. Instruction should incorporate other related language arts standards into the instruction on research writing. (Writing Strategies Standards 1.2, 1.3, 1.4, 1.6; Listening and Speaking Standard 2.2; Reading Standards 2.4, 2.7. The content standards for history–social science, science, and mathematics are rich sources of topics for research reports.)

Instructional Delivery

Many of the concepts and procedures used in research writing are new to sixth-grade students. Carefully delivered instruction over a long period of time is the key to teaching the concepts and procedures effectively, ensuring that students will have a strong foundation for coming school years.

1. The guidelines listed previously suggest a great deal more teacher-student interaction than do most traditional approaches to instruction in writing research reports. Teachers and library media teachers should model strategies such as those described and then closely monitor student progress through the application of each strategy, giving feedback and additional assistance when required.

2. A good scaffolding device to help students acquire mastery of research writing is initially to have groups work together in writing a single research report. To do so reduces considerably the need for students to develop a topic, find sources, record information on cards, organize, and create formal bibliographies. If this approach is used, however, students should also write individual research reports after the successful completion of a group report. (Students can still work cooperatively on some aspects of individual reports, such as revising or editing.)

Assessment

Entry-Level Assessment

1. *Entry-Level Assessment for Instructional Planning.* Students must know how to find and use reference materials as a prerequisite to meaningful instruction in writing research reports. Before beginning such instruction, the teacher should work with the library media teacher to develop an assignment for assessing students' proficiency in using source material. The students are asked to write a report that requires them to find answers to factual questions (e.g., finding three or four

Chapter 4
Content Standards
and Instructional
Practices—
Grades Four
Through Eight

Sixth Grade

Curricular and
Instructional
Profile

Assessment
(Continued)

Monitoring
Student
Progress

Post-test
Assessment

Universal
Access

Reading
Difficulties
or Disabilities

Advanced
Learners

different sources telling how the American explorer Meriwether Lewis died). Such sources might include an encyclopedia, a book on Lewis and Clark, an Internet search, and a query to the Lewis and Clark Museum in St. Louis.

2. *Monitoring Student Progress Toward the Instructional Objective.* Adhering to the clear stages of instruction, such as those listed previously for developing index cards, provides an opportunity to assess incrementally students' progress toward the research report standard. The teacher should adjust instruction according to the results of assessment. For instance, if the students have not located and catalogued an adequate number of sources prior to prewriting, instruction should be postponed briefly while the teacher gives further assistance and guidance in using source material.

3. *Post-test Assessment Toward the Standard.* A final research report presented in manuscript form is the best and most direct assessment for this standard. The individually written report, rather than a group report, serves as the summative evaluation tool.

1. *Students with Reading Difficulties or Disabilities.* The recommended accommodation for these students is access to the regular language arts curriculum through careful, systematic instruction in key concepts and strategies, such as those described previously. In addition, these students may require additional teacher or peer support (or both) with difficult procedures, such as developing a well-organized outline and organizing index cards to fit the outline. In addition, topics for students may vary, allowing research on topics that are more familiar.

2. *Students Who Are Advanced Learners.* Instruction can be differentiated for these students by:

   a. Assisting them in their development of higher-level research questions based on key words from taxonomies of thinking skills
   b. Directing them to more sophisticated and specialized source material (through the library media teacher)
   c. Encouraging them to incorporate more advanced elements into their reports (such as those found in the standards for higher grade levels)

Note: These students require knowledge of the fundamentals of writing research reports, as do other students, and sometimes need assistance in finding closure on a project because of propensity to explore topics in great depth.

Chapter 4
Content Standards
and Instructional
Practices—
Grades Four
Through Eight

Sixth Grade

Curricular and
Instructional
Profile

**Universal
Access**
(Continued)

English Learners

3. *Students Who Are English Learners.* Although all writing assignments are likely to be challenging for English learners, research reports may be especially difficult, given the additional requirements of reading source materials and cataloguing the results for planning purposes. Accordingly, the teacher may wish to:

a. Direct English learners to source materials written at a level they can manage.

b. Use clear, simple instructional language to teach the basic concepts and procedures of research report writing. During any cooperative learning sessions, care should be taken to distribute English learners among the groups.

c. Provide English learners with feedback at every stage of developing their research reports. They need guidance in organizing, finding reference materials, and revising and editing.

d. Expose English learners to several models of the types of research reports they are expected to write.

e. Provide additional instruction in how to incorporate quotations and citations into their reports appropriately.

f. Assess English learners at every stage of the research report. Editing is an important stage that teachers often overlook, partly because of the grammar mistakes they make and partly because it is the last stage in the research report process. Teachers need to make sure that they save time to assess this stage along with the other important stages of the research report.

**Instructional
Materials**

Instructional materials should include a liberal quantity of material that teachers can use to teach concepts and procedures for research report writing. For instance, instructional materials should include detailed examples of developing index cards or another systematic approach to creating bibliographies. They should also include detailed guides to resources particularly useful for this standard (such as web sites or references written below grade level for English learners and students who have reading difficulties).

Chapter 4
Content Standards
and Instructional
Practices—
Grades Four
Through Eight

Sixth Grade

English–Language Arts Content Standards

Reading

1.0 Word Analysis, Fluency, and Systematic Vocabulary Development

Students use their knowledge of word origins and word relationships, as well as historical and literary context clues, to determine the meaning of specialized vocabulary and to understand the precise meaning of grade-level-appropriate words.

Word Recognition

1.1 Read aloud narrative and expository text fluently and accurately and with appropriate pacing, intonation, and expression.

Vocabulary and Concept Development

1.2 Identify and interpret figurative language and words with multiple meanings.

1.3 Recognize the origins and meanings of frequently used foreign words in English and use these words accurately in speaking and writing.

1.4 Monitor expository text for unknown words or words with novel meanings by using word, sentence, and paragraph clues to determine meaning.

1.5 Understand and explain "shades of meaning" in related words (e.g., *softly* and *quietly*).

2.0 Reading Comprehension (Focus on Informational Materials)

Students read and understand grade-level-appropriate material. They describe and connect the essential ideas, arguments, and perspectives of the text by using their knowledge of text structure, organization, and purpose. The selections in *Recommended Readings in Literature, Kindergarten Through Grade Eight* illustrate the quality and complexity of the materials to be read by students. In addition, by grade eight, students read one million words annually on their own, including a good representation of grade-level-appropriate narrative and expository text (e.g., classic and contemporary literature, magazines, newspapers, online information). In grade six, students continue to make progress toward this goal.

Structural Features of Informational Materials

2.1 Identify the structural features of popular media (e.g., newspapers, magazines, online information) and use the features to obtain information.

2.2 Analyze text that uses the compare-and-contrast organizational pattern.

Comprehension and Analysis of Grade-Level-Appropriate Text

2.3 Connect and clarify main ideas by identifying their relationships to other sources and related topics.

Chapter 4
Content Standards
and Instructional
Practices—
Grades Four
Through Eight

Sixth Grade

English–Language
Arts Content
Standards

2.4 Clarify an understanding of texts by creating outlines, logical notes, summaries, or reports.

2.5 Follow multiple-step instructions for preparing applications (e.g., for a public library card, bank savings account, sports club, league membership).

Expository Critique

2.6 Determine the adequacy and appropriateness of the evidence for an author's conclusions.

2.7 Make reasonable assertions about a text through accurate, supporting citations.

2.8 Note instances of unsupported inferences, fallacious reasoning, persuasion, and propaganda in text.

3.0 Literary Response and Analysis

Students read and respond to historically or culturally significant works of literature that reflect and enhance their studies of history and social science. They clarify the ideas and connect them to other literary works. The selections in *Recommended Readings in Literature, Kindergarten Through Grade Eight* illustrate the quality and complexity of the materials to be read by students.

Structural Features of Literature

3.1 Identify the forms of fiction and describe the major characteristics of each form.

Narrative Analysis of Grade-Level-Appropriate Text

3.2 Analyze the effect of the qualities of the character (e.g., courage or cowardice, ambition or laziness) on the plot and the resolution of the conflict.

3.3 Analyze the influence of setting on the problem and its resolution.

3.4 Define how tone or meaning is conveyed in poetry through word choice, figurative language, sentence structure, line length, punctuation, rhythm, repetition, and rhyme.

3.5 Identify the speaker and recognize the difference between first- and third-person narration (e.g., autobiography compared with biography).

3.6 Identify and analyze features of themes conveyed through characters, actions, and images.

3.7 Explain the effects of common literary devices (e.g., symbolism, imagery, metaphor) in a variety of fictional and nonfictional texts.

Literary Criticism

3.8 Critique the credibility of characterization and the degree to which a plot is contrived or realistic (e.g., compare use of fact and fantasy in historical fiction).

Writing

1.0 Writing Strategies

Students write clear, coherent, and focused essays. The writing exhibits students' awareness of the audience and purpose. Essays contain formal introductions, supporting evidence, and conclusions. Students progress through the stages of the writing process as needed.

Organization and Focus

1.1 Choose the form of writing (e.g., personal letter, letter to the editor, review, poem, report, narrative) that best suits the intended purpose.

1.2 Create multiple-paragraph expository compositions:
   a. Engage the interest of the reader and state a clear purpose.
   b. Develop the topic with supporting details and precise verbs, nouns, and adjectives to paint a visual image in the mind of the reader.
   c. Conclude with a detailed summary linked to the purpose of the composition.

1.3 Use a variety of effective and coherent organizational patterns, including comparison and contrast; organization by categories; and arrangement by spatial order, order of importance, or climactic order.

Chapter 4
Content Standards
and Instructional
Practices—
Grades Four
Through Eight

Sixth Grade

English–Language
Arts Content
Standards

Research and Technology

1.4 Use organizational features of electronic text (e.g., bulletin boards, databases, keyword searches, e-mail addresses) to locate information.

1.5 Compose documents with appropriate formatting by using word-processing skills and principles of design (e.g., margins, tabs, spacing, columns, page orientation).

Evaluation and Revision

1.6 Revise writing to improve the organization and consistency of ideas within and between paragraphs.

2.0 Writing Applications (Genres and Their Characteristics)

Students write narrative, expository, persuasive, and descriptive texts of at least 500 to 700 words in each genre. Student writing demonstrates a command of standard American English and the research, organizational, and drafting strategies outlined in Writing Standard 1.0.

Using the writing strategies of grade six outlined in Writing Standard 1.0, students:

2.1 Write narratives:

    a. Establish and develop a plot and setting and present a point of view that is appropriate to the stories.

    b. Include sensory details and concrete language to develop plot and character.

    c. Use a range of narrative devices (e.g., dialogue, suspense).

2.2 Write expository compositions (e.g., description, explanation, comparison and contrast, problem and solution):

    a. State the thesis or purpose.

    b. Explain the situation.

    c. Follow an organizational pattern appropriate to the type of composition.

    d. Offer persuasive evidence to validate arguments and conclusions as needed.

2.3 Write research reports:

    a. Pose relevant questions with a scope narrow enough to be thoroughly covered.

    b. Support the main idea or ideas with facts, details, examples, and explanations from multiple authoritative sources (e.g., speakers, periodicals, online information searches).

    c. Include a bibliography.

2.4 Write responses to literature:

    a. Develop an interpretation exhibiting careful reading, understanding, and insight.

    b. Organize the interpretation around several clear ideas, premises, or images.

    c. Develop and justify the interpretation through sustained use of examples and textual evidence.

2.5 Write persuasive compositions:

    a. State a clear position on a proposition or proposal.

    b. Support the position with organized and relevant evidence.

    c. Anticipate and address reader concerns and counterarguments.

Written and Oral English Language Conventions

The standards for written and oral English language conventions have been placed between those for writing and for listening and speaking because these conventions are essential to both sets of skills.

1.0 Written and Oral English Language Conventions

Students write and speak with a command of standard English conventions appropriate to this grade level.

Sentence Structure

1.1 Use simple, compound, and compound-complex sentences; use effective coordination and subordination of ideas to express complete thoughts.

Chapter 4
Content Standards
and Instructional
Practices—
Grades Four
Through Eight

Sixth Grade

English–Language
Arts Content
Standards

Grammar

1.2 Identify and properly use indefinite pronouns and present perfect, past perfect, and future perfect verb tenses; ensure that verbs agree with compound subjects.

Punctuation

1.3 Use colons after the salutation in business letters, semicolons to connect independent clauses, and commas when linking two clauses with a conjunction in compound sentences.

Capitalization

1.4 Use correct capitalization.

Spelling

1.5 Spell frequently misspelled words correctly (e.g., *their, they're, there*).

Listening and Speaking

1.0 Listening and Speaking Strategies

Students deliver focused, coherent presentations that convey ideas clearly and relate to the background and interests of the audience. They evaluate the content of oral communication.

Comprehension

1.1 Relate the speaker's verbal communication (e.g., word choice, pitch, feeling, tone) to the nonverbal message (e.g., posture, gesture).

1.2 Identify the tone, mood, and emotion conveyed in the oral communication.

1.3 Restate and execute multiple-step oral instructions and directions.

Organization and Delivery of Oral Communication

1.4 Select a focus, an organizational structure, and a point of view, matching the purpose, message, occasion, and vocal modulation to the audience.

1.5 Emphasize salient points to assist the listener in following the main ideas and concepts.

1.6 Support opinions with detailed evidence and with visual or media displays that use appropriate technology.

1.7 Use effective rate, volume, pitch, and tone and align nonverbal elements to sustain audience interest and attention.

Analysis and Evaluation of Oral and Media Communications

1.8 Analyze the use of rhetorical devices (e.g., cadence, repetitive patterns, use of onomatopoeia) for intent and effect.

1.9 Identify persuasive and propaganda techniques used in television and identify false and misleading information.

2.0 Speaking Applications (Genres and Their Characteristics)

Students deliver well-organized formal presentations employing traditional rhetorical strategies (e.g., narration, exposition, persuasion, description). Student speaking demonstrates a command of standard American English and the organizational and delivery strategies outlined in Listening and Speaking Standard 1.0.

Using the speaking strategies of grade six outlined in Listening and Speaking Standard 1.0, students:

2.1 Deliver narrative presentations:
   a. Establish a context, plot, and point of view.
   b. Include sensory details and concrete language to develop the plot and character.
   c. Use a range of narrative devices (e.g., dialogue, tension, or suspense).

2.2 Deliver informative presentations:
   a. Pose relevant questions sufficiently limited in scope to be completely and thoroughly answered.
   b. Develop the topic with facts, details, examples, and explanations from multiple authoritative sources (e.g., speakers, periodicals, online information).

Chapter 4
Content Standards
and Instructional
Practices—
Grades Four
Through Eight

2.3 Deliver oral responses to literature:

a. Develop an interpretation exhibiting careful reading, understanding, and insight.

b. Organize the selected interpretation around several clear ideas, premises, or images.

c. Develop and justify the selected interpretation through sustained use of examples and textual evidence.

2.4 Deliver persuasive presentations:

a. Provide a clear statement of the position.

b. Include relevant evidence.

c. Offer a logical sequence of information.

d. Engage the listener and foster acceptance of the proposition or proposal.

2.5 Deliver presentations on problems and solutions:

a. Theorize on the causes and effects of each problem and establish connections between the defined problem and at least one solution.

b. Offer persuasive evidence to validate the definition of the problem and the proposed solutions.

151

Chapter 4
Content Standards
and Instructional
Practices—
Grades Four
Through Eight

Seventh Grade

Standards and Instruction

The content standards for the seventh grade mark a distinctive transition from the sixth grade and the earlier grades in at least two important ways. First, the transition from learning to read to reading to learn is complete. By the time students enter the seventh grade, they should have mastered reading aloud narrative and expository text fluently and accurately, with appropriate pacing, intonation, and expression. For students who have not mastered the previous standard, intensive and systematic instruction in word recognition is imperative. To be able to provide such remediation, teachers may need additional training, for many seventh-grade teachers have not been trained to teach developmental reading skills.

The second reason seventh-grade standards are distinctive is that they are decidedly more sophisticated, subtle, and intricate than those for previous grades. For example, students are required to identify and trace the development of an author's argument, write reports that use the formal research process, deliver persuasive oral presentations that employ well-articulated evidence, and analyze characterization as suggested through a character's thoughts, words, speech patterns, and actions. In some cases the standards are new and complex, such as

the requirement to articulate the expressed purposes and characteristics of different forms of prose, including the short story, novel, novella, and essay.

The strands to be emphasized at the seventh-grade level are listed below under the appropriate domains.

Reading

1.0 Word Analysis, Fluency, and Systematic Vocabulary Development
2.0 Reading Comprehension (Focus on Informational Materials)
3.0 Literary Response and Analysis

Writing

1.0 Writing Strategies
2.0 Writing Applications (Genres and Their Characteristics)

Written and Oral English-Language Conventions

1.0 Written and Oral English-Language Conventions

Listening and Speaking

1.0 Listening and Speaking Strategies
2.0 Speaking Applications (Genres and Their Characteristics)

Chapter 4
Content Standards
and Instructional
Practices—
Grades Four
Through Eight

Seventh Grade

Standards and
Instruction

The following sections profile focus areas within each of the strands and identify content and instructional connections across domains, strands, and standards.

Reading   Word Analysis, Fluency, and Systematic Vocabulary Development

Vocabulary and Concept Development

At this level the development of vocabulary used in literary works or seventh-grade content areas is emphasized. Students must also identify idioms, analogies, metaphors, and similes in prose and poetry and continue to clarify word meanings through definitions, examples, restatements, and contrasts.

Extensive opportunities to read are essential to vocabulary development. A student's vocabulary typically doubles between the fourth grade and the eighth grade as a direct result of how much a student reads. The more students read, the more their vocabulary increases. Although extensive independent reading is the primary means of increasing vocabulary, a need for teacher-directed vocabulary instruction still exists. New and important vocabulary should be taught and reviewed cumulatively and periodically during the school year. Without cumulative reviews and practice in context, vocabulary gains are likely to be temporary. Teachers should also provide students with opportunities to work with word derivations from Greek, Latin, and Anglo-Saxon roots and affixes in reading assignments.

Reading   Reading Comprehension (Focus on Informational Materials)

Although teachers have always taught reading-comprehension skills in relation to informational texts, the standards focus more attention on this aspect of the language arts curriculum, especially on expository rather than narrative reading. In the school setting informational texts are generally textbooks or reference works but can also include magazines, newspapers, online information, instructional manuals, consumer workplace and public documents, signs, and selections listed in *Recommended Readings in Literature, Kindergarten Through Grade Eight* (California Department of Education 1996a). Instructional strategies used to help students comprehend informational materials are often different for literary texts. In a departmentalized school, responsibility for improving the reading comprehension of instructional materials should be shared with teachers of all subjects, particularly teachers of history–social science and science.

Strategies for comprehending informational materials in the seventh grade are focused on (1) use and analysis of categories of informational materials (e.g., consumer and workplace documents, textbooks, newspapers, instructional manuals); and (2) assessment of an author's argument. Because both standards involve a cluster of challenging skills, systematic instruction and ample practice are required to become proficient. Instructional guidelines for evaluating an author's argument include:

- Selecting and using, during initial instruction, examples of an author's arguments that are not complex and

Chapter 4
Content Standards
and Instructional
Practices—
Grades Four
Through Eight

Seventh Grade

Standards and
Instruction

sophisticated but simple and straightforward

- Providing students with a procedural facilitator, such as a think sheet that maps for students the basic structure of an argument (e.g., the main problem, the author's position, statements in support of the author's position, statements against the author's position) and allows them to record and map the author's argument
- Scheduling ample opportunities throughout the year for students to read increasingly more complex arguments
- Providing systematic feedback to students on their analysis and evaluation of an author's arguments
- Integrating the evaluation of an author's arguments in reading-comprehension activities with writing activities in which students develop their own arguments about a particular topic of interest

Reading   Literary Response and Analysis

The increased sophistication and intricacy of the standards are readily apparent in the literary response and analysis strand. For example, students are required to:

- Articulate the express purposes and characteristics of different forms of prose (e.g., short story, novel, novella, essay).
- Identify events that advance the plot and determine how each event explains past or present actions or foreshadows future actions.
- Analyze characterization as delineated through a character's thoughts, words, speech patterns, and actions;

the narrator's description; and the thoughts, words, and actions of other characters.

- Identify and analyze recurring themes across works (e.g., the value of bravery, loyalty, and friendship; the effects of loneliness).
- Contrast points of view (e.g., first and third person, limited and omniscient, subjective and objective) in narrative text and explain how they affect the overall theme of the work.

The level of sophistication required by the standards calls for instruction that is both deep and diligent and allows students ample opportunity to scrutinize a particular work. Selection of literary works is important. Teachers should select works that are appropriate to the age and reading level of the students and are varied in culture and themes. In addition, the works must also lend themselves to exploring with the students how events advance the plot; how each event explains past or present actions or foreshadows future actions; and how a character's thoughts, words, speech patterns, and actions reveal characterization. Once the literary features and devices that are part of a particular work become clear, the teacher may introduce other more complex and varied literary works in which such features and devices are used.

Grade-level literary selections of various genres and lengths representing a variety of authors and cultures can be found in district-adopted anthologies. *Recommended Readings in Literature, Kindergarten Through Grade Eight* (California Department of Education 1996a) provides extensive lists of such selections.

Extensive independent reading, which in the seventh grade increasingly takes place outside the classroom, is an impor-

Chapter 4
Content Standards
and Instructional
Practices—
Grades Four
Through Eight

Seventh Grade

Standards and
Instruction

tant element of the language arts curriculum. The standards require that by the end of middle school, students will have read one million words annually on their own, including a good representation of narrative (classic and contemporary literature) and expository (magazines, newspapers, online) instructional materials. One million words translate to about 15 to 20 minutes of reading per day.

Instructional formats and strategies used for outside reading have much in common with those used in teaching core literature works but differ significantly. Student choice is a more important element in outside reading and may result in less-diverse selections because young readers typically choose to focus on a single author, topic, or genre for a period of time. Their reading should not be limited to works of fiction or nonfiction but should include magazines, especially those in areas of special interest to the students, newspapers, and online sources. A variety of methods are available to assess reading done outside the classroom, including student-maintained reading logs and book reports in various formats. According to the standard, the instruction should be focused on the reading itself rather than on the final report on reading.

Independent reading significantly improves a student's reading comprehension and vocabulary and increases familiarity with models of good writing and conventions of writing and spelling. It also serves an important affective purpose; that is, to develop a lifelong appreciation for reading for pleasure and information. Recent research indicates that the volume of reading also affects general cognitive development.

Writing   Writing Strategies

Seventh-grade students are expected to continue to develop strategies for organizing and giving focus to their writing. Increased emphasis is given to documentation of support (e.g., support for all statements and claims through the use of anecdotes, descriptions, facts and statistics, specific examples) and the extension of strategies (e.g., note taking, outlining, summarizing).

Students are expected to write research reports. They should be instructed in all phases of the research process, from identifying topics to preparing bibliographies, and should be expected to locate relevant information in electronic as well as printed texts. Further, they should be able to produce documents with a word-processing program and organize information gathered in the research process. (The guidelines for writing in the sixth grade are applicable in the seventh grade as well.)

Writing   Writing Applications (Genres and Their Characteristics)

Writing in the seventh grade focuses less on narrative writing (writing to tell a story) and more on multiparagraph expository compositions. Specifically, students are expected to write texts of between 500 and 700 words (two or three typed, double-spaced pages) in these categories: interpretations of literature, research reports, persuasive compositions, and summaries.

155

Chapter 4
Content Standards
and Instructional
Practices—
Grades Four
Through Eight

Seventh Grade

Standards and
Instruction

Written and Oral English-Language Conventions

Seventh-grade students are expected to have a general command of English-language conventions when they speak and write. Curriculum emphases at this grade level include sentence structure (e.g., proper placement of modifiers and use of the active voice); grammar (e.g., proper use of infinitives and participles, clear pronouns and antecedents); punctuation (e.g., correct use of hyphens, dashes, brackets, and semicolons); and spelling (e.g., applying the spelling of bases and affixes to derivatives).

Although most of the standards are also included at earlier grade levels, many students in the seventh grade have not yet mastered the standards and will require continued support and guidance in the form of remedial instruction that should:

- Involve teacher direction and guidance, with clear examples being offered in simplified contexts (e.g., use of pronouns with clear referents in abbreviated passages) before students are required to work in more complex contexts (e.g., multiple paragraphs with multiple pronouns and referents).
- Provide extensive opportunities to receive instruction and feedback from teachers or peers throughout the year and as a frequent small part of lessons or class periods.
- Emphasize the accurate use of conventions in student writing and speaking.
- Hold students to a high level of performance because the conventions are fundamental to proficient performance on other standards (e.g., writing strategies, writing applications).

Listening and Speaking
Listening and Speaking Strategies

Listening Strategies

Although listening and speaking are frequently paired, they represent decidedly different skills. An accomplished speaker may be a poor listener and vice versa. In the classroom, listening instruction is often concerned as much with behavior management ("Eyes up front, please") as with systematic skills in comprehending and evaluating oral information. The standards define specific listening skills to be taught in seventh grade. For example, students are expected to ask appropriate questions designed to elicit needed information and discern the speaker's point of view. As for electronic journalism, students are expected to be able to recognize techniques used to affect the viewer.

Speaking Strategies

Language arts teachers have traditionally provided a variety of speaking opportunities in informal settings (e.g., small-group discussions, cooperative learning activities) and more formal settings (e.g., individual or group presentations to the class). In many cases, however, instruction in speaking has been less structured and less detailed and has occupied less class time than instruction in reading and writing. The standards provide a detailed outline for an appropriate instructional program in speaking. Seventh-grade students are expected to employ traditional rhetorical strategies to deliver well-organized formal narrative, research, and persuasive presentations as well as oral summaries of articles and books. The standards identify for teachers the speaking skills and strategies that

Chapter 4
Content Standards
and Instructional
Practices—
Grades Four
Through Eight

Seventh Grade

Standards and
Instruction

accompany each type of oral presentation. For example, students are expected to describe complex major and minor characters in a narrative presentation. Students making a research presentation are expected to use their own words to convey their message.

Because the same genres appear in the writing applications at this grade level, writing and speaking activities might be combined. For example, students might write a persuasive composition and deliver an oral persuasive presentation on the same topic.

Listening and Speaking
Speaking Applications (Genres and Their Characteristics)

Like sixth-grade students, those in the seventh grade are expected to deliver well-organized formal presentations that employ traditional rhetorical strategies. Specifically, students are required to deliver narrative, research, and persuasive presentations as well as oral summaries of articles and books. They are expected to demonstrate a range of speaking skills and strategies that includes, for example, describing complex major and minor characters and a definite setting; using a range of appropriate strategies, including dialogue, suspense, and naming of specific narrative actions; using their own words, except for material quoted from the source, in an oral summary; and including evidence generated through the formal research process for a research presentation.

Content and Instructional Connections

The teacher can help students integrate mastery of standards across domains, strands, and academic disciplines by having students:

1. Analyze the differences in structure and purpose between various categories of informational materials (e.g., textbooks, newspapers, instructional manuals, signs).
2. Examine informational materials for an organizational structure that balances all aspects of the composition and uses effective transitions between sentences to unify important ideas.
3. Identify informational materials in which statements and claims are supported by anecdotes, descriptions, facts and statistics, and specific examples.
4. Create materials in which credit for quoted and paraphrased information in a bibliography is given and a consistent and sanctioned format and methodology are used for citations.
5. Revise writing to improve organization and word choice after checking the logic of ideas and precision of vocabulary.

Please see Appendix B for examples of standards that span domains and strands.

157

Chapter 4
Content Standards
and Instructional
Practices—
Grades Four
Through Eight

Seventh Grade

Curricular and Instructional Profile

Conventions Standard 1.3

DOMAIN	STRAND	SUBSTRAND	STANDARD
Written and Oral English-Language Convention	1.0 Written and oral English-language conventions		1.3 Identify all parts of speech and types and structure of sentences.

Prerequisite standard. **Sixth-Grade Written and Oral English-Language Conventions Standard 1.1:** Use simple, compound, and compound-complex sentences.

Corequisite standard. **Seventh-Grade Writing Strategies Standard 1.7:** Revise writing to improve organization and word choice.

Curricular and Instructional Decisions

Instructional Objective	Use sophisticated but appropriate sentence structures in oral and written discourse.
Instructional Design	At this level a challenge for students is to use sentence structures more sophisticated than simple kernel-sentence types but not excessively complex or convoluted. Instruction should, therefore, focus on options for combining kernel sentences in various ways and the rhetorical impact and appropriateness of those various combinations. To achieve a balance, instruction should address both sentence combining and decombining. A focus on sentence combining alone can easily, if inadvertently, create the impression that longer, more complex sentence structures are inherently or universally better than simpler sentence structures.

Chapter 4
Content Standards
and Instructional
Practices—
Grades Four
Through Eight

Seventh Grade

Curricular and
Instructional
Profile

**Instructional
Design**
(Continued)

Ultimately, students should be expected to develop a sense of appropriate sentence structures well enough to apply that sense to revisions of their own drafts. Initially, however, students should work on combining (and decombining and recombining) contrived sentences, which can be selected judiciously to illustrate specific possibilities for improvement. (Sentences contrived for revision can be taken from student writing examples or created by decombining sentences from texts students will read.)

The advantages to teaching sentence structure initially in this way are as follows:

- When all students are looking at and working with the same set of examples, teachers can conduct efficient whole-class instruction based on those examples.
- Teachers can correct work or otherwise evaluate student work more easily and give feedback when all students work initially with the same set of examples.
- Teachers can ensure that they cover several important classes or categories of sentence combining when examples are chosen specifically to illustrate those classes or categories.
- The examples used during initial instruction give teachers and students a solid basis of reference as individual student work is being revised.

Consider, for instance, the following example of student writing:

> Cowboys in Uruguay and Argentina are called gauchos. The gauchos are found in the country. They live and work in grass-covered prairies. Some gauchos herd cattle in the pampas. They do not make much money. Gauchos wear colorful outfits. They carry large knives and they drink a beverage called maté. It's a type of tea.

Initially, teachers should demonstrate possible improvements in the writing sample while discussing with students the relative advantages or effects of each possibility. For example, students might compare the differences in emphasis between Example 1 and Example 2:

Example 1. Gauchos, who are the cowboys of Uruguay and Argentina, live throughout the countryside.

Example 2. Across the countryside in the pampas of Uruguay and Argentina, you find cowboys called gauchos.

Which choice is better suited to a paragraph about gauchos? Why? What other options for sentence combining are possible? Which options illustrate trying to put too much into a sentence? How would the sense of Example 1 change if the commas were removed?

In short, instruction should address the strategies that good writers use—consciously or otherwise—by making such strategies overt and clear for students. Instruction should demonstrate the techniques by which secondary ideas are subordinated to primary, important ideas in strong, active sentences. Most critically, instruction should

159

Chapter 4
Content Standards
and Instructional
Practices—
Grades Four
Through Eight

Seventh Grade

Curricular and
Instructional
Profile

Instructional Design (Continued)

emphasize the relationships among ideas in kernel and complex sentences to ensure that students appreciate that conventions (e.g., the use of commas in dependent clauses) support the communication of ideas.

Instructional Delivery

Teachers should direct initial instruction in strategies for developing complex sentence structures and for evaluating competing structures. For such instruction to be meaningful, it must center on active discourse between teachers and students. The challenge for many students at this level is not so much to combine sentences as such but to do so judiciously in relation to specific purposes of communication. Teacher demonstrations and evaluations of thinking critically out loud are indispensable to effective instruction.

Assessment

Entry-Level Assessment

Monitoring Student Progress

Post-test Assessment

1. *Entry-Level Assessment for Instructional Planning.* Brief in-class compositions on well-defined topics should give teachers a satisfactory overview of the relative sophistication with which students manipulate sentence structures.

2. *Monitoring Student Progress Toward the Instructional Objective.* All written and oral assignments provide opportunities for ongoing assessment of this standard. Students should be prompted to focus on good sentence structures in all assignments that follow the initial instruction on this topic.

3. *Post-test Assessment Toward the Standard.* The best type of summative evaluation comes from specifically evaluating sentence structures in conjunction with authentic assignments in writing and speaking that address the writing and speaking standards.

Universal Access

Reading Difficulties or Disabilities

1. *Students with Reading Difficulties or Disabilities.* Students with reading difficulties or disabilities often use long strings of primitive kernel sentences in their writing. They may run a number of these sentences together without punctuation, splice them with commas, or join them with repeated use of conjunctions like *and* or *but*. In turn, many of the sentences are likely to overuse passive and intransitive verbs. When necessary, teachers should be prepared to begin instruction in sentence combining at the students' level. In addition, these students will probably take longer to make the transition from predominantly simple sentences to the wider use of longer, more appropriate complex sentences.

Chapter 4
Content Standards
and Instructional
Practices—
Grades Four
Through Eight

Seventh Grade

Curricular and
Instructional
Profile

Universal Access
(Continued)

Advanced Learners

2. *Students Who Are Advanced Learners.* The highest-performing students are the ones most likely to be able to learn about language for its own sake and benefit from that learning. For instance, they can investigate in depth the relationships between grammatical dependency and nuances in meaning and be challenged, for example, to come up with contrasting sentence pairs, such as the following:

Teenagers, who don't drive well, should pay higher insurance rates.

Teenagers who don't drive well should pay higher insurance rates.

English Learners

3. *Students Who Are English Learners*
Students with restricted proficiency in English will require intensive English-language instruction above and beyond that found in the regular language arts program. The type of explicit strategy instruction described previously for lower-performing students will help English learners as well. They might be exempted from some regular classroom work in sentence combining to provide more instructional time for intense work on well-formed grammatical kernel sentences.

Instructional Materials

Instructional materials should provide for a very wide range of student achievement levels in the seventh grade. Publishers will always be safe in providing *more* resources for a given set of standards—such as those for sentence combining and related conventions—than one might think sufficient for average students. (It is far easier for teachers to elect to not use some resources than to create them from scratch or to find them.) For instance, teachers should have the option of drawing from a rich variety of sample writing—examples of good and poor writing—to use as the basis for instruction in sentence combining.

161

Chapter 4
Content Standards
and Instructional
Practices—
Grades Four
Through Eight

Seventh Grade

English–Language Arts Content Standards

Reading

1.0. Word Analysis, Fluency, and Systematic Vocabulary Development

Students use their knowledge of word origins and word relationships, as well as historical and literary context clues, to determine the meaning of specialized vocabulary and to understand the precise meaning of grade-level-appropriate words.

Vocabulary and Concept Development

1.1 Identify idioms, analogies, metaphors, and similes in prose and poetry.

1.2 Use knowledge of Greek, Latin, and Anglo-Saxon roots and affixes to understand content-area vocabulary.

1.3 Clarify word meanings through the use of definition, example, restatement, or contrast.

2.0 Reading Comprehension (Focus on Informational Materials)

Students read and understand grade-level-appropriate material. They describe and connect the essential ideas, arguments, and perspectives of the text by using their knowledge of text structure, organization, and purpose. The selections in *Recommended Readings in Literature, Kindergarten Through Grade Eight* illustrate the quality and complexity of the materials to be read by students. In addition, by grade eight, students read one million words annually on their own, including a good representation of grade-level-

appropriate narrative and expository text (e.g., classic and contemporary literature, magazines, newspapers, online information). In grade seven, students make substantial progress toward this goal.

Structural Features of Informational Materials

2.1 Understand and analyze the differences in structure and purpose between various categories of informational materials (e.g., textbooks, newspapers, instructional manuals, signs).

2.2 Locate information by using a variety of consumer, workplace, and public documents.

2.3 Analyze text that uses the cause-and-effect organizational pattern.

Comprehension and Analysis of Grade-Level-Appropriate Text

2.4 Identify and trace the development of an author's argument, point of view, or perspective in text.

2.5 Understand and explain the use of a simple mechanical device by following technical directions.

Expository Critique

2.6 Assess the adequacy, accuracy, and appropriateness of the author's evidence to support claims and assertions, noting instances of bias and stereotyping.

3.0 Literary Response and Analysis

Students read and respond to historically or culturally significant works of literature that

Chapter 4
Content Standards
and Instructional
Practices—
Grades Four
Through Eight

Seventh Grade

English–Language
Arts Content
Standards

reflect and enhance their studies of history and social science. They clarify the ideas and connect them to other literary works. The selections in *Recommended Readings in Literature, Kindergarten Through Grade Eight* illustrate the quality and complexity of the materials to be read by students.

Structural Features of Literature

3.1 Articulate the expressed purposes and characteristics of different forms of prose (e.g., short story, novel, novella, essay).

Narrative Analysis of Grade-Level-Appropriate Text

3.2 Identify events that advance the plot and determine how each event explains past or present action(s) or foreshadows future action(s).

3.3 Analyze characterization as delineated through a character's thoughts, words, speech patterns, and actions; the narrator's description; and the thoughts, words, and actions of other characters.

3.4 Identify and analyze recurring themes across works (e.g., the value of bravery, loyalty, and friendship; the effects of loneliness).

3.5 Contrast points of view (e.g., first and third person, limited and omniscient, subjective and objective) in narrative text and explain how they affect the overall theme of the work.

Literary Criticism

3.6 Analyze a range of responses to a literary work and determine the extent to which the literary elements in the work shaped those responses.

Writing

1.0. Writing Strategies

Students write clear, coherent, and focused essays. The writing exhibits students' awareness of the audience and purpose. Essays contain formal introductions, supporting evidence, and conclusions. Students progress through the stages of the writing process as needed.

Organization and Focus

1.1 Create an organizational structure that balances all aspects of the composition and uses effective transitions between sentences to unify important ideas.

1.2 Support all statements and claims with anecdotes, descriptions, facts and statistics, and specific examples.

1.3 Use strategies of notetaking, outlining, and summarizing to impose structure on composition drafts.

Research and Technology

1.4 Identify topics; ask and evaluate questions; and develop ideas leading to inquiry, investigation, and research.

1.5 Give credit for both quoted and paraphrased information in a bibliography by using a consistent and sanctioned format and methodology for citations.

1.6 Create documents by using word-processing skills and publishing programs; develop simple databases and spreadsheets to manage information and prepare reports.

Evaluation and Revision

1.7 Revise writing to improve organization and word choice after checking the logic of the ideas and the precision of the vocabulary.

2.0 Writing Applications (Genres and Their Characteristics)

Students write narrative, expository, persuasive, and descriptive texts of at least 500 to 700 words in each genre. The writing demonstrates a command of standard American English and the research, organizational, and drafting strategies outlined in Writing Standard 1.0.

Using the writing strategies of grade seven outlined in Writing Standard 1.0, students:

2.1 Write fictional or autobiographical narratives:

a. Develop a standard plot line (having a beginning, conflict, rising action, climax, and denouement) and point of view.

b. Develop complex major and minor characters and a definite setting.

c. Use a range of appropriate strategies (e.g., dialogue; suspense; naming of specific narrative action, including movement, gestures, and expressions).

2.2   Write responses to literature:

a. Develop interpretations exhibiting careful reading, understanding, and insight.

b. Organize interpretations around several clear ideas, premises, or images from the literary work.

c. Justify interpretations through sustained use of examples and textual evidence.

2.3   Write research reports:

a. Pose relevant and tightly drawn questions about the topic.

b. Convey clear and accurate perspectives on the subject.

c. Include evidence compiled through the formal research process (e.g., use of a card catalog, *Reader's Guide to Periodical Literature*, a computer catalog, magazines, newspapers, dictionaries).

d. Document reference sources by means of footnotes and a bibliography.

2.4   Write persuasive compositions:

a. State a clear position or perspective in support of a proposition or proposal.

b. Describe the points in support of the proposition, employing well-articulated evidence.

c. Anticipate and address reader concerns and counterarguments.

2.5   Write summaries of reading materials:

a. Include the main ideas and most significant details.

b. Use the student's own words, except for quotations.

c. Reflect underlying meaning, not just the superficial details.

Written and Oral English Language Conventions

The standards for written and oral English language conventions have been placed between those for writing and for listening and speaking because these conventions are essential to both sets of skills.

1.0   Written and Oral English Language Conventions

Students write and speak with a command of standard English conventions appropriate to the grade level.

Sentence Structure

1.1   Place modifiers properly and use the active voice.

Grammar

1.2   Identify and use infinitives and participles and make clear references between pronouns and antecedents.

1.3   Identify all parts of speech and types and structure of sentences.

1.4   Demonstrate the mechanics of writing (e.g., quotation marks, commas at end of dependent clauses) and appropriate English usage (e.g., pronoun reference).

Punctuation

1.5   Identify hyphens, dashes, brackets, and semicolons and use them correctly.

Capitalization

1.6   Use correct capitalization.

Spelling

1.7   Spell derivatives correctly by applying the spellings of bases and affixes.

Chapter 4
Content Standards
and Instructional
Practices—
Grades Four
Through Eight

Seventh Grade

English–Language
Arts Content
Standards

Listening and Speaking

1.0. Listening and Speaking Strategies

Deliver focused, coherent presentations that convey ideas clearly and relate to the background and interests of the audience. Students evaluate the content of oral communication.

Comprehension

1.1 Ask probing questions to elicit information, including evidence to support the speaker's claims and conclusions.

1.2 Determine the speaker's attitude toward the subject.

1.3 Respond to persuasive messages with questions, challenges, or affirmations.

Organization and Delivery of Oral Communication

1.4 Organize information to achieve particular purposes and to appeal to the background and interests of the audience.

1.5 Arrange supporting details, reasons, descriptions, and examples effectively and persuasively in relation to the audience.

1.6 Use speaking techniques, including voice modulation, inflection, tempo, enunciation, and eye contact, for effective presentations.

Analysis and Evaluation of Oral and Media Communications

1.7 Provide constructive feedback to speakers concerning the coherence and logic of a speech's content and delivery and its overall impact upon the listener.

1.8 Analyze the effect on the viewer of images, text, and sound in electronic journalism; identify the techniques used to achieve the effects in each instance studied.

2.0 Speaking Applications (Genres and Their Characteristics)

Students deliver well-organized formal presentations employing traditional rhetorical strategies (e.g., narration, exposition, persuasion, description). Student speaking demonstrates a command of standard American English and the organizational and delivery strategies outlined in Listening and Speaking Standard 1.0.

Using the speaking strategies of grade seven outlined in Listening and Speaking Standard 1.0, students:

2.1 Deliver narrative presentations:

a. Establish a context, standard plot line (having a beginning, conflict, rising action, climax, and denouement), and point of view.

b. Describe complex major and minor characters and a definite setting.

c. Use a range of appropriate strategies, including dialogue, suspense, and naming of specific narrative action (e.g., movement, gestures, expressions).

2.2 Deliver oral summaries of articles and books:

a. Include the main ideas of the event or article and the most significant details.

b. Use the student's own words, except for material quoted from sources.

c. Convey a comprehensive understanding of sources, not just superficial details.

2.3 Deliver research presentations:

a. Pose relevant and concise questions about the topic.

b. Convey clear and accurate perspectives on the subject.

c. Include evidence generated through the formal research process (e.g., use of a card catalog, *Reader's Guide to Periodical Literature*, computer databases, magazines, newspapers, dictionaries).

d. Cite reference sources appropriately.

2.4 Deliver persuasive presentations:

a. State a clear position or perspective in support of an argument or proposal.

b. Describe the points in support of the argument and employ well-articulated evidence.

165

Chapter 4
Content Standards
and Instructional
Practices—
Grades Four
Through Eight

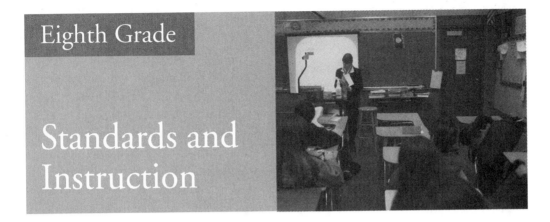

Eighth Grade

Standards and Instruction

Eighth grade marks the beginning of yet another significant transition for students—that of preparing for the high school years. The content standards for this grade signify the readiness required of students preparing for the secondary content in grades nine through twelve. Not surprisingly, the eighth-grade standards represent an important culmination of curriculum activities emphasized throughout grades four through eight.

The strands to be emphasized at the eighth-grade level are listed in the adjacent column under the appropriate domains.

The following sections profile focus areas within each of the strands and identify content and instructional connections across domains, strands, and standards.

Reading

1.0   Word Analysis, Fluency, and Systematic Vocabulary Development
2.0   Reading Comprehension (Focus on Informational Materials)
3.0   Literary Response and Analysis

Writing

1.0   Writing Strategies
2.0   Writing Applications (Genres and Their Characteristics)

Written and Oral English-Language Conventions

1.0   Written and Oral English-Language Conventions

Listening and Speaking

1.0   Listening and Speaking Strategies
2.0   Speaking Applications (Genres and Their Characteristics)

Chapter 4
Content Standards
and Instructional
Practices—
Grades Four
Through Eight

Eighth Grade

Standards and
Instruction

Reading — Word Analysis, Fluency, and Systematic Vocabulary Development

Eighth-grade students apply the vocabulary skills developed in earlier grades in more sophisticated contexts. The strategies for vocabulary instruction discussed in the seventh grade continue to apply in the eighth grade.

Reading — Reading Comprehension (Focus on Informational Materials)

Although teachers have always taught reading-comprehension skills in relation to informational texts, the content standards at this level focus more attention on that segment of the language arts curriculum. The term *informational materials* refers not just to nonfiction works such as biographies but to a variety of reading that is expository rather than narrative. In the school setting informational texts are generally textbooks or reference works but may include a host of print and nonprint materials. Instructional strategies used with information materials are often different from those used to comprehend literary texts. In a departmentalized school, responsibility for improving reading comprehension of instructional materials should be shared by teachers of all subjects, particularly teachers of history–social science and science.

Seventh-grade students study the structural features of consumer materials (warranties, contracts, product information, and instructional manuals). The seventh-grade focus on the cause-and-effect pattern in expository text is replaced in the eighth grade by the pattern of a proposal and its support. In addition,

students should be able to explain the use of a complex mechanical device.

Students are expected to demonstrate their ability to grapple with the treatment, scope, and organization of ideas by finding similarities and differences between texts. They are also expected to compare an original text with a summary to determine whether it accurately captures the main ideas, includes critical details, and conveys the underlying meaning. Finally, students are expected to evaluate the unity, logic, internal consistency, and structural patterns of text.

This framework recommends a strategy of helping students master these relatively sophisticated aspects of reading informational discourse; that is, contrasting good examples of various concepts with poor examples.

Reading — Literary Response and Analysis

This strand of the reading domain is designed to ensure that eighth-grade students are thoroughly familiar with the basic elements of story grammar. Specifically, students are required to (1) evaluate the structural elements of the plot; (2) compare and contrast the motivations and reactions of literary characters; (3) analyze the relevance of the setting; (4) identify and analyze recurring themes; and (5) identify elements of the writer's style.

As to the structural features of literature, eighth-grade students are expected to understand the different kinds of prose. They are also expected to understand the purposes and characteristics of different kinds of poetry (e.g., ballad, lyric, couplet, epic, sonnet).

Extensive independent reading, which in the eighth grade increasingly takes place outside the classroom, is an important

167

Chapter 4
Content Standards
and Instructional
Practices—
Grades Four
Through Eight

element of the language arts curriculum. The standards require that by the end of middle school, students will have read one million words annually on their own, including a good representation of narrative (classic and contemporary literature) and expository (magazines, newspapers, online) instructional materials. One million words translate to about 15 to 20 minutes of reading per day.

Instructional formats and strategies used for outside reading have much in common with those used in teaching core literature works but differ significantly. Student choice is a more important element in outside reading and may result in fewer diverse selections because young readers typically choose to focus on a single author, topic, or genre for a period of time. Their reading should not be limited to works of fiction or nonfiction but should include magazines, especially those in areas of special interest to the students, newspapers, and online sources. A variety of methods are available to assess reading done outside the classroom, including student-maintained reading logs and book reports in various formats. According to the standard, instruction should be focused on the reading itself rather than on the final report on the reading.

Independent reading significantly improves students' reading comprehension and vocabulary and increases their familiarity with models of good writing and conventions of writing and spelling. It also serves an important affective purpose; that is, in helping to develop a lifelong appreciation for reading for pleasure and information. Recent research indicates that the volume of reading also affects general cognitive development (Cunningham and Stanovich 1998).

Writing   Writing Strategies

Writing strategies called for in the eighth grade differ in degree from those used in the seventh grade. Students' writing should continue to be characterized by a controlling thesis well supported by details or evidence from the text but should now begin to display more sophistication and polish, including such features as transitions, parallelism, and a consistent point of view.

When conducting research with the aid of technology, students are expected to build on the foundation of research and technological skills developed in the earlier grades. Eighth-grade students should be able to plan and conduct multiple-step information searches, using Internet-based resources. They should be taught how to achieve an effective balance between researched information and original ideas in their written or oral presentations, a difficult issue for middle school students. Teachers need to assist students in evaluating data and evidence and matching them with thesis statements. Students need frequent opportunities to grasp the idea of preponderance of evidence versus isolated data. The importance of a thesis statement—a single, generalized statement that drives the entire work—cannot be overemphasized. Students with weak language arts skills may not recognize their need to have something to say before they can write a composition. If so, they may be helped by being encouraged to think of speaking as writing out loud because they often find themselves able to articulate and organize thoughts more easily in speech than in writing. Such oral statements can be bridges to the creation of a written thesis statement.

All of these across-the-board standards for writing strategies can be taught *initially*

Chapter 4
Content Standards
and Instructional
Practices—
Grades Four
Through Eight

Eighth Grade

Standards and
Instruction

in isolation. For instance, teachers can initially focus on a skill such as paraphrasing before requiring students to incorporate that skill into their written compositions. Doing so reduces the cognitive and organizational burden on students to incorporate all aspects of writing into an assigned composition. The standards warn, however, against teaching writing concepts in isolation without immediately incorporating them into writing assignments.

Writing Writing Applications (Genres and Their Characteristics)

Eighth-grade students should continue to produce major texts of 500 to 700 words (two to three pages, typed and double-spaced) in these categories: fictional or autobiographical narratives, responses to literature, research reports, and persuasive compositions.

The eighth-grade standards describe the more sophisticated elements now expected in student writing. For example, in writing narratives, students in the seventh grade are expected to develop the standard elements of plot (e.g., beginning, conflict, rising action). But in the eighth grade students are expected to go beyond the structural elements (e.g., to reveal the writer's attitude about the subject). However, the depth and duration of the instruction provided should be adjusted to the achievement level of the students in a given classroom. Well-developed instructional units have long been used in California for many categories of writing, although the titles may be slightly different (e.g., autobiographical incident, report of information).

The seventh-grade requirement to write summaries of reading materials no longer appears in the eighth grade, and two new

categories of writing are introduced: (1) documents related to career development, including simple business letters and job applications; and (2) technical documents that explain a complex operation or situation (e.g., design a system, operate a tool, or develop the bylaws of an organization).

Instruction in the business-related documents should go beyond the mechanics and conventional forms for such writing to include important rhetorical considerations, such as clear attention to the audience and purpose, clarity and succinctness, consideration of all appropriate variables, and coherence and logical sequencing.

Written and Oral English-Language Conventions

Eighth-grade students are expected to have mastered four of the five subsections in this standard: grammar, punctuation, capitalization, and spelling. Only in the fifth subsection, sentence structure, is new learning introduced. In that area students are expected to vary sentence types and sentence openings, use parallel structures appropriately, and indicate relationships between ideas by using such devices as subordination, coordination, and apposition.

Students' strengths and deficits in using English-language conventions are likely to vary considerably in the eighth grade. An important skill to be learned in improving that use is to train the eye and ear to recognize errors in conventions found in reading and writing. Extensive student experience in reading and writing helps to build those skills. Teachers should provide models of both outstanding and poor use of written conventions and help students develop editing skills. Explicit instruction in the conventions is also needed. Indi-

169

Chapter 4
Content Standards
and Instructional
Practices—
Grades Four
Through Eight

Eighth Grade

Standards and
Instruction

vidualized instructional software can be used to address efficiently the problem of significant differences among students in their ability to use conventions.

Skills students possess in mechanics and conventions are most often described in relation to writing. But, as the title of this strand indicates, the skills also apply to speaking. In addition to learning correct speech, students should recognize that the structures of spoken language are generally more informal than the structures of writing and depend on audience and purpose. They should be able to recognize instances in which formal standard English is required.

Listening and Speaking
Listening and Speaking Strategies

Many of the skills and strategies used in speaking are the same as those for writing (e.g., organizing information for audience and purpose; including an introduction, transitions, a logically developed body, and an appropriate conclusion; using correct language and grammar). Some of the rhetorical considerations, however, are unique to oral communications. In speaking, students should be able to match their voice modulation, tone, and pacing to the purpose of the presentation. Explicit instruction in speaking skills must go well beyond the traditional three elementary rules of speaking: speak audibly, speak clearly, and maintain eye contact with your audience.

Students are expected to use audience feedback in both speaking and listening. After listening to verbal cues and observing nonverbal cues, students are expected to be able to modify their original plan of organization to clarify meaning and counter potential opposition. They should be able to ask relevant questions concern-

ing a speaker's content, delivery, and purpose and evaluate the credibility of a speaker. Students are also expected to continue to analyze and evaluate media presentations, noting various techniques used by graphic artists, advertisers, and electronic journalists to influence the viewer.

Listening and Speaking
Speaking Applications (Genres and Their Characteristics)

The speaking applications discussed in the seventh grade reappear in the eighth grade: narrative, research, and persuasive presentations, which are areas of focus in writing as well. Students should, therefore, deliver some of their written compositions orally. Doing so is efficient in the use of instructional time and effective because it makes overt the differences and similarities between written and oral presentations.

Oral responses to reading shift from an expository focus in the seventh grade, when students deliver oral summaries of articles and books, to a literary focus in the eighth grade, when students interpret their reading orally and analyze it. Eighth-grade students are also expected to recite, with expression, poems of four to six stanzas, sections of speeches, or dramatic soliloquies.

Content and Instructional Connections

The teacher can help students integrate mastery of standards across domains, strands, and academic disciplines by having students:

1. Use word meanings within the appropriate context and show an ability to verify those meanings by definition, restatement, example, comparison, or contrast.

Chapter 4
Content Standards
and Instructional
Practices—
Grades Four
Through Eight

Eighth Grade

Standards and
Instruction

2. Use vocabulary, concepts, and writing related to the science, history–social science, and mathematics standards in some activities and assignments.

3. Compare and contrast motivations and reactions of literary characters from different historical eras or cultures who confront similar situations or conflicts.

4. Establish coherence within and among paragraphs through effective transitions, parallel structures, and similar writing techniques.

5. Achieve an effective balance between researched information and original ideas.

6. Revise writing for word choice, appropriate organization, consistent point of view, and transitions between paragraphs, passages, and ideas.

7. Write narratives, employing narrative and descriptive strategies.

8. Use correct punctuation, capitalization, and spelling.

9. Organize information to match the message, vocabulary, voice modulation, expression, and tone to the audience and purpose.

10. Deliver narrative presentations.

Please see Appendix B for examples of standards that span domains and strands.

171

Chapter 4
Content Standards
and Instructional
Practices—
Grades Four
Through Eight

Eighth Grade

Curricular and Instructional Profile

Writing Standard 2.4

DOMAIN	STRAND	SUBSTRAND	STANDARD
Writing	2.0 Writing applications (genres and their characteristics)		2.4 Write persuasive compositions.

Prerequisite standards. **Seventh-Grade Writing Strategies Standard 1.3:** Use strategies of notetaking, outlining, and summarizing.

Seventh-Grade Writing Applications Standard 2.4(a): State a clear position in support of a proposition.

Seventh-Grade Written and Oral English-Language Conventions Standard 1.4: Demonstrate the mechanics of writing and appropriate English usage.

Corequisite standards. **Eighth-Grade Writing Strategies Standards 1.1, 1.3.**

Standard 1.1: Create compositions that establish a controlling impression, have a coherent thesis, and end with a clear and well-supported conclusion.

Standard 1.3: Support conclusions with paraphrases, quotations, and opinions from authorities.

Curricular and Instructional Decisions

Instructional Objective	Write a well-structured persuasive composition, using rhetorical devices, relevant evidence, and responses to readers' counterclaims.
Instructional Design	Initial instruction should begin with students reading examples of persuasive writing. The examples may be of professional writing or student writing and should vary in quality to enhance students' ability to evaluate critically and understand fully the elements of persuasive discourse. An example of poor writing can demonstrate an obvious failure to anticipate and address a reader's response to

Chapter 4
Content Standards
and Instructional
Practices—
Grades Four
Through Eight

Eighth Grade

Curricular and
Instructional
Profile

**Instructional
Design**
(Continued)

the arguments put forth. A strong example that powerfully illustrates this concept should also be used.

The number of examples should vary according to student mastery of the persuasive text structures. Although students should be familiar with the elements of persuasive discourse by this time, the level of previous knowledge is likely to vary. Fewer examples should be used with students who already have a good mastery of the text structure and more examples with students who do not.

After their critical reading of persuasive texts, students should have a good command of the basic elements of text structure common to most similar texts. They can then apply that understanding to writing their own persuasive compositions. The instruction in writing persuasive compositions should follow the same steps in the writing process used for all written compositions:

- Students should first plan their compositions and outline their arguments, possible reader objections to their arguments, and their own responses to those objections.
- During the revision phase of writing, teachers should focus on the elements of revision emphasized in the standards for this level as well as the standards for grammar and usage and manuscript form.

If teachers anticipate that students will have significant difficulty in writing a persuasive composition, they should consider having all students write on the same topic or have half of them take the *pro* position and half the *con* position on an issue. This approach offers more opportunities for students to help one another with the writing process and makes it easier for teachers to evaluate compositions, giving them more time to deliver additional instruction when needed.

Once students have successfully completed a persuasive composition, teachers can turn their attention to having the students deliver the same composition orally. Doing so saves instructional time that would otherwise be required to start from scratch to develop an oral persuasive argument. Moreover, teachers can focus directly on the rhetorical elements unique to oral presentations (e.g., gestures, intonation).

Note: Students will have an opportunity to develop an oral presentation from scratch elsewhere because the standards call for delivering an oral descriptive presentation but not for writing descriptive discourse.

Initially, students may be allowed to read their oral presentations and then work gradually toward delivering presentations from notes.

Chapter 4
Content Standards
and Instructional
Practices—
Grades Four
Through Eight

Eighth Grade

Curricular and
Instructional
Profile

**Instructional
Delivery**

Teachers introduce new concepts, using models and detailed strategies for acquiring new skills and knowledge. They should explicitly identify the elements of good discourse in argument and persuasion before the students analyze good and poor models.

The greatest number of students will experience success with the standards if teachers plan for scaffolded instruction, with varying levels of assistance being provided before students are expected to apply their knowledge and skill independently. A simple scaffolding device, for example, is a think sheet that students use during the prewriting stage of writing. The think sheet shows the basic outline for argument or persuasion discourse, helping to ensure that students do not omit crucial elements during their planning and helping them prepare better drafts.

Another scaffolding device particularly well suited to writing instruction is peer-mediated instruction or cooperative learning. This approach not only gives students additional instructional opportunities as they assist one another but helps establish the writer-reader relationship in a manner more realistic than having students write principally for the teacher.

Note: Caution is in order regarding peer-mediated instruction. As with all scaffolded instruction, peer-mediated instruction should be gradually eliminated for each topic taught to ensure that each student learns to use skill and knowledge completely and independently. Ultimately, students should be held individually accountable for meeting standards.

Assessment

Entry-Level
Assessment

1. *Entry-Level Assessment for Instructional Planning.* The nature of the material at this level makes it impractical to pretest students formally for prerequisite knowledge or knowledge of upcoming instruction. Each time new instruction begins, teachers should assess students' entry knowledge informally and briefly with questions or very short assignments (such as a short in-class writing assignment, which can indicate a great deal about student knowledge of several standards).

Monitoring
Student
Progress

2. *Monitoring Student Progress Toward the Instructional Objective.* All assignments can serve to assess student progress. Teachers must examine performance on such assignments and analyze the results to discover areas that require more explicit instruction, an alternative instructional strategy, or other supportive instructional methods.

Post-test
Assessment

3. *Post-test Assessment Toward the Standard.* State-required or district-required formal assessments give part of the picture of how well students achieve the standards. In addition, the

Chapter 4
Content Standards
and Instructional
Practices—
Grades Four
Through Eight

Eighth Grade

Curricular and
Instructional
Profile

Assessment
(Continued)

assignments that teachers use to grade students give a more complete picture of achievement. For example, examination of a written composition in final form should be part of the summative evaluation for students. That evaluation should assess individual accountability on assignments that students complete on their own rather than those completed cooperatively.

**Universal
Access**

Reading
Difficulties
or Disabilities

1. *Students with Reading Difficulties or Disabilities.* Students are likely to encounter two major obstacles to meeting the standards for persuasive discourse as well as many other standards at this level. First, difficulties in reading can forestall critical and analytical reading of appropriate grade-level examples of persuasive writing. Alternative reading material below grade level may be substituted. Although these students may not achieve the desired goals as to reading level, they should be able to reach other standards as their reading level improves. In addition, the use of aides or peer-mediated instruction can provide the students with additional assistance in their study of difficult vocabulary and syntax in their reading assignments.

As much as possible, struggling readers should be encouraged to work on reading fluency itself as an ongoing activity outside the language arts classroom. They might be helped by being tutored or by receiving assistance in study hall or in classes designed to address more serious reading problems.

Other obstacles for lower performers at this level are writing mechanics in general and handwriting and spelling in particular. Research shows that students identified as having learning disabilities are often preempted from success in writing because the cognitive requirements of writing mechanics are too demanding.

General education teachers may be limited in accommodating major deficiencies they observe in their students' use of writing mechanics. Such students can benefit from peer-mediated, scaffolded instruction and from any outside support that can be arranged. Ultimately, the most successful accommodation for students at this level may be word processing or typing. Additional strategies may include the use of oral presentations, dramas, models, or dictation.

Advanced
Learners

2. *Students Who Are Advanced Learners.* Higher-performing students can follow the same curriculum as their normally achieving peers but should do so in greater depth and complexity and with more independence. Their persuasive arguments can be longer, more sophisticated, or better re-

175

Chapter 4
Content Standards
and Instructional
Practices—
Grades Four
Through Eight

**Universal
Access**
(Continued)

searched. Those who have mastered text structures can work on more complex writing involving a mixture of structures and can study the rhetorical devices and organizational patterns commonly found in speeches that can be used to recast their essays. Students can also be asked to argue both sides of an issue or be paired with another highly able student in a debate-style arrangement.

English Learners

3. *Students Who Are English Learners*

a. English learners benefit from specific instruction concerning argumentation.

b. English learners should be taught to avoid relying on such common slang words as *guy, kid, by the way,* and *stuff* as well as such general words as *thing, nice,* and *kind* in their writing.

c. English learners will experience difficulty in paraphrasing because they lack depth of vocabulary. They should be taught how to incorporate quotations into their texts to support their arguments and to reference appropriately and correctly.

d. Because students will present opposing views and explain why their view is better than that of others, they must be taught such grammatical structures as comparisons. Transitional devices (such as *first, second, to conclude,* and *in summary*) might also be taught.

e. English learners should be encouraged to practice before giving an oral presentation and should be allowed to use a prop or visual that will aid them during their presentation.

f. Teachers should provide corrective feedback consistently at the revising and editing stages to help English learners develop their English skills.

g. Teachers must provide students with straightforward assessments of their proficiency in English at every stage of instruction so that students understand what they can do to improve.

**Instructional
Materials**

Instructional materials should be provided in abundance for teachers to use with students who possess a broad range of abilities. Instead of presenting ideas for working with special-needs students in a sentence or two, for example, the instructional materials should provide many ready-to-go items for additional practice and instructional opportunities for English learners and students with learning difficulties. Similarly, several substantial resources or alternate assignments should be provided for high-performing students. Teachers cannot realistically be expected to invest long hours in finding or developing those resources.

Chapter 4
Content Standards
and Instructional
Practices—
Grades Four
Through Eight

Eighth Grade

English–Language Arts Content Standards

Reading

1.0 Word Analysis, Fluency, and Systematic Vocabulary Development

Students use their knowledge of word origins and word relationships, as well as historical and literary context clues, to determine the meaning of specialized vocabulary and to understand the precise meaning of grade-level-appropriate words.

Vocabulary and Concept Development

1.1 Analyze idioms, analogies, metaphors, and similes to infer the literal and figurative meanings of phrases.

1.2 Understand the most important points in the history of English language and use common word origins to determine the historical influences on English word meanings.

1.3 Use word meanings within the appropriate context and show ability to verify those meanings by definition, restatement, example, comparison, or contrast.

2.0 Reading Comprehension (Focus on Informational Materials)

Students read and understand grade-level-appropriate material. They describe and connect the essential ideas, arguments, and perspectives of the text by using their knowledge of text structure, organization, and purpose. The selections in *Recommended*

Readings in Literature, Kindergarten Through Grade Eight illustrate the quality and complexity of the materials to be read by students. In addition, students read one million words annually on their own, including a good representation of narrative and expository text (e.g., classic and contemporary literature, magazines, newspapers, online information).

Structural Features of Informational Materials

2.1 Compare and contrast the features and elements of consumer materials to gain meaning from documents (e.g., warranties, contracts, product information, instruction manuals).

2.2 Analyze text that uses proposition and support patterns.

Comprehension and Analysis of Grade-Level-Appropriate Text

2.3 Find similarities and differences between texts in the treatment, scope, or organization of ideas.

2.4 Compare the original text to a summary to determine whether the summary accurately captures the main ideas, includes critical details, and conveys the underlying meaning.

2.5 Understand and explain the use of a complex mechanical device by following technical directions.

2.6 Use information from a variety of consumer, workplace, and public documents to explain a situation or decision and to solve a problem.

177

Chapter 4
Content Standards
and Instructional
Practices—
Grades Four
Through Eight

Expository Critique

2.7   Evaluate the unity, coherence, logic, internal consistency, and structural patterns of text.

3.0   Literary Response and Analysis

Students read and respond to historically or culturally significant works of literature that reflect and enhance their studies of history and social science. They clarify the ideas and connect them to other literary works. The selections in *Recommended Readings in Literature, Kindergarten Through Grade Eight* illustrate the quality and complexity of the materials to be read by students.

Structural Features of Literature

3.1   Determine and articulate the relationship between the purposes and characteristics of different forms of poetry (e.g., ballad, lyric, couplet, epic, elegy, ode, sonnet).

Narrative Analysis of Grade-Level-Appropriate Text

3.2   Evaluate the structural elements of the plot (e.g., subplots, parallel episodes, climax), the plot's development, and the way in which conflicts are (or are not) addressed and resolved.

3.3   Compare and contrast motivations and reactions of literary characters from different historical eras confronting similar situations or conflicts.

3.4   Analyze the relevance of the setting (e.g., place, time, customs) to the mood, tone, and meaning of the text.

3.5   Identify and analyze recurring themes (e.g., good versus evil) across traditional and contemporary works.

3.6   Identify significant literary devices (e.g., metaphor, symbolism, dialect, irony) that define a writer's style and use those elements to interpret the work.

Literary Criticism

3.7   Analyze a work of literature, showing how it reflects the heritage, traditions, attitudes, and beliefs of its author. (Biographical approach)

Writing

1.0   Writing Strategies

Students write clear, coherent, and focused essays. The writing exhibits students' awareness of audience and purpose. Essays contain formal introductions, supporting evidence, and conclusions. Students progress through the stages of the writing process as needed.

Organization and Focus

1.1   Create compositions that establish a controlling impression, have a coherent thesis, and end with a clear and well-supported conclusion.

1.2   Establish coherence within and among paragraphs through effective transitions, parallel structures, and similar writing techniques.

1.3   Support theses or conclusions with analogies, paraphrases, quotations, opinions from authorities, comparisons, and similar devices.

Research and Technology

1.4   Plan and conduct multiple-step information searches by using computer networks and modems.

1.5   Achieve an effective balance between researched information and original ideas.

Evaluation and Revision

1.6   Revise writing for word choice; appropriate organization; consistent point of view; and transitions between paragraphs, passages, and ideas.

2.0   Writing Applications (Genres and Their Characteristics)

Students write narrative, expository, persuasive, and descriptive essays of at least 500 to 700 words in each genre. Student writing demonstrates a command of standard American English and the research, organizational, and drafting strategies outlined in Writing Standard 1.0.

Chapter 4
Content Standards
and Instructional
Practices—
Grades Four
Through Eight

Eighth Grade

English–Language
Arts Content
Standards

Using the writing strategies of grade eight outlined in Writing Standard 1.0, students:

2.1 Write biographies, autobiographies, short stories, or narratives:

a. Relate a clear, coherent incident, event, or situation by using well-chosen details.

b. Reveal the significance of, or the writer's attitude about, the subject.

c. Employ narrative and descriptive strategies (e.g., relevant dialogue, specific action, physical description, background description, comparison or contrast of characters).

2.2 Write responses to literature:

a. Exhibit careful reading and insight in their interpretations.

b. Connect the student's own responses to the writer's techniques and to specific textual references.

c. Draw supported inferences about the effects of a literary work on its audience.

d. Support judgments through references to the text, other works, other authors, or to personal knowledge.

2.3 Write research reports:

a. Define a thesis.

b. Record important ideas, concepts, and direct quotations from significant information sources and paraphrase and summarize all perspectives on the topic, as appropriate.

c. Use a variety of primary and secondary sources and distinguish the nature and value of each.

d. Organize and display information on charts, maps, and graphs.

2.4 Write persuasive compositions:

a. Include a well-defined thesis (i.e., one that makes a clear and knowledgeable judgment).

b. Present detailed evidence, examples, and reasoning to support arguments, differentiating between facts and opinion.

c. Provide details, reasons, and examples, arranging them effectively by anticipating and answering reader concerns and counterarguments.

2.5 Write documents related to career development, including simple business letters and job applications:

a. Present information purposefully and succinctly and meet the needs of the intended audience.

b. Follow the conventional format for the type of document (e.g., letter of inquiry, memorandum).

2.6 Write technical documents:

a. Identify the sequence of activities needed to design a system, operate a tool, or explain the bylaws of an organization.

b. Include all the factors and variables that need to be considered.

c. Use formatting techniques (e.g., headings, differing fonts) to aid comprehension.

Written and Oral English Language Conventions

The standards for written and oral English language conventions have been placed between those for writing and for listening and speaking because these conventions are essential to both sets of skills.

1.0 Written and Oral English Language Conventions

Students write and speak with a command of standard English conventions appropriate to this grade level.

Sentence Structure

1.1 Use correct and varied sentence types and sentence openings to present a lively and effective personal style.

1.2 Identify and use parallelism, including similar grammatical forms, in all written discourse to present items in a series and items juxtaposed for emphasis.

179

Chapter 4
Content Standards
and Instructional
Practices—
Grades Four
Through Eight

Eighth Grade

English–Language
Arts Content
Standards

1.3 Use subordination, coordination, apposition, and other devices to indicate clearly the relationship between ideas.

Grammar

1.4 Edit written manuscripts to ensure that correct grammar is used.

Punctuation and Capitalization

1.5 Use correct punctuation and capitalization.

Spelling

1.6 Use correct spelling conventions.

Listening and Speaking

1.0 Listening and Speaking Strategies

Students deliver focused, coherent presentations that convey ideas clearly and relate to the background and interests of the audience. They evaluate the content of oral communication.

Comprehension

1.1 Analyze oral interpretations of literature, including language choice and delivery, and the effect of the interpretations on the listener.

1.2 Paraphrase a speaker's purpose and point of view and ask relevant questions concerning the speaker's content, delivery, and purpose.

Organization and Delivery of Oral Communication

1.3 Organize information to achieve particular purposes by matching the message, vocabulary, voice modulation, expression, and tone to the audience and purpose.

1.4 Prepare a speech outline based upon a chosen pattern of organization, which generally includes an introduction; transitions, previews, and summaries; a logically developed body; and an effective conclusion.

1.5 Use precise language, action verbs, sensory details, appropriate and colorful

modifiers, and the active rather than the passive voice in ways that enliven oral presentations.

1.6 Use appropriate grammar, word choice, enunciation, and pace during formal presentations.

1.7 Use audience feedback (e.g., verbal and nonverbal cues):
   a. Reconsider and modify the organizational structure or plan.
   b. Rearrange words and sentences to clarify the meaning.

Analysis and Evaluation of Oral and Media Communications

1.8 Evaluate the credibility of a speaker (e.g., hidden agendas, slanted or biased material).

1.9 Interpret and evaluate the various ways in which visual image makers (e.g., graphic artists, illustrators, news photographers) communicate information and affect impressions and opinions.

2.0 Speaking Applications (Genres and Their Characteristics)

Students deliver well-organized formal presentations employing traditional rhetorical strategies (e.g., narration, exposition, persuasion, description). Student speaking demonstrates a command of standard American English and the organizational and delivery strategies outlined in Listening and Speaking Standard 1.0.

Using the speaking strategies of grade eight outlined in Listening and Speaking Standard 1.0, students:

2.1 Deliver narrative presentations (e.g., biographical, autobiographical):
   a. Relate a clear, coherent incident, event, or situation by using well-chosen details.
   b. Reveal the significance of, and the subject's attitude about, the incident, event, or situation.
   c. Employ narrative and descriptive strategies (e.g., relevant dialogue,

Chapter 4
Content Standards
and Instructional
Practices—
Grades Four
Through Eight

Eighth Grade

English–Language
Arts Content
Standards

specific action, physical description, background description, comparison or contrast of characters).

2.2 Deliver oral responses to literature:

a. Interpret a reading and provide insight.
b. Connect the students' own responses to the writer's techniques and to specific textual references.
c. Draw supported inferences about the effects of a literary work on its audience.
d. Support judgments through references to the text, other works, other authors, or personal knowledge.

2.3 Deliver research presentations:

a. Define a thesis.
b. Record important ideas, concepts, and direct quotations from significant information sources and paraphrase and summarize all relevant perspectives on the topic, as appropriate.

c. Use a variety of primary and secondary sources and distinguish the nature and value of each.
d. Organize and record information on charts, maps, and graphs.

2.4 Deliver persuasive presentations:

a. Include a well-defined thesis (i.e., one that makes a clear and knowledgeable judgment).
b. Differentiate fact from opinion and support arguments with detailed evidence, examples, and reasoning.
c. Anticipate and answer listener concerns and counterarguments effectively through the inclusion and arrangement of details, reasons, examples, and other elements.
d. Maintain a reasonable tone.

2.5 Recite poems (of four to six stanzas), sections of speeches, or dramatic soliloquies, using voice modulation, tone, and gestures expressively to enhance the meaning.

Content Standards and Instructional Practices

Grades Nine Through Twelve

By the twelfth grade students are expected each year to read independently two million words of running text. . . . For many students that amount of independent reading will not occur without strategic and systematic guidance in their selection of text and reinforcement of independent reading habits.

Many of the general topics in the standards for grades nine through twelve are similar to those for the earlier grades. For instance, the standards continue to emphasize reading informational and literary text critically, writing compositions according to major text structures and genres, and making oral presentations. By the twelfth grade students are expected each year to read independently two million words of running text (see page 209 in this chapter). That amount is twice that called for in earlier grades. The content of the reading should include a wide variety of

Chapter 5
Content Standards
and Instructional
Practices—
Grades Nine
Through Twelve

classic and contemporary literature, magazines, newspapers, and online information. For many students that amount of independent reading will not occur without strategic and systematic guidance in their selection of text and reinforcement of independent reading habits. The goal of two million words of annual independent reading should be a logical extension of the eighth-grade goal of one million words.

Comprehension standards for informational materials and literature require that students demonstrate more sophisticated strategies as they analyze, evaluate, and elaborate on what is read, critique the credibility of information, and compare works and provide evidence to support ideas. A major difference between the standards for grades nine through twelve and those for earlier grade levels is that all reading in the ninth through twelfth grades takes place in conjunction with grade-appropriate materials, which become increasingly long and complex as students advance.

Writing and oral presentations also become more sophisticated and complex in grades nine through twelve.

Writing and oral presentations also become more sophisticated and complex in grades nine through twelve. By the ninth grade students have had plentiful opportunities to read and compose narrative, expository, persuasive, and descriptive text. (See the discussion on writing as a process at the beginning of Chapter 3.) Composition standards in grades nine through

twelve require that writers combine the individual text genres to produce texts of at least 1,500 words each (see pages 195 and 211 in this chapter). Concurrently, writers apply and refine their command of the writing process and writing conventions.

Many standards for grades nine through twelve are either unique to those grades or receive far greater emphasis than in earlier grades. Such standards include:

- Strong emphasis on research-based discourse (writing and delivering research-based compositions and oral presentations and reading research discourse critically)
- Incorporating technology into the language arts as a tool for conducting research or creating finished manuscripts and multimedia presentations
- Focus on analytically critiquing a variety of media
- Greater emphasis on the language arts as applied to work and careers (e.g., conducting interviews, filling out job applications, writing business letters, performing technical writing)

As in previous grades new comprehension and writing strategies to assist readers in their understanding and use of written language will require instruction. Students will need explicit instruction as they learn and apply more sophisticated and complex strategies.

183

Chapter 5
Content Standards
and Instructional
Practices—
Grades Nine
Through Twelve

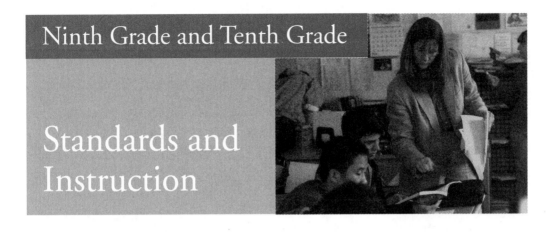

Ninth Grade and Tenth Grade

Standards and Instruction

I n the ninth and tenth grades, students continue to apply the knowledge and skills acquired in the earlier grades but in more refined and sophisticated ways. In some cases standards address new goals, such as mastering appropriate interviewing techniques. Regardless, emphasis continues to be centered on analyzing literature in greater depth, analyzing career-related and other informational discourse, completing more complex writing assignments, and giving more extensive oral presentations. The strands to be emphasized at the ninth-grade and tenth-grade levels are listed in the adjacent column under the appropriate domains.

The following sections profile focus areas within each of the strands.

Reading

1.0 Word Analysis, Fluency, and Systematic Vocabulary Development
2.0 Reading Comprehension (Focus on Informational Materials)
3.0 Literary Response and Analysis

Writing

1.0 Writing Strategies
2.0 Writing Applications (Genres and Their Characteristics)

Written and Oral English-Language Conventions

1.0 Written and Oral English-Language Conventions

Listening and Speaking

1.0 Listening and Speaking Strategies
2.0 Speaking Applications (Genres and Their Characteristics)

Chapter 5
Content Standards
and Instructional
Practices—
Grades Nine
Through Twelve

**Ninth Grade and
Tenth Grade**

Standards and
Instruction

Reading **Word Analysis,
Fluency, and
Systematic Vocabulary
Development**

Applying etymological and morphological knowledge to word meanings continues to be emphasized, particularly words derived from Greek, Roman, and Norse mythology. Students also distinguish between the denotative and connotative meanings of words and learn about the power of connotative meanings.

Instruction in word derivation should take place throughout the year as a relatively small part of several lessons. In addition, all work in vocabulary study should be reviewed cumulatively and periodically throughout the year. New vocabulary—especially when it represents new conceptual knowledge—is rarely acquired without such review. Often, students at this level may study word derivations independently, but their work should be closely monitored by the teacher.

Because the standards for the ninth and tenth grades emphasize Greek, Roman, and Norse mythology as sources for word derivations, some reading assignments should involve those topics.

Reading **Reading
Comprehension**

Comprehension and analysis of informational materials have not been focused on in language arts instruction at the high school level. Instead, emphasis has traditionally been placed on the study of literary works. Although anthologies of literature now provide many nonfiction selections (and suggested learning activities to accompany the selections), teachers may need to expand classroom collections of expository readings of various lengths. In addition, effective strategies for studying expository texts vary somewhat from the strategies used for narrative texts (fiction and biography). For example, students need to recognize the structural features and organization unique to nonnarrative texts, such as the use of headings and subheadings. Much of the expository reading done in high school is taken from textbooks and related academic readings assigned in classes other than English class. Therefore, teachers in all disciplines should share responsibility for student achievement in this area.

Students are expected to develop critical-thinking skills appropriate in all academic areas, such as:

- Synthesizing the content and ideas from several sources focused on a single issue or written by a single author
- Producing evidence of comprehension by paraphrasing ideas and connecting them to other sources and to related topics
- Extending ideas presented in primary or secondary sources through original analysis, evaluation, and elaboration

In the ninth and tenth grades, the structural features of workplace documents (e.g., business letters, memos, minutes, and procedural manuals) receive primary attention in contrast to the focus on consumer materials in the eighth grade. In addition, students are required to demonstrate their ability to follow the types of sophisticated technical directions found in advanced software programs or Internet resources. Students are likely to experience difficulties with technology guides because the terminology is unclear or the material is not well written or user-friendly. Instruction should help students identify the reasons for technological material to be difficult to follow. Moreover, the instruction should tie into students' own expository writing.

185

Chapter 5
Content Standards
and Instructional
Practices—
Grades Nine
Through Twelve

**NInth Grade and
Tenth Grade**

Standards and
Instruction

Students in the ninth and tenth grades are required to produce bibliographies of reference materials, using a variety of documents. Students preparing research reports in high school most frequently use the works-cited model (including only reference sources quoted or otherwise referred to in the student work) rather than the more extensive bibliography (including all materials used for background and research). Within the text students more frequently use a parenthetical model (author-date) rather than endnotes or footnotes. For students to understand and appreciate the function of reference citations, they should consider the types of problems researchers would have if one or more elements were missing from a citation or reference. Acceptable formats for presenting this information include the guidelines published by the Modern Language Association and by the American Psychological Association. Whichever is selected, it should be used meticulously and consistently throughout the document.

Reading Literary Response and Analysis

The literary response and analysis strand is an area of comfort and expertise for English teachers at the high school level. Indeed, the opportunity to share literary works with students is a common motivating force in a person's decision to become a high school English teacher.

Typically, novels are the core texts for literary analysis in high school and are supplemented with short stories, essays, and poetry. Teachers should note that current anthologies of literature are much more than compilations of short stories and poems and offer a wealth of instructional strategies and activities, many of which integrate several language arts standards. To meet the demanding requirements dictated by those standards, teachers must ensure that many student assignments and activities serve more than a single purpose in the curriculum.

In reading literary pieces, students in the ninth and tenth grades should analyze such elements as the following:

- Character, interactions among characters, and interactions between characters and plot
- Time and sequence (e.g., foreshadowing and flashbacks)
- Comparison of universal themes in several works
- Literary elements, such as figurative language, allegory, and symbolism
- Ambiguities, contradictions, and ironies in the text
- Voice or persona (point of view)

Although the elements of literature at this level are fundamental and have been targeted in the earlier grades, many are sophisticated concepts that require explicit instruction in strategies before mastery can be achieved. For instance, figurative language holds a cluster of challenging concepts. The goal here for students is not simply to define literary elements but to understand them in depth as an aid to reading and creating expressive discourse of their own. As a scaffolding technique, students should be prompted to look for very specific elements in reading. (*Example:* "Look for the metaphor in which something is compared to birds. Also, look at the imagery the narrator uses to describe her garden.")

By the end of high school, students are expected to be familiar with the purposes and characteristics of the major genres of literature. These standards identify the grade-level focus as follows: grade seven—prose; grade eight—poetry; grades nine and ten—drama; and grades eleven and twelve—subgenres that span genres, such as satire.

Chapter 5
Content Standards
and Instructional
Practices—
Grades Nine
Through Twelve

Ninth Grade and
Tenth Grade

Standards and
Instruction

One feature of this standard takes place largely outside the classroom. Students in the ninth and tenth grades are expected to read independently about one and one-half million words annually. (One million words are expected to be read annually by the end of the eighth grade and two million words annually by the end of the twelfth grade.) For the grade-level reader, two million words translate to about 11 pages per day or one 335-page book each month.

Although instructional formats and strategies used for outside reading have much in common for formats and strategies used in teaching core literature works, there are significant differences. The students' choices are more important in outside reading and may result in less diverse selections because young readers typically choose to focus on a single author, topic, or genre for a period of time. Reading should not be limited to works of fiction or nonfiction but should include magazines, especially those of special interest to the students; newspapers; and online sources. A variety of methods are available to assess reading done outside the classroom, including student-maintained reading logs and book reports in various formats. In relation to the standard, the instructional focus should be placed on the reading itself rather than on the final report on the reading.

Independent reading significantly improves a student's reading comprehension and vocabulary and increases familiarity with models of good writing and conventions of writing and spelling. It also serves an important affective purpose; that is, to develop a lifelong appreciation for reading for pleasure and information. Recent research indicates that the volume of reading also affects general cognitive development.

Writing   Writing Strategies

At this level writing extends the emphasis in earlier grades on establishing a coherent controlling theme that conveys a clear and distinctive perspective on the subject and maintains a consistent tone and focus throughout the piece of writing. Coherence can be a difficult concept for many students. On occasion students should work cooperatively in revising for coherence, using scaffolded think sheets as guides for helping one another obtain useful feedback and revise text. They are likely to need continuing assistance in developing themes that are clear and neither too broad nor too narrow for their targeted document's purpose and length.

This standard also includes requirements in research and technology. Students in the ninth and tenth grades should be competent in:

- Using clear, nontrivial research questions and suitable research methodology from primary and secondary sources
- Synthesizing information from multiple sources to support the thesis
- Identifying complexities, discrepancies, and differing perspectives in the researched information
- Embedding quotations and citations skillfully and using bibliographic conventions appropriately

Students are also expected to use advanced publishing software to create final documents. Ready access to technology hardware, software, and Internet-based resources is a prerequisite to student proficiency in this area. As with reading for information, responsibility for instruction in research and technology skills in high school might be shared with teachers of other disciplines that require such skills.

187

Chapter 5
Content Standards
and Instructional
Practices—
Grades Nine
Through Twelve

NInth Grade and
Tenth Grade

Standards and
Instruction

Writing   Writing Applications

This standard identifies the kinds of writing that students in the ninth and tenth grades are expected to produce. These writing assignments allow students to apply the general strategies of organization and focus, revision, and research methodology described in the standard.

The specific genres or text structures practiced in the eighth grade continue in the ninth and tenth grades, with increasing sophistication and length. When appropriate, student texts should be 1,500 words in length (about five to six pages, typed and double-spaced).

The most important considerations for teaching students to write various text structures are:

1. Interrelating different standards that all address the same text structure
2. Providing models of each text structure, including examples of student writing
3. Identifying the critical elements of each text structure for students
4. Providing instructional opportunities to learn about writing for a variety of purposes and helping students achieve a sense of audience

Written and Oral English-Language Conventions

Conventions emphasized at this level include:

- Sentence and paragraph structure: main and subordinate clauses, phrases, parallel structure, consistency of verb tenses, placement of modifiers
- Punctuation: semicolons, colons, ellipses, hyphens
- Grammar and usage, diction, syntax
- Correct spelling
- Manuscript conventions: title page, pagination, spacing and margins
- Appropriate citations for source and support material

These standards are mostly the continuation of standards from earlier grade levels. Some students will need explicit remedial instruction for some standards that were previously introduced but not mastered. The use of individualized instructional software is one way in which teachers can efficiently address individual student deficits.

Many students will need help with some aspect of the conventions standards. Although certain standards should require very little instruction (e.g., manuscript conventions), some usage topics will most likely plague many students (e.g., whether to use *affect* or *effect*; case of pronouns).

Listening and Speaking
Listening and Speaking Strategies

Generally, these standards fall into two categories, delivering oral communications and analyzing oral and media communications. (*Note:* Not all of the standards are listed. See the *English–Language Arts Content Standards* for the complete list.)

Delivering Oral Communications

- Apply standard structural elements of expressive discourse.
- Use various visual aids and electronic media.
- Use devices of oral rhetoric (intonation, gestures, eye contact).
- Produce concise notes for extemporaneous oral presentations.

Analyzing Oral and Media Presentations

- Compare how different media cover the same event.

Chapter 5
Content Standards
and Instructional
Practices—
Grades Nine
Through Twelve

Ninth Grade and
Tenth Grade

Standards and
Instruction

- Compare significant historical speeches and the rhetorical devices used.
- Analyze structural elements of oral and media presentations.
- Analyze rhetorical elements.
- Analyze orally presented arguments.
- Evaluate the aesthetic effects and techniques of media presentations.

The basic structural elements of oral presentations overlap significantly with written expression: logical patterns of organization, techniques for developing introductions and conclusions, development of a clear thesis, and so on. For that reason instruction should be made efficient by addressing the structural elements in conjunction with oral and written expression. Students can present orally the compositions they have written, giving them an opportunity to focus on the types of rhetorical elements unique to speech.

So that students can be assisted in analyzing oral and media presentations, they should first be taught the basic structures of such presentations through the use of models and formal instruction. They are thereby equipped with the tools they need for their own analyses. For example, students might first read a script for a situation comedy and then watch other comedies, evaluating the extent to which basic elements recur and identifying the elements of tone, timing, and delivery that contribute to creating humor.

Listening and Speaking
Speaking Applications

Students are required to deliver presentations of the following types: narrative (autobiographical or fictional); expository (research); oral responses to literature; argument or persuasion; and descriptive.

Most of the genres in the standards for oral presentations are also targets of standards at other levels and within other domains. Such strongly related standards at this level should be taught in conjunction with one another. Some oral presentations should be carefully prepared and rehearsed; others should be extemporaneous.

Students in the ninth and tenth grades are also required to apply appropriate interviewing techniques. This skill is useful in information gathering, such as interviewing a Vietnam veteran about wartime experiences, and also relates directly to students' future career and job opportunities. Students should be provided with background scenarios for interviews and then can work on interview techniques in cooperative learning groups. Interviews are good examples of activities that combine listening and speaking skills.

Text structures and skills in listening and reading are connected in the same way in which speaking and writing are connected. Just as reading comprehension is more than decoding and pronunciation, listening is more than simply hearing spoken words. Students in the ninth and tenth grades are expected to analyze and evaluate a speaker's arguments and tone and the techniques used to create them. The use of comparison and contrast is an effective instructional strategy to help students note the key features in oral presentations. For example, students might compare and contrast Lincoln's "Gettysburg Address" and Martin Luther King's "I Have a Dream" or Shakespeare's *Henry V* and Kenneth Branagh's 1990 film version of that play. Students are also required to evaluate the clarity, quality, and effectiveness of live speakers (including their peers) and of media presentations.

Please see Appendix B for examples of standards that span domains and strands.

189

Chapter 5
Content Standards
and Instructional
Practices—
Grades Nine
Through Twelve

Ninth Grade and Tenth Grade

Curricular and Instructional Profile

Reading Standard 1.3

DOMAIN	STRAND	SUBSTRAND	STANDARD	
Reading	1.0 Word analysis, fluency, and systematic vocabulary development	Vocabulary and concept development	1.3	Identify Greek, Roman, and Norse mythology and use the knowledge to understand the origin and meaning of new words.

Prerequisite standards. **Seventh-Grade Word Analysis, Fluency, and Systematic Vocabulary Development Standards 1.2, 1.3.**

Standard 1.2: Use knowledge of Greek, Latin, and Anglo-Saxon roots and affixes to understand content-area vocabulary.

Standard 1.3: Clarify word meanings through the use of definition, example, restatement, or contrast.

Corequisite standard. **Ninth-Grade and Tenth-Grade Word Analysis, Fluency, and Systematic Vocabulary Development Standard 1.1:** Identify and use the literal and figurative meanings of words and understand word derivations.

Curricular and Instructional Decisions

Instructional Objective	Develop vocabulary systematically, applying etymology and morphology, with particular emphasis being given to the contributions of Greek, Roman, and Norse mythology to English vocabulary.
Instructional Design	Beginning in the fourth grade, standards have emphasized the use of internal etymological and morphological cues as well as external context cues. Therefore, students should be very familiar with contributions that morphological and etymological cues can make to vocabulary development.

Chapter 5
Content Standards
and Instructional
Practices—
Grades Nine
Through Twelve

**NInth Grade and
Tenth Grade**

Curricular and
Instructional
Profile

Instructional Design
(Continued)

In the ninth and tenth grades, that emphasis extends to analyzing words according to etymology and morphology, specifically to the contributions of Greek, Roman, and Norse mythology to the English language. Such an analysis should include comparing literal etymological meanings with meanings currently in use. Words (e.g., roots) selected for initial instruction can lead to many other words, all of which contain that meaning (e.g., *solar, solstice, solarium*). Other useful roots can then be introduced (e.g., *fortune,* a word derived from Fortuna, Roman goddess of luck and vengeance; or *cloth,* derived from one of the three sisters of fate in Greek mythology, Clotho, who spun the thread of life in her spindle).

Words derived from mythology are often based on proper names, such as Narcissus as the basis for *narcissistic.* Students can study this category of word derivation beyond mythology as well. For instance, the word *maverick* is derived from the name of a Texas cattle rancher (Samuel A. Maverick), who did not brand his calves.

Instructional Delivery

Many tools are available to students for working independently and successfully on morphological and etymological word derivations. Textbooks should supply the fundamentals for the study of derivations and effective activities for independent application. Several trade books found in the reference section of most bookstores also address the vocabulary and conceptual development standards well (e.g., books on word origins, morphemically based vocabulary books, dictionaries). Many of the tools are also available through the Internet.

Throughout the year teachers, by themselves or with the aid of textbooks, should briefly review the fundamentals of instruction in derivations and particularly useful affixes and roots.

Assessment

Entry-Level
Assessment

1. *Entry-Level Assessment for Instructional Planning.* Students can be tested on their knowledge of high-frequency prefixes, suffixes, and some nonword bases. Tasks should include (a) asking students the meanings of some of the morphological elements; and (b) giving students some meanings and asking them to identify parts that correspond. Students should also be evaluated on their ability to break a word into its component parts.

Monitoring
Student
Progress

2. *Monitoring Student Progress Toward the Instructional Objective.* The most important characteristic of monitoring student progress in areas such as vocabulary (and oral and written language conventions) is *cumulative* monitoring; that is, checking periodically to determine whether students have

191

Chapter 5
Content Standards
and Instructional
Practices—
Grades Nine
Through Twelve

Assessment
(Continued)

Post-test
Assessment

retained the knowledge and skill learned throughout the school year. If they have not, teachers should provide additional opportunities for study and review.

3. *Post-test Assessment Toward the Standard.* Students should demonstrate their ability to extract the meanings of unfamiliar words through internal morphological and etymological cues (as well as context cues). They should show their work by indicating which meanings of which word parts led them to their inferences of word meanings.

**Universal
Access**

Reading
Difficulties
or Disabilities

Advanced
Learners

1. *Students with Reading Difficulties or Disabilities.* Some students may require more instruction and practice than do others in extracting meanings. Support should be provided through scaffolded activities, explicit instruction, and peer assistance.

2. *Students Who Are Advanced Learners.* These students can be expected not only to work on systematic vocabulary development independently but also to conduct sophisticated analyses of words. (*Note:* The morphology and derivation of many words are not always clear. For example, linguistic experts are uncertain about the derivation and morphological makeup of the word *embarrassed.*) Advanced students can investigate such words and offer hypotheses regarding their derivation and makeup, citing evidence and sources to support those hypotheses. These students can also investigate esoteric derivations, such as the relationship between the Latin meaning of *port* and words such as *inopportune* and *porterhouse steak.* Applications involving sophisticated linguistic puzzles also offer challenges to highly motivated students.

English Learners

3. *Students Who Are English Learners.* English learners often acquire the meaning of new words without being able to use them because they have not learned the grammatical rules governing usage and lack knowledge of the specific contexts in which the words are used. For instance, they may learn the meanings of such sophisticated words as *torrid, pungent,* and *umbrage* without having any idea how to use them in communication. (Consider, for instance, the learner who wrote, "She burned her tongue on the *torrid* food.") Teachers should provide English learners with information concerning not only the origins of words but also the use of words. English learners need to be helped to use the words appropriately in sentences. English learners often have great difficulty in acquiring more basic academic words (such as *comprise, denote, signify, summarize,* and *mention*) than words of Greek, Latin, and Old Norse derivation. However, they benefit from instruction in the

Chapter 5
Content Standards
and Instructional
Practices—
Grades Nine
Through Twelve

**NInth Grade and
Tenth Grade**

Curricular and
Instructional
Profile

Universal Access (Continued)

academic words, which appear in great number in middle school and high school textbooks. They also benefit from increased exposure to the words, opportunities to use them, and feedback as to usage.

Instructional Materials

Instructional materials should provide teachers with substantial means for teaching all the standards related to the more conventional language arts instruction: vocabulary, grammar and usage, spelling, capitalization, and punctuation. Students at this level will differ in their ability to use the conventions. Instructional materials should, therefore, be focused on independent activities that can be assigned as needed.

193

Chapter 5
Content Standards
and Instructional
Practices—
Grades Nine
Through Twelve

Ninth Grade and Tenth Grade

English–Language Arts Content Standards

Reading

1.0 Word Analysis, Fluency, and Systematic Vocabulary Development

Students apply their knowledge of word origins to determine the meaning of new words encountered in reading materials and use those words accurately.

Vocabulary and Concept Development

1.1 Identify and use the literal and figurative meanings of words and understand word derivations.

1.2. Distinguish between the denotative and connotative meanings of words and interpret the connotative power of words.

1.3 Identify Greek, Roman, and Norse mythology and use the knowledge to understand the origin and meaning of new words (e.g., the word *narcissistic* drawn from the myth of Narcissus and Echo).

2.0 Reading Comprehension (Focus on Informational Materials)

Students read and understand grade-level-appropriate material. They analyze the organizational patterns, arguments, and positions advanced. The selections in *Recommended Literature, Grades Nine Through Twelve* (1990) illustrate the quality and complexity of the materials to be read by students. In addition, by grade twelve, students read two million words annually on their own,

including a wide variety of classic and contemporary literature, magazines, newspapers, and online information. In grades nine and ten, students make substantial progress toward this goal.

Structural Features of Informational Materials

2.1 Analyze the structure and format of functional workplace documents, including the graphics and headers, and explain how authors use the features to achieve their purposes.

2.2 Prepare a bibliography of reference materials for a report using a variety of consumer, workplace, and public documents.

Comprehension and Analysis of Grade-Level-Appropriate Text

2.3 Generate relevant questions about readings on issues that can be researched.

2.4 Synthesize the content from several sources or works by a single author dealing with a single issue; paraphrase the ideas and connect them to other sources and related topics to demonstrate comprehension.

2.5 Extend ideas presented in primary or secondary sources through original analysis, evaluation, and elaboration.

2.6 Demonstrate use of sophisticated learning tools by following technical directions (e.g., those found with graphic calculators and specialized software programs and in access guides to World Wide Web sites on the Internet).

Chapter 5
Content Standards
and Instructional
Practices—
Grades Nine
Through Twelve

NInth Grade and
Tenth Grade

English–Language
Arts Content
Standards

Expository Critique

2.7 Critique the logic of functional documents by examining the sequence of information and procedures in anticipation of possible reader misunderstandings.

2.8 Evaluate the credibility of an author's argument or defense of a claim by critiquing the relationship between generalizations and evidence, the comprehensiveness of evidence, and the way in which the author's intent affects the structure and tone of the text (e.g., in professional journals, editorials, political speeches, primary source material).

3.0   Literary Response and Analysis

Students read and respond to historically or culturally significant works of literature that reflect and enhance their studies of history and social science. They conduct in-depth analyses of recurrent patterns and themes. The selections in *Recommended Literature, Grades Nine Through Twelve* illustrate the quality and complexity of the materials to be read by students.

Structural Features of Literature

3.1 Articulate the relationship between the expressed purposes and the characteristics of different forms of dramatic literature (e.g., comedy, tragedy, drama, dramatic monologue).

3.2 Compare and contrast the presentation of a similar theme or topic across genres to explain how the selection of genre shapes the theme or topic.

Narrative Analysis of Grade-Level-Appropriate Text

3.3 Analyze interactions between main and subordinate characters in a literary text (e.g., internal and external conflicts, motivations, relationships, influences) and explain the way those interactions affect the plot.

3.4 Determine characters' traits by what the characters say about themselves in narration, dialogue, dramatic monologue, and soliloquy.

3.5 Compare works that express a universal theme and provide evidence to support the ideas expressed in each work.

3.6 Analyze and trace an author's development of time and sequence, including the use of complex literary devices (e.g., foreshadowing, flashbacks).

3.7 Recognize and understand the significance of various literary devices, including figurative language, imagery, allegory, and symbolism, and explain their appeal.

3.8 Interpret and evaluate the impact of ambiguities, subtleties, contradictions, ironies, and incongruities in a text.

3.9 Explain how voice, persona, and the choice of a narrator affect characterization and the tone, plot, and credibility of a text.

3.10 Identify and describe the function of dialogue, scene designs, soliloquies, asides, and character foils in dramatic literature.

Literary Criticism

3.11 Evaluate the aesthetic qualities of style, including the impact of diction and figurative language on tone, mood, and theme, using the terminology of literary criticism. (Aesthetic approach)

3.12 Analyze the way in which a work of literature is related to the themes and issues of its historical period. (Historical approach)

Writing

1.0   Writing Strategies

Students write coherent and focused essays that convey a well-defined perspective and tightly reasoned argument. The writing demonstrates students' awareness of the audience and purpose. Students progress through the stages of the writing process as needed.

Organization and Focus

1.1 Establish a controlling impression or coherent thesis that conveys a clear and distinctive perspective on the subject and maintain a consistent tone and focus throughout the piece of writing.

Chapter 5
Content Standards
and Instructional
Practices—
Grades Nine
Through Twelve

Ninth Grade and
Tenth Grade
English–Language
Arts Content
Standards

1.2 Use precise language, action verbs, sensory details, appropriate modifiers, and the active rather than the passive voice.

Research and Technology

1.3 Use clear research questions and suitable research methods (e.g., library, electronic media, personal interview) to elicit and present evidence from primary and secondary sources.

1.4 Develop the main ideas within the body of the composition through supporting evidence (e.g., scenarios, commonly held beliefs, hypotheses, definitions).

1.5 Synthesize information from multiple sources and identify complexities and discrepancies in the information and the different perspectives found in each medium (e.g., almanacs, microfiche, news sources, in-depth field studies, speeches, journals, technical documents).

1.6 Integrate quotations and citations into a written text while maintaining the flow of ideas.

1.7 Use appropriate conventions for documentation in the text, notes, and bibliographies by adhering to those in style manuals (e.g., *Modern Language Association Handbook, The Chicago Manual of Style*).

1.8 Design and publish documents by using advanced publishing software and graphic programs.

Evaluation and Revision

1.9 Revise writing to improve the logic and coherence of the organization and controlling perspective, the precision of word choice, and the tone by taking into consideration the audience, purpose, and formality of the context.

2.0 Writing Applications (Genres and Their Characteristics)

Students combine the rhetorical strategies of narration, exposition, persuasion, and description to produce texts of at least 1,500 words each. Student writing demonstrates a command of standard American English and the research, organizational, and drafting strategies outlined in Writing Standard 1.0.

Using the writing strategies of grades nine and ten outlined in Writing Standard 1.0, students:

2.1 Write biographical or autobiographical narratives or short stories:

   a. Relate a sequence of events and communicate the significance of the events to the audience.

   b. Locate scenes and incidents in specific places.

   c. Describe with concrete sensory details the sights, sounds, and smells of a scene and the specific actions, movements, gestures, and feelings of the characters; use interior monologue to depict the characters' feelings.

   d. Pace the presentation of actions to accommodate changes in time and mood.

   e. Make effective use of descriptions of appearance, images, shifting perspectives, and sensory details.

2.2 Write responses to literature:

   a. Demonstrate a comprehensive grasp of the significant ideas of literary works.

   b. Support important ideas and viewpoints through accurate and detailed references to the text or to other works.

   c. Demonstrate awareness of the author's use of stylistic devices and an appreciation of the effects created.

   d. Identify and assess the impact of perceived ambiguities, nuances, and complexities within the text.

2.3 Write expository compositions, including analytical essays and research reports:

   a. Marshal evidence in support of a thesis and related claims, including information on all relevant perspectives.

   b. Convey information and ideas from primary and secondary sources accurately and coherently.

   c. Make distinctions between the relative value and significance of specific data, facts, and ideas.

Chapter 5
Content Standards
and Instructional
Practices---
Grades Nine
Through Twelve

**Ninth Grade and
Tenth Grade**

English–Language
Arts Content
Standards

d. Include visual aids by employing appropriate technology to organize and record information on charts, maps, and graphs.

e. Anticipate and address readers' potential misunderstandings, biases, and expectations.

f. Use technical terms and notations accurately.

2.4 Write persuasive compositions:

a. Structure ideas and arguments in a sustained and logical fashion.

b. Use specific rhetorical devices to support assertions (e.g., appeal to logic through reasoning; appeal to emotion or ethical belief; relate a personal anecdote, case study, or analogy).

c. Clarify and defend positions with precise and relevant evidence, including facts, expert opinions, quotations, and expressions of commonly accepted beliefs and logical reasoning.

d. Address readers' concerns, counter-claims, biases, and expectations.

2.5 Write business letters:

a. Provide clear and purposeful information and address the intended audience appropriately.

b. Use appropriate vocabulary, tone, and style to take into account the nature of the relationship with, and the knowledge and interests of, the recipients.

c. Highlight central ideas or images.

d. Follow a conventional style with page formats, fonts, and spacing that contribute to the documents' readability and impact.

2.6 Write technical documents (e.g., a manual on rules of behavior for conflict resolution, procedures for conducting a meeting, minutes of a meeting):

a. Report information and convey ideas logically and correctly.

b. Offer detailed and accurate specifications.

c. Include scenarios, definitions, and examples to aid comprehension (e.g., troubleshooting guide).

d. Anticipate readers' problems, mistakes, and misunderstandings.

Written and Oral English Language Conventions

The standards for written and oral English language conventions have been placed between those for writing and for listening and speaking because these conventions are essential to both sets of skills.

1.0 Written and Oral English Language Conventions

Students write and speak with a command of standard English conventions.

Grammar and Mechanics of Writing

1.1 Identify and correctly use clauses (e.g., main and subordinate), phrases (e.g., gerund, infinitive, and participial), and mechanics of punctuation (e.g., semicolons, colons, ellipses, hyphens).

1.2 Understand sentence construction (e.g., parallel structure, subordination, proper placement of modifiers) and proper English usage (e.g., consistency of verb tenses).

1.3 Demonstrate an understanding of proper English usage and control of grammar, paragraph and sentence structure, diction, and syntax.

Manuscript Form

1.4 Produce legible work that shows accurate spelling and correct use of the conventions of punctuation and capitalization.

1.5 Reflect appropriate manuscript requirements, including title page presentation, pagination, spacing and margins, and integration of source and support material (e.g., in-text citation, use of direct quotations, paraphrasing) with appropriate citations.

Chapter 5
Content Standards
and Instructional
Practices—
Grades Nine
Through Twelve

Listening and Speaking

1.0 Listening and Speaking Strategies

Students formulate adroit judgments about oral communication. They deliver focused and coherent presentations of their own that convey clear and distinct perspectives and solid reasoning. They use gestures, tone, and vocabulary tailored to the audience and purpose.

Comprehension

1.1 Formulate judgments about the ideas under discussion and support those judgments with convincing evidence.

1.2 Compare and contrast the ways in which media genres (e.g., televised news, news magazines, documentaries, online information) cover the same event.

Organization and Delivery of Oral Communication

1.3 Choose logical patterns of organization (e.g., chronological, topical, cause and effect) to inform and to persuade, by soliciting agreement or action, or to unite audiences behind a common belief or cause.

1.4 Choose appropriate techniques for developing the introduction and conclusion (e.g., by using literary quotations, anecdotes, references to authoritative sources).

1.5 Recognize and use elements of classical speech forms (e.g., introduction, first and second transitions, body, conclusion) in formulating rational arguments and applying the art of persuasion and debate.

1.6 Present and advance a clear thesis statement and choose appropriate types of proof (e.g., statistics, testimony, specific instances) that meet standard tests for evidence, including credibility, validity, and relevance.

1.7 Use props, visual aids, graphs, and electronic media to enhance the appeal and accuracy of presentations.

1.8 Produce concise notes for extemporaneous delivery.

1.9 Analyze the occasion and the interests of the audience and choose effective verbal and nonverbal techniques (e.g., voice, gestures, eye contact) for presentations.

Analysis and Evaluation of Oral and Media Communications

1.10 Analyze historically significant speeches (e.g., Abraham Lincoln's "Gettysburg Address," Martin Luther King, Jr.'s "I Have a Dream") to find the rhetorical devices and features that make them memorable.

1.11 Assess how language and delivery affect the mood and tone of the oral communication and make an impact on the audience.

1.12 Evaluate the clarity, quality, effectiveness, and general coherence of a speaker's important points, arguments, evidence, organization of ideas, delivery, diction, and syntax.

1.13 Analyze the types of arguments used by the speaker, including argument by causation, analogy, authority, emotion, and logic.

1.14 Identify the aesthetic effects of a media presentation and evaluate the techniques used to create them (e.g., compare Shakespeare's *Henry V* with Kenneth Branagh's 1990 film version).

2.0 Speaking Applications (Genres and Their Characteristics)

Students deliver polished formal and extemporaneous presentations that combine the traditional rhetorical strategies of narration, exposition, persuasion, and description. Student speaking demonstrates a command of standard American English and the organizational and delivery strategies outlined in Listening and Speaking Standard 1.0.

Chapter 5
Content Standards
and Instructional
Practices—
Grades Nine
Through Twelve

NInth Grade and
Tenth Grade

English–Language
Arts Content
Standards

Using the speaking strategies of grades nine
and ten outlined in Listening and Speaking
Standard 1.0, students:

2.1. Deliver narrative presentations:

   a. Narrate a sequence of events and
   communicate their significance to
   the audience.

   b. Locate scenes and incidents in
   specific places.

   c. Describe with concrete sensory
   details the sights, sounds, and smells
   of a scene and the specific actions,
   movements, gestures, and feelings of
   characters.

   d. Pace the presentation of actions to
   accommodate time or mood
   changes.

2.2 Deliver expository presentations:

   a. Marshal evidence in support of a
   thesis and related claims, including
   information on all relevant perspectives.

   b. Convey information and ideas from
   primary and secondary sources
   accurately and coherently.

   c. Make distinctions between the
   relative value and significance of
   specific data, facts, and ideas.

   d. Include visual aids by employing
   appropriate technology to organize
   and display information on charts,
   maps, and graphs.

   e. Anticipate and address the listener's
   potential misunderstandings, biases,
   and expectations.

   f. Use technical terms and notations
   accurately.

2.3 Apply appropriate interviewing
techniques:

   a. Prepare and ask relevant questions.

   b. Make notes of responses.

   c. Use language that conveys maturity,
   sensitivity, and respect.

   d. Respond correctly and effectively to
   questions.

   e. Demonstrate knowledge of the
   subject or organization.

   f. Compile and report responses.

   g. Evaluate the effectiveness of the
   interview.

2.4 Deliver oral responses to literature:

   a. Advance a judgment demonstrating a
   comprehensive grasp of the significant ideas of works or passages
   (i.e., make and support warranted
   assertions about the text).

   b. Support important ideas and
   viewpoints through accurate and
   detailed references to the text or to
   other works.

   c. Demonstrate awareness of the
   author's use of stylistic devices and an
   appreciation of the effects created.

   d. Identify and assess the impact of
   perceived ambiguities, nuances, and
   complexities within the text.

2.5 Deliver persuasive arguments (including
evaluation and analysis of problems and
solutions and causes and effects):

   a. Structure ideas and arguments in a
   coherent, logical fashion.

   b. Use rhetorical devices to support
   assertions (e.g., by appeal to logic
   through reasoning; by appeal to
   emotion or ethical belief; by use of
   personal anecdote, case study, or
   analogy).

   c. Clarify and defend positions with
   precise and relevant evidence,
   including facts, expert opinions,
   quotations, expressions of commonly
   accepted beliefs, and logical reasoning.

   d. Anticipate and address the listener's
   concerns and counterarguments.

2.6 Deliver descriptive presentations:

   a. Establish clearly the speaker's point of
   view on the subject of the presentation.

   b. Establish clearly the speaker's
   relationship with that subject
   (e.g., dispassionate observation,
   personal involvement).

   c. Use effective, factual descriptions of
   appearance, concrete images, shifting
   perspectives and vantage points, and
   sensory details.

199

Chapter 5
Content Standards
and Instructional
Practices—
Grades Nine
Through Twelve

Eleventh Grade and Twelfth Grade

Standards and Instruction

The standards for the eleventh and twelfth grades are the pinnacle of all the standards for the language arts. Most of the standards at this level are sophisticated extensions of the knowledge and skills previously targeted in the earlier grades. They highlight several interrelationships among the different domains of language arts: reading, writing, written and oral English-language conventions, and speaking and listening. The strands to be emphasized at the eleventh-grade and twelfth-grade levels are listed in the adjacent column under the appropriate domains.

The following sections profile focus areas within each of the strands.

Reading

1.0 Word Analysis, Fluency, and Systematic Vocabulary Development
2.0 Reading Comprehension (Focus on Informational Materials)
3.0 Literary Response and Analysis

Writing

1.0 Writing Strategies
2.0 Writing Applications (Genres and Their Characteristics)

Written and Oral English-Language Conventions

1.0 Written and Oral English-Language Conventions

Listening and Speaking

1.0 Listening and Speaking Strategies
2.0 Speaking Applications (Genres and Their Characteristics)

Chapter 5
Content Standards
and Instructional
Practices—
Grades Nine
Through Twelve

**Eleventh Grade
and Twelfth
Grade**

Standards and
Instruction

Reading **Word Analysis,
Fluency, and
Systematic Vocabulary
Development**

Etymology and morphology are the basis for systematically building vocabulary at this level. The standards emphasize using those strategies to attack terms from political science, history–social science, science, and mathematics. Once more, however, issues of teacher responsibility arise in a departmentalized school. English teachers may wonder how much time in English class should be devoted to acquiring the vocabulary of other disciplines. Shared responsibility is obviously an ideal solution. Regardless, English teachers should discuss the etymological and morphological principles that help students access meaning.

Vocabulary development should periodically occupy a small portion of classroom time in the eleventh and twelfth grades. Most students should be able to study word derivations independently. Teachers should continue to direct students' attention to external context cues for meaning.

Reading **Reading
Comprehension**

Informational reading in the twelfth grade is focused on public documents (e.g., policy statements, speeches, debates, platforms). In addition to the documents, public statements contained in formal speeches and informal interviews offer abundant opportunities for students to practice the analytic and evaluative skills described in this standard. Point-of-view essays in news magazines and editorials in newspapers are rich sources of additional instructional materials. The strongest emphasis at the content level is directed to

evaluating and verifying facts and arguments. At the structural level students analyze the ways in which clarity of meaning interacts with elements such as word choice, organization, and syntax.

The focus of the standards in this strand relates closely to the standards in writing (e.g., writing reports on historical investigations); speaking (e.g., delivering multimedia presentations); and listening (e.g., identifying logical fallacies in oral arguments). Therefore, instruction should capitalize on those relationships by addressing similar elements from different domains at one time. To do so contributes not only to efficiency but also to learning about important rhetorical considerations in more depth. For instance, students will understand the elements of persuasion in the greatest depth if they not only read persuasive discourse critically but also employ those elements in their own writing and oral presentations.

Reading **Literary Response
and Analysis**

By the end of high school, students are expected to be familiar with the purposes and characteristics of the major genres of literature. Reading Standard 3.0, Literary Response and Analysis, identifies the grade-level emphasis as follows: grade seven—prose; grade eight—poetry; grades nine and ten—drama; and grades eleven and twelve—subgenres that span genres, such as satire and parody.

In these culminating years this standard is focused on analyzing the historical genres and literary traditions of American literature and world literature. The traditional emphasis on British literature in the twelfth grade has been expanded to include works from other countries. Some of the novels or selections students read should be drawn from historically or

201

Chapter 5
Content Standards
and Instructional
Practices—
Grades Nine
Through Twelve

culturally significant works of literature that reflect and enhance their studies of history–social science at this level.

Whether reading American or world literature, students in the eleventh and twelfth grades are expected to:

- Contrast the major literary forms and characteristics of the major literary periods.
- Relate literary works and authors to major themes and issues of their eras.
- Analyze the philosophical, political, religious, ethical, and social influences that have shaped characters, plots, and themes.

Students at this level are expected to achieve more advanced and sophisticated standards. For the more challenging literary concepts, they need clear explanations and elaborations from teachers, together with extensive support throughout the process of acquiring thorough knowledge of such concepts.

Traditionally, literary evaluation has emphasized quality literature. Although that emphasis should remain, instructional benefits can occasionally be gained from exposure to less worthy examples of literature. For instance, to appreciate fully the concept of satire as a subgenre, students should read an example of satire in which the author has not consistently separated the literal and satirical levels of the discourse.

The standards for both reading comprehension (focus on informational materials) and literary response and analysis require that "by grade twelve students read two million words annually on their own, including a wide variety of classic and contemporary literature, magazines, newspapers, and online information" (see pages 193 and 209 in this chapter). Two million words translate to about 11 pages a day or about one 335-page book each month. (Independent reading is discussed in greater detail in the literary response and analysis strand for the ninth and tenth grades.)

Writing   Writing Strategies

Organization and Focus

Students should demonstrate full knowledge of the basic elements of discourse (e.g., audience) as well as more advanced literary devices, such as irony. They should be able to write well-structured arguments with good support and employ rhetorical devices and visual aids to enhance meaning. Their use of language should be fresh and natural.

Research and Technology

Students should use a variety of research strategies (e.g., experiments, interviews) and organize research information in systematic ways (e.g., through the development of an annotated bibliography). They should also integrate databases, graphics, and spreadsheets into word-processing documents. Students are likely to need relatively brief but intense and explicit instruction in merging or importing various types of application files into word-processing documents. Although these activities fall into the language arts area of writing, classroom instruction and student activities may take place in a variety of subject-matter classes.

Evaluation and Revision

Although students at this level should be familiar with all phases of the writing process, the standards focus on revising text to highlight voice, improve sentence variety and style, and enhance subtlety of meaning and tone. The standards within this strand should be addressed as students work on their compositions for the

Chapter 5
Content Standards
and Instructional
Practices—
Grades Nine
Through Twelve

**Eleventh Grade
and Twelfth
Grade**

Standards and
Instruction

writing applications strand and their presentations for the speaking applications strand.

Writing   Writing Applications

Text structures in this category found at earlier grade levels are fictional, auto-biographical, and biographical narratives and responses to literature. In the eleventh and twelfth grades, the standards require students to work with the structures at a more sophisticated level. When appropri-ate, student texts should be about 1,500 words in length (five to six pages, typed and double-spaced).

Three new types of composition are introduced in the eleventh and twelfth grades. The first type is reflective composi-tion. Although it resembles an autobiogra-phy, it focuses on exploring the signifi-cance of personal experience or concerns. A critical component is maintaining the appropriate balance between describing an incident and relating it to more abstract ideas. Like autobiographical writing, reflective writing has long been a focus of writing instruction in California's high schools. Instructional support materials should be readily available to assist the students.

Reports on historical investigation, the second type of composition, are new to this standard. Students are required to use primary and secondary sources to compare different points of view regarding a single historical event and explain the reasons for the similarities and differences. This activity is obviously appropriate in history–social science classes as well as in English classes.

The third new type of composition acknowledges the issues of students' approaching graduation from high school (i.e., filling out job applications and writing résumés). Although conventional style and format are still taught, equal emphasis is given to broader issues of content, such as tone, clarity, and appro-priateness for the audience and purpose.

Students will need less initial instruc-tion for familiar writing genres than they will for those structures introduced at this level. Accordingly, the teacher may wish to:

- Interrelate different standards that address the same text structure when possible. For instance, the standards include both writing and presenting orally a report on a historical investigation.

- Provide models of each text struc-ture, including examples of student writing. Some of the models used may be of lesser quality so that the impact of poor structures on the audience can be demonstrated.

- Identify explicitly for students the critical elements of each text struc-ture. Students are unlikely to have sufficient prior knowledge of the critical elements of a good multi-media presentation, for example. They need to become thoroughly familiar with such elements before they attempt to integrate them into challenging and time-consuming presentations. For instance, it is crucial to resist the temptation to put more emphasis on the "bells and whistles" of a multimedia presenta-tion than on the effective communi-cation of a theme.

- Have students do some cooperative work throughout the varying phases of the writing process to provide additional instructional opportuni-ties and help students achieve a sense of audience.

This standard also requires students to deliver multimedia presentations, a task

203

Chapter 5
Content Standards
and Instructional
Practices—
Grades Nine
Through Twelve

that clearly integrates reading, writing, and speaking and listening. Students are expected to synthesize information from a wide range of materials, including media sources, and create a culminating presentation that integrates text, images, and sound. Important elements in the process are the selection of an appropriate medium for each component of the presentation and the skillful use of the selected media. To combine the requirements of several standards, students may wish to adapt a composition they have already written for use in the multimedia presentation.

Access to an adequate number of computers and appropriate software is obviously a prerequisite to students' meeting this standard. In some schools English teachers may need to work with other colleagues and departments to coordinate the use of equipment and training to accomplish this task.

Written and Oral English-Language Conventions

In the eleventh and twelfth grades, more emphasis is given to using standard oral and written language conventions than to teaching them. Students are expected to control their use of grammar, paragraph and sentence structure, and diction. In addition, their written work should be legible and edited to follow standard conventions for spelling, capitalization, and punctuation. Writing should also reflect appropriate manuscript requirements.

For many students explicit instruction will probably be necessary for some of the content in this section. Individual instruction or peer-mediated instruction is appropriate for many students needing remedial work on conventions, such as improvement in legible writing and

capitalization. Use of individualized instructional software remains a valuable remediation strategy.

Listening and Speaking

Listening and Speaking Strategies

Comprehension

At this level emphasis is given to analyzing media presentations of various types (e.g., advertisements, speeches, film, news) to help students recognize the strategies being used to inform, persuade, or entertain.

Organization and Delivery of Oral Communication

Most of the standards at this level concentrate on structural elements and rhetorical techniques. Some elements and techniques apply to several areas of language arts, such as rhetorical questions, parallelism, concrete images, figurative language, and irony. Others, such as gesture, movement, vocalization, and rehearsal strategies, are unique to oral presentations. Students should use standard English for clarity but recognize when informal language is effective and when technical language is needed. At this culminating level students are required to use classic and contemporary forms of logical argument, including inductive and deductive reasoning and reasoning from analogies.

Analysis and Evaluation of Oral and Media Communications

Students critique oral presentations, particularly media presentations, to evaluate rhetorical techniques as they relate to the purpose of the presentation, either stated or implied. In addition, they are required to analyze the arguments presented, a skill that requires some direct

Chapter 5
Content Standards
and Instructional
Practices—
Grades Nine
Through Twelve

Eleventh Grade
and Twelfth
Grade

Standards and
Instruction

instruction. They should recognize common logical fallacies, such as false causality, red herrings, and bandwagoning. Fallacies are best taught in contrast to standard logical principles of premises and conclusions.

Listening and Speaking
Speaking Applications

Students are required to deliver polished formal and extemporaneous reflective presentations, oral reports on historical investigations, oral responses to literature, multimedia presentations, and recitations of poems, selections from speeches, or dramatic soliloquies. Except for recitations of poetry, these same types of presentations are targeted in the standards for the eleventh and twelfth grades within the writing applications strand. Even at this level students may find it challenging to deliver oral presentations to a large group. The challenge can be made less frightening and more successful when teachers:

- Allow students to deliver presentations initially to a small group of other students in a cooperative work group.
- Postpone extemporaneous presentations until after the students have delivered oral presentations from fully written documents. A tactic for teaching students to present extemporaneous—or nearly extemporaneous—presentations is first to make brief outlines of major points on a variety of topics.
- Allow students to present orally a discourse they had originally developed as a written composition. This approach also makes instruction more efficient and encourages a comparison between the same discourse as a written document and as a speech. Students will make some relatively minor changes in their written compositions to make them more effective in speech. For example, they will probably want to break some complex sentences into simpler structures as a general tactic for giving speeches and as an aid to varying intonation.
- Help students develop strong introductions that will capture the interest of their audience.

Please see Appendix B for examples of standards that span domains and strands.

205

Chapter 5
Content Standards
and Instructional
Practices—
Grades Nine
Through Twelve

Eleventh Grade and Twelfth Grade

Curricular and Instructional Profile

Reading Standard   3.8

DOMAIN	STRAND	SUBSTRAND	STANDARD
Reading	3.0 Literary response and analysis	Literary criticism	3.8 Analyze the clarity and consistency of political assumptions in a selection of literary works or essays on a topic (political approach).

Prerequisite standard. **Ninth-Grade and Tenth-Grade Literary Response and Analysis Standard 3.12:** Analyze the way in which a work of literature is related to the themes and issues of its historical period (historical approach).

Corequisite standards. **Eleventh-Grade and Twelfth-Grade Literary Response and Analysis Standards 3.1, 3.3.**

Standard 3.1: Analyze characteristics of subgenres that are used in poetry, prose, and so forth.

Standard 3.3: Analyze the ways in which irony, tone, and mood achieve specific rhetorical and aesthetic purposes.

Eleventh-Grade and Twelfth-Grade Writing Applications Standard 2.2: Write responses to literature.

Eleventh-Grade and Twelfth-Grade Speaking Applications Standard 2.3: Deliver oral responses to literature.

Curricular and Instructional Decisions

Instructional Objective	Analyze the clarity and consistency of political assumptions in a selection of literary works or essays on a particular topic.
Instructional Design	A crucial element in achieving this objective is the assumption that students possess reasonably thorough knowledge about a given political topic. Although that knowledge can be obtained in con-

Chapter 5
Content Standards
and Instructional
Practices---
Grades Nine
Through Twelve

**Eleventh Grade
and Twelfth
Grade**

Curricular and
Instructional
Profile

Instructional Design (Continued)

junction with literary criticism activities, it is more efficient for learning that it take place through the coordination of the standards for the eleventh and twelfth grades and those for the ninth and tenth grades. For example, one of the approaches to literary criticism in the ninth-grade and tenth-grade standards is historical. Accordingly, students might visit a topic at that level (e.g., establishment of labor unions) with a historical emphasis, then revisit the topic in the eleventh and twelfth grades, using more sophisticated sources to learn the background necessary to conduct meaningful literary criticism through a political approach.

If readings are selected carefully, further economy in meeting ambitious standards can be achieved. For example, students might read some of Blake's *Songs of Innocence* for background on child-labor abuses in England that contributed to the formation of labor unions there. Work with such literature can contribute to achieving other standards related to literary response and analysis as well.

Students will learn that the contents of *Songs of Innocence* are not innocent and contribute to the students' understanding of one way in which irony achieves a rhetorical effect. Simultaneously, students analyze characteristics of a variety of poems and other reading selections as part of their overall analysis of characteristics of the subgenres found within basic genres. Instruction should include portions of several other literary standards as well. The sequencing and selection of reading material can simultaneously influence the effectiveness and efficiency of instruction.

One group of writing standards requires students to write responses to literature. When they have read several selections and have demonstrated their understanding of the political approach to literary criticism—either in an informal way or through class discussion or more formal assessments—the next logical step for students to take is to write a formal literary critique emphasizing responses to literature singled out in the writing standards.

Instructional Delivery

Objective, thorough literary criticism is not easy to achieve. Instruction should begin with a clear notion of what literary criticism is and how the approach currently under study (i.e., political) differs from approaches taught in earlier grades (e.g., historical). A good way to frame the instruction is to have students first read examples of political literary criticism before going to source selections and eventually writing a formal critique.

Teachers should provide substantial guidance throughout this sequence, particularly in the form of explicit instruction in the elements of literary criticism unique to the political approach.

207

Chapter 5
Content Standards
and Instructional
Practices—
Grades Nine
Through Twelve

**Eleventh Grade
and Twelfth
Grade**

Curricular and
Instructional
Profile

Assessment

Entry-Level
Assessment

Monitoring
Student
Progress

Post-test
Assessment

1. *Entry-Level Assessment for Instructional Planning.* Formal pretesting at this level is neither practical nor necessary. However, important prior knowledge assumed as prerequisite for instruction should be tested informally. For example, if instruction in a political approach to literary criticism assumes background knowledge of history, students should be tested on that knowledge. The assessments can also serve as a mechanism for allowing students to review what they learned earlier.

2. *Monitoring Student Progress Toward the Instructional Objective.* Throughout the year the activities students participate in provide multiple opportunities for ongoing evaluation of progress toward achieving standards. The crucial aspect of testing at this level is not the nature of the tests as much as how teachers use the results to make changes in the curriculum and instruction. For instance, if several students are having great difficulty with literary criticism, teachers should provide more scaffolded learning opportunities than they might do otherwise (e.g., procedural facilitators, such as think sheets).

3. *Post-test Assessment Toward the Standard.* No single source of assessment can give a complete picture of student achievement of the standards. The types of tests required by the school district or the state contribute partially to the picture. Final independently produced compositions and oral presentations provide substantial significant data on achievement as well. For this standard in particular, a final written critique of a literary work is the best criterion-referenced assessment tool.

**Universal
Access**

Reading
Difficulties
or Disabilities

Advanced
Learners

1. *Students with Reading Difficulties or Disabilities.* Doing sophisticated critical analyses of literature and writing about them are extremely challenging for students with disabilities or other learning difficulties. They will be helped enormously if teachers provide the substantial and explicit guidance previously recommended. Teachers should read more challenging literary selections to the whole class. Lower-performing students may require significant support from peers while analyzing some literary selections. For very low performing students, the standards for writing sophistication may be adapted.

2. *Students Who Are Advanced Learners.* Advanced students may be exempted from the substantial and explicit instruction described previously if they demonstrate a satisfactory grasp of the concepts being taught. Independent study might be useful provided guidance by the teacher is available as needed.

Chapter 5
Content Standards
and Instructional
Practices—
Grades Nine
Through Twelve

**Eleventh Grade
and Twelfth
Grade**

Curricular and
Instructional
Profile

**Universal
Access**
(Continued)

(Advanced learners still need instruction and should not be expected to teach themselves.) Extending those students' learning to include the political analysis of writings about present-day concerns might prove to be stimulating, especially if students are thereby allowed to express their thoughts in genuine forums.

English Learners

3. *Students Who Are English Learners*

a. Teachers need to provide English learners with models of the types of literary analyses the learners are expected to produce. Also recommended are exercises that will help the learners acquire the grammatical structures and vocabulary needed to perform the analyses and consistent feedback on the quality and accuracy of the learners' written work.

b. Because English learners may not have access to the same cultural knowledge as English speakers do in order to analyze political assumptions, teachers may need to provide the learners with additional information.

c. English learners may not have acquired the grammatical structures and vocabulary needed to complete literary analyses. For instance, they may not have learned how to use the present tense to discuss specific types of literary texts. (Note how the present tense is used in this sentence: Hamlet *dies* and his son *seeks* revenge.) English learners require additional information on verb tense as well as instruction in introducing and incorporating short and long quotations into text to support literary analyses and in analyzing texts rather than merely summarizing them.

d. As the learners acquire advanced academic vocabulary, they should be guided in the appropriate use of the words in their writing.

**Instructional
Materials**

Instructional materials should provide the following:

1. A sufficient number of examples of the genres targeted at this level that span reading, writing, and speaking

2. Procedural facilitators (i.e., devices designed to help facilitate acquisition of new knowledge and skills)

3. Reading selections coordinated to address more than a single standard

4. Examples of explicit strategies for achieving important standards

5. Substantial, significant resources for helping teachers accommodate a wide range of student achievement

209

Chapter 5
Content Standards
and Instructional
Practices—
Grades Nine
Through Twelve

Eleventh Grade and Twelfth Grade

English–Language Arts Content Standards

Reading

1.0. Word Analysis, Fluency, and Systematic Vocabulary Development

Students apply their knowledge of word origins to determine the meaning of new words encountered in reading materials and use those words accurately.

Vocabulary and Concept Development

1.1 Trace the etymology of significant terms used in political science and history.

1.2 Apply knowledge of Greek, Latin, and Anglo-Saxon roots and affixes to draw inferences concerning the meaning of scientific and mathematical terminology.

1.3 Discern the meaning of analogies encountered, analyzing specific comparisons as well as relationships and inferences.

2.0 Reading Comprehension (Focus on Informational Materials)

Students read and understand grade-level-appropriate material. They analyze the organizational patterns, arguments, and positions advanced. The selections in *Recommended Readings in Literature, Grades Nine Through Twelve* illustrate the quality and complexity of the materials to be read by students. In addition, by grade twelve, students read two million words annually on their own, including a wide variety of classic and contemporary literature, magazines, newspapers, and online information.

Structural Features of Informational Materials

2.1 Analyze both the features and the rhetorical devices of different types of public documents (e.g., policy statements, speeches, debates, platforms) and the way in which authors use those features and devices.

Comprehension and Analysis of Grade-Level-Appropriate Text

2.2 Analyze the way in which clarity of meaning is affected by the patterns of organization, hierarchical structures, repetition of the main ideas, syntax, and word choice in the text.

2.3 Verify and clarify facts presented in other types of expository texts by using a variety of consumer, workplace, and public documents.

2.4. Make warranted and reasonable assertions about the author's arguments by using elements of the text to defend and clarify interpretations.

2.5 Analyze an author's implicit and explicit philosophical assumptions and beliefs about a subject.

Chapter 5
Content Standards
and Instructional
Practices—
Grades Nine
Through Twelve

Eleventh Grade
and Twelfth
Grade

English–Language
Arts Content
Standards

Expository Critique

2.6   Critique the power, validity, and
truthfulness of arguments set forth in
public documents; their appeal to both
friendly and hostile audiences; and the
extent to which the arguments anticipate and address reader concerns and
counterclaims (e.g., appeal to reason, to
authority, to pathos and emotion).

3.0   Literary Response and Analysis

Students read and respond to historically or
culturally significant works of literature that
reflect and enhance their studies of history and
social science. They conduct in-depth analyses
of recurrent themes. The selections in *Recommended Readings in Literature, Grades Nine
Through Twelve* illustrate the quality and
complexity of the materials to be read by
students.

Structural Features of Literature

3.1   Analyze characteristics of subgenres
(e.g., satire, parody, allegory, pastoral)
that are used in poetry, prose, plays,
novels, short stories, essays, and other
basic genres.

Narrative Analysis of Grade-Level-
Appropriate Text

3.2   Analyze the way in which the theme or
meaning of a selection represents a view
or comment on life, using textual
evidence to support the claim.

3.3.   Analyze the ways in which irony, tone,
mood, the author's style, and the
"sound" of language achieve specific
rhetorical or aesthetic purposes or both.

3.4.   Analyze ways in which poets use
imagery, personification, figures of
speech, and sounds to evoke readers'
emotions.

3.5.   Analyze recognized works of American
literature representing a variety of
genres and traditions:

a.   Trace the development of American
literature from the colonial period
forward.

b.   Contrast the major periods, themes,
styles, and trends and describe how
works by members of different
cultures relate to one another in
each period.

c.   Evaluate the philosophical, political,
religious, ethical, and social influences of the historical period that
shaped the characters, plots, and
settings.

3.6   Analyze the way in which authors
through the centuries have used
archetypes drawn from myth and
tradition in literature, film, political
speeches, and religious writings
(e.g., how the archetypes of banishment
from an ideal world may be used to
interpret Shakespeare's tragedy
Macbeth).

3.7   Analyze recognized works of world
literature from a variety of authors:

a.   Contrast the major literary forms,
techniques, and characteristics of the
major literary periods (e.g., Homeric
Greece, medieval, romantic,
neoclassic, modern).

b.   Relate literary works and authors to
the major themes and issues of their
eras.

c.   Evaluate the philosophical, political,
religious, ethical, and social influences of the historical period that
shaped the characters, plots, and,
settings.

Literary Criticism

3.8   Analyze the clarity and consistency of
political assumptions in a selection of
literary works or essays on a topic
(e.g., suffrage, women's role in organized labor). (Political approach)

3.9   Analyze the philosophical arguments
presented in literary works to determine
whether the authors' positions have
contributed to the quality of each work
and the credibility of the characters.
(Philosophical approach)

211

Chapter 5
Content Standards
and Instructional
Practices—
Grades Nine
Through Twelve

Eleventh Grade
and Twelfth
Grade

English–Language
Arts Content
Standards

Writing

1.0 Writing Strategies

Students write coherent and focused texts that convey a well-defined perspective and tightly reasoned argument. The writing demonstrates students' awareness of the audience and purpose and progression through the stages of the writing process.

Organization and Focus

1.1 Demonstrate an understanding of the elements of discourse (e.g., purpose, speaker, audience, form) when completing narrative, expository, persuasive, or descriptive writing assignments.

1.2 Use point of view, characterization, style (e.g., use of irony), and related elements for specific rhetorical and aesthetic purposes.

1.3 Structure ideas and arguments in a sustained, persuasive, and sophisticated way and support them with precise and relevant examples.

1.4 Enhance meaning by employing rhetorical devices, including the extended use of parallelism, repetition, and analogy; the incorporation of visual aids (e.g., graphs, tables, pictures); and the issuance of a call for action.

1.5 Use language in natural, fresh, and vivid ways to establish a specific tone.

Research and Technology

1.6 Develop presentations by using clear research questions and creative and critical research strategies (e.g., field studies, oral histories, interviews, experiments, electronic sources).

1.7 Use systematic strategies to organize and record information (e.g., anecdotal scripting, annotated bibliographies).

1.8 Integrate databases, graphics, and spreadsheets into word-processed documents.

Evaluation and Revision

1.9 Revise text to highlight the individual voice, improve sentence variety and style, and enhance subtlety of meaning and tone in ways that are consistent with the purpose, audience, and genre.

2.0 Writing Applications (Genres and Their Characteristics)

Students combine the rhetorical strategies of narration, exposition, persuasion, and description to produce texts of at least 1,500 words each. Student writing demonstrates a command of standard American English and the research, organizational, and drafting strategies outlined in Writing Standard 1.0.

Using the writing strategies of grades eleven and twelve outlined in Writing Standard 1.0, students:

2.1 Write fictional, autobiographical, or biographical narratives:

   a. Narrate a sequence of events and communicate their significance to the audience.

   b. Locate scenes and incidents in specific places.

   c. Describe with concrete sensory details the sights, sounds, and smells of a scene and the specific actions, movements, gestures, and feelings of the characters; use interior monologue to depict the characters' feelings.

   d. Pace the presentation of actions to accommodate temporal, spatial, and dramatic mood changes.

   e. Make effective use of descriptions of appearance, images, shifting perspectives, and sensory details.

2.2 Write responses to literature:

   a. Demonstrate a comprehensive understanding of the significant ideas in works or passages.

   b. Analyze the use of imagery, language, universal themes, and unique aspects of the text.

   c. Support important ideas and viewpoints through accurate and detailed references to the text and to other works.

Chapter 5
Content Standards
and Instructional
Practices—
Grades Nine
Through Twelve

Eleventh Grade
and Twelfth
Grade

English–Language
Arts Content
Standards

d. Demonstrate an understanding of the author's use of stylistic devices and an appreciation of the effects created.

e. Identify and assess the impact of perceived ambiguities, nuances, and complexities within the text.

2.3 Write reflective compositions:

a. Explore the significance of personal experiences, events, conditions, or concerns by using rhetorical strategies (e.g., narration, description, exposition, persuasion).

b. Draw comparisons between specific incidents and broader themes that illustrate the writer's important beliefs or generalizations about life.

c. Maintain a balance in describing individual incidents and relate those incidents to more general and abstract ideas.

2.4 Write historical investigation reports:

a. Use exposition, narration, description, argumentation, exposition, or some combination of rhetorical strategies to support the main proposition.

b. Analyze several historical records of a single event, examining critical relationships between elements of the research topic.

c. Explain the perceived reason or reasons for the similarities and differences in historical records with information derived from primary and secondary sources to support or enhance the presentation.

d. Include information from all relevant perspectives and take into consideration the validity and reliability of sources.

e. Include a formal bibliography.

2.5 Write job applications and resumés:

a. Provide clear and purposeful information and address the intended audience appropriately.

b. Use varied levels, patterns, and types of language to achieve intended effects and aid comprehension.

c. Modify the tone to fit the purpose and audience.

d. Follow the conventional style for that type of document (e.g., resumé, memorandum) and use page formats, fonts, and spacing that contribute to the readability and impact of the document.

2.6 Deliver multimedia presentations:

a. Combine text, images, and sound and draw information from many sources (e.g., television broadcasts, videos, films, newspapers, magazines, CD-ROMs, the Internet, electronic media-generated images).

b. Select an appropriate medium for each element of the presentation.

c. Use the selected media skillfully, editing appropriately and monitoring for quality.

d. Test the audience's response and revise the presentation accordingly.

Written and Oral English-Language Conventions

The standards for written and oral English language conventions have been placed between those for writing and for listening and speaking because these conventions are essential to both sets of skills.

1.0 Written and Oral English-Language Conventions

Students write and speak with a command of standard English conventions.

1.1 Demonstrate control of grammar, diction, and paragraph and sentence structure and an understanding of English usage.

1.2 Produce legible work that shows accurate spelling and correct punctuation and capitalization.

1.3 Reflect appropriate manuscript requirements in writing.

213

Chapter 5
Content Standards
and Instructional
Practices—
Grades Nine
Through Twelve

Eleventh Grade
and Twelfth
Grade
English–Language
Arts Content
Standards

Listening and Speaking

1.0 Listening and Speaking Strategies

Students formulate adroit judgments about oral communication. They deliver focused and coherent presentations that convey clear and distinct perspectives and demonstrate solid reasoning. They use gestures, tone, and vocabulary tailored to the audience and purpose.

Comprehension

1.1 Recognize strategies used by the media to inform, persuade, entertain, and transmit culture (e.g., advertisements; perpetuation of stereotypes; use of visual representations, special effects, language).

1.2 Analyze the impact of the media on the democratic process (e.g., exerting influence on elections, creating images of leaders, shaping attitudes) at the local, state, and national levels.

1.3 Interpret and evaluate the various ways in which events are presented and information is communicated by visual image makers (e.g., graphic artists, documentary filmmakers, illustrators, news photographers).

Organization and Delivery of Oral Communication

1.4 Use rhetorical questions, parallel structure, concrete images, figurative language, characterization, irony, and dialogue to achieve clarity, force, and aesthetic effect.

1.5 Distinguish between and use various forms of classical and contemporary logical arguments, including:
   a. Inductive and deductive reasoning
   b. Syllogisms and analogies

1.6 Use logical, ethical, and emotional appeals that enhance a specific tone and purpose.

1.7 Use appropriate rehearsal strategies to pay attention to performance details, achieve command of the text, and create skillful artistic staging.

1.8 Use effective and interesting language, including:
   a. Informal expressions for effect
   b. Standard American English for clarity
   c. Technical language for specificity

1.9 Use research and analysis to justify strategies for gesture, movement, and vocalization, including dialect, pronunciation, and enunciation.

1.10 Evaluate when to use different kinds of effects (e.g., visual, music, sound, graphics) to create effective productions.

Analysis and Evaluation of Oral and Media Communications

1.11 Critique a speaker's diction and syntax in relation to the purpose of an oral communication and the impact the words may have on the audience.

1.12 Identify logical fallacies used in oral addresses (e.g., attack *ad hominem*, false causality, red herring, overgeneralization, bandwagon effect).

1.13 Analyze the four basic types of persuasive speech (i.e., propositions of fact, value, problem, or policy) and understand the similarities and differences in their patterns of organization and the use of persuasive language, reasoning, and proof.

1.14 Analyze the techniques used in media messages for a particular audience and evaluate their effectiveness (e.g., Orson Welles' radio broadcast "War of the Worlds").

2.0 Speaking Applications (Genres and Their Characteristics)

Students deliver polished formal and extemporaneous presentations that combine traditional rhetorical strategies of narration, exposition, persuasion, and description. Student speaking demonstrates a command of standard American English and the organizational and delivery strategies outlined in Listening and Speaking Standard 1.0.

Chapter 5
Content Standards
and Instructional
Practices—
Grades Nine
Through Twelve

**Eleventh Grade
and Twelfth
Grade**

English–Language
Arts Content
Standards

Using the speaking strategies of grades eleven and twelve outlined in Listening and Speaking Standard 1.0, students:

2.1 Deliver reflective presentations:

a. Explore the significance of personal experiences, events, conditions, or concerns, using appropriate rhetorical strategies (e.g., narration, description, exposition, persuasion).

b. Draw comparisons between the specific incident and broader themes that illustrate the speaker's beliefs or generalizations about life.

c. Maintain a balance between describing the incident and relating it to more general, abstract ideas.

2.2 Deliver oral reports on historical investigations:

a. Use exposition, narration, description, persuasion, or some combination of those to support the thesis.

b. Analyze several historical records of a single event, examining critical relationships between elements of the research topic.

c. Explain the perceived reason or reasons for the similarities and differences by using information derived from primary and secondary sources to support or enhance the presentation.

d. Include information on all relevant perspectives and consider the validity and reliability of sources.

2.3 Deliver oral responses to literature:

a. Demonstrate a comprehensive understanding of the significant ideas of literary works (e.g., make assertions about the text that are reasonable and supportable).

b. Analyze the imagery, language, universal themes, and unique aspects of the text through the use of rhetorical strategies (e.g., narration, description, persuasion, exposition, a combination of those strategies).

c. Support important ideas and viewpoints through accurate and detailed references to the text or to other works.

d. Demonstrate an awareness of the author's use of stylistic devices and an appreciation of the effects created.

e. Identify and assess the impact of perceived ambiguities, nuances, and complexities within the text.

2.4 Deliver multimedia presentations:

a. Combine text, images, and sound by incorporating information from a wide range of media, including films, newspapers, magazines, CD-ROMs, online information, television, videos, and electronic media-generated images.

b. Select an appropriate medium for each element of the presentation.

c. Use the selected media skillfully, editing appropriately and monitoring for quality.

d. Test the audience's response and revise the presentation accordingly.

2.5 Recite poems, selections from speeches, or dramatic soliloquies with attention to performance details to achieve clarity, force, and aesthetic effect and to demonstrate an understanding of the meaning (e.g., Hamlet's soliloquy "To Be or Not to Be").

Assessment of Proficiency in the Language Arts

Taken together [the three purposes of assessment] provide a road map to achieving the standards: the starting place, the routes to take, the points at which to change routes, and the destination.

Ideally, assessment and instruction are linked inextricably within any curriculum. The key to using assessment effectively and efficiently in a program of instruction is to recognize above all that different types of assessment tools must be used for different purposes. The assessments most crucial to achieving the language arts content standards are the following:

- *Entry-level assessment:* Do students possess crucial prerequisite skills and knowledge expected at their grade level? Do they already know some of the material to be taught?
- *Monitoring of progress:* Are students progressing adequately toward achieving the standards? Do they need reteaching? Is emphasis on

216

Chapter 6
Assessment
of Proficiency
in the
Language Arts

specific instructional components needed in the next series of lessons or units?

- *Summative assessment:* Have students achieved the goals defined by a given standard or group of standards?

Although many other purposes exist for assessment, the three just listed are critical to this framework because they inform instruction. Taken together, they provide a road map to achieving the standards: the starting place, the routes to take, the points at which to change routes, and the destination. Assessment to inform instruction does not, however, address other purposes of assessment, such as supplying diagnostic information to qualify students for special programs outside the classroom setting. The discussion in this chapter also summarizes the Statewide Pupil Assessment System, including the statewide standards-based summative assessment initiated in 1998—the Standardized Testing and Reporting Program (STAR).

Teachers may have well-founded apprehensions about assessment; some may even be convinced that successfully achieving the standards requires a large amount of testing. But if language arts programs and textbooks fully integrate assessment and instruction, most assessment activities—especially the monitoring of progress—will contribute to learning and will not usurp precious instructional time.

Characteristics of Assessment Across Grade Levels

No single measure or method of assessment can provide the scope of information needed to achieve all three purposes listed previously. Except for contributing to informing instruction, the three types of assessment do not apply equally across all grade levels. The content and specific skills

and strategies, more discrete in the early grades, become progressively more complex and intertwined in the advanced grades. Therefore, the differences require different tasks. In the sections that follow, the differences in emphasis that assessment should accommodate are described for the three grade-level clusters: kindergarten through grade three, grades four through eight, and grades nine through twelve. In addition, examples of what and when to assess are indicated for kindergarten through grade three and grades four through eight. These examples are based on the English–language arts content standards.

Assessment in Kindergarten Through Grade Three

Entry-Level Assessment

These assessments are used to determine the proficiency of individual students or groups of students according to a specific standard or prerequisite skill or knowledge. This determination informs the teacher what needs to be included in upcoming lessons or in preteaching or reteaching lessons. In some instances these more discrete assessments will help the teacher locate the level of the instructional program the students should enter. Entry-level assessment should not prevent a student from participating in grade-level instruction. Instead, teachers should use the information gained from entry-level assessment to offer supplemental instruction in specific areas while including all students in grade-level instruction.

Monitoring of Progress

These assessments focus on the general skills and knowledge students are to acquire according to the standards. Through tests developed by publishers, teachers, or

217

Chapter 6
Assessment
of Proficiency
in the
Language Arts

districts and arranged as periodic assessments for all students, the domains and
strands of the standards are assessed at the
end of each major set of lessons. The tests,
which are curriculum embedded, should
be administered and scored frequently by
the teacher. The results should be analyzed
for each student and classroom on the
basis of established levels that identify
1) who is at mastery; and (2) what percent
of students are at mastery. And the results
should influence how teachers modify or
emphasize parts of the curriculum.

Summative Assessment

These assessments include quarterly,
midyear, and end-of-the-year tests developed by the publisher and the school
district. They are used to determine
whether the student has mastered the
content and to document long-term
growth. The state-required assessment,
STAR, also functions as a summative
assessment for grades two and three.
Long-term outcomes should be the focus
of summative assessment. For instance,
blending words enables the long-term
outcome of decoding words accurately
and in turn enables fluency and meaningful reading comprehension. Similarly,
kindergarten students should be assessed
on phonemic awareness.

**Examples of What and When to Assess,
Kindergarten Through Grade Three**

Because of the large number of skills
and strategies students are to acquire in
each grade, a critical decision has to be
made to determine what knowledge to
assess and when. In the early grades key
indicators or predictors can be used to
identify students making adequate
progress toward literacy standards and
those likely to have continued difficulty in
learning to read. Those key indicators are
derived largely from research on students
who learn to read easily in comparison
with those who do not. Knowledge of

letter names, phonemic segmentation, the
reading of nonsense words, and fluency in
oral reading are examples of the predictors
or key indicators (Good, Simmons, and
Smith 1998). Several commercial measures are available to provide reliable
information about students' ability to
recognize letters and to segment words
into phonemes. When used in timed
conditions, the measures can also be
reliably used to assess students' rate of
progress over time. The purpose of the
measures is to identify students who need
additional instruction and assess the
effectiveness of instruction over time.

An important caveat is that some of the
measures are indicators or predictors of
reading difficulty but do not translate
directly into instructional objectives. For
example, although the ability to name
letters is highly correlated with later
reading achievement (Adams 1990), that
ability should not be the exclusive focus of
instruction (National Research Council
1998). It is important to distinguish
between (1) identification of children at
risk of reading difficulty; and (2) instruction. For example, although the ability to
read nonsense words is a strong predictor
for students who will learn to read easily,
teaching the reading of nonsense words as
part of the first-grade curriculum is not
recommended. Knowledge of letter-sound
correspondences and ability to blend those
sounds into words are assessed by measur-
ing the student's ability to read nonsense
words and are stringent indicators of
students' acquisition and application of
letter sounds and ability to blend sounds.

The table on the following page offers
suggestions for some of the important
measures available to teachers to inform
them of their effectiveness in the delivery
of the instructional program and the
progress of their students toward mastery
of the standards.

In the early grades key indicators or predictors can be used to identify students making adequate progress toward literacy standards and those likely to have continued difficulty in learning to read.

Measure	Description	Grade			
		K	One	Two	Three
Phoneme awareness	Detect rhyme. Count syllables. Match initial sounds. Count phonemes.	Spring	Fall/ winter	Only if needed	Only if needed
Phoneme deletion	Initial sounds Final sounds First sound of a consonant blend Embedded sound of a consonant blend	Spring	Fall/ winter	Only if needed	Only if needed
Phoneme segmentation	Segment sounds. Count phonemes.	Spring	Fall/ winter	Only if needed	Only if needed
Beginning phonics	Alphabet names Consonant sounds	Spring	Only if needed	Only if needed	Only if needed
Phonics	Reading of nonsense words Other decoding Spelling		Fall/ winter/ spring Every 4–6 weeks until mastery	Fall/ winter/ spring Every 4–6 weeks until mastery	Only if needed
Oral reading (fluency)	Words correct per minute on grade-level text		Spring Earlier as needed	3–6 times per year	3–6 times per year
Reading comprehension*	Main idea Author's point of view Analysis Inference		Fall/ winter/ spring Every 8–10 weeks	Fall/ winter/ spring Every 6–8 weeks	Fall/ winter/ spring Every 6–8 weeks
Vocabulary	Antonyms Synonyms Multiple meanings Context meanings		Every 8–10 weeks	Every 6–8 weeks	Every 6–8 weeks
Spelling	Unit words Regular/irregular words Word patterns Single and multisyllabic words Sentence structure		Every 8–10 weeks	Every 6–8 weeks	Every 6–8 weeks
Conventions	Punctuation Capitalization Grammar Penmanship		Every 8–10 weeks	Every 6–8 weeks	Every 6–8 weeks
Writing	Narratives (fictional and autobiographical) Organization/focus Single paragraph Topic sentence Facts/details Expository descriptions Friendly letter		Twice per year	Twice per year	Twice per year

*End-of-unit tests developed by publishers or teachers

219

Chapter 6
Assessment
of Proficiency
in the
Language Arts

Assessment in Grades Four Through Eight

Entry-Level Assessment

In these grades the quantity and variety of prerequisite knowledge reach a point at which it is impractical to pretest for more than the most essential prior knowledge and skills. Gradually, the emphasis changes to evaluating the extent to which students already have knowledge of planned content and the need students may have for instructional support.

Monitoring of Progress

Regularly scheduled testing of progress is still appropriate, especially in fourth through sixth grades. But many forms of informal progress testing are also appropriate, useful, and relatively easy to use. Written products, both draft and final, and oral presentations students do as a part of their class assignments should be scored and used to determine progress toward mastery of standards.

Summative Assessment

These assessments include quarterly, midyear, and end-of-the-year tests developed by the publisher and the school district. They are used to determine whether the student has mastered the content and to document long-term growth. The state-required assessment, STAR, also functions as a summative assessment. Long-term outcomes should be the focus of summative assessment. Consequently, in the areas of writing applications, listening, and speaking not covered by the STAR, the school district or school may need to establish summative assessment for each genre of writing and speaking at each grade level that can be scored by teachers using district rubrics.

Examples of What and When to Assess, Grades Four Through Eight

Assessment of skills development is much less specific in grades four through eight. However, many of the assessment areas from earlier grades apply at this level. Fluency in oral reading is a reliable indicator for students in grades four through six and for middle school students whose oral reading fluency is significantly below grade level. Assessments should be conducted to assist in determining the next steps for instruction and in planning interventions as necessary.

The table on the following page offers suggestions for some of the important measures available to teachers to inform them of their effectiveness in the delivery of the instructional program and the progress of their students toward mastery of the standards.

220

Chapter 6
Assessment
of Proficiency
in the
Language Arts

Measure	Description	Grade				
		Four	Five	Six	Seven	Eight
Oral reading (fluency)	Words correct per minute on grade-level text	3–4 times per year	2–3 times per year	1–2 times per year	As needed	As needed
Reading comprehension*	Main idea Author's point of view Inference Analysis Critique/criticism	At the end of unit of study	At the end of unit of study	At the end of unit of study	At the end of unit of study	At the end of unit of study
Vocabulary	Multiple meanings Word origins Context meanings Metaphors, similes, analogies	Every 4–6 weeks	Every 4–6 weeks	Every 4–6 weeks	Every 4–6 weeks	Every 4–6 weeks
Spelling	Derivations Multisyllabic words	Every 4–6 weeks	Every 4–6 weeks	Every 4–6 weeks	Every 4–6 weeks	Every 4–6 weeks
Conventions	Sentence structure Punctuation Capitalization Grammar Penmanship	Every 4–6 weeks	Every 4–6 weeks	Every 4–6 weeks	Every 4–6 weeks	Every 4–6 weeks
Writing	Narratives and responses to literature Expository compositions and research reports Persuasive compositions Documents	At least twice per year	At least twice per year	At least twice per year	At least twice per year	At least twice per year

*End-of-unit tests developed by publishers or teachers

221

Chapter 6
Assessment
of Proficiency
in the
Language Arts

Assessment in Grades Nine Through Twelve

Entry-Level Assessment

Teachers need to attend closely to student performance in the early weeks of the school year to determine student strengths and weaknesses relative to given standards. Entering ninth graders and new students should be assessed with a variety of measures, including standardized tests, which may be used to determine entry-level skills. Some students may require more extensive assessment of strengths and weaknesses, including the use of specialized testing.

Monitoring of Progress

Tests for monitoring progress, as described for grades four through eight, are most appropriate throughout these grades. Instructional materials should emphasize which tasks double as instructional and progress assessment tasks, along with guidelines to assist teachers as they make data-based decisions. Because of the added complexities of the complete reading and language arts curriculum and the number of students assigned to each teacher at these grade levels, teachers should develop systems to organize records of student test scores and analyze regularly the progress each student is making toward achieving mastery of the grade-level standards.

Summative Assessment

Each summative assessment at this level should assess several standards at once. The semester course tests that teachers give in English classes should be aligned to reflect how well students are meeting the expectations of end-of-year mastery of grade-level standards. As with the previous grade levels, the state STAR program will offer annual assessments. Teachers in grades nine through twelve should routinely assess students' proficiency in all the writing applications appropriate for each grade level—a process similar to that used in grades four through eight.

Assessments of specific skills are less frequent in the high school years except for assessments of students who read and write significantly below grade level (i.e., two grade levels or more below a student's current grade level) and for whom a plan of intervention has been established. Schoolwide writing assessments, commonly conducted in these grades once a year, are a source of information on student achievement not typically available elsewhere. Most important, teachers in grades nine through twelve determine mastery of content standards by assessing the students' increasingly sophisticated language arts skills and knowledge through an examination of their reading and writing skills and strategies in the context of literature and informational text.

Similarities of Assessments Across Grade Levels

All three types of assessments used to inform instruction share some critical characteristics across grade levels:

Entry-Level Assessment

The exact purpose of each item of assessment should be clear: Do the students have the prerequisite skills needed? Do they already know the planned content? To what extent? The results of entry-level assessments help guide the teacher in setting the course of initial instruction and determining modifications for specific students or groups of students.

Monitoring of Progress

The most critical guideline for the monitoring of progress is that it should occur at frequent intervals and that the assessment data should be used quickly to adjust instruction. Each subtest should have established or agreed-on cutoff scores to indicate what score equates to mastery (e.g., a score of eight out of 10 items indicates mastery). Collecting and acting on information frequently during instruction is a sign of a highly effective program. In an effort to ensure the progress of every student, the data should be examined by individual students and classroom groups. Because the monitoring of progress is a collaborative, professional activity, the data should be shared among teachers at the same grade level and should be analyzed to identify student needs and determine what strategies are working most effectively.

Everything students do during instruction provides an opportunity for monitoring their progress. For the classroom teacher and site administrator to be able to use the assessment information across

> It is virtually impossible to overstate the importance of using performance data as the basis for making well-informed adjustments to instruction.

classrooms by grade level, this type of assessment requires (1) the use of standardized procedures to administer the test; (2) the standardization of test form; (3) the use of standardized scoring procedures with agreed-on answer keys and interpretation guides (e.g., established cutoff scores for indicating mastery level); and (4) a procedure for the use of the information to determine instructional needs and appropriate interventions for each student.

It is virtually impossible to overstate the importance of using performance data as the basis for making well-informed adjustments to instruction. Teachers need a solid basis for answering such questions as the following:

- Should I move ahead? Or should I spend a little more time on the current phase of instruction?
- Are students able to practice and apply what they have learned adequately through independent activities? Or do I need to provide additional, specific instruction?
- Can I accelerate the planned instruction for some or all students, given that there is sufficient evidence of student mastery? If so, what is the best way to proceed?

Summative Assessment

The most critical aspect of all summative assessment is that it measures generalization and transference of skills and knowledge required for mastery of grade-level standards. For example, if one summative evaluation in the early grades involves a test of decoding a list of words, some or all of those words should be new to students (words not previously used extensively in decoding tasks). If a summative assessment in later grades involves reading a passage and answering comprehension questions, students should

223

Chapter 6
Assessment
of Proficiency
in the
Language Arts

not have read the measurement passages previously. If students are to write a critical review of a literary work in high school, they should analyze and evaluate a new reading selection.

Many teachers are concerned about teaching to the test. Summative assessments did not guide the development of the standards; rather, the standards provide the basis for developing or selecting summative assessments. Further, summative assessments aligned with the standards and the curriculum are not mere reflections of retained knowledge but can be the most valid and reliable indicators of depth of understanding as demonstrated through generalization and transference.

Statewide Pupil Assessment System

A major component of California's statewide testing system is the Standardized Testing and Reporting (STAR) Program. For reading and the language arts, STAR, along with the Assessment of Applied Academic Skills currently under development, is the statewide system for summative assessment.

Standardized Testing and Reporting Program

STAR consists of three parts: (1) a standardized norm-referenced test; (2) an augmentation test aligned with the English–language arts content standards; and (3) a standardized, norm-referenced primary language assessment. Characteristics of the STAR Program are that it:

- Requires the assessment of all students in English with a test approved by the State Board of Education
- Assesses achievement in reading, spelling, written expression, and

mathematics in grades two through eight and reading, writing, mathematics, history–social science, and science in grades nine through eleven

- Requires testing of academic achievement in the primary language for limited-English-proficient students enrolled for fewer than 12 months (optional thereafter)
- Generates the results of testing for individual students and reports to the public the results for schools, school districts, counties, and the state
- Disaggregates the results by grade level as to English proficiency, gender, and economic disadvantage for reporting to the public
- Provides both norm-referenced and standards-based results

The State Board of Education has adopted performance levels to be used in reporting the results of the augmented test: advanced, proficient, and basic, with an additional level designated as below basic. The levels correspond with those used by the National Assessment of Educational Progress. The augmented test addresses all the categories of the content standards except direct writing, listening, and speaking.

Additional Components

Several additional components of the Statewide Pupil Assessment System enacted into law were being developed when this framework was being prepared for publication. The components include the following:

- Development of performance standards that define levels of student performance at each grade level in each of the areas in which the content standards have been adopted. "Performance standards gauge the degree to which the student has met the content standards and the degree to which a school or school district has met the content standards" (*Education Code* Section 60603[h]).

- Assessment of applied academic skills, based on the content and performance standards, that "requires students to demonstrate their knowledge of, and ability to apply, academic knowledge and skills in order to solve problems and communicate" in grades four, five, eight, and ten. "It may include . . . writing an essay, conducting an experiment, or constructing a diagram or model" (*Education Code* Section 60603[b]).

- Adoption of a test to measure the development of reading, speaking, and writing skills in English for students whose primary language is not English.

The Golden State Examination Program completes the assessment picture in California. It provides a measure of student achievement in several academic subjects normally taken at the middle school and high school levels. Participation in this program is voluntary, and students who do well on the tests receive a special honors designation. Work is under way to align the Golden State Examination with the content standards in the four core areas.

Summary of the Chapter

Each of the three distinct types of assessment described previously—entry-level assessment, monitoring of progress, and summative assessment—contributes substantially to informing effective instruction. In particular the monitoring of progress can play a key role in developing and delivering curricula and instruction that effectively lead to the achievement of the goals embedded in the standards. This framework places substantial emphasis on integrating an assessment system with curriculum and instruction. Therefore, assessment and instruction must be interrelated in ways that minimize the loss of instructional time and maximize the potential for assessment measures themselves to contribute to meaningful learning.

Universal Access to the Language Arts Curriculum

The ultimate goal of language arts programs in California is to ensure access to high-quality curriculum and instruction for all students in order to meet or exceed the state's English–language arts content standards.

The diversity of California's students presents unique opportunities and significant challenges for instruction. Students come to school with a wide variety of skills, abilities, and interests as well as varying proficiency in English and other languages. The wider the variation of the student population in each classroom, the more complex becomes the teacher's role in organizing high-quality curriculum and instruction in the language arts and ensuring that each student has access according to the student's current level of achievement. The ultimate goal of language arts programs in California is to ensure access to high-quality curriculum and instruction for all students in order to meet or exceed the state's English–language arts content standards. To reach that goal, teachers need assistance in assessing and using the results of that assessment for planning programs, differentiating curriculum and instruction, using grouping strategies effectively, and implementing other strategies for meeting the needs of students with reading difficulties, special education students, advanced learners, English learners, and students with combinations of special needs.

Procedures that may be useful in planning for universal access are to:

- Assess each student's understanding at the start of instruction and continue to do so frequently as instruction advances, using the results of *assessment* for program placement and planning.
- *Diagnose* the nature and severity of the student's difficulty and modify curriculum and instruction accordingly when students have trouble with the language arts.
- Engage in careful organization of resources and instruction and *planning* to adapt to individual needs. A variety of good teaching strategies that can be used according to the situation should be prepared.
- *Differentiate* when necessary as to depth, complexity, novelty, or pacing and focus on the language arts standards and the key concepts within the standards that students must master to move on to the next grade level.
- Employ *flexible grouping* strategies according to the students' needs and achievement and the instructional tasks presented.
- *Enlist help* from others, such as reading specialists, special education specialists, parents, aides, other teachers, community members, administrators, counselors, and diagnosticians when necessary and explore technology or other instruc-

What the student
already knows in
the language arts
should form the
basis for further
learning and
study.

tional devices or instructional materials, such as Braille text, as a way to respond to students' individual needs.

Alignment of Assessment and Instruction

One of the first tasks required of a school district is to determine its students' achievement levels in the language arts so that each student or group of students can be offered a structured language arts program leading to the attainment of all of the content standards. What the student already knows in the language arts should form the basis for further learning and study.

Assessment is the key to ensuring that all students are provided with language arts instruction designed to help the students progress at an appropriate pace from what they already know to higher levels of learning. Knowing which standards have been mastered, teachers can better plan the instructional program. For a variety of reasons, gaps often appear in what has been learned by students with special needs. The gaps can be discovered through assessment, and instruction can be designed to remediate specific weaknesses without slowing down the students' entire language arts program.

Successful Diagnostic Teaching

Students who have trouble in reading and writing are at risk of failing to meet the standards, becoming discouraged, and eventually dropping out of school. The teacher should try to determine the cause of the learning difficulties. Contributing factors might include a lack of foundation skills; limited-English proficiency; uncorrected errors; confusing, inadequate, or inappropriate instructional resources or instruction; or an undiagnosed specific learning disability. A teacher can use the results of assessment and classroom observations to determine what interventions should be tried in the classroom and whether to refer the students to a student success team (student study team) or seek assistance from specialists. Most learning difficulties can be corrected with good diagnostic teaching that combines repetition of instruction, focus on key skills and understanding, and practice. For some students modification of the curriculum or instruction (or both) may be required to accommodate differences in communication modes, physical skills, or learning abilities.

To plan appropriate intervention strategies for helping students who are experiencing learning difficulties, teachers should consider the degree of severity according to the three following major groups (Kame'enui and Simmons 1998):

Benchmark Group

Students in the benchmark group are generally making good progress toward the standards but may be experiencing temporary or minor difficulties. Although the needs of these students are not critical, they must be addressed quickly to prevent the students from falling behind. Often, the teacher can reteach a concept in a different way to an individual or a group of students or schedule a study group to provide additional learning time. Occasionally, parents can be enlisted to reinforce learning at home. Ideally, instructional resources will be organized in ways that make it easy for parents to do so. Some students may need periodic individual assistance, the help of a reading

specialist, or other types of support to ensure that they succeed in the regular classroom. Once the concept or procedure has been grasped correctly by the student, additional practice is usually helpful.

Strategic Group

Students in the strategic group may be one to two standard deviations below the mean according to the results of standardized testing. However, their learning difficulties, which must be examined with systematic and, occasionally, intensive and concentrated care, can often be addressed by the regular classroom teacher with minimal assistance within the classroom environment. A student success team might be called on to discuss appropriate support for the student. In addition to reteaching a concept, the teacher may wish to provide specific assignments over a period of time for students to complete with a peer or tutor or by themselves at home. Regular study groups working before or after school, in the evenings, or on weekends can provide an effective extension of the learning time. Some students may need to schedule extended blocks of time for the study of language arts to master difficult content. Others may require specific accommodations and modifications to the classroom environment, curriculum, or instruction as identified in the students' 504 plan. Special education students may need special modifications of curriculum or instruction, as specified in their individualized education program, to enable them to participate successfully in a mainstream classroom.

Intensive Group

Students in the intensive group are seriously at risk as indicated by their extremely and chronically low performance on one or more measures. The greater the number of measures and the lower the performance, the greater is their risk. These students perform well below the mean and should be referred to a student success team for a thorough discussion of options. A referral to special education may be advisable. If eligible for special education services, these students will be given an individualized education program, which will describe the most appropriate services for the student. Often, specialized assistance will be available through the special education referral, perhaps including intensive intervention by a qualified specialist, tutoring, services of a classroom assistant, specialized materials or equipment, changes in assessment procedures, or modification of the curriculum or instruction.

Planning for Special Needs Students

Experienced teachers develop a repertoire of successful instructional strategies to be used in special situations or with specific groups of students. Many of the strategies can be explicitly taught or can be embedded in the instructional materials to help teachers plan differentiated instruction. To establish successful instructional strategies for all students, the teacher should:

1. Establish a safe and supportive environment in which the students are encouraged to talk and ask questions freely when they do not understand.
2. Use a wide variety of ways to explain a concept or assignment. When appropriate, the concept or assignment may be depicted in graphic or pictorial form, with manipulatives, or with real objects to accompany oral and written instructions.
3. Provide assistance in the specific and general vocabulary to be used for each lesson prior to the lesson, using reinforcement or additional practice afterward. Instructional resources and instruction should be monitored for ambiguities or language that would be confusing, such as idioms.
4. Set up tutoring situations that offer additional assistance. Tutoring by a qualified teacher is optimal. Peer or cross-age tutoring should be so designed not to detract from the instructional time of either the tutor or tutee and should be supervised.
5. Extend the learning time by establishing a longer school day, weekend classes, and intersession or summer classes.
6. Enlist the help of parents at home when possible.
7. Establish special sessions to prepare students for unfamiliar testing situations.
8. Ask each student frequently to communicate his or her understanding of the concept or assignment. Students should be asked to verbalize or write down what they know, thereby providing immediate insight into their thinking and level of understanding. In addition, students should be encouraged to confer about each other's understanding of the concept being taught and the class work or homework assignments, particularly if the students are not fully proficient in English.
9. Check frequently for understanding in a variety of ways. When a

student does not understand, analyze why.

10. Allow students to demonstrate their understanding and abilities in a variety of ways while reinforcing modes of communication that will be used on standardized tests.

Differentiation Through Pacing and Complexity

Advanced students and those with learning difficulties in the language arts often require systematically planned differentiation to ensure that curriculum and instruction are appropriately challenging. The strategies for modification of curriculum and instruction for special education or at-risk students are similar to those used for advanced learners and can be considered variations along four dimensions: pacing, depth, complexity, and novelty. Two dimensions will be discussed here, pacing and complexity. For additional discussion see *Differentiating the Core Curriculum and Instruction to Provide Advanced Learning Opportunities* (California Department of Education 1994).

Use of Pacing

Pacing is perhaps the most commonly used strategy for differentiation. That is, the teacher slows down or speeds up instruction. This strategy can be simple, effective, and inexpensive for many students with special needs (Benbow and Stanley 1996; Geary 1994). The instructional pace of the advanced learner can be accelerated if the assessment indicates mastery of significant portions of the standards. Students can be helped to move on to the content standards for the next grade level.

For students experiencing difficulty in the language arts, the same content might be extended over twice as long a period of time for additional reinforcement in the more difficult concepts. Alternatively, some students with attention deficits respond better to shorter, more frequent episodes of instruction. A key element in slowing down instruction is to ensure that the content remains rigorous, that the students move ahead as quickly as they can, and that the instruction leads to mastery of the content standards within a reasonable amount of time.

Use of Complexity

Modifying instruction as to *complexity* requires more training and skill on the part of the teacher and the provision of instructional materials that lend themselves to such variations. For advanced students it means enriched instruction that encourages students to address topics, time periods, or connections across disciplines not normally expected at that grade level.

For students experiencing difficulty in the language arts, the teacher should focus on the key concepts within the standards and eliminate confusing activities or variables. The lessons should be even more organized and sequential and be focused on the most important concepts. Instruction is not thereby watered down. Instead, it is distilled to ensure that instructional time is used to help students understand the fundamental concepts or skills needed to master later standards.

Differentiation for special needs students is sometimes criticized by those who say that struggling students never progress to the more interesting or complex assignments. This argument is often used to move struggling students along or involve them in complex assignments, even though they have not mastered the basics they

[Instruction] is distilled to ensure that instructional time is used to help students understand the fundamental concepts or skills needed to master later standards.

need to understand the assignments. This framework advocates a focus on the standards and frequent assessment to ensure that students are not just passed along without the skills they will need to be successful in subsequent grades. Struggling students are expected to learn the key concepts well so that they can develop a foundation on which further understanding can be built.

Grouping as an Aid to Instruction

Research shows that what students are taught has a far greater effect on their achievement than how they are grouped (Mosteller, Light, and Sachs 1996). The first focus of educators should always be on the quality of instruction; grouping is a secondary concern. This framework recommends that educators use common sense about grouping. Grouping is a tool and an aid to instruction, not an end in itself. As a tool it should be used flexibly to ensure that all students achieve the standards. Instructional objectives should always be based on the standards and should dictate grouping strategies. It is perfectly appropriate, even advisable, to group those students who do not understand a concept or skill and to find time to reteach the concept or skill in a different way and provide additional practice. At the same time those students might be participating with a more heterogeneous mix of students in other classroom activities.

In another setting teachers may discover that they have a group of students in a grade who have mastered the standards for that grade and are ready to go on to the standards for the next grade. It is appropriate and advisable to group those students for as long as the grouping meets

their needs and to provide the needed accelerated instruction. To promote maximum learning, the teacher should ensure that assessment is frequent, that high-quality instruction is always provided, and that the students are frequently moved into appropriate instructional groups according to their needs.

Special Modifications for Special Education Students

Educators who wish to help children with difficulties in a particular domain need to know about the course of typical development in that domain, about the specific cognitive abilities that are crucial at various points in development, about the cognitive abilities in which a particular child is weak, and about how to best develop these abilities. (Spear-Swerling and Sternberg 1998, 400)

Students eligible for special education services often have specific needs described in an individualized education program. Special resources may be available to the students to help them meet the standards, including personnel (e.g., reading specialists, speech and hearing therapists, psychologists, and classroom aides). Assistive devices, such as wheelchairs, walkers, tape recorders, sound-amplification devices, and regular or Braille word processors, can accommodate a student's physical challenges so that the curriculum is accessible.

Specific learning disabilities that manifest themselves as deficits in language arts achievement can be difficult to diagnose and at times difficult to remedy. The approach recommended in this framework, with its focus on "first best teaching," including frequent assessment,

> Grouping is a tool and an aid to instruction, not an end in itself.

systematic and explicit instruction in the building blocks of word recognition and reading comprehension, and modifications of curriculum as needed, should result in many more students reading. It should significantly reduce the number of students identified as having learning problems or learning disabilities. No single approach is as effective in teaching students to read, particularly in teaching those who have difficulty in reading, as systematic, explicit instruction emphasizing phonemic awareness, decoding, and phonics.

Nevertheless, some students with learning disabilities affecting the processing of oral or written language, usually phonology, will be atypical in reading acquisition. For those students a thorough diagnosis of what they can and cannot do is helpful. The assessment should be conducted by a learning specialist who understands thoroughly the typical process students go through when learning to read. The specialist should also understand the specific areas of cognitive functioning in which learning-disabled students may have difficulty and ways in which instruction can be adapted. The specialist can then work with the regular classroom teacher to implement specific strategies, which might include changes in the sequence of instruction, the methods of instruction, the pacing of instruction, or the materials used. The strategies might also include variations in assessment techniques (e.g., allowing more time for a student who processes or produces written language more slowly). Regardless of the modifications made, however, the focus should always be placed on helping students meet the language arts content standards to the best of their ability and frequently assessing their progress in attaining the standards.

Differentiated Instruction for Advanced Learners

Advanced learners are students who demonstrate or are capable of demonstrating performance in the language arts at a level significantly above the performance of their peers. They may include (1) students formally identified by a school district as gifted and talented pursuant to *Education Code* Section 52200; and (2) other students who have not been formally identified as gifted and talented but demonstrate outstanding capacity or actual performance in the language arts. This situation is especially true in California, where each district sets its own criteria for identifying gifted and talented students, where the percentage of students so identified varies, and where each district may choose whether to identify on the basis of ability in language arts. The research studies cited in this framework use the term *gifted students,* which is defined in most areas outside California in a more standardized way in accordance with nationally normed tests of achievement or intelligence. In that context the term usually refers to the small number of students who score at the highest percentiles on the test.

Standards-based education offers opportunities for students who have the motivation, interest, or ability in the language arts to excel. Several research studies have demonstrated the importance of setting high standards for all students, including gifted students. The content standards in the language arts have provided students with goals worth reaching for and identify the point at which skills and knowledge should be mastered. The natural corollary is that

When standards
are mastered,
students should
either move on
to standards at
higher grade
levels or focus
on unlearned
material not
covered by the
standards.

when standards are mastered, students should either move on to standards at higher grade levels or focus on unlearned material not covered by the standards.

A research study (Shore et al. 1991) examined whether any evidence exists to support 101 common practices in gifted education and found that very few practices were supported by solid evidence. However, the study also found that a combination of acceleration (in which students move on to material above grade level) and enrichment (in which students study topics in more depth or complexity or study related topics not covered in the normal curriculum) is supported by the research and results in improved achievement for gifted students.

How to group advanced learners has been controversial. In a longitudinal study (Delcourt et al. 1994) of grouping arrangements for over 1,000 elementary-age students, it was found that gifted students receiving an enriched and accelerated curriculum delivered in special schools, special day classes, and pullout programs made statistically significant improvement in achievement in the language arts, mathematics, science, and history–social science in comparison with gifted students who did not receive such programming.

The only type of programming arrangement that did not result in statistically significant improvement in achievement was enrichment offered in the regular heterogeneously grouped classroom. The reason for the lack of success was that even with the best of intentions, teachers did not have enough time to deliver the advanced or enriched curriculum for the gifted students that had been planned. Because most gifted students in California are served in the regular heterogeneously grouped classroom, teachers must ensure that enrichment or acceleration occurs when advanced students are instructed in

a heterogeneous group, as argued for persuasively in the study (Delcourt et al. 1994). A previous study (California Department of Education 1994) provides an outline on how to differentiate instruction for advanced students regardless of how they are grouped. In referencing that study, we do not mean to suggest that all gifted students be homogeneously grouped. Decisions on how to group students should be made locally. However, the Delcourt study underscores the importance of providing support for teachers so that they can effectively meet the individual needs of all students in their classrooms.

Instructional Programs for English Learners

California's diverse student population comes from many different ethnic groups, speaks a variety of languages and dialects, varies in English proficiency, and comes to school with a variety of experiences, academic and nonacademic. A 1997 report issued by the California Department of Education revealed that 1.4 million students enrolled in California public schools used a primary language other than English and were identified as limited-English proficient (LEP). More than 100 languages (other than English) were found to be represented. The top four languages and percentages of LEP students were Spanish (81 percent), Vietnamese (3 percent), Hmong (2 percent), and Cantonese (2 percent).

English learners have as their goal developing proficiency in English and in the concepts and skills contained in the *English–Language Arts Content Standards*. Because of recent changes in California law, instruction for most English learners must be presented "overwhelmingly in English." To learn English and achieve mastery of the English–language arts content standards, students must participate in instructional programs that combine skill and concept development in both English literacy and the English language. For those students whose parents have chosen a program that teaches literacy in the primary language, students must work to achieve the same standards contained in the *English–Language Arts Content Standards*. Appropriate modifications should be made for the language of instruction.

In a structured English immersion program, instruction in reading and writing for English learners should not be delayed until the students have mastered oral English. Effective early instruction in English literacy, as described in Chapter 3, must be incorporated into a program of English-language development from the very beginning. Students must be provided significant support to be successful in the language arts. Such support includes the preteaching of essential elements of lesson vocabulary and language structure and additional assistance after the lesson during the school day and after school. Instruction in oral and written academic language for English learners is a critical element that must be specifically designed, planned, scheduled, and taught. It includes direct instruction and experiences for students in English phonology, morphology, syntax, and semantics and supports students as they move toward English proficiency.

Instructional programs for English learners should be planned according to the students' assessed levels of literacy in English and their primary language as well as their proficiency in English. English-language proficiency progresses from the students' initial contact with formal instruction in English to the point at which their use of English compares with that of their native English-speaking peers. Because of differing academic backgrounds and ages, some students can be expected to progress more quickly and others to require more support in the English–language arts program. Instructional materials contain assessment tools to diagnose students' proficiency in listening, speaking, reading, and writing in English and to assist teachers in planning initial instruction, monitoring progress, and conducting summative evaluations.

Three groups of English learners must be considered in program planning: students in kindergarten through grade two; those in grades three through twelve who are literate in their primary language; and those in grades three through twelve who have limited prior academic experience or literacy in their primary language. Typically, primary students who are learning English can participate fully in classroom language arts instruction if provided appropriate reading and writing supports and instruction in oral language. Students in grades three through twelve who have strong literacy skills in their primary language can be expected to transfer many of those skills to English and to progress rapidly in learning English. And students in grades three through twelve with limited prior schooling will require intensive support in beginning literacy instruction as well as in learning English.

Instruction and Support in Reading and Writing

Students in kindergarten through grade two. Students who begin to learn reading and writing in English in the primary grades should participate fully in the classroom program and receive additional support to achieve the English–language

Instruction in
reading and
writing for English
learners should
not be delayed
until the students
have mastered
oral English.

Additional
instructional
support must align
with classroom
instruction and
assist students in
learning the
specific vocabulary,
background
knowledge, and
language structures
needed to
succeed.

arts content standards. Whereas most English-speaking kindergartners enter school with 6,000 to 15,000 words in their English vocabulary, most English learners do not. Instruction in English is a critical component of the program for English learners and proceeds simultaneously with direct, explicit, and systematic instruction in reading and writing. Abundant opportunities to participate in oral language and speaking activities help students hear and develop the English sound system and lexicon and support the concurrent development of reading and writing with comprehension. Beginning instruction in reading, particularly in phonemic awareness, concepts about print, and vocabulary development commences immediately upon entry into school and supports the acquisition of English phonology and initial language structures. In kindergarten and the first grade, English learners progress to sound-symbol correspondence and formation of letters as they build vocabulary and an understanding of the features of the English language.

Full comprehension of text will be limited by the students' level of English proficiency and should be supported by additional exposure to and study of vocabulary and language patterns presented in the text. Students should receive preteaching in essential vocabulary, background information, and language patterns. A review of key lesson elements and assessment of the students' level of understanding should follow the lessons in reading and writing. As described at the beginning of this chapter, additional instructional time, differentiated instruction, flexible grouping, and smaller groups should provide students the support they need to succeed in the language arts. After-school programs, specialist teachers, and the judicious use of tutors and

paraprofessionals are other sources of support. Additional instructional support must align with classroom instruction and assist students in learning the specific vocabulary, background knowledge, and language structures needed to succeed.

Students in grades three through twelve. English learners entering school in grades three through twelve with strong literacy skills in their primary language are advantaged in that they can concentrate on acquiring and learning English rather than on receiving initial instruction in reading and writing. However, the greater cognitive demands of the academic program in those grades require that the students move quickly to more advanced English vocabulary and language structures. English-language development should be intensive and should emphasize the language students will need to know so that they profit from instruction in the language arts and other content areas at their grade level. Again, students will need additional support to learn English and to understand the vocabulary and language of instruction. School districts and schools need to consider additional allocations of instructional time to maximize students' opportunities to acquire language and participate in the overall language arts program.

Students who enter school in grades three through twelve with little prior schooling and limited English must be quickly identified and assessed to determine their level of reading and writing skills in their primary language and in English. Learning to read and write while concurrently learning English is a challenge for these students. School districts and schools need to structure the instructional program so that the students receive the instruction they require in literacy and language. The students require intensive, systematic instruction in oral and written language, including, for example, instruction in the use of common nouns, verbs, adjectives, and adverbs. They also need to learn common phrases, language patterns, and idiomatic expressions. Materials that address those skills, individualized instruction, and additional assistance and instructional time will be needed to support English learners who have limited academic experience. The materials must describe age-appropriate activities to teach reading and English-language development.

English-Language Development

Stages of instruction. From the earliest stages of their academic careers and in concert with instruction in reading and writing, English learners participate in an instructional program that supports their acquisition of informal English and teaches them the patterns of formal academic English. The instruction is designed to provide for students experiences with English that are understandable and meaningful and enable the students to communicate with peers and adults and thereby participate fully in the academic program. Students begin by learning basic social conventions, rudimentary classroom vocabulary, and ways to express personal and safety needs. They participate in language study in a variety of contexts ranging from informal classroom conversations to teacher-directed instruction in language forms and structures. Effective teachers use a variety of activities to introduce and reinforce language concepts (e.g., singing, presenting dramas, reading aloud, using visuals and props, and practicing simple phrases and vocabulary).

Teachers model and teach the language patterns and vocabulary needed to understand and participate in the study of the language arts and other content areas. They should not assume that students will use their newly acquired academic vocabulary in casual conversation. Instead, they should specifically plan student-to-student discussions in which the students are expected to practice their new vocabulary and understanding of language forms in substantive academic discussions. Students learn English phonology, morphology (including spelling and syllabication patterns), syntax, and semantics through teacher modeling, teacher-directed instruction, and classroom interaction. They build on classroom exposure and interaction with English sounds, word elements, sentence structure, and vocabulary through directed study and practice of the linguistic elements. Analysis of the elements of instruction and materials increases in sophistication as students progress through the grades and gain linguistic and academic competence. This purposeful study of the features of the English language, which involves instruction in oral and written language, is connected to the English–language arts content standards through the language arts and content-area instruction in which students participate daily.

Instructional opportunities and materials. Most important, teachers plan opportunities, supported by appropriate instructional materials, for students to produce language they have acquired, use language in academic interactions with peers and adults, and monitor and correct their oral and written language. Teachers create an environment in which students feel comfortable in risking the use of new and unfamiliar language. Instructional materials describe for teachers the linguistic features of the most commonly spoken languages as they differ from English (e.g., analysis of similar and dissimilar sounds). Teachers apply the understanding of similarities and differences among the languages in planning instruction and

English learners participate in an instructional program that supports their acquisition of informal English and teaches them the patterns of formal academic English.

Students should
receive specific,
constructive
feedback from
their teachers
regarding the
accuracy of their
oral and written
work and their
progress toward
mastery of
conventional
English.

use questioning and other strategies to foster substantive student discussion and participation. Emphasis is placed on the students' producing language in a variety of contexts and the teachers' eliciting student participation and thought.

Students should receive specific, constructive feedback from their teachers regarding the accuracy of their oral and written work and their progress toward mastery of conventional English. Teachers should analyze students' errors to determine development in oral and written English and plan appropriate instruction to improve competence. Instructional materials contain assessment tools that assist teachers in the analysis and specifically address instruction in those areas as related to grade-level English–language arts standards.

Instruction for English learners in academic language helps bring the students to a level of English proficiency comparable with that of their native English-speaking peers. English-language development occurs daily; is specifically identified within the curriculum of the school district and the school; and is

supported by high-quality instructional materials, a sufficient amount of instructional time, and professional development for teachers. Language development and literacy instruction are integrated with the basic instructional materials and should be specifically identified in the teacher's edition as differentiated instruction for students not fully proficient in English. For students in grades three through twelve who are just learning English, instructional materials should be specially designed to provide intensive and extensive English-language development. Included should be development in oral and written vocabulary, reading instruction (as described in this framework), and systematic instruction in the forms and features of English. Publishers are encouraged to develop materials for those districts that choose to have students spend most of their school day receiving such instruction. The purpose of differentiated instruction in English is to move English learners as quickly as possible through stages of language proficiency and to enable them to achieve mastery of the English–language arts content standards.

Responsibilities and Support for Proficiency in the Language Arts

8

Together, the [school] community members can help refocus the school or district priorities for reading, writing, listening, and speaking.

For students to meet grade-level content standards, comprehensive community systems of support should be developed to advocate a sustained focus on the development of language arts skills for every student. A support system for each school will help in the design, implementation, and evaluation of effective language arts instructional plans, classroom teaching strategies, instructional materials, and support systems for students with special needs.

Responsibilities of the School Community

The school community includes parents and families, classroom teachers and specialist teachers, library media teachers, tutors, paraprofessionals, preschool educators, local educational

Chapter 8
Responsibilities
and Support
for Proficiency
in the Language
Arts

agencies, school administrators, professional developers, and business, civic, and service organizations. Together, the community members can help refocus the school or district priorities for reading, writing, listening, and speaking.

The school community can participate in the development and implementation of a literacy plan for each school by:

- Insisting on a sustained *schoolwide and communitywide discussion* on students' achievement in the language arts
- Establishing *clear and measurable reading improvement goals* (*Example:* "Every student who is reading below grade level will be provided with a systematic intervention program no later than November 1 of each year." Or: "At Maple Street School the percentage of students reading at or above grade level will increase from 40 percent to 60 percent by June 1.")
- Implementing a *systematic process for the selection of instructional materials* based on comprehensive information, such as reviewing current and confirmed research or data provided by publishers or conducting pilot tests
- Providing an effective program of *professional development* based on current research and the English–language arts content standards for preservice, new, and continuing teachers
- Encouraging *parent involvement* in a variety of ways (e.g., through regular communication between parents and educators, multiple opportunities for volunteering, parent involvement in school decision making, collaboration with community support agencies)

- Ensuring the availability of well-stocked *classroom libraries and a well-equipped media center* to provide students with access to a variety of high-quality resources for language arts development
- Creating *partnerships* with business, civic, and service organizations and establishing service-learning projects to seek involvement and support for promoting literacy for all students.

Parents and Families

Parents are their children's first teachers. The child's home language and home literacy experiences form the basis of more formal language development in school. The involvement of parents in their children's early years is an important predictor of the children's success in school (McCollum and Russo 1993; Chavkin 1993; National Committee for Citizens in Education 1994) and is more important than economic status in predicting academic learning (Walberg 1984). The importance of parents' reading to their children is well documented (Anderson, Wilson, and Fielding 1988), and parents' conversations with children can be a rich source of language development.

In addition to support for early language development at home, parents can provide a stable source of support for their children's schooling. Recent studies indicate that most parents care deeply about their children's education but may not show their concerns in the same way (Valdés 1996; Gándara 1995). For example, some parents may show their support by voicing to their children consistent respect for the value of education. Other parents may support completion of homework or volunteer in the classroom. In addition, parents may serve in an advisory capacity on a school-site

239

Chapter 8
Responsibilities
and Support
for Proficiency
in the Language
Arts

council or manage activities in the library media center, such as the shelving and checking out of books. Classroom teachers or librarians can promote and expand parent involvement through family literacy events, visits by guest authors, summer reading programs, and book fairs. Regardless of the way in which parents or family members support education, they should always be made to feel welcome and know that their contributions are welcomed and appreciated.

Parents and families should be well informed about the language arts curriculum their children receive and the progress their children are making in learning to read, write, speak, and listen. The school and school district should provide outreach to inform parents and families about the English–language arts content standards, the district's curriculum and assessment programs, and the degree to which students in the school and district are mastering the standards in the language arts. Materials and programs should be organized so that parents and families can receive specific information and support for extending their children's learning at home. Parents and families should be made aware, as appropriate, of resources available to support their own literacy, such as Even Start or adult education. Ultimately, parents and families are the most essential partners in promoting the value of reading and writing and in providing the home support needed for children to master the standards in the language arts.

Classroom Teachers

The impact of an outstanding classroom teacher on a child's life can be dramatic. Good teachers are effective because they work hard at perfecting their teaching ability over a long period of time. Development of their craft comes from years of formal college training, experience in the classroom, periodic professional development, and an undying commitment to learning.

The demands on teachers in California are greater than ever before. More and more teachers are being called on to be reading teachers regardless of whether they have had formal training in teaching students how to read. In standards-based education teachers will be expected to help their students master areas of the curriculum that were previously attempted only by gifted students. Granted, class size has been reduced in most kindergarten through grade three classrooms in California. But in those classrooms and in classrooms for students in grades four through twelve, the diversity of students' prior experiences provides a challenge as teachers try to adapt instruction to a range of experience and ability.

To help teachers build expertise and find satisfaction in their work, ongoing professional development should target specific knowledge and skills. It should also provide consistent support for improved teaching through coaching, the pairing of teachers with a mentor or buddy, and collegial discussions about the design and implementation of effective language arts programs. Teachers should have a role in designing their own professional development, which should be planned and organized and should lead to long-term goals and be supported over time.

For new teachers the requirements for preparation and the support for their induction into the teaching profession are changing rapidly. For example, to earn a multiple-subjects teaching credential, teacher candidates must now pass the *Reading Instruction Competence Assessment (RICA),* which tests the knowledge, skills, and abilities of new teachers as related to

More and more teachers are being called on to be reading teachers regardless of whether they have had formal training in teaching students how to read.

Chapter 8
Responsibilities
and Support
for Proficiency
in the Language
Arts

teaching reading. Areas assessed include phonemic awareness; concepts about print; systematic, explicit phonics and other word-identification strategies; spelling instruction; vocabulary development; reading comprehension; student independent reading and its relationship to improved reading performance; relationships between reading, writing, and oral language; diagnosis of reading development; and the structure of the English language. Preservice programs specifically prepare teacher candidates for *RICA* as a part of their courses in reading instruction.

Specialist Teachers

Even with the most effective literacy instruction in place, some students, for a variety of reasons, struggle with reading or are unable to read at grade level. "Such students will require supplementary services, ideally from a reading specialist who provides individual or small-group intensive instruction that is coordinated with high-quality instruction from the classroom teacher" (National Research Council 1998, 12).

Reading specialists, resource specialists, and speech and language therapists are key individuals in the provision of supplementary services for students not achieving in reading and language arts as well as in the implementation of the overall language arts program. As knowledgeable and experienced teachers of reading and language, specialists can assume a leadership role in the school by modeling effective instruction, presenting professional development activities, organizing early intervention, assisting with assessment activities, consulting with classroom teachers, and facilitating schoolwide planning and decision making for the language arts. The role of specialists in supporting the work of classroom teachers

The role of
specialists in
supporting the
work of classroom
teachers is
especially
important as
teachers grapple
with the
implementation
of content
standards and
shifts in instruc-
tional materials
and practices.

is especially important as teachers grapple with the implementation of content standards and shifts in instructional materials and practices.

Most importantly, specialists play a key role in intervention by working with teachers to identify students who need assistance, conducting specialized assessments, and providing the extra instruction and support students need to master the language arts standards. Specialists "could specialize in knowledge about the cognitive processes involved in typical acquisition of academic skills, in knowledge about the ways in which children might go awry in acquiring important cognitive and academic skills, and in adapting instruction for children with a variety of cognitive and academic difficulties" (Spear-Swerling and Sternberg 1998, 401).

Library Media Teachers

The American Association of School Librarians and the Association for Educational Communications and Technology (1998) point to the importance of library media teachers as learning resource and technology specialists and instructional partners. When the library media teacher, who knows the learning resources, technologies, skills, and information problem-solving process, acts as a partner with the classroom teacher, who knows the students and the curricular content to be addressed, they expand students' learning opportunities and directly improve achievement (Lance, Welborn, and Hamilton-Pennell 1993). By codesigning and implementing resource-based learning and other cross-disciplinary projects, library media teachers and classroom teachers help students apply language arts skills to genuine information problems.

Particularly at the elementary school level but later too, library media teachers contribute to students' success in literary

241

Chapter 8
Responsibilities
and Support
for Proficiency
in the Language
Arts

response and analysis. The library media credential equips library media teachers with extensive background in literacy genres for children and young adults. They know the characteristics of different genres and authors; can easily connect books similar in setting, character, plot, or theme; and can work with teachers to locate useful examples of literary devices, such as simile, metaphor, and personification. In effectively conveying that aspect of reading comprehension to students, they are essential partners with classroom teachers.

Library media teachers, who are teachers primarily, have an additional credential that extends their expertise into literature, the research process, library management, and information technologies. The dynamic library field is changing with the advent of expanded information access afforded by the digital age. They can contribute to expanding students' literacy, information acquisition, and ability to become independent, self-directed learners. Library media teachers provide motivation to read and guidance in personal reading and reach out to the community and parents to encourage family literacy. They also teach students how to use the online catalog, how to locate information, how to think about what they have found in relation to what they need, and how to communicate what they have learned in print and in multimedia formats.

Tutors

Tutoring is *not* a substitute for teaching. Tutoring methods should complement professional teaching, not supplant it. Pinnel and Fountas (1997) conclude that effective tutoring embodies an organized, well-articulated system that includes strong leadership, quality training, appropriate instructional materials,

careful monitoring, alignment with classroom instruction, and communication among classroom teachers, tutors, and parents. Yet it is exactly in those areas that programs are often planned ineffectively or not at all (Topping 1998).

Among the goals of tutoring and other remedial programs are improved literacy skills (in both reading and writing), reading fluency and comprehension at grade level or above, significant gains in reading achievement, increased motivation, greater self-confidence in reading and writing, and ability to transfer literacy skills to other content areas. Some of the most effective tutoring activities are those that involve modeling and scaffolding and are adaptive to the individual student.

Because of the great number of tutoring approaches (e.g., pullout programs, after-school or before-school coaching classes, peer or cross-age tutoring, paired reading, and summer classes) and the variety of potential providers (e.g., reading specialists, credentialed teachers, trained paraprofessional, college students, trained volunteers, and cross-age peers), setting up a remedial program requires informed choices. Selection of the type of supplementary approach to be used and the type of tutor to be provided should be based primarily on the specific needs of students. For instance, students diagnosed with specific learning disabilities must be supported by specialized professionals adequately trained to work with such students. As stated in *Preventing Reading Difficulties in Young Children* (National Research Council 1998, 12), "Although volunteer tutors can provide valuable practice and motivational support for children learning to read, they should not be expected either to provide primary reading instruction or to instruct children with serious reading problems."

Tutoring is not a substitute for teaching. Tutoring methods should complement professional teaching, not supplant it.

Chapter 8
Responsibilities
and Support
for Proficiency
in the Language
Arts

Preschool
educators and
day-care providers
have a key
responsibility and
an opportunity to
provide literacy
experiences that
will help children
meet or exceed
language arts
standards in the
elementary school.

According to *Preventing Early School Failure* (1994), the tutoring programs with the best long-term success in effecting and maintaining achievement gains are those that use teachers rather than aides as tutors. Unfortunately, cost often restricts the use of that approach. Tutoring programs that employ paraprofessionals should be carefully planned and supervised. Available resources are also a factor in the selection of the type of supplementary services used. "However, more is not necessarily better; the cost effectiveness of elaborate training programs requiring many hours [to train tutors] must be considered" (Topping 1998, 48).

Ideally, success in reading can be enhanced for most students who need intervention through good learning experiences in preschool and kindergarten, a quality reading program in the early grades, brief intervention strategies or programs applied at critical points, and family support. A smaller proportion of students may require more extensive intervention strategies (Slavin, Karweit, and Wasik 1993).

Paraprofessionals

Opportunities for planning, ongoing communication, and collaboration with teachers are critical for all paraprofessionals, whether associated with the classroom or the library media center, to ensure coordinated, systematic programs for students. Regularly scheduled offerings for staff development specifically tailored to the needs of the paraprofessionals are also important to improving their skills and knowledge.

Research indicates that paraprofessionals can have a positive impact on student success when trained to provide structured one-on-one tutoring (Slavin, Karweit, and Wasik 1993). A collaborative model featuring open communication between

the classroom teacher, the specialist teacher, and the paraprofessional works well in maximizing the effectiveness of paraprofessionals. Critical to the success of this model is the ongoing training and coaching of the paraprofessional.

Similarly, bilingual paraprofessionals paired with monolingual teachers need time to communicate regularly with the classroom teacher under whose direction they work. The paraprofessionals and the teachers should discuss student needs and progress, alternative strategies, and the use of appropriate materials to help students access fully the core curriculum and acquire English.

Preschool Educators

Preschool educators and day-care providers have a key responsibility and an opportunity to provide literacy experiences that will help children meet or exceed language arts standards in the elementary school. Expectations for language arts learning in the preschool years are presented in *Teaching Reading* (California Department of Education 1996b). Language development is a fundamental element of success in literacy. Early childhood educators recognize that speaking and listening abilities are critical factors in young children's cognitive and social and emotional development. Young children begin to build a foundation for reading and writing through oral communication with adults and other children about everyday experiences. As young children make connections between spoken and written language, they extend their understanding to include symbolic forms used to capture speech.

Adults can aid language development in children by creating a language-rich environment that includes opportunities for language use and interaction, focused stimulation on particular language

243

Chapter 8
Responsibilities
and Support
for Proficiency
in the Language
Arts

features, routines that connect events and language, and social interaction between children (see *Fostering the Development of a First and a Second Language in Early Childhood,* California Department of Education 1998b). Such behaviors may be encouraged in the context of children's play, small-group exploration time, or individual (one-on-one) awareness or exploration activities.

The connection between language development and literacy for young children is featured in *Preventing Reading Difficulties in Young Children* (National Research Council 1998, 319–20):

> Research with preschoolers has demon-strated that (a) adult-child shared book reading that stimulates verbal interaction can enhance language (especially vocabulary) development and knowl-edge about concepts of print; and (b) activities that direct young children's attention to the sound structure within spoken words . . . and to the relations between print and speech can facilitate learning to read. These findings are buttressed by others showing that knowledge of word meanings, and understanding that print conveys meaning, phonological awareness, and some understanding of how printed letters code the sounds of language contribute directly to successful reading.

Preschool programs and day-care-home experiences must, therefore, ensure that children have abundant opportunities to listen to stories, converse, play with language through rhymes and literature, talk about a variety of words and their meanings, hear and repeat correct lan-guage structures, gain understanding of the rich and varied forms of print, learn letters of the alphabet, and practice reading and writing behaviors. *Preventing Reading Difficulties in Young Children* (National Research Council 1998, 171) encourages parents and preschool educa-tors to "spend time in one-on-one conver-sations with young children, read books with them, provide writing materials, support dramatic play that might incorpo-rate literacy activities, demonstrate the uses of literacy, and maintain a joyful, playful atmosphere around literacy activities." Those learning opportunities are important for all children, especially those limited in their exposure to literacy and vocabulary enrichment experiences before entering school.

For preschool programs to promote effectively children's language and literacy development, preschool educators must participate in ongoing professional development, collaborate with elementary school colleagues, and engage in support-ive interactions with families.

Local Educational Agencies

A major premise of local control within the state's educational system centers on the quality of instruction offered to all students. Local educational agencies (LEAs) should establish a special priority for preventing reading difficulties affecting students from families living in poverty, students with disabilities, and English learners—all of whom constitute the fastest-growing segment of America's school population. At the very least LEAs must set high standards for instruction and programs in the language arts. Determining what is of "high" instruc-tional quality should, however, result from research and demonstration and not from a consensus of opinion among content experts, curriculum organizations, or personnel in a state agency or local educational agency.

Local priorities are established within the requirements of state law and regula-tions by a school district governing board, whose members represent the electorate. A school district's accountability rests,

Chapter 8
Responsibilities
and Support
for Proficiency
in the Language
Arts

therefore, with the school board and the public. Through policy development an elected school board provides direction for the operation of a school system, including instruction. The school board is responsible for setting policy, and the administration is responsible for recommending policy to the school board and implementing adopted board policy. This process should include a data-based management system for analyzing, reporting, and representing student performance data as a critical factor in determining a school's success in the language arts.

School Administrators

The school principal must know the essential elements of a research-based language arts program. In addition, he or she must establish a culture within the school in which effective research-based programs are valued and demanded by teachers, parents, administrators, and other stakeholders.

The principals for kindergarten through grade three must establish the language arts, especially beginning reading, as a top priority for the curriculum. For grades four through eight and nine through twelve, the principals must establish the language arts as a priority for all students and implement a specially designed system of instruction (e.g., extended language arts or remedial reading support) for supporting students not proficient in the language arts. Although the school principal is responsible for staff support and resources, the deployment of these resources should be guided by the school's literacy plan and priorities. Such a plan must have as an integral part an accountability system at each grade level. As the school instructional leader, the principal should:

- Understand and provide staff with information about the English–language arts content standards and

research-based programs and interventions in the language arts. Provide staff with the time needed to discuss the standards and current research to establish and promote an understanding of instructional programs demonstrated to improve student achievement.

- Maximize and protect instructional time for the language arts and ensure that adequate personnel and resources are available to support program implementation.
- Provide time for monthly grade-level meetings that focus on assessing student work samples, progress-monitoring data, and articulation of the language arts standards throughout the school.
- Build reflective practice among all faculty by (1) providing guidance and informed feedback on classroom instruction; and (2) facilitating and encouraging structured dialogue among faculty members about results-oriented instruction and strategies to help every student meet grade-level standards.
- Provide leadership in defining and articulating the language arts program. A process should be established for (1) examining results for individual students; and (2) using data to identify program needs and to ensure that all students receive sufficient instruction and support to achieve mastery.
- Provide time for modeling effective instruction, training, and coaching teachers whenever possible. Time should also be provided for teachers to visit other classrooms at the school and at model implementation sites so that successful instruction can be observed.

Chapter 8
Responsibilities
and Support
for Proficiency
in the Language
Arts

- Monitor the implementation process and anticipate future opportunities, needs, and problems through frequent classroom visits.
- Establish schoolwide systems to ensure that students with special needs are (1) assessed early to determine need for additional and specialized instruction; (2) monitored to determine when and if additional support is needed; and (3) included in all state, school district, and schoolwide assessments.
- Establish a schoolwide system to ensure that students who are advanced learners and have exceeded standards are placed at appropriate levels of instruction and are working toward standards they have not yet mastered.
- Align the instructional methods, materials, and schedules across programs and personnel to maximize learning.

Professional Developers, University and College Partners, and Professional Organizations

Teachers well prepared to teach reading and the language arts are vital to the success of language arts instruction. The adoption of content standards and recent changes in assessment and instructional materials require teachers to gain new knowledge and alter classroom practices. Experienced teachers need support in learning and applying new curriculum and instructional strategies, and new teachers and teacher candidates need even greater support in learning to teach reading and the language arts as they acquire the fundamentals of teaching.

Professional developers from school districts, county offices of education, colleges and universities, and professional organizations are key individuals in the

support of new and experienced teachers. Their responsibility is to understand content standards, frameworks, and assessment in California and to teach new and continuing teachers about the key features of the educational landscape in the state. Professional organizations support teachers with publications that support current and confirmed research in language arts instruction and opportunities for networking and training. Funding for professional development and the support of new teachers has increased dramatically in recent years, providing schools and school districts with important opportunities to increase teacher knowledge and effectiveness in language arts instruction. Knowledgeable and collaborative leadership within schools, school districts, counties, and regions is necessary to marshal the resources necessary to train, support, and coach California's professional teaching staff adequately.

Business, Civic, and Service Organizations

Schools may create partnerships with a variety of public and private organizations and agencies to seek support and participation in the education of California's children. Many private companies and organizations have education departments that seek opportunities to work with youngsters. Schools are encouraged to (1) use those kinds of community resources to provide the additional adult support that students need to meet their literacy requirements; and (2) start to develop ideas about the workforce, careers, and students' relationships to their communities. Service-learning projects benefiting both partners can be established between schools and community organizations. When students work alongside others from their own communities to

Teachers well
prepared to teach
reading and the
language arts are
vital to the
success of
language arts
instruction.

Chapter 8
Responsibilities
and Support
for Proficiency
in the Language
Arts

At every grade level classroom collections should reflect a wide variety of reading interests, favorite authors, and topics related to the instructional program.

identify and solve local problems, they build civic responsibility and practice literacy skills. Literacy is improved when the students apply their language arts skills in their service-learning activities and perform research, read, write, and speak about their service projects and experiences. Through service-learning projects involving tutoring and mentoring, older students also support the literacy of younger students.

Partnerships with business, civic, and professional organizations can also serve to keep schools focused on their mission—learning and reaching the goals of the literacy improvement plan. As schools accomplish their literacy goals, they gain greater credibility and support in the community. In the face of increased social, technological, and cultural changes, a whole community can help educate a child or at least help ensure that every child will reach proficiency in the language arts standards.

Instructional Materials

Balanced, comprehensive language arts programs are based on high-quality learning materials—from basal series and literature to factual expository works in books and in other formats. A powerful language arts curriculum should engage students with literature written in English or translated from other languages. The high-quality materials should reflect the faces and resonate with the voices of learners in California, representing their diverse linguistic, cultural, and social backgrounds. Access to materials in the students' home languages promotes growth in concept development and academic language as the students acquire English as their second language.

Schools foster literacy when they ensure that students have access to extensive collections of high-quality, high-interest reading materials in the classroom, in the school library media center, in community libraries, and in the home to allow for daily teacher-directed and voluntary reading. Schools also enhance literacy when they provide students with access to other learning resources and technologies.

Classroom Resources

Children benefit from having age-appropriate and skill-reinforcing magazines, journals, and books in the classroom. At every grade level classroom collections should reflect a wide variety of reading interests, favorite authors, and topics related to the instructional program. In the primary grades classroom resources must include large numbers of highly readable books and other items that allow students to practice and reinforce their growing literacy. Classroom libraries are enhanced when students and teachers acquire outstanding, high-interest books by notable authors and illustrators for young people. The books may be borrowed from the school library media center or the public library. Frequent access to extensive school library collections is an effective way to maintain fresh classroom collections, allow students to select books of personal interest, and keep reading motivation high.

Classrooms are enhanced when supplied with adequate hardware, software, and Internet-based resources for students to use in language arts instruction. *Connect, Compute, and Compete* (California Department of Education 1996c) recommends a student-to-computer ratio of four to one and telecommunications access for students in every classroom and library. The recommendations are consistent with the federal technology goals: (1) modern computers and learning devices will be accessible to every student; (2) classrooms will be connected to one another and to the outside world; (3) educational software will be an integral part of the curriculum; and (4) teachers will be ready to use and teach with technology.

Collections in the Library Media Center

In addition to the classroom library, the school's library media center is a focal point of reading. The center's collection consists of learning resources and technologies carefully selected to meet the teaching and learning needs of teachers and their students and supports curriculum and instruction at the point of need. The collection should contain at least 20 books per student professionally selected in accordance with a district selection policy (American Association of School Librarians and the Association for Educational Communications and Technology 1998). The books should be classified and labeled and should be accessible, preferably on computer via an automated catalog. The collection should be up-to-date and contain a wide variety of high-quality expository works as well as a full range of narrative genres, from picture books to contemporary fiction. Also to be included are fantasy, historical fiction, science fiction, folklore, poetry, biography, career-related books and materials, and books representing many voices and diverse points of view.

Access to a well-developed book collection and electronic resources, selected with the guidance of a credentialed school library media teacher and housed in the school library media center, (1) allows teachers to help students broaden and extend their study of core

works; and (2) allows students to benefit from a broad spectrum of reading choices to meet their learning needs. Students should be given access to outstanding examples of multicultural literature across genres to extend literary response and analysis. The center should also provide the learning resources and technologies students need to pursue problem solving, thereby applying and deepening essential reading-comprehension skills. And the center should allow students to begin to develop the skills that will allow them to become independent, self-directed learners for the rest of their lives. Library media teachers, in collaboration with classroom teachers, teach the skills and strategies that allow students intellectual access to the resources.

Physical access to the collections in the library media center depends on:

- Having a sufficient number of qualified staff to keep the library open
- Having sufficient shelving space for the recommended number of books per student (20)
- Having the technology resources that allow for expanded access to information, including adequate hardware, software, and Internet access
- Developing flexibility in the schedule so that students can come to the library every day if they need to do so
- Developing policies that allow that books be taken home and multiple titles to be borrowed and that make the library a lively, welcoming center for the school as a reading community

The schedule should allow for whole-group visits, small-group work, and times for individual browsing, exploring, and voluntary, self-selected reading.

Library media teachers, in collaboration with classroom teachers, teach the skills and strategies that allow students intellectual access to the resources.

Development and Evaluation of Instructional Materials

All of the content standards for each grade level should be addressed in a coherent fashion, and the instructional materials should thoughtfully and logically address the development of skills and knowledge that build throughout the grade levels.

The *English–Language Arts Content Standards* provides the basic foundation for the design of instructional materials.* All of the content standards for each grade level should be addressed in a coherent fashion, and the instructional materials should thoughtfully and logically address the development of skills and knowledge that build throughout the grade levels so that the standards

---

*Education Code Section 60010(h): "Instructional materials means all materials that are designed for use by pupils and their teachers as a learning resource and help pupils to acquire facts, skills, or opinions or to develop cognitive processes. Instructional materials may be printed or nonprinted, and may include textbooks, technology-based materials, other educational materials, and tests."

can be mastered. The standards should be listed at the grade levels at which students are expected to have *mastered* the standards. Many standards will need to be *introduced* at earlier grade levels.

This framework recommends a minimum of two and one-half hours of language arts instruction daily in kindergarten through grade three. Because this time commitment constitutes the major portion of the instructional day, instructional materials should, particularly in kindergarten through grade three, address the content standards approved by the State Board of Education for other areas, especially history–social science and science, that can appropriately be taught within the language arts context. Portions of the history–social science and science content standards that do not lend themselves to instruction in a language arts context (e.g., investigation and experimentation activities) should not, however, be a part of the instructional time for the language arts.

The content of this framework is designed to provide a road map for designers and developers of instructional materials. The entire framework will be used to develop specific criteria for the adoption of instructional materials. Those criteria are approved by the State Board of Education at the beginning of the cycle for the development of materials. Although much of what appears in this framework reports on effective practices, the framework is not to be construed as containing definitive routes for every leg of the journey. For example, research on the importance of systematic and explicit phonics instruction as a beginning reading strategy establishes a general direction to follow in the lower grades. Although the developers of instructional materials are expected to examine the research on effective practices, they are not expected

to assume that there is only one correct way to implement the specifications in the standards. For example, the standards in kindergarten require students to learn letter names and sounds. The particular order in which that information is taught is not set in stone, and a definitive sequence for teaching letter names and sounds has not been established empirically.

Some reading programs recommend introducing letter names first because they are typically easier and more familiar to children. In other programs letter-sound relationships are taught before letter names. Similarly, the treatment of uppercase and lowercase letters has varied. In some programs both uppercase and lowercase letters are introduced concurrently; in others, the introduction of capital letters that are dissimilar to their respective lowercase letters is delayed. Despite such differences deciding what to teach first should be based on student success and efficient instruction.

Instructional materials must be constructed with great care because they play a major role in determining the content students learn. They need to be effective, reliable tools that empower the teacher to meet the instructional needs of all students, enabling them to meet or exceed the standards. The express intent of this framework is to provide research-based guidance when that guidance is available and to rely on validated principles of instruction when research has not addressed specific instructional procedures.

Importance of Systematic Instruction

To that end instruction needs to be systematic. *Systematic instruction* is defined as the carefully planned design and delivery

250

Chapter 9
Development
and Evaluation
of Instructional
Materials

of instruction that examines the nature of the objective to be learned and selects and sequences the essential skills and strategies necessary to achieve the objective by:

- Allocating sufficient time to essential skills
- Organizing information to minimize confusion that learners may experience
- Introducing new information in manageable and sequential units
- Identifying prerequisite skills and building on the prior knowledge of the learner
- Reviewing previously taught skills
- Integrating old knowledge strategically with new knowledge
- Progressing from skills in more easily managed contexts to more complex contexts
- Including modification, as necessary, for special-needs students

Instructional materials should describe specific ways for the teacher to address the learning needs of different students and thereby ensure access for all students to the core grade-level materials and instruction. Modifications for special-needs students should include instructional materials specifically designed to assist students who are below grade level in their development. The instructional materials should be designed to supplement classroom instruction. Students who have fallen behind should have access to and participate in grade-level instruction. They should also receive additional assistance in the form of review, reteaching, or tutoring supplemented by homework assignments in which review packets or units are used. Publishers may wish to identify those portions of earlier grade-level materials useful for review or to develop new material to reteach essential skills and concepts introduced in the earlier grades.

Criteria for Evaluating Instructional Materials

The major criteria that should be used in evaluating instructional materials are divided into five categories:

1. *Language arts content*—alignment with standards specified for kindergarten through grade twelve and described in detail in Chapter 3 through Chapter 5. For kindergarten through grade three, instructional materials should align with the content standards in history–social science and science as much as possible and may also support the content standards in mathematics. To the extent that the instructional materials include content extraneous to instruction in the Board-adopted standards in the four core areas, that content may not be fundamentally contrary to any of the standards and may not detract from the ability of teachers to teach readily and students to learn thoroughly the content specified in the standards.

2. *Program organization*—sequence and organization of the language arts program. Sequential organization of the language arts program provides structure concerning what students should learn each year and allows teachers to convey the language arts instruction efficiently and effectively. The content should be organized logically and presented in a manner consistent with providing all students an opportunity to achieve the essential knowledge and skills described in the standards.

3. *Assessment*—strategies, procedures, and tools presented in instructional materials for assessing what students know, how well they know it, and

251

Chapter 9
Development
and Evaluation
of Instructional
Materials

what they are able to do. Assessment tools should be provided by publishers as part of the instructional materials. They should assist teachers in using the results of assessment to plan and modify instruction designed to help all students meet or exceed the standards.

4. *Universal access*—practices supporting students with special learning needs whereby materials are designed to maximize the learning of all students, including special education students; students whose proficiency in English is significantly lower than that typical for age, classroom, or grade; and students whose achievement is significantly below or above that typical for age, classroom, or grade.

5. *Instructional planning and support*—instructional planning and support information and materials needed for a successful course of study, typically including a separate edition specifically designed for use by the teacher, that assist teachers in the implementation of the language arts program. Teacher support materials should be built into the instructional materials and should help teachers teach to the standards.

Instructional materials in the language arts must support teaching aligned with the standards. Materials that fail to meet the language arts content criteria in Category 1 will not be considered satisfactory for adoption. Only those materials that meet the Category 1 criteria will be evaluated under categories 2 through 5. In addition to the criteria in the five categories described in this chapter, all instructional materials must meet all applicable requirements contained in codes and regulations, including the "Standards for Evaluation of Instructional Materials with Respect to Social Content" developed to

implement *Education Code* sections 60040, 60041, 60042, and 60044.

Category 1— Language Arts Content

Textbooks, electronic learning resources, and other instructional materials should agree with the content in the *English–Language Arts Content Standards* and should reflect the information presented throughout this framework. Content should be carefully selected according to current confirmed research in language arts instruction. Some standards require much more teaching than others do. Although all standards are important, those that require extensive teaching and are clear prerequisites for later standards are essential. Cursory treatment of instruction in the priority standards is unacceptable. Careful attention should be given to the standards for early reading and the importance of the alphabetic writing system.

Students who meet or exceed the language arts standards will have developed the essential skills and knowledge necessary to be successful in all other content areas. For that reason publishers are encouraged to design materials that will allow for a total of two and one-half hours of language arts instruction daily in kindergarten through grade three. It is assumed that mathematics will also be allocated instructional time daily. Because this time allocation does not leave sufficient instructional time for the other content areas, publishers are strongly encouraged to address the content standards in science and history–social science within the time period for the language arts. Publishers should include outstanding children's literature as an integral part of language arts instruction at every grade level. They should also carefully select informational text in history–social science and science for reading instruction and practice as well as assignments in writing, listening, and speaking consistent with the grade-level standards in those content areas.

Category 2— Program Organization

The scope and sequence of the instructional materials should be aligned with the language arts content standards and, ideally, should reinforce the content standards in science, history–social science, and mathematics. Within a grade level standards do not have to be introduced and taught in exactly the sequence in which they appear in the *English–Language Arts Content Standards.* Publishers should select and develop a coherent structure for teaching to the standards that introduces the standards in a logical sequence and groups related standards into lessons, units, or chapters when those standards can be addressed simultaneously.

Instructional materials should be arranged to make the rate of learning and its effectiveness optimal and to enhance the likelihood of information being retained and generalized. Sequential, logical organization of language arts instruction that addresses all standards but allocates more time and emphasis to key standards throughout the grades will help students develop comprehensive skills and knowledge in the language arts.

The time and type of instruction allocated to the instructional standards and component skills must be differentiated according to the complexity and dimensions of the standards. Therefore, instructional units of varying lengths will be required to meet the individual standards or groups of standards. Units should not be fixed as to the number of units per week or the number of pages per unit. Some topics will require instruction over an extended

Instructional
materials should
be arranged to
make the rate of
learning and its
effectiveness
optimal and to
enhance the
likelihood of
information being
retained and
generalized.

period of time (e.g., teaching letter-sound correspondences is a continual daily activity during much of kindergarten).

Several principles of organization are discussed as follows:

Arrangement of a sequence of skills. Skills and standards should be sequenced within and across domains and academic disciplines. In the sequence of instruction, students should learn the component skills and then make the connections between skills and strategies. Important skills are integrated into a meaningful context within and across domains.

Instruction should be organized around major encompassing ideas. However, not all the concepts, skills, and strategies are of equal importance. The standards call for continuing, progressive growth over a broad range of concepts, skills and strategies. Major ideas are the concepts and principles that apply across a wide range of examples and contexts. Organizing instruction around the major ideas maximizes student learning because small ideas can often be best understood in relationship to larger umbrella concepts or major ideas. An example of a major idea in reading comprehension is *story grammar,* which describes the pattern of stories (*For example:* Who is the leading character? What is the problem? How does the character try to solve the problem? How is the problem finally resolved?). In addition, it helps children anticipate the plot of a narrative text.

Instruction should use a strand design. The construction of a language arts curriculum can be thought of as weaving together the strands of a strong rope. The power of instruction depends on (1) the strength of the individual strands; (2) the strategic integration of all strands; and (3) the effective binding or connecting of all strands. Instruction according to

253

Chapter 9
Development
and Evaluation
of Instructional
Materials

a strand design should include the following:

- The dimensions of a complex task are analyzed, and the strands are identified (e.g., in writing: content, organization and focus, grammar, punctuation, clarity, editing).
- The specific objectives within a strand are identified and sequenced individually.
- Cross-strand skills are integrated once learners are proficient in individual strand skills and strategies.
- Previously taught skills and strategies are reviewed cumulatively.
- The strands may be continued over the course of the year or may be discontinued at designated points. The instructional analysis of the content will prescribe the length of the instructional sequence. Whether additional instruction is necessary will be determined according to the proficiency of the learner.

The order in which information is presented in instructional materials can influence student learning. The recommended sequence to be followed in introducing content is to teach prerequisite skills and then build on those skills to develop more sophisticated skills and understandings.

Prerequisite skills are the information and applications that students need to complete a task. For example, to sound out the word *hum,* the student must know and be able to produce the sound represented by each of the letters, know that works are read from left to right, and be able to blend the sounds for each letter and then translate the blended sounds into a word said at normal rate. To complete the analogy "An architect is to a ruler as a plumber is to a _____," the student must first recognize the problem as an analogy calling for a missing word; know the meaning of *architect, ruler,* and *plumber;* and be familiar with the concept of tools. The student would also have to know that a wrench is a tool of a plumber.

Provisions for assessing students' knowledge of prerequisite skills and adequate guidance for the teacher in teaching critical prerequisite skills need to be incorporated into the instructional resources as additional manuals or by the identification of specific sections in manuals used in earlier grades. Instruction for students who do not know the prerequisite skills should be thorough. On the other hand students who know critical information should not be subjected to pointless exercises focusing on the same information.

The suggested sequence to be followed in introducing content is to:

- Introduce prerequisite skills before more advanced applications that require the use of those skills. The program should be designed so that the students can master the prerequisite skills before being required to apply those skills in the more advanced applications.
- Introduce the easier content before the more difficult content. When teaching students about several applications of a skill or concept, the teacher should not try to teach all of the applications at once. Instead, the teacher should begin with an easy application and progress to the more difficult ones. For example, in teaching students to identify words as nouns, the teacher should not initially include verbals—words that are partly nouns and partly verbs in function (e.g, *Running* is fun.).

Students who know critical information should not be subjected to pointless exercises focusing on the same information.

The transition
from initial
teacher-directed,
modeled,
prompted teaching
to independent
use of a new skill
or extended
application by the
student should
not be taken for
granted.

- Separate the introduction of content and strategies likely to be confused. The more similar the characteristics of two items, the more likely it is that students will confuse them. For example, the letters *b* and *d* are similar in shape and sound, and the words *where* and *were* are similar in letters, content, and sound. As a rule the teacher should have the students practice with one item or application so that they master and are comfortable with that item before a second similar item is introduced.
- Introduce information that has greater utility before information with less utility. When letter-sound correspondences are introduced, those that appear more frequently should be introduced before those that appear less frequently. For example, the letters *s*, *r*, *m* and *d* appear in more words than the letters *v*, *q*, *x* and *z*.
- Control the amount of new information so that it is comfortably and reasonably challenging for students. Students should learn new information at a rate that requires effort but is not overwhelming. When too much information is presented at one time, learning can be slowed because confusion may result, causing the students to adopt inappropriate guessing strategies.

Clear communication by the teacher. The words and examples a teacher uses during instruction need to be carefully planned so that students apprehend and understand the concept that the teacher is trying to communicate. Clarity is in part facilitated by carefully guiding the vocabulary and language structures teachers use. The words used to explain new information must be known to the students.

Similarly, language forms must be appropriate to the skill levels and ages of the students. For example, in teaching young students phonological skills, the words *first*, *middle*, and *last* are commonly used. Teachers must ensure that kindergartners understand those words. Further, the examples used in teaching a concept should be carefully designed to rule out likely misinterpretations. For example, if the color *red* is being taught and the teacher shows a red towel, a red shirt, and a red hat, a naïve student might logically think that red refers to the material and not to the color. And if, in the learning of more complex vocabulary, the student encounters only this example ("Chad had an innate understanding of how to talk with strangers; he quickly made them feel at ease"), the student could quite possibly misinterpret the word *innate*.

Assistance to students during transitions. The transition from initial teacher-directed, modeled, prompted teaching to independent use of a new skill or extended application by the student should not be taken for granted. Merely demonstrating a complex strategy or application and then requiring students to apply that strategy is often not realistic. The transition can be provided by gradually changing the design of tasks and examples or by changing the level of assistance the teacher provides. Careful monitoring and assistance by the teacher should occur as students make the transition from guided instruction to independent work and mastery.

Adequate practice and review. Practice and review, when thoughtfully planned and organized, are critical ingredients of efficient instruction. They are not synonymous with "drill and kill." Students should not practice what is not challenging and what they have already mastered. A carefully planned review of instructional

255

Chapter 9
Development
and Evaluation
of Instructional
Materials

materials enables the teacher to focus on student performance rather than on the time-consuming creation of activities for extra practice. Students will vary widely in the amount of practice required. Put differently, not all students require the same amount of practice and review to master and maintain what they are learning.

Instructional materials should be designed so that teachers can readily provide the practice needed by students. Clear provisions should be made about how to accelerate or enrich instruction for advanced learners who need less practice and how to provide extra practice for learners who have difficulty acquiring skills and knowledge.

Factors to be considered when planning practice and review are that the review must be *sufficient, distributed, cumulative* and *varied*:

- *Sufficient review* involves the amount of practice needed for the student to acquire and become facile with the new information.
- *Distributed review* refers to providing the practice over a period of time to facilitate retention. When distributed review is not scheduled, instruction becomes less efficient because students forget information learned earlier.
- *Cumulative review* is the means by which students learn when to apply new learning. The new content is mixed with similar content previously taught. Sufficient review and distributed review provide the student with practice in how to do something. The cumulative review provides practice in *when* to apply the skills. Cumulative practice is very important because it is the vehicle by which likely confusions can be preempted. For example, if students have already

learned the letters *b* and *d* and *p* is introduced, the practice exercise would include all three letters so that the teacher can provide the student with the opportunity to practice and receive feedback in identifying all three similar letters.

Without cumulative review students are likely to misapply new strategies. For example, when students initially learn to punctuate sentences that begin with a dependent clause by placing a comma after the dependent clause (e.g., After the game ended, the sun came out), they will often begin placing commas in all sentences with dependent clauses, even when not needed (e.g., The sun came out, after the game ended). Providing students with punctuation exercises that include sentences that do not need commas gives students practice on when to use the new skill.

- *Varied review* refers to providing a range of meaningful activities that reinforce learning.

Make connections. Instructional resources must also make connections for students. For example, as students learn about a declarative sentence, they should be asked explicitly to practice writing that type of sentence and integrate it with other writing activities. Similarly, if students practice writing sentences with correct punctuation and capitalization but never apply those skills in larger contexts or for authentic purposes, the instruction becomes fragmented and the skills seemingly without purpose. The goal in designing instruction must, therefore, be to ensure that component parts (skills, strategies, structures) are (1) identified; (2) carefully sequenced according to their complexity and utility and used in more advanced applications; (3) developed to mastery; and (4) progressively and purposefully connected and then incorporated in authentic writing exercises.

Category 3—
Assessment

As described throughout this framework, frequent assessment is the key to planning instruction that is appropriate to students' needs and to determining whether students are meeting or exceeding standards. (Assessment is fully described in Chapter 6.) Instructional materials should furnish tasks and exercises to assess student learning. Measures should be available to inform instruction at entry level, monitor progress during instruction, and evaluate mastery of information on completion of instruction.

Assessment should help teachers learn what students know and how well they know it. Frequent assessment should be included to help teachers determine whether students are learning and retaining what has been taught. Because assessment measures what students have been taught, the tasks in the assessment should parallel those in the instructional materials.

Category 4—
Universal Access

Instructional materials should present comprehensive guidance for teachers in providing effective, efficient instruction for all their students. The materials must be constructed to meet the needs of those who enter school with less-developed vocabulary and language background and those with a more sophisticated language background. Suggestions and procedures for meeting the instructional needs of students with special learning needs must not be superficial and lack a central focus or be mere afterthoughts to the main focus

of instruction. Materials should not be so constructed that extensive modifications are necessary for the teacher to meet the learning needs of a full range of students.

English learners need materials to help them (1) master the standards of language arts—notably, to read, write, and speak at academically proficient levels; and (2) learn to understand, speak, and use their new language of English to accomplish purposes ranging from the personal to the academic and professional. Accordingly, instructional materials will need to provide specific support for English learners in lessons in reading and writing and to contain specific instruction in English-language development, including phonology, morphology, syntax, and semantics.

Students need materials to study English explicitly and other materials to support them as they learn to read and write. The materials are mutually reinforcing in that both have the same eventual goal; however, each type is unique in its specific content and learning objectives. Ideally, materials for kindergarten through grade two or three should integrate the development of both literacy and the English language. For students arriving in this country or learning English in grades three or four and beyond, materials may include separate strands of instruction for literacy and language development.

For advanced students publishers should include suggestions or materials for students who need an enriched or accelerated program. Materials may provide suggestions for the teacher to use to help students study a particular author, theme, or concept in more depth. Strategies for students to conduct independent research projects or to do a more critical analysis than that normally included at a particular grade would be helpful. Reminders for

257

Chapter 9
Development
and Evaluation
of Instructional
Materials

teachers of standards at higher grade levels would also be useful in helping teachers provide a challenge for all students.

Category 5— Instructional Planning and Support

The application of instructional design principles in constructing instructional materials is important in providing students with a successful and efficient learning experience. A final organizational issue is that of the format of the materials rather than the arrangement of the content. The teacher resource materials should provide a clear road map for the teacher to follow in delivering instruction. There should be a planning guide to all of the materials contained in the program. They should describe for teachers what is to be taught, how it is to be taught, and when it is to be taught. Further, they should be organized so that the learning objectives are clearly discernible and the relation of the parts of the lesson to the objective clear and coherent. The materials should clearly explain to teachers how the objectives and activities relate to skills within the standards or to the standards themselves. Language and terms from the standards should be used whenever appropriate. Lesson plans and suggestions for organizing materials for the lesson should be clear, and critical components of the lesson should be prioritized and designated as such. Extraneous resources and activities should be kept to a minimum and should not detract from teaching to the standards or contradict the standards.

Usually, a teacher's edition is included that contains important support and planning information for teachers. These materials should be organized and described in a clear and coherent manner so that the connections of all the component parts of a program are apparent. They should explain what each component of the program is and how to use it in a particular lesson or set of lessons. A list of all components of the program should be included as well as a list of materials required for each lesson or unit. The publisher should identify which components of the program are necessary to teach at each grade level and which are optional. If instructional materials come with assessment or instructional tools or informational technology resources, technical support and suggestions for appropriate use must be included. The teacher's manual or guide should explain when to use the tools. If included, electronic learning resources should be an integral part of the program.

High-quality literature and informational reading selections should be included at every grade level. The teacher resource materials should provide background information about the reading selection, including author, context, content, and illustrations, if any. Instructions for the teacher on salient features of the reading material and suggestions on how to use each reading selection in the lesson or lessons should also be included. A list of books for independent reading that span at least two proficiency levels and match the topic of the unit should be included so that classroom teachers and library media teachers can acquire them for their libraries. Specific guidance for teachers on how to use texts at different levels to increase reading fluency would be helpful.

Instructional practices recommended in the instructional materials should be based on current and confirmed research wherever such research exists. If all students are to have access to reaching high levels of proficiency in the English–language arts content standards, the time available for language arts instruction will have to be used efficiently. Instruction is more efficient when it is presented explicitly than implicitly. The modeling of strategies to solve problems can make instructional time more effective for learners. Research suggests that students in general and students whose achievement is below grade level in particular benefit from having good strategies made conspicuous for them provided great care is taken to ensure that the strategies are designed to result in widely transferable knowledge of their application. Publishers should include examples of common student misconceptions or mistakes and how to address them. Options for instructional strategies should be described, including information about instruction that can be best delivered in a whole-group setting, as well as suggestions for teaching activities that lend themselves to small groups, pairs of students, or individual work.

Parental involvement in the language arts program supports classroom learning.

Homework suggestions should extend or reinforce classroom instruction or provide additional practice and should be varied enough so that the teacher can differentiate homework assignments according to students' needs. Because parents should be informed about standards, instruction, and their children's progress toward meeting the standards, materials should include suggestions on how to explain student assessment data and involve parents so that they may better support the achievement of their children in language arts.

A format that clearly distinguishes the role of the teacher from that of the student is also recommended. Materials should be formatted so that additional examples of a skill or strategy for review or reteaching or extension or acceleration suggested for advanced learners are easy to locate. The goal to be achieved is to make examples easily accessible to the teacher for moment-to-moment adjustments in response to learner performance so that all students can be assisted to meet or exceed the standards as efficiently as possible.

Appendix A

Matrix for the English–Language Arts Content Standards, by Grade

Domain, Strand, Substrand	K	1	2	3	4	5	6	7	8	9	10	11	12
READING													
Word Analysis, Fluency, and Systematic Vocabulary Development:													
Concepts about print	X	X											
Phonemic awareness	X	X											
Decoding and word recognition	X	X	X	X									
Word recognition					X	X	X						
Vocabulary and concept development	X	X	X	X	X	X	X	X	X	X	X	X	X
Reading Comprehension:													
Structural features of informational materials	X	X	X	X	X	X	X	X	X	X	X	X	X
Comprehension and analysis of grade-level-appropriate text	X	X	X	X	X	X	X	X	X	X	X	X	X
Expository critique						X	X	X	X	X	X	X	X
Literary Response and Analysis:													
Structural features of literature				X	X	X	X	X	X	X	X	X	X
Narrative analysis of grade-level-appropriate text	X		X	X	X	X	X	X	X	X	X	X	X
Literary criticism						X	X	X	X	X	X	X	X

Appendix A

Matrix for the
English–Language
Arts Content
Standards,
by Grade

Appendix A (Continued)

Domain, Strand, Substrand	K	1	2	3	4	5	6	7	8	9	10	11	12
WRITING													
Writing Strategies:													
Organization and focus	X	X	X	X	X		X	X	X	X	X	X	X
Penmanship	X	X	X	X	X								
Research			X	X	X								
Research and technology						X	X	X	X	X	X	X	X
Evaluation and revision			X	X	X	X	X	X	X	X	X	X	X
Writing Applications (Genres and Their Characteristics)	X	X	X	X	X	X	X	X	X	X	X	X	X
WRITTEN AND ORAL ENGLISH-LANGUAGE CONVENTIONS													
Written and Oral English-Language Conventions:												X	X
Sentence structure	X	X	X	X	X	X	X	X	X				
Grammar			X	X	X	X	X	X	X	X			
Punctuation		X	X	X	X	X	X	X					
Capitalization		X	X	X	X	X	X	X					
Spelling		X	X	X	X	X	X	X	X	X			
Punctuation and capitalization									X				
Grammar and mechanics of writing										X	X		
Manuscript form										X	X		

Appendix A (Continued)

261

Appendix A
Matrix for the
English–Language
Arts Content
Standards,
by Grade

Domain, Strand, Substrand	K	1	2	3	4	5	6	7	8	9	10	11	12
LISTENING AND SPEAKING — Listening and Speaking Strategies:													
Comprehension	X	X	X	X	X	X	X	X	X	X	X	X	X
Organization and delivery of oral communication		X	X	X	X	X	X	X	X	X	X	X	X
Analysis and evaluation of oral and media communications				X	X	X	X	X	X	X	X	X	X
Speaking Applications (Genres and Their Characteristics)	X	X	X	X	X	X	X	X	X	X	X	X	X

Appendix B

Representative Content Standards and Instructional Connections for the Language Arts

The tables contained in this appendix illustrate representative content standards that span domains and present opportunities for critical instructional and content connections reinforcing, extending, and generalizing learning. The standards represent knowledge and skills that should first be taught independently but can be combined or connected in lessons to gain instructional efficiency and enhance learning.

Note: Some of the content standards have been abbreviated.

Kindergarten

Standards-based instructional topics	Reading	Writing	Written and oral English-language conventions	Listening and speaking
Concepts about print and writing strategies: letter names and letter formation	1.6 Recognize and name all uppercase and lowercase letters of the alphabet.	1.4 Write uppercase and lowercase letters of the alphabet independently.		
Phonemic awareness, decoding, and spelling: consonant-vowel-consonant words	1.9 Blend vowel-consonant sounds orally to make words or syllables. 1.14 Match all consonant and short-vowel sounds to appropriate letters. 1.15 Read simple one-syllable words.	1.2 Write consonant-vowel-consonant words.	1.2 Spell words, using prephonetic knowledge, sounds of the alphabet, and knowledge of letter names.	
Narrative text: elements of stories	2.4 Retell familiar stories. 3.3 Identify characters, settings, and important events.			1.2 Speak in complete, coherent sentences. 2.3 Relate a creative story in a logical sequence.

First Grade

Appendix B
Representative
Content Standards
and Instructional
Connections
for the Language
Arts

Standards-based instructional topics	Reading	Writing	Written and oral English-language conventions	Listening and speaking
Decoding, spelling, and writing strategies: phonetically regular words of three to four letters	1.10 Generate the sounds from all letters and letter patterns and blend those sounds into recognizable words. 1.11 Read common irregular sight words.		1.8 Spell three- and four-letter short vowel words and grade-level-appropriate sight words correctly.	
Narrative text structure	2.2 Respond to *who, what, when, where,* and *how* questions. 2.7 Retell the central ideas of expository or narrative passages. 3.1 Identify plot, setting, and characters in a story as well as the beginning, middle, and ending.	2.1 Write brief narratives describing an experience.		2.2 Retell stories, using basic story grammar and relating the sequence of story events by answering *who, what, when, where, why,* and *how* questions.

Appendix B
Representative
Content Standards
and Instructional
Connections
for the Language
Arts

Second Grade

Standards-based instructional topics	Reading	Writing	Written and oral English-language conventions	Listening and speaking
Decoding and spelling	1.1 Recognize and use knowledge of spelling patterns (e.g., diphthongs, special vowel spellings) when reading.		1.8 Spell basic short-vowel, long-vowel, r-controlled, and consonant-blend patterns correctly.	
Narrative text structure	3.1 Compare and contrast plots, settings, and characters presented by different authors. 3.3 Compare and contrast different versions of the same stories that reflect different cultures.	1.1 Group related ideas and maintain a consistent focus. 2.1 Write a brief narrative based on experience, moving through a logical sequence of events and describing the setting, characters, objects, and events in detail.		1.8 Retell stories, using characters, plot, setting. 2.1 Recount experiences or present stories, moving through a logical sequence of events and describing story elements.

Appendix B
Representative
Content Standards
and Instructional
Connections
for the Language
Arts

Third Grade

Standards-based instructional topics	Reading	Writing	Written and oral English-language conventions	Listening and speaking
Word recognition and spelling	1.1 Use knowledge of complex word families (e.g., *ight*) to decode unfamiliar words. 1.2 Decode regular multisyllabic words.		1.8 Spell correctly one-syllable words that have blends, contractions, compounds, orthographic patterns, and common homophones.	
Reading and speaking fluency	1.3 Read aloud narrative and expository text fluently and accurately and with appropriate intonation, pacing, and expression.			1.9 Read prose and poetry aloud with fluency, rhythm, and pace, using appropriate intonation and vocal patterns to emphasize important passages.
Writing conventions and speaking applications		1.1 Write a single paragraph. 2.1 Write narratives. 2.2 Write descriptions. 2.3 Write personal and formal letters, thank-you notes, and invitations.	1.1 Use complete and correct declarative, interrogative, imperative, and exclamatory sentences in writing and speaking.	2.1 Make brief narrative presentations. 2.2 Present dramatic interpretations. 2.3 Make descriptive presentations.
Narratives		2.1 Write narratives, providing a context, well-chosen details, and insight into why incidents are memorable.		2.1 Make brief narrative presentations, providing a context, well-chosen details, and insight into why an incident is memorable.

Appendix B
Representative
Content Standards
and Instructional
Connections
for the Language
Arts

Third Grade (Continued)

Standards-based instructional topics	Reading	Writing	Written and oral English-language conventions	Listening and speaking
Expository text	2.5 Distinguish the main idea and supporting details in expository text.	1.1 Write a single paragraph, developing a topic sentence and include supporting facts and details. 1.4 Revise drafts to improve the coherence and logical progression of ideas by using an established rubric.		
Descriptive text		2.2 Write descriptions that use concrete details to present and support unified impressions of people, places, things, or experiences.		2.3 Make descriptive presentations that use concrete sensory details to set forth and support unified impressions of people, places, things, or experiences.

Appendix B
Representative
Content Standards
and Instructional
Connections
for the Language
Arts

Fourth Grade

Standards-based instructional topics	Reading	Writing	Written and oral English-language conventions	Listening and speaking
Narrative text structure	1.1 Read narrative and expository text aloud with grade-appropriate fluency and accuracy and with appropriate pacing, intonation, and expression. 3.2 Identify the main events of the plot, their causes, and the influence of each event on future actions.	2.1 Write narratives that relate ideas, observations, or recollections of an event or experience; provide a context; use sensory details; and provide insight.	1.1 Use simple and compound sentences in writing and speaking.	2.1 Make narrative presentations that relate ideas, observations, or recollections about events and provide a context and insight. 2.3 Deliver oral summaries of articles and books that contain the main ideas of the event and the most significant details.
Informational text structure	2.1 Identify structural patterns found in informational text (compare and contrast, cause and effect, order, proposition, and support).	1.2 Create multiple-paragraph compositions that provide an introductory paragraph, establish and support a central idea with a topic sentence, include supporting paragraphs, and conclude with a summary paragraph.	1.1 Use simple and compound sentences in writing and speaking. 1.2 Combine short, related sentences with appositives, participial phrases, and so forth.	2.2 Make informational presentations that frame a key question, include facts and details, and incorporate more than one source of information.

Appendix B
Representative
Content Standards
and Instructional
Connections
for the Language
Arts

Fifth Grade

Standards-based instructional topics	Reading	Writing	Written and oral English-language conventions	Listening and speaking
Analysis of media as information source	1.1 Read aloud narrative and expository text fluently and with appropriate pacing, intonation and expression. 2.1 Understand how text features (e.g., format, graphics, sequence, diagrams) make information accessible and usable.	1.2 Create multiple-paragraph compositions that establish a topic in sequence or chronological order, provide details and transitional expressions, and offer a concluding summary paragraph. 2.3 Write research reports about important ideas, issues, or events by framing questions that direct the investigation, establishing a controlling idea or topic, and developing the topic with simple facts, details, examples, and explanations.	1.1 Correctly use prepositional phrases, appositives, and independent and dependent clauses; use transitions and conjunctions to connect ideas. 1.5 Spell frequently misspelled words correctly (e.g., *their, they're, there*).	1.8 Analyze media as sources for information, entertainment, persuasion, interpretation of events, and transmission of culture. 2.2 Deliver informative presentations about an important idea, issue, or event by framing questions to direct the investigation.

Appendix B
Representative
Content Standards
and Instructional
Connections
for the Language
Arts

Sixth Grade

Standards-based instructional topics	Reading	Writing	Written and oral English-language conventions	Listening and speaking
Expository compositions	1.1 Read aloud narrative and expository text fluently and accurately and with appropriate pacing, intonation, and expression.	1.2 Create multiple-paragraph expository compositions. Engage the reader, state a clear purpose, develop the topic, and conclude with a detailed summary.	1.1 Use simple, compound, and compound-complex sentences; use effective coordination and subordination of ideas to express complete thoughts.	1.4 Select a focus, an organizational structure, and a point of view, matching the purpose, message, occasion, and vocal modulation to the audience.
	1.4 Monitor expository text for unknown words or words with novel meanings by using word, sentence, and paragraph clues to determine meaning.	1.3 Use a variety of effective and coherent organizational patterns.	1.2 Identify and properly use indefinite pronouns and present perfect, past perfect, and future perfect verb tenses; ensure that verbs agree with compound subjects.	2.2 Deliver informative presentations. Pose relevant questions sufficiently limited in scope to be completely and thoroughly answered and develop the topic with facts, details, examples, and so forth.
	2.6 Determine the adequacy and appropriateness of evidence for an author's conclusions.	1.6 Revise writing to improve the organization and consistency of ideas within and between paragraphs.	1.4 Use correct capitalization.	2.5 Deliver presentations on problems and solutions. Theorize on the cause and effect of each problem and establish connections. Offer persuasive evidence.
		2.2 Write expository compositions (e.g., description, explanation, comparison and contrast, problem and solution).	1.5 Spell frequently misspelled words correctly (e.g., *their*, *they're*, *there*).	

Appendix B
Representative
Content Standards
and Instructional
Connections
for the Language
Arts

Seventh Grade

Standards-based instructional topics	Reading	Writing	Written and oral English-language conventions	Listening and speaking
Reading comprehension	1.1 Identify idioms, analogies, metaphors, and similes in prose and poetry. 1.2 Use knowledge of Greek, Latin, and Anglo-Saxon roots and affixes to understand content-area vocabulary. 1.3 Clarify word meanings through the use of definition, example, restatement, or contrast. 2.1 Understand and analyze the differences in structure and purpose between various categories of informational materials.	1.3 Use notetaking, outlining, and summarizing to impose structure on composition drafts. 1.4 Identify topics; ask and evaluate questions; and develop ideas leading to inquiry, investigation, and research. 1.6 Create documents by using word-processing skills and publishing programs. Develop simple databases and spreadsheets to manage information and prepare reports.	1.3 Identify all parts of speech and types and structure of sentences.	1.2 Determine the speaker's attitude toward the subject. 2.1 Deliver narrative presentations. Establish a context, standard plot line, and point of view.

Appendix B
Representative
Content Standards
and Instructional
Connections
for the Language
Arts

Eighth Grade

Standards-based instructional topics	Reading	Writing	Written and oral English-language conventions	Listening and speaking
Comparison and contrast—similarities and differences	2.1 Compare and contrast the features and elements of consumer materials to gain meaning from documents. 2.3 Find similarities and differences between texts in the treatment, scope, or organization of ideas. 3.3 Compare and contrast motivations and reactions of literary characters from different historical eras who confront similar situations or conflicts.	1.6 Revise writing for word choice; appropriate organization; consistent point of view; and transitions between paragraphs, passages, and ideas. 2.2 Write responses to literature. Support judgments through references to the text, other works, other authors, or personal knowledge. 2.5 Write documents related to career development. Present information purposefully and succinctly and meet the needs of the intended audience.	1.1 Use correct and varied sentence types and sentence openings to present a lively and effective personal style. 1.4 Edit written manuscripts to ensure that correct grammar is used. 1.5 Use correct punctuation and capitalization.	2.1 Deliver narrative presentations. Employ narrative and descriptive strategies (e.g., comparison or contrast of characters). 2.2 Deliver oral responses to literature. Interpret a reading and provide insight. 2.2 Deliver oral responses to literature. Support judgments through references to the text, other works, other authors, or personal knowledge.

Appendix B
Representative
Content Standards
and Instructional
Connections
for the Language
Arts

Ninth and Tenth Grades

Standards-based instructional topics	Reading	Writing	Written and oral English-language conventions	Listening and speaking
Expository (research) discourse	2.2 Prepare a bibliography of reference materials for a report, using a variety of consumer, workplace, and public documents.	1.3 Use clear research questions and suitable research methods to elicit and present evidence from primary and secondary sources.	1.0 Write and speak with a command of standard English conventions.	2.2 Deliver expository presentations.
	2.3 Generate relevant questions about reading on issues that can be researched.	1.4 Develop the main ideas within the body of the composition through supporting evidence.	1.5 Reflect appropriate manuscript requirements, including integration of source and support material with appropriate citations.	
	2.4 Synthesize the content from several sources or works by a single author dealing with a single issue. Paraphrase the ideas and connect them to other sources and related topics to demonstrate comprehension.	1.5 Synthesize information from multiple sources and identify complexities and discrepancies in the information and the different perspectives found in each medium.		
	2.5 Extend ideas presented in primary or secondary sources through original analysis, evaluation, and elaboration.	1.6 Integrate quotations and citations into a written text while maintaining the flow of ideas.		
		1.7 Use appropriate conventions for documentation in the text, notes, and bibliographies by adhering to those in style manuals.		
		2.3 Write expository compositions, including analytical essays and research reports.		

Appendix B
Representative
Content Standards
and Instructional
Connections
for the Language
Arts

Ninth and Tenth Grades (Continued)

Standards-based instructional topics	Reading	Writing	Written and oral English-language conventions	Listening and speaking
Argument and persuasion	2.7 Critique the logic of functional documents by examining the sequence of information and procedures in anticipation of possible reader misunderstandings. 2.8 Evaluate the credibility of an author's argument or defense of a claim by critiquing the evidence and the way in which the author's intent affects the structure and tone of the text.	2.4 Write persuasive compositions.		1.1 Formulate judgments about the ideas under discussion and support those judgments with convincing evidence. 1.3 Choose logical patterns of organization to inform and persuade by soliciting agreement or action or to unite audiences behind a common belief or cause. 2.5 Deliver persuasive arguments (including evaluation and analysis of problems and solutions and causes and effects).
Technology	2.6 Demonstrate use of sophisticated learning tools by following technical directions.	1.8 Design and publish documents by using advanced publishing software and graphic programs.		

Appendix B
Representative
Content Standards
and Instructional
Connections
for the Language
Arts

Eleventh and Twelfth Grades

Standards-based instructional topics	Reading	Writing	Written and oral English-language conventions	Listening and speaking
Responses to literature	3.1 Analyze characteristics of subgenres that are used in poetry, prose, plays, novels, short stories, essays, and other basic genres. 3.2 Analyze the way in which the theme or meaning of a selection represents a view or comment on life, using textual evidence to support the claim. 3.3 Analyze the ways in which irony, tone, mood, the author's style, and the "sound" of language achieve specific rhetorical or aesthetic purposes or both. *Note:* Standards 3.4–3.9 also connect across domains.	2.2 Write responses to literature.		2.3 Deliver oral responses to literature.
Fundamentals of discourse	2.1 Analyze both the features and the rhetorical devices of different types of public documents and the way in which authors use those features and devices.	1.1 Demonstrate an understanding of the elements of discourse when completing narrative, expository, persuasive, or descriptive writing assignments.	1.1 Demonstrate control of grammar, diction, paragraph and sentence structure, and an understanding of English usage.	1.4 Use rhetorical questions, parallel structure, concrete images, figurative language, characterization, irony, and dialogue to achieve clarity, force, and aesthetic effect.

Appendix B
Representative
Content Standards
and Instructional
Connections
for the Language
Arts

Eleventh and Twelfth Grades (Continued)

Standards-based instructional topics	Reading	Writing	Written and oral English-language conventions	Listening and speaking
Fundamentals of discourse (Continued)	2.2 Analyze the way in which clarity of meaning is affected by the patterns of organization, hierarchical structures, repetition of the main ideas, syntax, and word choice in the text.	1.2 Use point of view, characterization, style, and related elements for specific rhetorical and aesthetic purposes.		1.5 Distinguish between and use various forms of classical and contemporary logical arguments.
	2.3 Verify and clarify facts presented in other types of expository texts by using a variety of consumer, workplace, and public documents.	1.3 Structure ideas and arguments in a sustained, persuasive, and sophisticated way and support them with precise and relevant examples.		1.6 Use logical, ethical, and emotional appeals that enhance a specific tone and purpose.
	2.4 Make warranted and reasonable assertions about the author's arguments by using elements of the text to defend and clarify interpretations.	1.4 Enhance meaning by employing rhetorical devices, including the extended use of parallelism, repetition, and analogy, the incorporation of visual aids, and the issuance of a call for action.		1.7 Use appropriate rehearsal strategies to pay attention to performance details, achieve command of the text, and create skillful artistic staging.
	2.5 Analyze an author's implicit and explicit philosophical assumptions and beliefs about a subject.	1.5 Use language in natural, fresh, and vivid ways to establish a specific tone.		1.8 Use effective and interesting language.
				1.9 Use research and analysis to justify strategies for gesture, movement, and vocalization, including dialect, pronunciation, and enunciation.
				1.10 Evaluate when to use different kinds of effects to create effective productions.

Glossary of Selected Terms

alphabetic principle. The assumption underlying an alphabetic writing system that each speech sound or phoneme of a language has its own distinctive graphic representation.

automaticity. The ability to recognize a word (or series of words) in text effortlessly and rapidly.

capitalization. The act of writing or printing a particular word (e.g., a proper noun) and using an uppercase (capital) letter of the alphabet for the first letter of the word.

concepts about print. Insights about the ways in which print works. Basic concepts about print include identification of a book's front and back covers and title page; directionality (knowledge that readers and writers move from left to right, top to bottom, front to back); spacing (distance used to separate words); recognition of letters and words; connection between spoken and written language; understanding of the function of capitalization and punctuation; sequencing and locating skills.

decodable texts. Reading materials that provide an intermediate step between words in isolation and authentic literature. Such texts are designed to give students an opportunity to learn to use their understanding of phonics in the course of reading connected text. Although decodable texts may contain sight words that have been previously taught, most words are wholly decodable on the basis of the letter-sound and spelling-sound correspondences taught and practiced in phonics lessons.

decoding. A series of strategies used selectively by readers to recognize and read written words. The reader locates cues (e.g., letter-sound correspondences) in a word that reveal enough about it to help in pronouncing it and attaching meaning to it.

description. One of the four traditional forms of composition in speech and writing. Its purpose is to provide a verbal picture of a character, event, setting, and so forth.

editing. The process of reviewing text in draft form to check for correctness of the mechanics and conventions of writing (e.g., spelling, grammar, punctuation, capitalization, and format).

encoding. Transferring oral language into written language.

environmental print. Any print found in the physical environment, such as street signs, billboards, labels, business signs.

etymology. The study of the history of words.

explicit instruction. The intentional design and delivery of information by the teacher to the students. It begins with (1) the teacher's modeling or demonstration of the skill or strategy; (2) a structured and substantial opportunity for students to practice and apply newly taught skills and knowledge under the teacher's direction and guidance; and (3) an opportunity for feedback.

exposition. One of the four traditional forms of composition in speech and writing. Its purpose is to set forth or explain.

expository text. A traditional form of written composition that has as its primary purpose explanation of the communication of details, facts, and discipline- or content-specific information.

fluency. The clear, easy, and quick written or spoken expression of ideas; freedom from word-identification problems that might hinder comprehension in silent reading or the expression of ideas in oral reading; automaticity.

formative evaluation. The gathering of data during the time a program is being developed to guide the development process.

genre. A term used to classify literary works, such as novel, mystery, historical fiction, biography, short story, poem.

grammar. The system of rules for the use of language; the study of the collection of specific spoken and written conventions that exist in a language.

graphic organizer. A visual representation of facts and concepts from a text and their relationships within an organized frame. Graphic organizers are effective tools for thinking and learning. They help teachers and students represent abstract or implicit information in more concrete form, depict the relationships among facts and concepts, aid in organizing and elaborating ideas, relate new information with prior knowledge, and effectively store and retrieve information.

independent practice. The phase of instruction that occurs after skills and strategies have been explicitly taught and practiced under teacher direction or supervision. Independent practice involves the application of newly taught skills in familiar formats or tasks and reinforces skill acquisition.

informational text and materials. Text that has as its primary purpose the communication of technical information about a specific topic, event, experience, or circumstance. Informational text is typically found in the content areas (e.g., science, history–social science) in grades four through twelve.

interactive writing. A shared writing experience used to assist emergent readers in learning to read and write. With help from the teacher, students dictate sentences about a shared experience, such as a story, movie, or event. The teacher stretches each word orally so that students can distinguish its sounds and letters as they use chart paper to write the letter while repeating the sound. After each word has been completed, the teacher and students reread it. The students take turns writing letters to complete the words and sentences. The completed charts are posted on the wall so that the students can reread them or rely on them for standard spelling.

learning center or station. A location within a classroom in which students are presented with instructional materials, specific directions, clearly defined objectives, and opportunities for self-evaluation.

listening comprehension. The act or ability of understanding what a speaker is saying and seizing the meaning.

literary analysis. The study or examination of a literary work or author.

literary criticism. The result of literary analysis; a judgment or evaluation of a work or a body of literature.

Matthew effect. The "rich-get-richer, poor-get-poorer" effects embedded in the educational process. The term is derived from Matthew's Gospel.

minilesson. Direct instruction on specific topics or skills. This direct and explicit instruction can also be conducted to benefit students who need more information or further clarification of skills or topics already taught. The lessons or series of lessons are connected to the broader goal of getting students to become independent readers and writers. They are presented briefly and succinctly on the assumption that such information will be added to the set of ideas, strategies, and skills to be drawn upon as needed.

morpheme. A linguistic unit of relatively stable meaning that cannot be divided into smaller meaningful parts; the smallest meaningful part of a word.

narration. One of the four traditional forms of composition in speech and writing. Its purpose is to tell a story or give an account of something dealing with sequences of events and experiences.

narrative. A story or narrated account of actual or fictional events.

onset and rime. Intersyllabic units that are smaller than words and syllables but larger than phonemes. The *onset* is the portion of the syllable that precedes the vowel (e.g., in the word *black* the onset is *bl*). The *rime* is the portion of the syllable including any vowels and consonants that follow (e.g., in the word *black* the rime is *ack*). Although not all syllables or words have an onset, all do have a rime (e.g., the word or syllable *out* is a rime without an onset).

orthographic. Pertains to *orthography*, the art or study of correct spelling according to established usage.

peer editing. A form of collaborative learning in which students work with their peers in editing a piece of writing.

persuasion. One of the four traditional forms of composition in speech and writing. Its purpose is to move a reader by argument or entreaty to a belief, position, or course of action.

phonemes. The smallest units of speech that distinguish one utterance or word from another in a given language (e.g., the /r/ in *rug* or the /b/ in *bug*.)

phonemic awareness. The insight that every spoken word is made up of a sequence of phonemes or speech sounds. This insight is essential for learning to read an alphabetic language because these elementary sounds or phonemes are represented by letters. Without phonemic awareness phonics makes no sense; consequently, the spelling of words can be learned only by rote.

phonemic awareness instruction. Teaching awareness of words, syllables, and phonemes along a developmental continuum that includes rhyming, recognition and production, isolation, blending, matching of phonemes, segmentation, and substitution. Early phonemic instruction should focus on exploration of the auditory and articulatory structure of spoken language, not on letter-sound correspondences.

phonics. A system of teaching reading and spelling that stresses basic symbol-sound relationships and their application in decoding words.

predictable text. Reading material that supports the prediction of certain features of text. Text is predictable when it enables students to predict quickly and easily what the author is going to say and how the author is going to say it on the basis of their knowledge of the world and of language. Predictable books can also contain rhythmical, repetitive, or cumulative patterns; familiar stories or story lines; familiar sequences; or a good match between illustrations and text.

prewriting. The initial creative and planning stage of writing, prior to drafting, in which the writer formulates ideas, gathers information, and considers ways in which to organize a piece of writing.

primary language. The first language a child learns to speak.

print-rich environment. An environment in which students are provided many opportunities to interact with print and an abundance and variety of printed materials are available and accessible. Students have many opportunities to read and be read to. In such an environment reading and writing are modeled by the teacher and used for a wide variety of authentic everyday purposes.

punctuation. The appropriate use of standard marks, such as periods, commas, and semicolons, in writing and printing to separate words into sentences, clauses, and phrases to clarify meaning.

reading comprehension. The ability to apprehend meaning from print and understand text. At a literal level comprehension is the understanding of what an author has written or the specific details provided in a text. At a higher-order level, comprehension involves reflective and purposeful understanding that is thought-intensive, analytic, and interpretive.

recreational reading. Voluntary or leisure reading for which students use self-selected texts that can be read comfortably and independently.

retelling. The paraphrasing of a story in a student's own words to check for comprehension. Sometimes, retelling can be followed by questions to elicit further information.

revising. The process of changing a piece of writing to improve clarity for its intended audience and make certain that it accomplishes its stated purpose.

scaffolding. The temporary support, guidance, or assistance provided to a student on a new or complex task. For example, students work in partnership with a more advanced peer or adult who scaffolds the task by engaging in appropriate instructional interactions designed to model, assist, or provide necessary information. The interactions should eventually lead to independence.

schema. A reader's organized knowledge of the world that provides a basis for comprehending, learning, and remembering ideas in stories and texts.

self-monitoring. Students learn to monitor their own reading behaviors and use appropriate strategies to decode and comprehend text effectively.

sentences:
   Declarative—a sentence that makes a statement.
   Exclamatory—a sentence that makes a vehement statement or conveys strong or sudden emotion.
   Imperative—a sentence that expresses a command or request.
   Interrogative—a sentence that asks a question or makes an inquiry.

sentence structure. The formal pattern or grouping of words that make up a sentence, are grammatically dependent on one another, and convey an idea or message.

sight vocabulary/sight words. Words that are read automatically on sight because they are familiar to the reader.

spelling. The forming of specific words with letters in the correct order according to established usages; orthography.

spelling, temporary/invented. An emergent writer's attempt to spell a word phonetically when the spelling is unknown. Temporary spelling is a direct reflection of the writer's knowledge and understanding of how words are spelled. By engaging students in thinking actively and reflectively about the sounds of words and their spellings, temporary spelling lays a strong cognitive foundation for both formal spelling and phonics. It does *not,* however, eliminate the need for learning how to spell correctly. Support for temporary spelling should be combined with formal instruction in spelling to move students toward rapid growth in word recognition and correct spelling.

story frame/map. A graphic organizer of major events and ideas from a story to help guide students' thinking and heighten their awareness of the structure of stories. The teacher can model this process by filling out a chart on an overhead while reading. Or students can complete a chart individually or in groups after a story is read, illustrating or noting characters, setting, compare/contrast, problem/solution, climax, conflict, and so forth.

story grammar. The important elements that typically constitute a story. In general the elements include plot, setting, characters, conflict or problem, attempts or resolution, twist or complication, and theme.

structured/guided practice. A phase of instruction that occurs after the teacher explicitly models, demonstrates, or introduces a skill or strategy. In this phase students practice newly learned skills or strategies under teacher supervision and receive feedback on performance. This critical interactive phase involves teachers and students.

summative evaluation. An overall assessment or decision regarding a program.

syllabication. The division of words into syllables, the minimal units of sequential speech sounds composed of a vowel sound or a vowel-consonant combination.

systematic instruction. The strategic design and delivery of instruction that examines the nature of the objective to be learned and selects and sequences the essential skills, examples, and strategies necessary to achieve the objective by (1) allocating sufficient time to essential skills; (2) scheduling information to minimize confusion on the part of the learner; (3) introducing information in manageable and sequential units; (4) identifying prerequisite skills and building on prior knowledge of the learner; (5) reviewing previously taught skills; (6) strategically integrating old knowledge with new knowledge; and (7) progressing from skills in easier, manageable contexts to more complex contexts.

text difficulty (relative to student's ability):

- The *independent reading level* is the level of reading material a child can easily read independently with high comprehension, few problems with word identification, and an accuracy rate of 95–100 percent.
- The *instructional reading level* is the level of reading material a child can read successfully with instruction and support and an accuracy rate of 90–94 percent.
- The *frustration reading level* is the level of reading material a child can read with an accuracy rate of 89 percent or less. At this level "reading skills break down, fluency disappears, errors in word recognition are numerous, comprehension is faulty, recall is sketchy, and signs of emotional tension and discomfort become evident" (statement of the Committee on the Prevention of Reading Difficulties of Young Children, quoted in Harris and Sipay 1975, 213).

vocabulary and concept development. Instruction in the meaning of new words and concepts. Vocabulary instruction is most effective when specific information about the definitions of words is accompanied by attention to their usages and meanings across contexts. The development of an extensive reading vocabulary is a necessary phase of good comprehension.

web. A graphic organizer used to involve students in thinking about and planning what they will study, learn, read about, or write about within a larger topic. A teacher may begin with a brainstorming discussion of topics related to a particular theme and then represent subtopics through the use of a web drawn on the board. Webbing can be used to encourage students to consider what they know about each subtopic or what they want to know.

word attack (or word analysis). Refers to the process used to decode words. Students are taught multiple strategies to identify a word. This sequence progresses from decoding of individual letter-sound correspondences, letter combinations, phonics analysis and rules, and syllabication rules to analyzing structural elements (including prefixes, suffixes, and roots). Advanced word-analysis skills include strategies for identifying multisyllabic words.

word play. A child's manipulation of sounds and words for language exploration and practice or for pleasure (using alliteration, creating rhymes, singing songs, clapping syllables, and so forth).

word recognition. The identification and subsequent translation of the printed word into its corresponding sound, leading to accessing the word's meaning.

writing as a process (or process writing). The process used to create, develop, and complete a piece of writing. Depending on the purpose and audience for a particular piece of writing, students are taught to use the stages of prewriting, drafting, revising, editing, and publishing.

Works Cited

Adams, M. J. 1990. *Beginning to Read: Thinking and Learning About Print.* Cambridge: Massachusetts Institute of Technology Press.

American Association of School Librarians and the Association for Educational Communications and Technology. 1998. *Information Power: Building Partnerships for Learning.* Chicago: American Library Association.

Anderson, R. C.; P. T. Wilson; and L. G. Fielding. 1988. "Growth in Reading and How Children Spend Their Time Outside of School," *Reading Research Quarterly,* Vol. 23, No. 3, 285–303.

Baker, S. K.; D. C. Simmons; and E. J. Kame'enui. 1998. "Vocabulary Acquisition: Research Bases," in *What Reading Research Tells Us About Children with Diverse Learning Needs.* Edited by D. C. Simmons and E. J. Kame'enui. Mahwah, N.J.: Lawrence Erlbaum Associates.

Bay Area Reading Task Force. 1997. *A Reading-Writing-Language Source Book for the Primary Grades.* San Francisco: University School Support for Educational Reform.

Beck, I., et al. 1997. *Questioning the Author: An Approach for Enhancing Student Engagement with Text.* Newark, Del.: International Reading Association.

Benbow, C. P., and J. C. Stanley. 1996. "Inequity in Equity: How 'Equity' Can Lead to Inequity for High-Potential Students," *Psychology, Public Policy and Law,* Vol. 2, 249–92.

Bloom, B. S., ed. 1985. *Developing Talent in Young People.* New York: Ballantine Books.

California Department of Education. 1990. *Recommended Literature, Grades Nine Through Twelve.* Sacramento: California Department of Education.

California Department of Education. 1994. *Differentiating the Core Curriculum and Instruction to Provide Advanced Learning Opportunities.* Sacramento: California Department of Education.

California Department of Education. 1995. *Every Child a Reader: The Report of the California Reading Task Force.* Sacramento: California Department of Education.

California Department of Education. 1996a. *Recommended Readings in Literature, Kindergarten Through Grade Eight* (Revised annotated edition). Sacramento: California Department of Education.

California Department of Education. 1996b. *Teaching Reading: A Balanced, Comprehensive Approach to Teaching Reading in Prekindergarten Through Grade Three.* Sacramento: California Department of Education.

California Department of Education. 1996c. *Connect, Compute, and Compete: The Report of the California Education Technology Task Force.* Sacramento: California Department of Education.

California Department of Education. 1998a. *English–Language Arts Content Standards for California Public Schools, Kindergarten Through Grade Twelve.* Sacramento: California Department of Education.

California Department of Education. 1998b. *Fostering the Development of a First and a Second Language in Early Childhood.* Sacramento: California Department of Education.

Note: The publication data in this section were supplied by the Curriculum Frameworks and Instructional Resources Office, California Department of Education. Questions about the availability of the references or the accuracy of the data should be addressed to that office, telephone (916) 657-3023.

Calkins, L. 1996. "Motivating Readers," ERIC Clearinghouse on Assessment and Evaluation (No. SP525606), *Instructor,* Vol. 106, No. l, 32–33.

Carroll, J. B. 1963. "A Model of School Learning," *Teachers College Record,* Vol. 64, 723–33.

Carroll, J. B. 1989. "The Carroll Model: A 25-Year Retrospective and Prospective View," *Educational Researcher,* Vol. 18, No. 1, 26–31.

Chall, J.; V. Jacobs; and L. Baldwin. 1990. *The Reading Crisis: Why Poor Children Fall Behind.* Cambridge: Harvard University Press.

Chard, D. J.; D. C. Simmons; and E. J. Kame'enui. 1998. "Word Recognition: Research Bases," in *What Reading Research Tells Us About Children with Diverse Learning Needs.* Edited by D. C. Simmons and E. J. Kame'enui. Mahwah, N.J.: Lawrence Erlbaum Associates.

Chavkin, Nancy F. 1993. "School Social Workers Helping Multi-Ethnic Families, Schools, and Communities Join Forces," in *Families and Schools in a Pluralistic Society.* Edited by N. F. Chavkin. Albany: State University of New York Press.

Cornwall, A., and H. Bawden. 1992. "Reading Disabilities and Aggression: A Critical Review," *Journal of Learning Disabilities,* Vol. 25, 281–88.

Corson, D. 1995. *Using English Words.* Dordrecht, Netherlands: Kluwer.

Cunningham, A. E., and K. E. Stanovich. 1998. "What Reading Does for the Mind," *American Educator: The Unique Power of Reading and How to Unleash It,* Vol. 22, Nos. 1 and 2, 8–15.

Cunningham, P. M. 1998. "The Multisyllabic Word Dilemma: Helping Students Build Meaning, Spell, and Read 'Big' Words," *Reading and Writing Quarterly,* Vol. 14, 189–218.

Delcourt, M. A. B., et al. 1994. *Evaluation of the Effects of Programming Arrangements on Student Learning Outcomes.* Charlottesville: University of Virginia.

Dickinson, D. K., and M. W. Smith. 1994. "Long-Term Effects of Preschool Teachers' Book Readings on Low-Income Children's Vocabulary and Story Comprehension," *Reading Research Quarterly,* Vol. 29, No. 2, 104–22.

Drucker, P. F. 1993. "The Rise of the Knowledge Society," *The Wilson Quarterly,* Vol. 17, 52–72.

Ediger, M. 1988. "Motivation in the Reading Curriculum," ERIC Clearinghouse on Assessment and Evaluation (No. CS009424).

Ehri, L. 1994. "Development of the Ability to Read Words: Update," in *Theoretical Models and Processes of Reading.* Edited by R. Ruddell, M. Ruddell, and H. Singer. Newark, Del.: International Reading Association.

Ehri, L. C., and S. McCormick. 1998. "Phases of Word Learning: Implications for Instruction with Delayed and Disabled Readers," *Reading and Writing Quarterly,* Vol. 14, 135–63.

Eisenberg, M., and R. Berkowitz. 1990. *Information Problem Solving: The Big Six Skills Approach to Library and Information Skills Instruction.* Norwood, N.J.: Ablex.

Felton, R. H., and P. P. Pepper. 1995. "Early Identification and Intervention of Phonological Deficits in Kindergarten and Early Elementary Children at Risk for Reading Disability," *School Psychology Review,* Vol. 24, 405–14.

Fuchs, L. S., et al. 1993. "Formative Evaluation of Academic Progress: How Much Growth Can We Expect?" *School Psychology Review,* Vol. 22, No. 1, 27–48.

Gambrell, L. B., et al. 1996. *Elementary Students' Motivation to Read.* Reading Research Report No. 52. Athens, Ga.: National Reading Research Center.

Gándara, P. 1995. *Over the Ivy Walls: The Educational Mobility of Low-Income Chicanos.* Albany: State University of New York Press.

Gardner, H. 1983. *Frames of Mind: The Theory of Multiple Intelligences.* New York: Basic Books.

Geary, D. C. 1994. *Children's Mathematical Development: Research and Practical Applications.* Washington, D.C.: American Psychological Association.

Goldenberg, C. 1992-93. "Instructional Conversations: Promoting Comprehension Through Discussion," *The Reading Teacher,* Vol. 46, 316–26.

Good, R. III; D. C. Simmons; and S. Smith. 1998. "Effective Academic Interventions in the United States: Evaluating and Enhancing the Acquisition of Early Reading Skills," *School Psychology Review,* Vol. 27, No. 1, 45–56.

Greene, J. F. 1998. "Another Chance: Help for Older Students with Limited Literacy," *American Educator: The Unique Power of Reading and How to Unleash It,* Vol. 22, Nos. 1 and 2, 74–79.

Hanson, R. A., and D. Farrell. 1995. "The Long-Term Effects on High School Seniors of Learning to Read in Kindergarten," *Reading Research Quarterly,* Vol. 30, No. 4, 908–33.

Hasbrouck, J. E., and G. Tindal. 1992. "Curriculum-Based Oral Reading Fluency Norms for Students in Grades 2 Through 5," *Teaching Exceptional Children,* Vol. 24, 41–44.

Hunter, M., and G. Barker. 1987. "If at First . . . : Attribution Theory in the Classroom," *Educational Leadership,* Vol. 45, No. 2, 50–53.

Juel, C. 1988. "Learning to Read and Write: A Longitudinal Study of 54 Children from First Through Fourth Grades," *Journal of Educational Psychology,* Vol. 80, 437–447.

Kame'enui, E. J. 1996. "Shakespeare and Beginning Reading: 'The Readiness Is All,'" *Teaching Exceptional Children,* Vol. 28, No. 2, 77–81.

Kame'enui, E. J., and D. C. Simmons. 1998. "Beyond Effective Practice to Schools as Host Environments: Building and Sustaining a Schoolwide Intervention Model in Reading," *Oregon School Study Council Bulletin,* Vol. 41, No. 3, 3–24.

Lance, K. C.; L. Welborn; and C. Hamilton-Pennell. 1993. *The Impact of School Library Media Centers on Academic Achievement.* San Jose, Calif.: Hi Willow Research and Publishing.

Lipson, M. Y., and K. K. Wixson. 1986. "Reading Disability Research: An Interactionist Perspective," *Review of Educational Research,* Vol. 56, 111–36.

Loertscher, D. 1998. *Reinvent Your School Library in the Age of Technology: A Guide for Principals and Superintendents.* San Jose, Calif.: Hi Willow Research and Publishing.

Lyon, G. R., and V. Chhabra. 1996. "The Current State of Science and the Future of Specific Reading Disability," *Mental Retardation and Developmental Disabilities Research Reviews,* Vol. 2, 2–9.

Markell, M. A., and S. L. Deno. 1997. "Effects of Increasing Oral Reading: Generalization Across Reading Tasks," *The Journal of Special Education,* Vol. 31, No. 2, 233–50.

McCollum, H., and A. Russo. 1993. *Model Strategies in Bilingual Education: Family Literacy and Parent Involvement.* Washington, D.C.: United States Department of Education.

Moats, L. C. 1995. *Spelling: Development, Disability, and Instruction.* Baltimore: York Press.

Mosenthal, P. 1984. "The Problem of Partial Specification in Translating Reading Research into Practice," *The Elementary School Journal,* Vol. 85, No. 2, 199–227.

Mosenthal, P. 1985. "Defining Progress in Educational Research," *Educational Researcher,* Vol. 14, No. 9, 3–9.

Mosteller, F.; R. Light; and J. Sachs. 1996. "Sustained Inquiry in Education: Lessons from Skill Grouping and Class Size," *Harvard Educational Review,* Vol. 66, No. 4, 797–842.

Nagy, W. 1998. "Increasing Students' Reading Vocabularies." Presentation at the Commissioner's Reading Day Conference, Austin, Texas.

Works Cited

National Center to Improve the Tools of Educators. 1997. *Learning to Read, Reading to Learn—Helping Children to Succeed: A Resource Guide.* Washington, D.C.: American Federation of Teachers.

National Committee for Citizens in Education. 1994. *A New Generation of Evidence: The Family Is Critical to Students' Achievement.* Edited by A. T. Henderson and N. Berla. Washington, D.C.: National Committee for Citizens in Education.

National Research Council. 1998. *Preventing Reading Difficulties in Young Children.* Edited by M. S. Burns, P. Griffin, and C. E. Snow. Washington, D.C.: National Academy Press.

Pearson, P. D., and K. Camperell. 1985. "Comprehension in Text Structures," in *Theoretical Models and Processes of Reading.* Edited by H. Singer and R. B. Ruddell. Newark, Del.: International Reading Association

Pinnell, G. S., and I. C. Fountas. 1997. *Help America Read: A Handbook for Volunteers.* Portsmouth, N.H.: Heinemann.

Samuels, S. J. 1979. "The Method of Repeated Reading," *The Reading Teacher,* Vol. 32, 403–08.

Sanacore, J. 1988. "Linking Vocabulary and Comprehension Through Independent Reading," ERIC Clearinghouse on Assessment and Evaluation (No. CS009409).

Seidenberg, P. L. 1989. "Relating Text-Processing Research to Reading and Writing Instruction for Learning-Disabled Students," *Learning Disabilities Focus,* Vol. 5, No. 1, 4–12.

Shefelbine, J. 1991. *Encouraging Your Junior High Student to Read.* Bloomington, Ind.: ERIC Clearinghouse on Reading, English, and Communication.

Shefelbine, J. 1998. "Academic Language and Literacy Development." A paper presented at the Reading and English-Language Learner Forum. Sacramento: California Reading and Literature Project.

Shore, B. M., et al. 1991. *Recommended Practices in Gifted Education: A Critical Analysis.* New York: Teachers College Press.

Simmons, D. C., and E. J. Kame'enui. 1996. "A Focus on Curriculum Design: When Children Fail," in *Strategies for Teaching Children in Inclusive Settings.* Edited by E. Meyen, G. Vergason, and R. Whelan. Denver: Love Publishing.

Slavin, R. E.; N. L. Karweit; and B. A. Wasik, eds. 1993. *Preventing Early School Failure: Research, Policy, and Practice.* 1993. Boston: Allyn and Bacon.

Smith, S.; D. C. Simmons; and E. J. Kame'enui. 1998. "Phonological Awareness: Research Bases," in *What Reading Research Tells Us About Children with Diverse Learning Needs: Bases and Basics.* Edited by D. C. Simmons and E. J. Kame'enui. Mahwah, N.J.: Lawrence Erlbaum Associates.

Spandel, V. 1998. *Seeing with New Eyes: A Guidebook on Teaching and Assessing Beginning Writers* (Fourth edition). Portland, Ore.: Northwest Regional Educational Laboratory.

Spear-Swerling, L., and R. J. Sternberg. 1998. "Curing Our 'Epidemic' of Learning Disabilities," *Phi Delta Kappan,* Vol. 79, No. 5, 397–401.

Stanovich, K. E. 1986. "Matthew Effects in Reading: Some Consequences of Individual Differences in the Acquisition of Literacy," *Reading Research Quarterly,* Vol. 21, 360–407.

Stanovich, K. E. 1994. "Constructivism in Reading Education," *The Journal of Special Education,* Vol. 28, 259–74.

Topping, K. 1998. "Effective Tutoring in America Reads: A Reply to Wasik," *The Reading Teacher,* Vol. 52, No. 1, 42–50.

Valdés, G. 1996. *Con Respeto—Bridging the Distances Between Culturally Diverse Families and Schools.* New York: Teachers College Press.

Walberg, H. J. 1984. "Families as Partners in Educational Productivity," *Phi Delta Kappan,* Vol. 65, No. 6, 397–400.

Wells, G. 1986. *The Meaning Makers: Children Learning Language and Using Language to Learn.* Portsmouth, N.H.: Heinemann.

Werner, E. 1993. "Risk, Resilience, and Recovery: Perspectives from the Kauai Longitudinal Study," *Development and Psychopathology,* Vol. 5, 503–15.

White, E. B. 1952. *Charlotte's Web.* New York: Harper and Row.

Whitman, D., and T. Gest. 1995. "Welfare: The Myth of Reform." *U.S. News and World Report,* Vol. 118, No. 2, 30–33 and 36–39.

Yopp, H. K. 1988. "The Validity and Reliability of Phonemic Awareness Tests," *Reading Research Quarterly,* Vol. 23, No. 2, 159–77.

Additional References

Adams, M. J., et al. 1998. "The Elusive Phoneme: Why Phonemic Awareness Is So Important and How to Help Children Develop It," *American Educator: The Unique Power of Reading and How to Unleash It,* Vol. 22, Nos. 1 and 2, 18–29.

Adams, M. J.; R. Treiman; and M. Pressley. 1998. "Reading, Writing, and Literacy," in *Handbook of Child Psychology: Child Psychology in Practice* (Fifth edition). Vol. 4. Edited by I. E. Sigel and K. A. Renninger. New York: Wiley.

Advisory Task Force on Educator Preparation for Parent Involvement. 1998. *Preparing Educators for Partnerships with Families.* Sacramento: California Commission on Teacher Credentialing.

Allen, L. 1998. "An Integrated Strategies Approach: Making Word Identification Instruction Work for Beginning Readers," *The Reading Teacher,* Vol. 52, No. 3, 254–68.

Anderson, R. C., et al. 1985. *Becoming a Nation of Readers: The Report of the Commission on Reading.* Washington, D.C.: National Academy of Education, Commission on Education and Public Policy.

Anderson, R. C., and W. E. Nagy. 1991. "Word Meanings," in *Handbook of Reading Research.* Vol. 2. Edited by R. Barr, et al. New York: Longman.

Baker, L.; D. Scher; and K. Mackler. 1997. "Home and Family Influences on Motivations for Reading," *Educational Psychologist,* Vol. 32, No. 2, 69–82.

Ball, E. W., and B. A. Blachman. 1991. "Does Phoneme Awareness Training in Kindergarten Make a Difference in Early Word Recognition and Developmental Spelling?" *Reading Research Quarterly,* Vol. 26, No. 1, 49–66.

Barinaga, M. 1996. "Giving Language Skills a Boost," *Science,* Vol. 271, 27–28.

Barnett, W. S. 1995. "Long-Term Effects of Early Childhood Programs on Cognitive and School Outcomes," *The Future of Children,* Vol. 5, No. 3, 25–50.

Baumann, J. F., and E. J. Kame'enui. 1991. "Research on Vocabulary Instruction: Ode to Voltaire," in *Handbook of Research on Teaching the English Language Arts.* Edited by J. Flood, J. J. D. Lapp, and J. R. Squire. New York: Macmillan.

Beck, I., et al. 1996. "Questioning the Author: A Year-Long Classroom Implementation to Engage Students with Text," *The Elementary School Journal,* Vol. 96, 385–414.

Beck, I., et al. 1998. "Getting at the Meaning: How to Help Students Unpack Difficult Text," *American Educator: The Unique Power of Reading and How to Unleash It,* Vol. 22, Nos. 1 and 2, 66–71, 85.

Berninger, V. W., et al. 1994. "Developmental Skills Related to Writing and Reading Acquisition in the Intermediate Grades," *Reading and Writing: An Interdisciplinary Journal,* Vol. 6, 161–96.

Berthoff, A. E. 1984. "Recognition, Representation, and Revision," in *Rhetoric and Composition: A Sourcebook for Teachers and Writers.* Edited by R. Graves. Portsmouth, N.H.: Boynton Cook.

Blachman, B. A., et al. 1994. "Kindergarten Teachers Develop Phoneme Awareness in Low-Income, Inner-City Classrooms," *Reading and Writing: An Interdisciplinary Journal,* Vol. 6, 1–18.

Blachowicz, C. L. Z., and P. Fisher. 1996. *Teaching Vocabulary in All Classrooms.* Englewood Cliffs, N.J.: Merrill/Prentice Hall.

Note: The publication data in this section were supplied by the Curriculum Frameworks and Instructional Resources Office, California Department of Education. Questions about the availability of the references or the accuracy of the data should be addressed to that office, telephone (916) 657-3023.

Bus, A. G.; M. H. vanIJzendoorn; and A. D. Pellegrini. 1995. "Joint Book Reading Makes for Success in Learning to Read: A Meta-Analysis on Intergenerational Transmission of Literacy," *Review of Educational Research,* Vol. 65, 1–21.

Byrne, B., and R. Fielding-Barnsley. 1995. "Evaluation of a Program to Teach Phonemic Awareness to Young Children: A One- and Three-Year Follow-Up and a New Preschool Trial," *Journal of Educational Psychology,* Vol. 87, No. 3, 488–503.

California Commission on Teacher Credentialing, State Superintendent of Public Instruction, and State Board of Education. 1997. *California Standards for the Teaching Profession.* Sacramento: California Commission on Teacher Credentialing.

California Department of Education. 1996. *Practical Ideas for Teaching Writing as a Process at the Elementary School and Middle School Levels.* Edited by C. B. Olson. Sacramento: California Department of Education.

California Department of Education. 1997. *Practical Ideas for Teaching Writing as a Process at the High School and College Levels.* Edited by C. B. Olson. Sacramento: California Department of Education.

California State Board of Education. 1997. *A Blueprint for Professional Development for Teachers of Early Reading Instruction.* Sacramento: Comprehensive Reading Leadership Center, Sacramento County Office of Education.

Campbell, F. A., and C. T. Ramsey. 1995. "Cognitive and Social Outcomes for High-Risk African-American Students at Middle Adolescence: Positive Effects of Early Intervention," *American Educational Research Journal,* Vol. 32, 743–72.

Carlisle, J. F., and D. M. Nomanbhoy. 1993. "Phonological and Morphological Awareness in First-Graders," *Applied Psycholinguistics,* Vol. 14, 177–95.

Carnine, D.; J. Silbert; and E. J. Kame'enui. 1990. *Direct Instruction Reading.* Columbus, Ohio: Merrill Publishing Company.

Cunningham, A. E., and K. E. Stanovich. 1993. "Children's Literacy Environments and Early Word Recognition Subskills," *Reading and Writing: An Interdisciplinary Journal,* Vol. 5, 193–204.

Daneman, M. 1991. "Individual Differences in Reading Skills," in *Handbook of Reading Research* (Vol. 2). Edited by R. Barr, M. L. Kamil, P. B. Mosenthal, and P. D. Pearson. New York: Longman.

Defior, S., and P. Tudela. 1994. "Effect of Phonological Training on Reading and Writing Acquisition," *Reading and Writing,* Vol. 6, 299–320.

Delpit, L. D. 1986. "Skills and Other Dilemmas of a Progressive Black Educator," *Harvard Educational Review,* Vol. 56, 379–85.

Dillard, A. 1998. "What Reading Does for the Soul: A Girl and Her Books," *American Educator: The Unique Power of Reading and How to Unleash It,* Vol. 22, Nos. 1 and 2, 88–93.

Ehri, L. C. 1991. "Development of the Ability to Read Words," in *Handbook of Reading Research* (Vol. 2). Edited by R. Barr, et al. New York: Longman.

Ehrlich, M. F.; B. Kurtz-Costess; and C. Loridant. 1993. "Cognitive and Motivational Determinants of Reading Comprehension in Good and Poor Readers," *Journal of Reading Behavior,* Vol. 25, No. 4, 365–81.

Englert, C. S., et al. 1995. "The Early Literacy Project: Connecting Across the Literacy Curriculum," *Learning Disability Quarterly,* Vol. 18, 253–75.

Epstein, J. L. 1995. "School-Family-Community Partnerships: Caring for Children We Share," *Phi Delta Kappan,* Vol. 76, No. 9, 701–2.

Evertson, C. M., and C. H. Randolph. 1989. "Teaching Practices and Class Size: A New Look at an Old Issue," *Peabody Journal of Education,* Vol. 67, No. 1, 85–105.

Felton, R. H. 1992. "Early Identification of Children at Risk for Reading Disabilities," *Topics in Early Childhood Special Education,* Vol. 12, 212–29.

Additional
References

Fielding, L. G., and Pearson, P. D. 1994. "Synthesis of Research—Reading Comprehension: What Works," *Educational Leadership*, Vol. 51, No. 5, 62–7.

Fielding-Barnsley, R. 1997. "Explicit Instruction in Decoding Benefits Children High in Phonemic Awareness and Alphabet Knowledge," *Scientific Studies of Reading*, Vol. 1, No. 1, 85–98.

Fitzgerald, J. 1995. "English-as-a-Second-Language Learners' Cognitive Reading Processes: A Review of Research in the U.S.," *Review of Educational Research*, Vol. 65, 145–90.

Flower, L. 1979. "Writer-Based Prose: A Cognitive Basis for Problems in Writing," *College English*, Vol. 41, No. 1, 19–37.

Flower, L. 1985. *Problem-Solving Strategies for Writing*. New York: Harcourt Brace Jovanovich.

Foorman, B., et al. 1998. "The Role of Instruction in Learning to Read: Preventing Reading Failure in At-Risk Children," *Journal of Educational Psychology*, Vol. 90, 37–55.

Foster, K. C., et al. 1994. "Computer-Assisted Instruction in Phonological Awareness: Evaluation of the DaisyQuest Program," *Journal of Research and Development in Education*, Vol. 27, 126–37.

Gersten, R., and J. Woodward. 1995. "A Longitudinal Study of Transitional and Immersion Bilingual Education Programs in One District," *Elementary School Journal*, Vol. 95, 223–39.

Giles, H. C. 1997. "Parent Engagement As a School Reform Strategy," ERIC Clearinghouse on Urban Education (Digest 135).

Goldenberg, C. N., and R. Gallimore. 1991. "Local Knowledge, Research Knowledge, and Educational Change: A Case Study of Early [First-Grade] Spanish Reading Improvement," *Educational Researcher*, Vol. 20, No. 8, 2–14.

Guthrie, J. T., et al. 1996. "Growth of Literacy Engagement: Changes in Motivations and Strategies During Concept-Oriented Reading Instruction," *Reading Research Quarterly*, Vol. 31, 306–25.

Hart, B., and T. R. Risley. 1995. *Meaningful Differences in the Everyday Experience of Young American Children*. Baltimore: Paul H. Brookes Publishing Co.

Hiebert, E. H., et al. 1992. "Reading and Writing of First-Grade Students in a Restructured Chapter I Program," *American Educational Research Journal*, Vol. 29, 545–72.

Hillocks, G., Jr. 1986. *Research on Written Composition: New Directions for Teaching*. Urbana, Ill.: National Council for Teachers of English.

Hoover-Dempsey, K. V., and H. M. Sandler. 1997. "Why Do Parents Become Involved in Their Children's Education?" *Review of Educational Research*, Vol. 67, No. 1, 3–42.

Invernizzi, M., et al. 1997. "At-Risk Readers and Community Volunteers: A Three-Year Perspective," *Scientific Studies of Reading*, Vol. 1, 277–300.

Iverson, S., and W. E. Tunmer. 1993. "Phonological Processing Skills and the Reading Recovery Program," *Journal of Educational Psychology*, Vol. 85, 112–26.

Jimenez, R. T.; G. E. Garcia; and P. D. Pearson. 1996. "The Reading Strategies of Latina/o Students Who Are Successful Readers: Opportunities and Obstacles," *Reading Research Quarterly*, Vol. 31, 90–112.

Juel, C. 1991. "Beginning Reading," in *Handbook of Reading Research* (Vol. 2). Edited by R. Barr, M. L. Kamil, P. B. Mosenthal, and P. D. Pearson. New York: Longman.

Kuhn, M. R., and S. A. Stahl. 1998. "Teaching Children to Learn Word Meanings from Context: A Synthesis and Some Questions," *Journal of Literacy Research*, Vol. 30, No. 1, 119–38.

Leather, C. V., and L. A. Henry. 1994. "Working Memory Span and Phonological Awareness Tasks as Predictors of Early Reading Ability," *Journal of Experimental Child Psychology*, Vol. 58, 88–111.

Levy, B. A.; A. Nicholls; and D. Kohen. 1993. "Repeated Readings: Process Benefits for Good and Poor Readers," *Journal of Experimental Child Psychology,* Vol. 56, 303–27.

Liberman, I. Y.; D. Shankweiler; and A. M. Liberman. 1991. "The Alphabetic Principle and Learning to Read," in *Phonology and Reading Disability: Solving the Reading Puzzle.* Edited by D. Shankweiler and I. Y. Liberman. Ann Arbor: University of Michigan Press.

Lie, A. 1991. "Effects of a Training Program for Stimulating Skills in Word Analysis in First-Grade Children," *Reading Research Quarterly,* Vol. 26, No. 3, 234–50.

Louis, K. S.; H. M. Marks; and S. Kruse. 1996. "Teachers' Professional Community in Restructuring Schools," *American Educational Research Journal* (Vol. 33).

Lundberg, I.; J. Frost; and O. P. Petersen. 1988. "Effects of an Extensive Program for Stimulating Phonological Awareness in Preschool Children," *Reading Research Quarterly,* Vol. 23, 263–284.

Lyon, G. R. 1995. "Toward a Definition of Dyslexia," *Annals of Dyslexia,* Vol. 45, 3–27.

McGuinness, D.; C. McGuinness; and J. Donahue. 1996. "Phonological Training and the Alphabetic Principle: Evidence for Reciprocal Causality," *Reading Research Quarterly,* Vol. 30, 830-52.

McWhorter, J. 1998. *The Word on the Street: Fact and Fable about American English.* New York: Plenum.

Moats, L. C. 1998. "Teaching Decoding," *American Educator: The Unique Power of Reading and How to Unleash It,* Vol. 22, Nos. 1 and 2, 42–49, 95–96.

Moffett, J., and B. J. Wagner. 1991. *Student-Centered Language Arts, K–12.* Portsmouth, N.H.: Boynton Cook.

Morrow, L. M. 1992. "The Impact of a Literature-Based Program on Literacy, Achievement, Use of Literature, and Attitudes of Children from Minority Backgrounds," *Reading Research Quarterly,* Vol. 27, 250–75.

National Parent-Teacher Association. 1998. *National Standards for Parent/Family Involvement Programs.* Chicago: National Parent-Teacher Association.

National Research Council. 1999. *Starting Out Right: A Guide to Promoting Children's Reading Success.* Edited by M. S. Burns, P. Griffin, and C. E. Snow. Washington, D.C.: National Academy Press.

National Research Council and Institute of Medicine. 1997. *Improving Schooling for Language-Minority Children: A Research Agenda.* Edited by D. August and K. Hakuta. Washington, D.C.: National Academy Press.

Neuman, S. B. 1996. "Children Engaging in Storybook Reading: The Influence of Access to Print Resources, Opportunity, and Parental Interaction," *Early Childhood Research Quarterly,* Vol. 11, 495–513.

O'Connor, R. E.; J. R. Jenkins; and T. A. Slocum. 1995. "Transfer Among Phonological Tasks in Kindergarten: Essential Instructional Content," *Journal of Educational Psychology,* Vol. 87, 202–17.

Pearson, P. D., et al. 1992. "Developing Expertise in Reading Comprehension," in *What Research Says to the Teacher.* Edited by S. J. Samuels and A. E. Farstrup. Newark, Del.: International Reading Association.

Peitzman, F.; G. Gadda; and W. Walsh. 1988. *Teaching Analytical Writing.* Long Beach, Calif.: California Academic Partnership Program.

Perfetti, C. A., and S. Zhang. 1995. "The Universal Word Identification Reflex," in *The Psychology of Learning and Motivation* (Vol. 33). Edited by D. L. Medlin. San Diego: Academic Press.

Peterson, P. L.; S. J. McCarthey; and R. F. Elmore. 1996. "Learning from School Restructuring," *American Educational Research Journal,* Vol. 33, 119–53.

Phillips, L. M.; S. P. Norris; and J. M. Mason. 1996. "Longitudinal Effects of Early Literacy Concepts on Reading Achievement: A Kindergarten Intervention and Five-Year Follow-Up," *Journal of Literacy Research,* Vol. 28, 173–95.

Pressley, M.; J. Rankin; and L. Yokoi. 1996. "A Survey of Instructional Practices of Primary Teachers Nominated as Effective in Promoting Literacy," *The Elementary School Journal*, Vol. 96, 363–84.

Purcell-Gates, V.; E. McIntyre; and P. Freppon. 1995. "Learning Written Storybook Language in School: A Comparison of Low-SES Children in Skills-Based and Whole-Language Classrooms," *American Educational Research Journal*, Vol. 32, 659–85.

Robbins, C., and L. C. Ehri. 1994. "Reading Storybooks to Kindergartners Helps Them Learn New Vocabulary Words," *Journal of Educational Psychology*, Vol. 86, No. 1, 54–64.

Rosenshine, B., and C. Meister. 1994. "Reciprocal Teaching: A Review of the Research," *Review of Educational Research*, Vol. 64, No. 4, 479–530.

Ross, S. M., et al. 1995. "Increasing the Academic Success of Disadvantaged Children: An Examination of Alternative Early Intervention Programs," *American Educational Research Journal*, Vol. 32, 773–800.

Ruddell, R.; M. Rapp Ruddell; and H. Singer, eds. 1994. *Theoretical Models and Processes of Reading* (Fourth edition). Newark, Del.: International Reading Association.

Ryder, R. J., and M. F. Graves. 1994. "Vocabulary Instruction Presented Prior to Reading in Two Basal Readers," *Elementary School Journal*, Vol. 95, No. 2, 139–53.

Sacks, C. H., and J. R. Mergendoller. 1997. "The Relationship Between Teachers' Theoretical Orientation Toward Reading and Student Outcomes in Kindergarten Children with Different Initial Reading Abilities," *American Educational Research Journal*, Vol. 34, 721–39.

Shaughnessey, M. 1977. *Errors and Expectations: A Guide for the Teacher of Basic Writing*. New York: Oxford University Press.

Shefelbine, J. L. 1990. "Student Factors Related to Variability in Learning Word Meanings from Context," *Journal of Reading Behavior*, Vol. 22, No. 1, 71–97.

Shore, W. J., and F. T. Durso. 1990. "Partial Knowledge in Vocabulary Acquisition: General Constraints and Specific Detail," *Journal of Educational Psychology*, Vol. 82, 315–18.

Simmons, D. C., and E. J. Kame'enui, eds. 1998. *What Reading Research Tells Us About Children with Diverse Learning Needs: Bases and Basics*. Mahwah, N.J.: Lawrence Erlbaum Associates.

Sindelar, P. T.; L. Monda; and L. O'Shea. 1990. "Effects of Repeated Readings on Instructional- and Mastery-Level Readers," *Journal of Educational Research*, Vol. 83, 220–26.

Snider, V. E. 1995. "A Primer on Phonological Awareness: What It Is, Why It's Important, and How to Teach It," *School Psychology Review*, Vol. 24, 443–55.

Sommers, N. 1984. "Revision Strategies of Student Writers and Experienced Adult Writers," in *Rhetoric and Composition: A Sourcebook for Teachers and Writers*. Edited by R. Graves. Portsmouth, N.H.: Boynton Cook.

Spear-Swerling, L., and R. J. Sternberg. 1996. *Off Track: When Poor Readers Become Learning Disabled*. Boulder, Colo.: Westview Press.

Stanovich, K. E. 1993-94. "Romance and Reality," *The Reading Teacher*, Vol. 47, 280–90.

Stringfield, S. 1997. "Underlying the Chaos of Factors Explaining Exemplary U.S. Elementary Schools: The Case for High-Reliability Organizations," in *Restructuring and Quality: Problems and Possibilities for Tomorrow's Schools*. Edited by T. Townsend. London: Routledge.

Sulzby, E., and W. Teale. 1991. "Emergent Literacy," in *Handbook of Reading Research* (Vol. 2). Edited by R. Barr, M. L. Kamil, P. B. Mosenthal, and P. D. Pearson. New York: Longman.

Teddlie, C., and S. Stringfield. 1993. *Schools Make a Difference: Lessons Learned from a Ten-Year Study of School Effects*. New York: Teachers College Press.

Torgesen, J. K. 1998. "Catch Them Before They Fall: Identification and Assessment to Prevent Reading Failure in Young Children," *American Educator: The Unique Power of Reading and How to Unleash It,* Vol. 22, Nos. 1 and 2, 32–39.

Treiman, R. 1985. "Onsets and Rimes as Units of Spoken Syllables: Evidence from Children," *Journal of Experimental Child Psychology,* Vol. 39, 161–81.

Treiman, R.; S. Weatherston; and D. Berch. 1994. "The Role of Letter Names in Children's Learning of Phoneme-Grapheme Relations," *Applied Psycholinguistics,* Vol. 15, 97–122.

Vandervelden, M. C., and L. S. Siegel. 1995. "Phonological Recoding and Phoneme Awareness in Early Literacy: A Developmental Approach," *Reading Research Quarterly,* Vol. 30, 854–73.

Vellutino, F. R., et al. 1996. "Cognitive Profiles of Difficult-to-Remediate and Readily Remediated Poor Readers: Early Intervention as a Vehicle for Distinguishing Between Cognitive and Experiential Deficits as Basic Causes of Specific Reading Disability," *Journal of Educational Psychology,* Vol. 88, 601–38.

Wagner, R. K., et al. 1993. "Development of Young Readers' Phonological Processing Abilities," *Journal of Educational Psychology,* Vol. 85, 83–103.

Walker, D., et al. 1994. "Prediction of School Outcomes Based on Socioeconomic Status and Early Language Production," *Child Development,* Vol. 65, 606–21.

Wasik, B. A., and R. E. Slavin. 1993. "Preventing Early Reading Failure with One-to-One Tutoring: A Review of Five Programs," *Reading Research Quarterly,* Vol. 28, 178–200.

White, T. G.; M. F. Graves; and W. H. Slater. 1990. "Growth of Reading Vocabulary in Diverse Elementary Schools: Decoding and Word Meaning," *Journal of Educational Psychology,* Vol. 82, 281–90.

Whitehurst, G. J., et al. 1994. "Outcomes of an Emergent Literacy Intervention in Head Start," *Journal of Educational Psychology,* Vol. 86, 542–55.

Winik, L. W. 1998. "The Little Bookstore That Grew to a Thousand," *American Educator: The Unique Power of Reading and How to Unleash It,* Vol. 22, Nos. 1 and 2, 82–85.

Publications Available from the Department of Education

This publication is one of over 600 that are available from the California Department of Education. Some of the more recent publications or those most widely used are the following:

Item no.	Title (Date of publication)	Price
1372	Arts Work: A Call for Arts Education for All California Students (1997)	$11.25
1438	California School Accounting Manual, 1998 Edition	28.50
1398	California Year-Round Education Directory, 1997-98 (1998)	10.00
0488	Caught in the Middle: Educational Reform for Young Adolescents in California Public Schools (1987)	9.25
1373	Challenge Standards for Student Success: Health Education (1998)	10.00
1409	Challenge Standards for Student Success: Language Arts Student Work Addendum (1998)	12.75
1298	Challenge Standards for Student Success: Mathematics (1997)	15.75
1435	Challenge Standards for Student Success: Physical Education (1998)	8.50
1429	Challenge Standards for Student Success: Visual and Performing Arts (1998)	12.50
1290	Challenge Toolkit: Family-School Compact (1997)	9.95*
1439	Check It Out! Assessing School Library Media Programs (1998)	9.25
1281	Connect, Compute, and Compete: The Report of the California Education Technology Task Force (1996)	5.75
1093	Differentiating the Core Curriculum and Instruction to Provide Advanced Learning Opportunities (1994)	7.00
1389	English–Language Arts Content Standards for California Public Schools, Kindergarten Through Grade Twelve (1998)	9.25
1244	Every Child a Reader: The Report of the California Reading Task Force (1995)	5.25
1064	Health Framework for California Public Schools, Kindergarten Through Grade Twelve (1994)	10.00
1284	History–Social Science Framework for California Public Schools, 1997 Updated Edition (1997)	12.50
1245	Improving Mathematics Achievement for All California Students: The Report of the California Mathematics Task Force (1995)	5.25
1024	It's Elementary! Elementary Grades Task Force Report (1992)	9.00
1442	Joining Hands: Preparing Teachers to Make Meaningful Home-School Connections (1998)	13.25
1457	Mathematics Content Standards for California Public Schools, Kindergarten Through Grade Twelve (1999)	8.50
1065	Physical Education Framework for California Public Schools, Kindergarten Through Grade Twelve (1994)	7.75
1221	Practical Ideas for Teaching Writing as a Process at the Elementary School and Middle School Levels (1996)	18.00
1222	Practical Ideas for Teaching Writing as a Process at the High School and College Levels (1997)	18.00
0831	Recommended Literature, Grades Nine Through Twelve (1990)	8.00
1171	Recommended Readings in Literature, Kindergarten Through Grade Eight (Revised annotated edition) (1996)	10.00
0870	Science Framework for California Public Schools, Kindergarten Through Grade Twelve (1990)	9.50
1276	Teaching Reading: A Balanced, Comprehensive Approach to Teaching Reading in Prekindergarten Through Grade Three (1996)	5.75
1261	Visual and Performing Arts Framework for California Public Schools, Kindergarten Through Grade Twelve (1996)	15.00
1392	Work-Based Learning Guide (1998)	12.50
1390	Work Permit Handbook (1998)	13.00
1381	Workforce Career Development Model (1998)	9.50

*Other titles in the *Challenge Toolkit* series are *Outline for Assessment and Accountability Plans* (Item 1300), *Safe and Healthy Schools* (Item 1299), *School Facilities* (Item 1294), *Site-Based Decision Making* (Item 1295), *Service Learning* (Item 1291), *Student Activities* (Item 1292), and *Student Learning Plans* (Item no. 1296). Call 1-800-995-4099 for prices and shipping charges.

Orders should be directed to:

California Department of Education
CDE Press, Sales Office
P.O. Box 271
Sacramento, CA 95812-0271

Please include the item number and desired quantity for each title ordered. Shipping and handling charges are additional, and purchasers in California also add county sales tax.

Mail orders must be accompanied by a check, a purchase order, or a credit card number, including expiration date (VISA or MasterCard only). Purchase orders without checks are accepted from educational institutions, businesses, and governmental agencies. Telephone orders will be accepted toll-free (1-800-995-4099) for credit card purchases. *All sales are final.*

Prices are subject to change. Please call 1-800-995-4099 for current prices and shipping charges.

R99-021 003-0024-99 003-0025-99 300 10/99 130,350